**L**awrenceville
**P**ress

A Division of **EMC Publishing**

# A Guide to Programming in Java™

*Third Edition*

Jan Marrelli

The data files used in this text can be downloaded from:
**www.emcschool.net/Java3e (hardcover)**
**www.paradigmcollege.net/Java3e (softcover)**

Care has been taken to verify the accuracy of information presented in this book. However, the authors, editors, and publisher cannot accept responsibility for Web, e-mail, newsgroup, or chat room subject matter or content, or for consequences from application of the information in this book, and make no warranty, expressed or implied, with respect to its content.

**Trademarks**: Some of the product names and company names included in this book have been used for identification purposes only and may be trademarks or registered trade names of their respective manufacturers and sellers. The authors, editors, and publisher disclaim any affiliation, association, or connection with, or sponsorship or endorsement by, such owners.

We have made every effort to trace the ownership of all copyrighted material and to secure permission from copyright holders. In the event of any question arising as to the use of any material, we will be pleased to make the necessary corrections in future printings. Thanks are due to the aforementioned authors, publishers, and agents for permission to use the materials indicated.

ISBN 978-0-82196-213-8 (Hardcover)
ISBN 978-0-82196-214-5 (Softcover)

© 2012 by EMC Publishing, LLC
875 Montreal Way
St. Paul, MN 55102
E-mail: educate@emcp.com
Web site: www.emcp.com

Printed in the United States of America

20 19 18 17 16 15 14 13 12 11    1 2 3 4 5 6 7 8 9 10

# Preface

**W**e have strived to make this the clearest and most comprehensive Java text available. Our primary objective in this text is to present material in clear language with easy to follow examples. To meet this objective, we use our teaching experiences as well as the feedback, comments, and suggestions from other experienced instructors to determine how best to present programming concepts.

For the best classroom experience for both the student and the instructor, our comprehensive text book includes hands-on reviews, critical-thinking questions, and exercises of varying difficulty levels. Additionally, our Instructor Resources correlate directly to the text book and offer teaching hints for explaining difficult concepts, additional lessons and exercises, and a comprehensive question bank for creating tests, quizzes, and reviews. The Instructor Resources include the applications, case studies, and vocabulary from the text book, as well as answers to all the reviews and exercises.

It is our belief that learning to program offers the student an invaluable opportunity to develop problem-solving skills. The process of defining a problem, breaking it down into a series of smaller problems, and finally writing an application to solve it exercises a student's logical abilities. Additionally, the student is made aware of the capabilities and limitations of a computer and soon realizes that the programmer—the human element—is more important than the machine.

A Guide to Programming in Java is written for a one-term or two-term course. No previous programming experience is required or assumed. It is our goal that this text provide students the best possible introduction to programming using Java and to prepare them for further study in the IT/programming/computer science field.

## Design and Features

**Programming Concepts**   This text emphasizes the fundamental concepts of programming so that this knowledge can be applied to other programming languages.

**Problem Solving**   From the very beginning, students are taught to implement programming solutions with proper algorithm design and code conventions.

**Programming Style**   Throughout the text, proper programming style is emphasized so that students can make their applications easy to read, modify, and debug.

**Demonstration Applications and Runs**   Many demonstration applications are included, complete with sample runs, so that students are shown both proper programming techniques and the output actually produced by an application.

**Reviews**   Numerous reviews are presented throughout each chapter to provide immediate reinforcement of newly learned concepts. Solutions to the reviews are included on the Instructor Resources CD.

**Case Studies**   Most chapters end by stating a problem, developing an appropriate algorithm, and then implementing the solution. The process of specification, design, implementation, and debugging and testing is clearly outlined.

**Chapter Summaries**   Each chapter ends by summarizing the concepts and statements covered in the chapter.

**Vocabulary Sections**   Each chapter contains a vocabulary section that defines new terms. A separate section lists Java keywords, statements, and classes.

**Critical Thinking**   Written response questions that require critical thinking from the student are included at the end of each chapter.

**Exercises**   Each chapter includes a large set of exercises of varying difficulty, making them appropriate for students with a range of abilities. Most exercises include a demonstration run to help make clear what output is expected from the student's application. Exercises based on previous work are marked with a ✿ symbol. Answers to the exercises are included on the Instructor Resources CD.

**Appendices**   Appendix A includes a chart of Unicode symbols. Appendix B includes information on downloading an IDE and installing Java. Appendix C introduces applets and Web programming.

**Online Resources**   Students can download all the files needed to complete the reviews and exercises from www.emcschool.net/Java3e (hardcover) or www.paradigmcollege.net/Java3e (softcover). At this site, you will also find materials that complement and extend this text.

**Software**   The Java Development Kit (JDK) can be downloaded for free from:www.oracle.com. An IDE, such as JCreator or NetBeans will also have to be installed. Refer to Chapter 1 and Appendix B for more information. This text has been tested with Java SE 6 and Java SE 7.

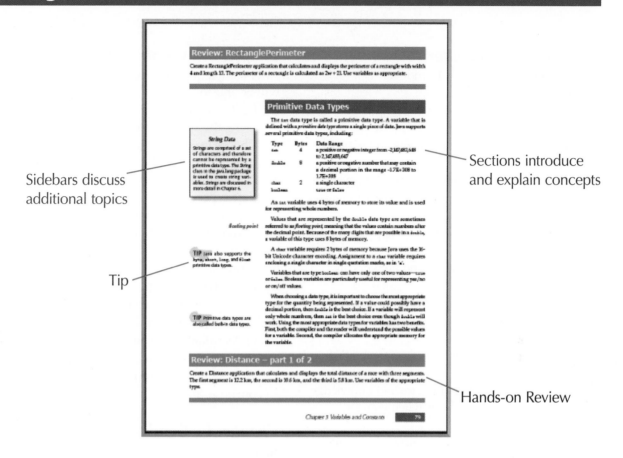

Sidebars discuss additional topics

Tip

Sections introduce and explain concepts

Hands-on Review

Within each chapter, you will find:

**Alternatives** – Other ways to perform actions.

**TIPs** – Additional information that complements the text.

**Sidebars** – Additional topics that complement the text.

**Text in the margin** – Indicates new terminology and subtopics.

**Reviews** – Concepts are presented, discussed, and then followed by a "hands-on" review that allows you to try out newly learned programming skills and knowledge. Some reviews stand alone, while others build on work completed in previous reviews. Therefore, it is recommended that the reviews are completed in the order in which they are presented.

The end of each chapter contains:

**Chapter Summaries** – Concepts covered in the chapter are reviewed.

**Critical Thinking Questions** – Critical thinking questions that will let you review and deepen your understanding of the concepts covered in the chapter.

**Vocabulary and Java Syntax Sections** – A list of new terms and definitions and a list of the Java syntax covered in the chapter.

# Chapter Expectations

## Chapter 1 – Computer Technology

After completing Chapter 1, students will be able to:

1. Compare and contrast various input, output, and storage devices.
2. Identify hardware components and explain their function.
3. Demonstrate knowledge of operating systems.
4. Discuss different computer classifications and compatibility issues.
5. Differentiate among the levels of programming languages.
6. Describe communication and networking components.
7. Understand the binary number system.
8. Describe how data is stored in memory and in files.
9. Use Internet services to access information and share resources.
10. Demonstrate proper etiquette and knowledge of acceptable use policies when using a network.
11. Discuss social and ethical issues associated with computer use.

## Chapter 2 – Introducing Java

After completing Chapter 2, students will be able to:

1. Define terminology associated with object-oriented programming.
2. Explain why Java is a widely used programming language.
3. Create Java applications.
4. Describe the process involved in executing a Java application.
5. Display and format program output.
6. Annotate code properly with comments, formatting, and indentation.
7. Explain the importance of using code conventions.
8. Demonstrate algorithm design as a problem-solving strategy.

## Chapter 3 – Variables and Constants

After completing Chapter 3, students will be able to:

1. Declare and initialize variables and constants using the appropriate data type.
2. Choose legal identifiers that follow good programming style.
3. Differentiate between primitive and abstract data types.
4. Explain how to access Java packages.
5. Demonstrate how to read data from an input stream.
6. Write numeric expressions.
7. Apply type casting.
8. Format numeric output.
9. Identify Java keywords.
10. Differentiate between syntax and logic errors.
11. Understand run-time exceptions.
12. Read and understand a problem description, purpose, and goals.

## Chapter 4 – Conditional Control Structures

After completing Chapter 4, students will be able to:

1. Demonstrate the use of decision structures to control the flow of a program.
2. Generate random numbers.
3. Write compound Boolean expressions.
4. Access methods in the Math class.
5. Modify existing code.
6. Develop code with correct and efficient use of conditional control structures.
7. Select appropriate test data.
8. Create and modify solutions to problems.

## Chapter 5 – Loop Structures and Strings

After completing Chapter 5, students will be able to:

1. Demonstrate the use of repetition control structures.
2. Explain how infinite loops can occur.
3. Differentiate between counters and accumulators.

4. Use various tools and techniques to debug an application.
5. Manipulate and compare strings using the String class and its methods.
6. Develop code with correct and efficient use of repetitive control structures.
7. Apply problem solving strategies.

## Chapter 6 – Methods

After completing Chapter 6, students will be able to:
1. Use top-down development and procedural abstraction to develop problem solutions.
2. Write methods.
3. Use method parameters.
4. Demonstrate the use of method overloading.
5. Return values from a method.
6. Write appropriate method documentation, including pre- and post-conditions.
7. Identify boundary cases and generate appropriate test data.
8. Describe code conventions that apply to methods.

## Chapter 7 – Classes and Object-Oriented Development

After completing Chapter 7, students will be able to:
1. Understand and instantiate objects.
2. Design and implement a class.
3. Apply functional decomposition.
4. Apply appropriate naming conventions to a class.
5. Explain the difference between accessor, modifier, and helper methods.
6. Write constructors.
7. Compare and contrast instance and class members.
8. Understand class specifications and the relationships among the classes.
9. Understand and implement a given class hierarchy.
10. Apply encapsulation.
11. Identify reusable code from existing code.

## Chapter 8 – Inheritance and Polymorphism

After completing Chapter 8, students will be able to:
1. Extend a class using inheritance.
2. Explain an is-a relationship.
3. Implement a subclass.
4. Define and demonstrate polymorphism.
5. Understand abstract classes.
6. Declare and implement an interface.
7. Extend existing code using inheritance.

## Chapter 9 – Arrays

After completing Chapter 9, students will be able to:
1. Describe types of problems that benefit from the use of arrays.
2. Create one and two dimensional arrays.
3. Include array parameters in a method declaration.
4. Understand how to implement arrays with meaningful indexes.
5. Apply offset array indexes.
6. Manipulate characters in a string.
7. Understand the digital code, Unicode.
8. Apply search algorithms to an array.
9. Use methods in the ArrayList class.
10. Demonstrate the use of the Wrapper classes.
11. Understand autoboxing and auto-unboxing.

## Chapter 10 – GUIS and Event-Driven Programming

After completing Chapter 10, students will be able to:
1. Design graphical user interfaces.
2. Use component classes in the Java swing package.
3. Create event-driven applications.
4. Control the layout of an interface using layout managers.
5. Use text fields and combo boxes to obtain user input.
6. Apply color and add images to an interface.

## Chapter 11 – Files and Exception Handling

After completing Chapter 11, students will be able to:

1. Use the File class to create objects that represent a file.
2. Write exception handlers.
3. Understand file streams.
4. Read the contents of an existing file.
5. Process numeric data.
6. Create an output file stream.
7. Explain the object serialization and deserialization processes.

## Chapter 12 – Recursion and Advanced Algorithms

After completing Chapter 12, students will be able to:

1. Implement the selection sort algorithms.
2. Sort objects using the Comparable interface.
3. Implement the insertion sort algorithm.
4. Define and demonstrate recursion.
5. Implement the merge sort algorithm.
6. Implement the binary search algorithm.
7. Explain the recursive technique, depth-first searching.
8. Analyze algorithms for efficiency.
9. Design and document sequential search algorithms.

## Chapter 13 – Data Structures

After completing Chapter 13, students will be able to:

1. Explain how data structures, such as stacks and queues, can be used to organize data.
2. Use and implement well known data structures.
3. Describe standard operations associated with data structures.
4. Choose appropriate data structures.
5. Differentiate between a LIFO and FIFO structure.

# Instructor Resources

Our Instructor Resources correlate directly to the textbook and provide all the additional materials required to offer students an excellent computer programming course. The Instructor Resources feature:

- **Lesson Plans**  Lessons in PDF format keyed to the chapters in the text. Each lesson includes assignments, teaching notes, worksheets, and additional topics.

- **Tutorials**  Flash movie files that provide animations to illustrate searching and sorting concepts. Each movie is keyed to the text.

- **PowerPoint Presentations**  Topics keyed to the text are in PowerPoint files for presentation.

- **Vocabulary**  Word files of the vocabulary presented in the text.

- **Rubrics**  Rubrics keyed to exercises in the text for assessment.

- **Worksheets**  Programming assignments that supplement the exercises in the text provide additional reinforcement of concepts.

- **Critical Thinking Answers**  Answers for the critical thinking questions presented in the text.

- **Data files**  All the files the student needs to complete the reviews and exercises in the text, as well as the files needed to complete the worksheets and tests.

- **EXAM**VIEW® **Assessment Suite**  Question banks keyed to the text and the popular **EXAM**VIEW® software are included to create tests, quizzes, and additional assessment materials.

- **Answer files**  Answers to the reviews, exercises, worksheets, and tests.

# Table of Contents

# Chapter 4 – Conditional Control Structures

# Chapter 5 – Loop Structures and Strings

# Chapter 6 – Methods

# Chapter 7 – Classes and Object-Oriented Development

# Chapter 12 – Recursion and Advanced Algorithms

# Chapter 13 – Data Structures

# Appendix A – Unicode

# Appendix B – Using JCreator

# Appendix C – Applets and Web Programming

# Index

# Chapter 1
# Computer Technology

## Key Concepts

Installing Java
Desktop and mobile computing
Hardware components
Operating systems
Computer classifications and compatibility issues
Programming languages
Networks
Number systems
Files and folders

Storage devices
Internet services
Downloading files
Safe computing
Internet privacy issues
Social and ethical issues
Ergonomics
Environmental issues

## Getting Started with Java

*Java* is a programming language and computing platform that was first released in 1995. It is the underlying technology that is used in many utilities, games, and applications. Java runs on millions of personal computers and mobile devices. Because of its wide-spread use, there are lots of applications and websites that will not work unless the Java Runtime Environment (JRE) is installed on the computer.

Java is a free download from www.oracle.com. The latest version of Java is Java SE (Standard Edition) 7. To develop Java applications and applets you need to install the JDK (Java Development Kit):

**TIP** Java applets are introduced in Appendix C.

- When you download the JDK, the JRE is installed. The JRE consists of the Java Virtual Machine (JVM), Java platform core classes, and supporting Java platform libraries.

- The Java Virtual Machine helps run Java applications.

- The Java Plug-in software is a component of the Java Runtime Environment (JRE). The Java Plug-in software is not a stand-alone program and cannot be installed separately.

To develop Java applications, you will also need to install an Integrated Development Environment (IDE), such as *JCreator* or *NetBeans*. An IDE provides a workspace that allows for editing, compiling, and running of source code. Refer to Appendix B for more information about installing Java and downloading JCreator and other IDEs.

You will start creating Java applications in Chapter 2.

## Desktop and Mobile Computing

Computers come in many sizes and with a variety of features. A *desktop computer* and its components are designed to fit on or under a desk:

Mobile computing devices, such as notebooks, tablet PCs, handhelds, and smartphones, contain long-lasting batteries and wireless technology that allow them to be portable:

Mobile computing devices also include *wearable computers*, which are used in many occupations. For example, a wearable scanner can be placed or worn on the back-of-the-hand, freeing up a warehouse operator's hands to move packages or products, improving efficiency and productivity. They are also used to monitor health problems, such as heart rate and respiration flow.

### Mainframes and Supercomputers

A mainframe is a large computer system that supports multiuser applications and tasks that require the storage and processing of huge amounts of information. Large corporations, airlines, banks, government agencies, and universities use mainframes.

A supercomputer is the fastest and most powerful type of computer. Supercomputers focus on executing a few programs as fast as possible and are used for weather forecasting and nuclear energy research.

## Computer Hardware

The physical components of the computer, such as the monitor and base unit, are referred to as *hardware*:

**input devices**

- *Input devices*, such as a keyboard, mouse, microphone, DVD drive, and digital camera are used to enter data into the computer.

- *Peripheral devices*, such as printers, webcams, and microphones, are added to make a computer more versatile. A peripheral device either has a wireless connection or is attached to a *port* on the computer. There are different types of ports, such as serial, parallel, FireWire, USB, and Bluetooth ports.

- Computers process data into meaningful, useful information. Processed data is conveyed using *output devices*. Monitors and printers display data, DVD+RWs, disk drives, and memory keys store data, and speakers communicate audio output.

### Printers

A laser printer uses a laser and toner to generate characters and graphics on paper. An ink-jet printer uses an ink cartridge to place very small dots of ink onto paper to create characters and graphics.

The base unit also contains the *motherboard*, which is the main circuit board. The motherboard contains several components:

*expansion boards*

- *Expansion boards* are circuit boards that connect to the motherboard to add functionality to the computer. Examples include sound cards and video adapters.

- The *CPU (Central Processing Unit)* or processor processes data and controls the flow of data between the computer's other units. Within the CPU is the *ALU (Arithmetic Logic Unit)*, which can perform arithmetic and logic operations. It can also make comparisons, which is the basis of the computer's decision-making power. The ALU is so fast that the time needed to carry out a single addition is measured in nanoseconds (billionths of a second). The speed at which a CPU can execute instructions is determined by the computer's *clock rate*. The clock rate is measured in *megahertz* (*MHz*, million of cycles per second) or *gigahertz* (*GHz*, billion of cycles per second).

*clock rate, megahertz gigahertz*

- A *bus* is a set of circuits that connect the CPU to other components. The data bus transfers data between the CPU, memory, and other hardware devices on the motherboard. The *address bus* carries memory addresses that indicate where the data is located and where the data should go. A *control bus* carries control signals. All data flows through the CPU:

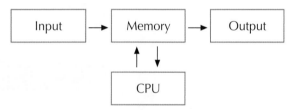

**Real-time Clock**

A battery chip called a real-time clock keeps track of the date and time in a computer even when the computer is off.

**TIP** Intel and AMD are two processor manufacturers.

- Memory in the form of *integrated circuits (ICs)* stores data electronically. *ROM (Read Only Memory)* contains the most basic operating instructions for the computer. The data in ROM is a permanent part of the computer and cannot be changed. *RAM (Random Access Memory)*, also called primary or main memory, is memory where data and instructions are stored temporarily. Data stored in RAM can be written to *secondary memory*, which includes any type of storage media, such as a hard disk, memory key, or DVD+RW. Secondary memory must be copied into primary memory before it is processed by the CPU. SRAM (Static Random Access Memory) is high-speed memory referred to as *cache* (pronounced "cash"). This memory is used to store frequently used data so that it can be quickly retrieved by an application.

**Integrated Circuits**

Integrated circuits, also called chips, are created from silicon wafers which are etched with intricate circuits and coated with a metallic oxide that allows the circuits to conduct electricity. The silicon wafers are housed in special plastic cases that have metal pins. The pins allow the integrated circuits to be plugged into circuit boards.

# Operating Systems and Environment

Computers also contain programs, or software. *Applications software* is written by programmers to perform a specific task, such as a word processor. *Operating system* (OS) software is run automatically when the computer is turned on and is used to control processing and peripherals, run application software, and control input and output, among other tasks. Operating systems include Windows, Mac OS X, Unix, and Linux. Java applications are *platform-independent*, which means they can run on most major operating systems.

*environment*

*Environment* refers to a computer's hardware and software configuration. For example, a Windows 7 environment means that the computer is running a version of the Windows 7 OS software and hardware includes a 1GHz processor or better, 1GB of RAM or more, and at least 16 GB of hard disk space available. The hardware requirements are based on what will be needed to allow the OS software to properly manage the computer's tasks. The term platform is sometimes synonymous with environment. Most environments run an OS with a graphical user interface (GUI). For example:

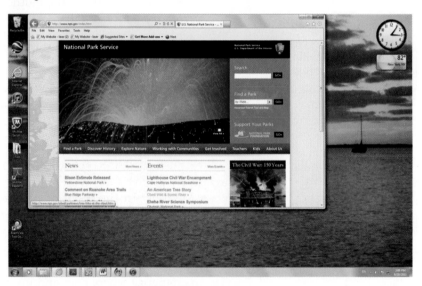

*Windows 7 Operating System*

*utility program*

OS functions are implemented through *utility programs* which have one clearly defined task. Utility programs manage input and output, read and write to memory, manage the processor, maintain system security, and manage files and disks. A *device driver* is one type of utility program. Device drivers are needed for printing, viewing graphics, using a CD/ DVD drive, and using peripherals in general. Some utility programs load when the computer starts and are called *memory-resident* because they are always in memory. Features are added to an OS by incorporating utility programs to perform tasks that are in addition to the tasks required to run the computer. For example, an OS intended for a desktop or notebook environment will often include utilities for backing up the computer, restoring files, and other tools for improving performance:

*device driver*

*memory-resident*

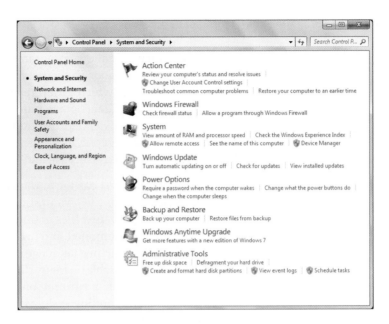

*Windows 7 Utilities*

# Programming Languages

A *programming language* is a set of words, codes, and symbols that allow a programmer to give instructions to the computer. Many programming languages exist, each with their own rules, or syntax, for writing these instructions.

*low-level programming languages*

Programming languages can be classified as low-level and high-level languages. *Low-level programming languages* include machine language and assembly language. Machine language, which is referred to as a first generation programming language, can be used to communicate directly with the computer. However, it is difficult to program in machine language because the language consists of 0s and 1s to represent the status of a switch (0 for off and 1 for on). Assembly language uses the same instructions and structure as machine language but the programmer is able to use meaningful names or abbreviations instead of numbers. Assembly language is referred to as a second generation programming language.

## Fourth and Fifth Generation Languages

Fourth generation languages (4GL), such as SQL, have higher English-like instructions than most high-level languages and are typically used to access databases. Fifth generation languages are used for artificial intelligence.

*High-level programming languages*, which are often referred to as third generation programming languages (3GL), were first developed in the late 1950s. High-level programming languages have English-like instructions and are easier to use than machine language. High-level programming languages include Fortran, C, Basic, COBOL, and Pascal. In order for the computer to understand a program written in a high-level language, programmers convert the source code into machine language using a compiler or an interpreter. A *compiler* is a program that converts an entire program into machine code before the program is executed. An *interpreter* translates and executes an instruction before moving on to the next instruction in the program.

**object-oriented programming**

In the 1980s, *object-oriented programming* (OOP) evolved out of the need to better develop complex programs in a systematic, organized approach. The OOP approach allows programmers to create modules that can be used over and over again in a variety of programs. These modules contain code called classes, which group related data and actions. Properly designed classes encapsulate data to hide the implementation details, are versatile enough to be extended through inheritance, and give the programmer options through polymorphism. Object-oriented languages include Java, C++, Visual C#, Visual F#, and Visual Basic.

As mentioned earlier in the chapter, Java applications are platform-independent. In the Java programming language, all source code is first written in plain text files ending with the .java extension. Those source files are then compiled into .class files. A .class file contains *bytecodes*, which is the machine language of the Java Virtual Machine (JVM). Because the JVM is available on many different operating systems, the same .class files are capable of running on Microsoft Windows, Linux, Mac OS, and other major operating systems:

## Networks

A *network* is a combination of hardware and software that allows computers to exchange data and share software and devices, such as printers. Networks are widely used by businesses, universities, and other organizations because a network:

- allows users to reliably share and exchange data.

- can reduce costs by sharing devices such as printers.

- offers security options including password protection to restrict access to certain files.

- simplifies file management through centralized software updates and file backups.

- provides communication tools such as e-mail for network users.

Networks are classified by their size, architecture, and topology. A common size classifications is *LAN (Local-Area Network)*, which is a network used to connect devices within a small area such as a building or a campus. A *WAN (Wide-Area Network)* is used to connect devices over large geographical distances. A WAN can be one widespread network or it can be a number of LANs linked together.

*Chapter 1 Computer Technology*

The computers and other devices in a LAN each contain an expansion card called a *network interface card*:

*Network interface card*

## Transmission Media

Computers must be connected in order to transmit data between the nodes. Cable transmission media includes twisted-pair wiring, coaxial cable, and fiber optic cable.

Wireless transmission media includes infrared signals, broadcast radio, cellular radio, microwaves, and communications satellites.

The amount of data and the speed at which data can travel over a media is called bandwidth, which is measured in bits per second (bps). Each transmission media has a specific length or range restriction, data transmission rate, and cost.

A cable plugs into the adapter card to connect one device to another to form a LAN. Cables are not required for network cards that have wireless capabilities. Network interface cards are available for desktop and mobile computers and take various other forms including an adapter card, a PC card, or a Flash memory card.

Along with the physical, or hardware, aspects of setting up a network, there is also the software aspect. A *network operating system* is software that allow users and devices to communicate over the network. The operating system installed must be capable of supporting networking functions, such as security access features and support for multiple users. Operating systems capable of network functions are available for Linux, Windows, Unix, and Mac. The network architecture, discussed next, must also be considered when choosing a network OS.

Network architecture includes the type of computers on the network and determines how network resources are handled. Two common models are peer-to-peer and client/server. In a *peer-to-peer network*, each computer on the network is considered equal in terms of responsibilities and resource sharing. A *client/server network* consists of a group of computers, called *clients*, connected to a server. A *server* is a computer with more RAM, a larger hard disk, and sometimes multiple CPUs that is used to manage network functions.

**topology**
**node**

Physical *topology* refers to the arrangement of the nodes on a network. A *node* is a location on the network with a device capable of processing information, such as a computer or a printer. There are three common physical topologies:

**bus topology**

- The *bus topology* is a physical LAN topology that uses a single central cable, called the bus or backbone to attach each node directly:

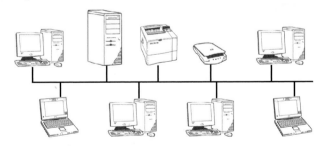

*LAN using a bus topology*

- In a *star topology*, each node is attached to a *hub*, which is a device that joins communication lines at a central location on the network:

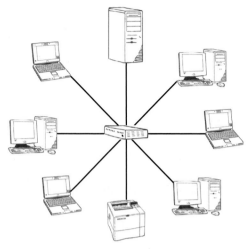

*LAN using a star topology*

- In a *ring topology*, each node is connected to form a closed loop. A LAN with a ring topology can usually cover a greater distance than a bus or star topology:

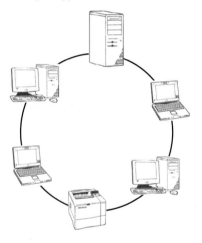

*LAN using a ring topology*

- *Wireless networks* use high frequency radio waves or infrared signals instead of cables to transmit data. A router/wireless access point device is used to allow nodes to transfer data wirelessly.

Another type of topology is *logical topology*, which refers to the way data is passed between the nodes on a network. A LAN's logical topology is not always the same as its physical topology.

Network users are given a user name and password to log on to a network through a computer connected to the network. Users are also assigned a level of access to maintain security. Network users should follow a certain etiquette referred to as *netiquette*:

*netiquette*

- Do not attempt to access the account of another user without authorization.

- Do not share your password, and change it periodically.

- Use appropriate subject matter and language, and be considerate of other people's beliefs and opinions.

## Number Systems

*binary number system*

The electrical circuits on an IC have one of two states, off or on. Therefore, the *binary number system* (base 2), which uses only two digits (0 and 1), was adopted for use in computers. To represent numbers and letters, a code was developed with eight binary digits grouped together to represent a single number or letter. Each 0 or 1 in the binary code is called a *bit* (BInary digiT) and an 8-bit unit is called a *byte*.

*bit*
*byte*

*base 10*

Our most familiar number system is the decimal, or *base 10*, system. It uses ten digits: 0 through 9. Each place represents a power of ten, with the first place to the left of the decimal point representing $10^0$, the next place representing $10^1$, the next $10^2$, and so on (remember that any number raised to the zero power is 1). In the decimal number 485, the 4 represents $4 \times 10^2$, the 8 represents $8 \times 10^1$, and the 5 represents $5 \times 10^0$. The number 485 represents the sum $4 \times 100 + 8 \times 10 + 5 \times 1$ (400 + 80 + 5):

| Decimal | Base 10 Equivalent |
|---------|--------------------|
| 485 | $4 \times 10^2 + 8 \times 10^1 + 5 \times 10^0 = 400 + 80 + 5$ |

*base 2*

The binary, or *base 2*, system works identically except that each place represents a power of two instead of a power of ten. For example, the binary number 101 represents the sum $1 \times 2^2 + 0 \times 2^1 + 1 \times 2^0$ or 5 in base ten. Some decimal numbers and their binary equivalents are:

| Decimal | Binary | Base 2 Equivalent | | |
|---------|--------|-------------------|-----|-----|
| 0 | 0 | $= 0 \times 2^1 + 0 \times 2^0$ | $= 0 \times 2 + 0 \times 1$ | $= 0 + 0$ |
| 1 | 1 | $= 0 \times 2^1 + 1 \times 2^0$ | $= 0 \times 2 + 1 \times 1$ | $= 0 + 1$ |
| 2 | 10 | $= 1 \times 2^1 + 0 \times 2^0$ | $= 1 \times 2 + 0 \times 1$ | $= 2 + 0$ |
| 3 | 11 | $= 1 \times 2^1 + 1 \times 2^0$ | $= 1 \times 2 + 1 \times 1$ | $= 2 + 1$ |
| 4 | 100 | $= 1 \times 2^2 + 0 \times 2^1 + 0 \times 2^0$ | $= 1 \times 4 + 0 \times 2 + 0 \times 1$ | $= 4 + 0 + 0$ |

*base 16*

The hexadecimal system is used to represent groups of four binary digits. The *hexadecimal*, or *base 16*, system is based on 16 digits: 0 through 9, and the letters A through F representing 10 through 15 respectively. Each place represents a power of sixteen. For example, the hexadecimal number 1F represents the sum $1 \times 16^1 + 15 \times 16^0$. Some decimal numbers and their hexadecimal equivalents are:

| Decimal | Binary | Hexadecimal | Base 16 Equivalent | | |
| --- | --- | --- | --- | --- | --- |
| 0 | 0000 0000 | 0 | $= 0 \times 16^0$ | $= 0 \times 1$ | $= 0$ |
| 10 | 0000 1010 | A | $= 10 \times 16^0$ | $= 10 \times 1$ | $= 10$ |
| 25 | 0001 1001 | 19 | $= 1 \times 16^1 + 9 \times 16^0$ | $= 1 \times 16 + 9 \times 1$ | $= 16 + 9$ |
| 30 | 0001 1110 | 1E | $= 1 \times 16^1 + 14 \times 16^0$ | $= 1 \times 16 + 14 \times 1$ | $= 16 + 14$ |

For clarity, a non-base 10 number should have the base subscripted after the number. For example, to show the difference between 100 in base 10 and 100 in base 2 (which represents 4), the base 2 number should be written as $100_2$.

*Unicode*

Every letter of an alphabet (Latin, Japanese, Cherokee, and so on) and symbols of every culture (=, @, ½, and so on) have been given a representation in a digital code called Unicode. *Unicode* uses a set of sixteen 1s and 0s to form a 16-bit binary code for each symbol. For example, the uppercase letter V is Unicode 00000000 01010110, which can be thought of as the base 10 number 86 ($86_{10}$). Lowercase v has a separate code of 00000000 01110110, or $118_{10}$.

## Storing Data in Memory

*megabyte*
*gigabyte*

Computer memory is measured in bytes. For example, a computer might have 1GB of RAM. In computers and electronics *MB* stands for *megabytes* where mega represents $2^{20}$ or 1,048,576 bytes and *GB* stands for *gigabytes*, which is $2^{30}$ or 1,073,741,820 bytes.

*address*

Data stored in memory is referred to by an address. An *address* is a unique binary representation of a location in memory. Therefore, data can be stored, accessed, and retrieved from memory by its address. For data to be addressable in memory, it must usually be at least one byte in length. For example, to store JIM in memory each character is converted to Unicode and stored in two bytes of memory with each memory location designated by its address:

|  | J | I | M |
| --- | --- | --- | --- |
| binary code | 01001010 | 01001001 | 01001101 |
| memory address | 01 | 10 | 11 |

Because JIM is a character string, it will probably be stored in adjacent memory addresses.

*words*

Bits grouped in units of 16 to 64 (2 to 8 bytes) are called *words*. Data stored in a word is also located by an address. The size of a word depends on the computer system.

*overflow error*

The binary representation of an integer number is usually stored in four bytes of memory. Because an integer is stored in four bytes, the range of integers that can be stored is –2,147,483,648 to 2,147,483,647. An *overflow error* occurs when the number of bits that are needed to represent the integer is greater than the size of four bytes.

*real numbers*

*Real numbers*, also called *floating point numbers*, are numbers that contain decimal points. The binary representation of a real number is usually 4 to 8 bytes of memory. The binary number 111.10 is equivalent to the real decimal number 7.5 and is stored in memory as the binary number $0.11110 \times 2^3$. In this form, the bits that represent the mantissa (fractional part) are stored in one section of a word and the exponent, in this example $3$ ($11_2$), is stored in another section of the word:

| 0 | 0 | 0 | 0 | 0 | 0 | 1 | 1 | 1 | 1 | 0 | 0 | 0 | 0 | 1 | 1 |

mantissa          exponent

*roundoff error*

The overflow problem discussed for integers can also occur in real numbers if the part of the word storing the exponent is not large enough. A *roundoff error* occurs when there are not enough bits to store the mantissa.

## What is a File?

A *file* is related data stored on a persistent media. A file can be an application (program) or the product of an application. For example, a word processor application is used to create document files. A file is stored on a persistent media so that it is retained even after the computer or computerized device is turned off. A file can be used over and over again whenever the data it stores is needed.

### Extensions

Common extensions include:

.class - compiled Java file
.gif - GIF image file
.java - Java file
.odt - Open Document file
.xlsx - Excel file
.zip - compressed file

**TIP** The original form the file is saved in is referred to as the *native* format.

A file is really just 1s and 0s because it is stored in binary code. Computers are programmed to translate bytes and words into symbols. Depending on the file type, these symbols are either human-readable or computer-readable after translation. Human-readable files are called *text files*, and computer-readable files are called *binary files*. Simple files, such as a text document, can be measured in *kilobytes*, for example 64K. The K comes from the word *kilo* and represents $2^{10}$ or 1,024. Therefore, a 64K file uses 65,536 bytes ($64 \times 2^{10}$) of storage.

File types are distinguished by the *extension* that comes after the file name. An application adds a unique extension to the files it creates. For example, `MyResume.docx` is a document file type. A DOCX file is a file format created by Microsoft. A file named `TestData.txt` is a plain text file. A TXT file contains only letters, numbers, and common symbols readable by humans. An ODT file is an Open Document file format for saving documents such as text documents, spreadsheets, charts, and presentations. This standard was developed by the OASIS industry consortium and was based on the XML file format originally created by OpenOffice.org.

*folders*

*Folders* are used to organize commonly related files. A Java application consists of a series of files that are organized into a project folder:

Binary files are more complex than text files and often contain data for photos, formatted text, spreadsheets, sound, and so on. The disadvantage of binary files is that they require another application to interpret the contents. A binary file may have content similar to:

þ»ÿÿúªî¿þÿþûîûûü¾þ¨ÿ ÿÝþ_ÿÿ ÿwþuUuWÿw÷÷ÿ{þÿß¿ß÷ÿuWwwu÷uu

*A binary file is computer-readable*

### File Size Limitations

File size can be decreased or compressed using a compression program. This technique is often used to accommodate storage device and e-mail account limitations.

## Storage Devices

Storage devices use a persistent media to maintain files. These devices, which are also referred to as drives, mass storage, and auxiliary storage, can be categorized in three ways:

- internal, such as a hard disk, or external, such as a memory key
- removable or permanent media
- magnetic, optical, or solid state technology

Storage device technologies determine the media, size, and portability of a device. Magnetic technology uses a mechanical drive with tiny electromagnetic heads for reading and writing data to media. The media required with magnetic technology is a disk, usually made of aluminum or Mylar®, coated with iron oxide. The disk is either encased in hard plastic or several disks, called platters, are sealed in a case (hard disk). A data signal sent through the heads in the drive magnetize a bit of the media in one direction to store a 1 and in the other direction to store a 0.

Optical technology uses a drive with a laser and an optoelectronic sensor. The media required with optical technology is a compact or DVD disc made of polycarbonate plastic.

Solid state technology allows for the smallest, most portable storage devices because the technology requires no moving parts. The media is Flash memory, which consists of a grid with two tiny transistors at each cell. Each cell corresponds to a bit. Applying a charge to a cell stores a 0, while applying a stronger charge stores a 1. The grid of transistors is encased in hard plastic and is very small. Some devices can store 2MB or more within a package thinner and smaller than a quarter. Slightly larger media can store gigabytes of data. Encased media is often directly attached to a USB plug for use with a computer, or simply has conductive material imprinted so the media can slide into a digital camera slot.

Magnetic technology allows for storage devices that range in capacity up to many gigabytes (hard disk drives with many platters). Optical technology includes DVDs that can store at least 4GB of data. Solid-state devices store from 64KB of data to many gigabytes.

On a Windows computer, storage media is accessed using a drive letter, such a *D* or *E*. On a Macintosh computer, storage media is accessed through a drive name, such as *Macintosh HD*. On a personal computer, files are typically saved to the hard disk which is an internal storage device. It is always a good idea to back-up any files saved to the hard drive.

Storage media can be very sensitive. Care should be taken to avoid damaging files:

- Keep magnetic media away from magnets.
- Handle CD/DVDs by the center hole or by the edges.
- Store CD/DVDs in a jewel case or sleeve to prevent scratches.
- Keep media away from moisture and extreme temperatures.

### Storage Media

The capacity of storage media varies. For example, a CD has a storage capacity of 650 MB, and a DVD has a storage capacity of over 4GB.

### Blu-ray Disc

Blu-ray Disc is an optical disc storage media format that has the same dimensions as a CD or DVD. A dual layer Blu-ray Disc can store 50GB.

### Tera, Peta, Exa

As more and more data is stored electronically, file sizes become very large and require storage devices with very large capacities. TB (terabyte) is $2^{40}$ bytes or 1 trillion bytes, petabyte (PB) is $2^{50}$ bytes or 1,024 terabytes, and EB (exabyte) is $2^{60}$ bytes or 1,024 petabytes. Devices with TB storage capacities are gradually coming into use, especially for database files.

## Intranet, Extranet, Internet

*firewall*

An *intranet* is a network that is used by a single organization, such as a corporation or school, and is only accessible by authorized users. The purpose of an intranet is to share information. However, a firewall is also used to lock out unauthorized users. A *firewall* is a network security system that prevents unauthorized network access.

An *extranet* extends an intranet by providing various levels of accessibility to authorized members of the public. For example, a corporation may extend their intranet to provide access to specific information, such as their ordering system, to registered customers.

The largest and most widely accessed network is the *Internet*, a worldwide network of computers that is not controlled by any one organization. The Internet has had an undeniable impact on modern society because it allows users worldwide to communicate in a matter of seconds.

The Internet is actually numerous networks all linked together through routers. A *router* is a device that connects different network technologies. Networks connected to routers use *TCP/IP* (Transmission Control Protocol/Internet Protocol) software to communicate.

Computers on the Internet are either servers or clients. The client is sent information from a server. The client/server structure of the Internet is called interactive because the information accessed is a result of selections made by the user. For example, a computer with just minimal software for accessing the Internet is a client. The client user selecting options from the Internet is receiving the information from a server, a computer with additional software and files that is also connected to the Internet.

### History of the Internet

The Internet evolved from ARPANET, a network created in the late 1960s by the Department of Defense's ARPA (Advanced Research Projects Agency), and the theory of open architecture networking.

## Telecommunications

### PLC

PLC (power line communications) uses existing power grid networks to send broadband data communications. Internet connections are established by plugging a computer device into a power outlet.

*Telecommunications* is the transmitting and receiving of data. Data can be in various forms including voice and video. Telecommunications requires a modem or adapter and a line or cable. The speed of data transmission (sending) and receipt (receiving) is measured in *Kbps* (thousands of bits per second) or *Mbps* (millions of bits per second). Numerous telecommunications options are available, which vary in speed and cost:

- A **conventional modem** uses standard telephone lines to convert analog signals to digital data. A conventional modem is a 56 Kbps modem, which transmits data at 28.8 Kbps and 36.6 Kbps, and receives data at 56 Kbps. Today, most home and business users select options other than conventional modems if they are available in their area, due to the slow access time associated with conventional modems.

- A **DSL** (Digital Subscriber Line) modem uses standard telephone lines with data transmission up to 640 Kbps. Data receipt is from 1.5 Mbps to 9 Mbps. A DSL (Asymmetric DSL) is the most common form used.

- A **cable modem** transmits data through a coaxial cable television network. Data transmission is from 2 Mbps to 10 Mbps and data receipt is from 10 Mbps to 36 Mbps.

- **Leased/Dedicated lines** are used by many businesses and schools for Internet access. They allow for a permanent connection to the Internet that is always active. The cost of a leased line is usually a fixed monthly fee. A T-1 carrier is a type of leased line that transmits data at 1.544 Mbps.

- **ISDN** (Integrated Services Digital Network) is a digital telephone network provided by a local phone company. ISDN is capable of transmitting and receiving data at up to 64 Kbps. ISDN requires the use of an ISDN terminal adapter instead of a modem.

## Internet Services

Internet services include the World Wide Web, e-mail, and mailing lists. The *World Wide Web* (WWW), also called the *Web* is the most widely used Internet service. The Web can be used to search and access information available on the Internet. A *web browser* application, such as Microsoft Internet Explorer, provides a graphical interface to present information in the form of a website:

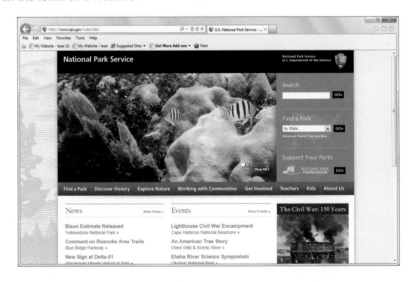

Another widely used Internet service is *e-mail* or *electronic mail*, which is the sending and receiving of messages and computer files over a communications network, such as a LAN (Local Area Network) or the Internet. E-mail can be received in a matter of seconds, even if the recipient is located half way around the world.

An e-mail address is required in order to send and receive e-mail messages. E-mail addresses are provided when you sign up with an ISP or an online service. A typical e-mail address is similar to:

christina@emcschool.net

user name — host or domain name — top-level domain

---

### Blog

Blog is short for weblog and is a type of website where users can post entries in a journal format.

### Feeds

Feeds, also known as RSS feeds, XML feeds, syndicated content, or web feeds, contain frequently updated content published by a website. They are typically used for news and blog websites. Feeds can also be used to deliver audio content, typically in MP3 format. This is referred to as podcasting.

### Digital Signature

A digital signature is a code that is attached to an electronic message to verify the authenticity of a website or e-mail message.

*Chapter 1 Computer Technology*

### E-mail Protocols

POP3 is an e-mail protocol that connects to an e-mail server to download messages to a local computer.

IMAP is an e-mail protocol that connects to an e-mail server to read message headers and then the user selects which e-mail messages to download to a local computer.

HTTP is used as an e-mail protocol when a web page is used to access an e-mail account.

E-mail software is also required for sending and receiving e-mail messages. An example of e-mail software is Outlook. Browser-based e-mail only requires a web browser and is available through sites such as Yahoo!, Google, and Hotmail.

Certain rules should be followed when composing e-mail messages

- Use manners. Include "please" and "thank you" and also properly address people you do not know as Mr., Ms., Mrs., Dr., and so on.
- Be concise.
- Be professional, which includes using the proper spelling and grammar.
- Re-read a message before it is sent. Always fill in the To box last to avoid sending a message before it is complete.

E-mail messages are not private. An e-mail message goes through several mail servers before it reaches the recipient, making it easily accessible for others to read. Therefore, sending e-mail messages requires following a certain etiquette:

- Send messages through your account only.
- Use appropriate subject matter and language.
- Be considerate of other people's beliefs and opinions.

### Spam

Along with personal and business messages, most people also receive a lot of "junk e-mail" or spam. Most e-mail software includes features to filter and block messages from specific senders.

When sending e-mail at work or school, it is important to remember that employers and school administrators have the right to read any e-mail messages sent over the corporate or school network, as well as the right to track online activity.

A *mailing list server* is a server that manages mailing lists for groups of users. Two mailing list servers are Listserv and Majordomo. Often users subscribe to mailing lists for discussion purposes. When a subscriber posts a message to a mailing list server, every subscriber receives a copy of the message. Subscribers are identified by a single name or e-mail address.

## Finding Information on the Web and Downloading Files

A *search engine* is a program that searches a database of web pages for keywords and then lists hyperlinks to pages that contain those keywords. Commonly used search engines include:

**Yahoo!** (www.yahoo.com)
**Google** (www.google.com)
**Bing** (www.bing.com)

### Search Engines

A search engine usually works by sending out an agent, such as spider. A spider is an application that gathers a list of available web page documents and stores this list in a database that users can search by keywords.

When displaying information, search engines often show "Sponsored Sites Results" first. These are sites that contain the information being searched for but have paid the search engine to list their sites at the top of the list.

A search engine can be queried to display specific web pages. *Search criteria* can include single words or phrases that are then used by the engine to determine a match. A *match* is a web page that contains the search criteria. Surrounding phrases with quotation marks finds web pages that contain the entire phrase. The more specific the search criteria, the better the chance the information will be found.

Most searches yield far too many matches to be useful. Limiting the number of matches to a reasonable number can usually be accomplished by using Boolean logic in the search criteria:

- The **+** (plus sign) is used in search criteria to limit a search to only web pages that contain all of the specified words. For example, a search for florida +hotel or florida hotel returns only links to pages containing both words. **AND** can be used in place of + in most search engines.

- **OR** can be used in most search engines to find web pages that contain any one of the words in the criteria. For example, the criteria florida OR hotel returns links to pages containing either of the words.

- The **–** (minus sign) is used to exclude unwanted web pages. For example, the search for shakespeare –play returns hyperlinks to pages containing the word shakespeare, but eliminates pages that also contain the word play. **NOT** can be used in place of – in most search engines.

Some search engines provide a *subject tree*, or *web directory*, which is a list of sites separated into categories. The term subject tree is used because many of the categories "branch" off into subcategories, such as technology or images. These subcategories allow the user to narrow their search.

Information on a website is sometimes in the form of a downloadable file. *Downloading* is the process of copying a file from a website to the user's computer. For example, virus definitions can be downloaded from an antivirus software company's website and software updates can be downloaded from the software company's website. When a file is downloaded, the user specifies where the file should be saved on the local computer. Files should only be downloaded from known, authentic websites since downloadable files are often associated with viruses.

**TIP** Just because a file is available on a website for download does not mean that it is legal to download the file. Downloading copyrighted files that have not been made freely available is a violation of copyright law.

If information from a website is to be referenced or quoted in a report, essay, or other document, a citation must be used to give credit to the original author and allow the reader to locate the cited information. A widely accepted form for citation is published by the Modern Language Association (MLA) in its publication *MLA Handbook for Writers of Research Papers, Seventh Edition.*

MLA

In general, a citation for material located at a website should look similar to:

> Author's Last Name, First Name. "Article Title." Site Title. Publisher Name, Last-updated date. Web. Access date. <URL>.

If no publisher name is available, n.p. should be used and if no publication date is listed, n.d. is used. A citation of a page on a website:

> Marrelli, J. "How to use Internet Explorer". *Lawrenceville Press - Download Data Files.* Lawrenceville Press, 23 Dec. 2010. Web. 15 May 2012.

**TIP** MLA no longer requires the use of URLs in MLA citations because Web sites are not static and typically documents can be located by searching the title in a search engine. If an instructor still requires the use of URLs, they are placed in angle brackets after the date of access.

# Internet Privacy Issues

The growth of the Internet has caused additional concerns about personal privacy. Searching for information on the Internet is not as anonymous as it might seem.

The collection of data about consumers visiting a website is a marketing technique known as *online profiling*. When a commercial website is visited, information about the user may be collected using various methods such as cookies or web beacons.

A *cookie* is a text file created by the server computer when a user enters information into a website. The cookie file is then stored on the user's computer and accessed each time the user visits that website. Cookies are often created when online purchases are made. Although cookies can only store information that the user has selected or entered, their use has raised concerns over privacy issues.

*Web beacons*, also called *web bugs* or *pixel tags*, are tiny, transparent graphics located on web pages or in e-mail messages that are used in combination with cookies to collect data about web page users or e-mail senders. Usually the monitoring is done by an outside advertising company. The information a web beacon collects includes the IP address of the computer, the URL being visited, the time the web page was viewed, the type of browser being used, and the cookie file.

Before providing a company with personal information through a website, check the site's privacy policy. A *privacy policy* is a legally binding document that explains how any personal information will be used.

The Internet has opened up access to many files that were previously inaccessible. To protect both the privacy of an individual and the accuracy of data stored about individuals, several laws have been passed:

- The **Electronic Communications Privacy Act of 1986 (ECPA)** makes it a crime to access electronic data without authorization. It also prohibits unauthorized release of such data.

- The **Electronic Freedom of Information Act of 1996 (E-FOIA)** requires federal government agencies to make certain agency information available for public inspection and is designed to improve public access to agency records by making more information available online.

- The **Children's Online Privacy Protection Act of 1998 (COPPA)** requires commercial websites that collect personal information from children under the age of 13 to obtain parental consent.

- The **Safety and Freedom through Encryption Act of 1999 (SAFE)** gives Americans the freedom to use any type of encryption to protect their confidential information.

Other laws have been passed that may invade the privacy of some to protect the safety of others. For example, the **Provide Appropriate Tools Required to Intercept and Obstruct Terrorism (PATRIOT) Act of 2001** gives law enforcement the ability to monitor individual's e-mail and web activity.

## Spyware

Spyware is software that uses the Internet to gather personal information from an unsuspecting user. Spyware is unknowingly downloaded and installed with another file, such as freeware or shareware programs.

## IP Address

An IP address is an identifier for a computer or device on a TCP/IP network.

**TIP** A website's privacy policy is typically found as a link at the bottom of the home page of a website.

## NET Act

The NET (No Electronic Theft) Act of 1997 closed a loophole in the law which allowed copyrighted material to be given away on the Internet without any legal penalty.

# Internet Acceptable Use Policy

Internet content, unproductive use, and copyright have prompted many schools and businesses to develop an Acceptable Use Policy or Internet Use Agreement. Acceptable Use Policies typically contain rules similar to:

- Use appropriate language.

- Do not reveal personal address or phone numbers.

- Do not access, upload, download, or distribute inappropriate materials.

- Do not access another user's account.

- Use of the network for private business is prohibited.

- Only administrator installed software may be used on the computers. Adding, deleting, or modifying installed software is not permitted.

# The Social and Ethical Implications of Computer Use

*information age*

The society in which we live has been so profoundly affected by computers that historians refer to the present time as the *information age*. This is due to the our ability to store and manipulate large amounts of information (data) using computers. As an information society, we must consider both the social and ethical implications of our use of computers. By ethical questions we mean asking what are the morally right and wrong ways to use computers.

*ergonomics*

*Ergonomics* is the science that studies safe work environments. Many health-related issues, such as carpal tunnel syndrome and computer vision syndrome (CVS), are related to prolonged computer use.

Power and paper waste are environmental concerns associated with computer use. Suggestions for eliminating these concerns include recycling paper and printer toner cartridges and turning off monitors and printers when not in use.

Employee monitoring is an issue associated with computers in the workplace. It is legal for employers to install software programs that monitor employee computer use. As well, e-mail messages can be read without employee notification.

As discussed in a previous section in the chapter, the invasion of privacy is a serious problem associated with computers. Because computers can store vast amounts of data we must decide what information is proper to store, what is improper, and who should have access to the information. Every time you use a credit card, make a phone call, withdraw money, reserve a flight, or register at school, a computer records the transaction. These records can be used to learn a great deal about you—where you have been, when you were there, and how much money was spent. Should this information be available to everyone?

Computers are also used to store information about your credit rating, which determines your ability to borrow money. If you want to buy a car and finance it at a bank, the bank first checks your credit records on a computer to determine if you have a good credit rating. If you purchase the car and then apply for automobile insurance, another computer will check to determine if you have traffic violations. How do you know if the information being used is accurate? The laws listed below have been passed to help ensure that the right to privacy is not infringed by the improper use of data stored in computer files:

- The **Fair Credit Reporting Act of 1970** gives individuals the right to see information collected about them for use by credit, insurance, and employment agencies. If a person is denied credit they are allowed to see the files used to make the credit determination. If any of the information is incorrect, the person has the right to have it changed. The act also restricts who may access credit files to only those with a court order or the written permission of the individual whose credit is being checked.

- The **Privacy Act of 1974** restricts the way in which personal data can be used by federal agencies. Individuals must be permitted access to information stored about them and may correct any information that is incorrect. Agencies must insure both the security and confidentiality of any sensitive information. Although this law applies only to federal agencies, many states have adopted similar laws.

- The **Financial Privacy Act of 1978** requires that a government authority have a subpoena, summons, or search warrant to access an individual's financial records. When such records are released, the financial institution must notify the individual of who has had access to them.

## Protecting Computer Software and Data

*copyright*
As society becomes more and more reliant on digital information, copyright and exposure to malicious code have become two important issues among computer users. *Copyright* is protection of digital information. Copyright infringement is the illegal use or reproduction of data (text, pictures, music, video, and so on). Laws, such as the NET Act (No Electronic Theft Act) of 1997, protect against copyright infringement. There have been several well-known cases of high penalties for individuals guilty of copyright infringement.

*piracy*
Copyright infringement includes duplication of computer software when copies are being used by individuals who have not paid for the software. This practice is called *piracy* when illegal copies are distributed. Developing, testing, marketing, and supporting software is an expensive process. If the software developer is then denied rightful compensation, the future development of all software is jeopardized. Therefore, it is important to use only legally acquired copies of software, and to not make illegal copies for others.

Malicious code comes in many forms and is delivered in many ways. A virus, a Trojan horse, and an Internet worm are three forms of malicious code. They can appear on a system through executable programs, scripts, macros, e-mails, and some Internet connections. One devastating effect of malicious code is the destruction of data.

*virus*

A *virus* is a program or series of instructions that can replicate without the user's knowledge. Often a virus is triggered to run when given a certain signal. For example, a virus might check the computer's clock and then destroy data when a certain time is reached. A virus is easily duplicated when the file is copied, which spreads it to other computers.

*Trojan horse*

A *Trojan horse* program appears as something else, usually a program that looks trustworthy. Running the program runs the malicious code

*worm*

and damages files on the computer. A *worm* is a program that is able to reproduce itself over a network. Worms are a threat because of the way they replicate and use system resources, sometimes causing the system to shut down.

*antivirus programs*

Malicious code has become so widespread that software called *antivirus programs* must be installed on computers and networks to detect and remove the code before it can replicate or damage data. Precautions can also be taken to prevent damage from malicious code:

- Update antivirus software. An antivirus program can only detect the viruses, Trojan horses, and worms it is aware of. Antivirus programs have a web link for updating the virus definitions on the computer containing the antivirus program.

- Do not open e-mail attachments without scanning for malicious code. One estimate states that 80% of virus infection is through e-mail.

*crackers, hackers*

Newspapers have carried numerous reports of *crackers*, or *hackers*, gaining access to large computer systems to perform acts of vandalism. This malicious act is illegal and can cause expensive damage. The Electronic Communications Privacy Act of 1986 specifically makes it a federal offense to access electronic data without authorization. Networks usually include a firewall, which is a combination of hardware and software, to help prevent unauthorized access.

The willful destruction of computer data is no different than any other vandalizing of property. Since the damage is done electronically the result is often not as obvious as destroying physical property, but the consequences are much the same. It is estimated that computer crimes cost billions of dollars each year.

*phishing*

*Phishing* is the act of sending an e-mail to a user falsely claiming to be a legitimate business in an attempt to trick the user into revealing personal information that could be used for crimes such as identity theft.

## The Ethical Responsibilities of an IT Professional

An *IT* (information technology) professional has responsibilities that relate to system reliability. System reliability involves installing and updating appropriate software, keeping hardware working and up-to-date, and maintaining databases and other forms of data. Governments, schools, and employers rely on IT professionals to maintain their computer systems.

In addition to ensuring system reliability, an IT professional must take responsibility for the ethical aspects of the career choice. For example, IT professionals involved in creating software must ensure, as best he or she can, the reliability of the computer software. This means the ethical responsibility of the IT professional includes using the appropriate tools and methods to test and evaluate programs before distribution. A special cause for concern is the increased use of computers to control potentially dangerous devices such as aircraft, nuclear reactors, or sensitive medical equipment.

IT professionals must also consider the impact they have on computer users. Web users for example often rely on data from websites providing real-time information. The information displayed is determined with a program written using a language that accesses a database. The IT professionals involved in such a project have the ethical responsibility to possibly millions of individuals for ensuring, as best they can, accurate data retrieval.

As capable as computers have proven to be, we must be cautious when allowing them to replace human beings in areas where judgement is crucial. As intelligent beings, we can often detect that something out of the ordinary has occurred which has not been previously anticipated and then take appropriate actions. Computers will only do what they have been programmed to do.

### IT Careers

The growth of computers, the Internet, and the Web have created many new job opportunities in the IT field. IT careers include data-entry operator, systems analyst, programmer, computer engineer, and technical support technician.

## Chapter Summary

Java is a programming language and computing platform. It is the underlying technology that is used in many utilities, games, and applications. To develop Java applications you need to install the JDK (Java Development Kit) and an Integrated Development Environment (IDE).

A desktop computer and its components are designed to fit on or under a desk. Mobile computers include notebooks, tablets, handhelds, smart phones, and wearables. A computer must run operating system (OS) software in order to control processing and peripherals, run application software, and control input and output, among other tasks.

A network is a combination of hardware and software that allows computers to exchange data and share software and devices, such as printers. Networks are classified by their size, architecture, topology, and protocol.

A programming language is a set of words, codes, and symbols that allows a programmer to communicate with the computer. Programming languages can be classified as low-level and high-level languages.

The electrical circuits on an IC have one of two states, off or on. Therefore, the binary number system (base 2), which uses only two digits (0 and 1), was adopted for use in computers. Our most familiar number system is the decimal or base 10 system. The binary number system is a base 2 system and the hexadecimal system is base 16.

Computer memory, file sizes, and storage device capacities are measured in bytes. In computers and electronics MB stands for megabytes, GB stands for gigabytes, and K stands for kilobytes.

A file is related data stored on a persistent media. A file is really just 1s and 0s because it is stored in binary code. Computers are programmed to translate bytes and words into symbols. File types are distinguished by the extension that comes after the file name. Folders are used to organize commonly related files.

Storage devices use a persistent media to maintain files. These devices, which are also referred to as drives, mass storage, and auxiliary storage, can be categorized as internal or external.

An intranet is a network that is used by a single organization and is only accessible by authorized users. A firewall is a network security system that prevents unauthorized network access. An extranet extends an intranet by providing various levels of accessibility to authorized members of the public. The largest and most widely accessed network is the Internet.

Telecommunications is the transmitting and receiving of data. Telecommunication options include a conventional modem, a DSL modem, a cable modem, leased/dedicated lines, and ISDN.

A search engine is a program that searches a database of web pages for keywords and then lists hyperlinks to pages that contain those keywords. Limiting the number of matches to a reasonable number can be accomplished using Boolean logic.

Information found at a website should be evaluated for accuracy. There are guidelines for citing electronic material on the Internet. The primary purpose of a citation is to give credit to the original author and allow the reader to locate the cited information.

The growth of the Internet has caused concerns about personal privacy. Online profiling, cookies, and web bugs are all areas of concern. To protect an individual's privacy, several laws have been passed. Concerns about Internet content, unproductive use, and copyright have prompted many schools and businesses to develop an Internet Use Agreement.

Historians refer to our present time as the information age. The potential for the use of computers to invade our right to privacy has prompted legislation to protect individuals. Piracy is the illegal act of duplicating software without permission. A virus is a computer file that erases data and can cause considerable damage.

Working as an IT (information technology) professional includes taking responsibility for the ethical aspects of a career choice. IT professionals must also consider the impact they have on computer users.

# Vocabulary

**Address** A unique binary representation of a location in memory.

**Address bus** Carries memory addresses that indicate data storage locations.

**ALU (Arithmetic Logic Unit)** The part of the CPU that handles arithmetic and logic operations.

**Antivirus program** Software installed on computers and networks to detect and remove viruses.

**Applications software** Program written to perform a specific task.

**Base unit** Housing that contains the motherboard, CD-RW/DVD drive, disk drive, and hard disk drive.

**Binary files** Computer-readable files.

**Binary number system** Number system used by computers that uses only digits 0 and 1. Also called base 2.

**Bit (BInary digiT)** A single 0 or 1 in binary code.

**Bus** A central network cable. Also a set of circuits that connect the CPU to other components.

**Bus topology** A physical LAN topology that uses a single central cable to attach each node directly.

**Byte** A group of 8 bits.

**Cable modem** A modem that transmits data through a coaxial cable television network.

**Cache** High-speed memory used to store frequently used data so that it can be quickly retrieved by an application.

**Client** A computer that is sent information from a server computer.

**Client/server network** A type of network that consists of a group of computers, called clients connected to a server computer.

**Clock rate** The speed at which a CPU can execute instructions, measured in megahertz or gigahertz.

**Compiler** A program that converts an entire program into machine code before the program is executed.

**Control bus** Carries control signals.

**Conventional modem** A modem that uses standard telephone lines to convert analog signals to digital data.

**Cookie** Text file created by the server computer when a user enters information into a website.

**Copyright** Protects a piece of work from reproduction without permission from the work's author.

**CPU (Central Processing Unit)** Processes data and controls the flow of data between the computer's other units. Also contains the ALU. Located on the motherboard.

**Cracker** Person who accesses a computer system without authorization.

**Cross-platform connectivity** The ability of one type of PC to link to and share data with a different type of PC.

**Dedicated line** *See* Leased line.

**Desktop computer** A computer designed to fit on or under a desk.

**Device driver** One type of utility program.

**Downloading** The process of copying a file from a website to the user's computer.

**DSL (Digital Subscriber Line) modem** A modem that uses standard telephone phone lines. ADSL is the most common form used.

**E-mail (electronic mail)** The sending and receiving of messages and electronic files over a communications network such as a LAN or the Internet.

**Environment** A computer's hardware and software configuration. Also referred to as platform. Environment types include desktop, multiuser, network, handheld, distributed, multiprocessing, and multitasking.

**Ergonomics** The science that studies safe work environments.

**Expansion boards** Circuit boards that connect to the motherboard to add functionality to the computer.

**Extension** Added after a file name to distinguish file types.

**Extranet** An extended intranet that provides various levels of access to authorized members of the public.

**File**  A collection of related data stored on a lasting medium.

**Firewall**  A network security system that prevents unauthorized network access.

**Folder**  Used to organize commonly related files.

**Gigabytes (GB)**  Approximately one billion bytes.

**Gigahertz (GHz)**  Billion of cycles per second.

**Hacker**  *See* Cracker.

**Handheld computer**  A mobile computing device.

**Hardware**  The physical components of the computer, such as the monitor and system unit.

**Hexadecimal system**  Number system based on 16 digits. Also called base 16.

**High-level programming languages**  Third generation programming languages that have English-like instructions.

**Hub**  A communication device that joins communication lines at a central location on the network.

**Information age**  Present time characterized by increasing dependence on the computer's ability to store and manipulate large amounts of information.

**Input device**  Device used to enter data and instructions into the computer.

**Integrated circuits (ICs)**  A silicon wafer with intricate circuits etched into its surface and then coated with a metallic oxide that fills in the etched circuit patterns. Also called a chip.

**Interactive**  Information accessed as a result of selections made by the user.

**Internet**  The largest and most widely accessed network.

**Interpreter**  A program that translates and executes an instruction before moving on to the next instruction in the program.

**Intranet**  A network that is used by a single organization and only accessible by authorized users.

**ISDN (Integrated Services Digital Network)**  A digital telephone network provided by a local telephone company.

**IT (Information Technology)**  A term that encompasses all aspects of computer-related technology.

**Java**  A programming language and computing platform that was first released in 1995.

**Kbps**  Thousands of bits per second.

**Kilobytes (K)**  Approximately a thousand bytes.

**LAN (Local Area Network)**  A network used to connect devices within a small area.

**Leased line**  A telecommunication option used for a permanent connection to the Internet that is always active.

**Logical topology**  Refers to the way in which data is passed between the nodes on a network.

**Low-level programming languages**  First and second generation programming languages including machine language and assembly language.

**Mailing list server**  A server that manages mailing lists for groups of users.

**Match**  A web page that contains the search criteria.

**Mbps**  Millions of bits per second.

**Megabytes (MB)**  Approximately one million bytes.

**Megahertz (MHz)**  Million of cycles per second.

**Memory-resident**  A program that is always in memory.

**Minus sign (–)**  Used in search criteria to exclude unwanted web pages.

**Modern Language Association (MLA)**  Organization that publishes standards used for citations.

**Motherboard**  The main circuit board inside the base unit.

**Netiquette**  The etiquette that should be followed when using a network.

**Network**  A combination of software and hardware that allows computers to exchange data and to share software and devices, such as printers.

**Network interface card**  A circuit board that goes into a computer or other device in a LAN.

**Network operating system**  Software that allows users and devices to communicate over a network.

**Node**  A location on the network capable of processing information, such as a computer or a printer.

**Object-oriented programming (OOP)** An approach to programming where modules are created that can be used over and over again.

**Online profiling** A marketing technique that collects online data about consumers.

**Operating system** Software that allows the user to communicate with the computer. Types include multiuser, multiprocessing, multitasking, multithreading, or real time.

**Output device** A device used to convey processed data.

**Overflow error** An error that occurs when the number of bits that are needed to represent the integer is greater than four bytes.

**Peer-to-peer network** A type of network that does not have a server.

**Peripheral device** A device attached to a PC.

**Phishing** The act of sending an e-mail to a user falsely claiming to be a legitimate business in an attempt to trick the user into revealing personal information that could be used for crimes such as identity theft.

**Piracy** Illegally copying or distributing software.

**Plus sign (+)** Used in search criteria to limit a search to only those web pages containing two or more specified words.

**Port** Used to attach a peripheral device to a computer.

**Privacy policy** A legally binding document that explains how any personal information will be used.

**Programming languages** A set of words, codes, and symbols that allows a programmer to communicate with the computer.

**RAM (Random Access Memory)** Memory that temporarily stores data and instructions. Also called primary or main memory.

**Real numbers** Numbers that contain decimal points. Also called floating point numbers.

**Ring topology** A physical LAN topology where each node is connected to form a closed loop.

**ROM (Read Only Memory)** Memory that stores data and is a permanent part of the computer.

**Roundoff error** An error that occurs when there are not enough bits to hold the mantissa.

**Router** A device that connects different network technologies.

**Search criteria** A single word or phrase that is used by the search engine to match web pages.

**Search engine** A program that searches a database of web pages for keywords and then lists hyperlinks to pages that contain those keywords.

**Secondary memory** Any type of storage media.

**Server** A computer used to manage network functions such as communication and data sharing.

**Smartphone** Cellular phone that is able to send and receive e-mail messages and access the Internet.

**SRAM (Static Random Access Memory)** High-speed memory referred to as cache.

**Star topology** A physical LAN topology where each node is attached to a hub.

**Storage devices** Devices that use persistent media to maintain files. Also referred to as drives, mass storage, and auxiliary storage.

**Subject tree** A list of sites separated into categories.

**TCP/IP (Transmission Control Protocol/Internet Protocol)** Software used by networks connected to routers to communicate.

**Telecommunications** The transmitting and receiving of data.

**Text files** Human-readable files.

**Topology** The physical or logical arrangement of the nodes on a network.

**Transmission media** The media that joins the nodes on a network to enable communication.

**Trojan horse** Malicious code in the form of a program that appears as something else, usually a program that looks trustworthy.

**Unicode** A digital code that uses a set of sixteen 1s and 0s to form a 16-bit binary code for each symbol.

**Utility program** Program run by the operating system to manage input and output, read and write to memory, manage the processor, maintain system security, and manage files and disks.

**Virus**  A program that is designed to reproduce itself by copying itself into other programs stored on a computer without the user's knowledge.

**WAN (Wide Area Network)**  A network used to connect computers over large geographical distances.

**Wearable computer**  A mobile computing device that is incorporated into clothing, eyewear, wrist-wear, and other wearables.

**Web**  *See* World Wide Web.

**Web beacon**  A tiny, transparent graphic located on a web page used to collect data about the web page user. Also called a web bug or pixel tag.

**Web browser**  Interprets an HTML document to display a web page.

**Web directory**  *See* Subject tree.

**Wireless network**  A type of network that does not require the use of cables.

**Word**  Bits grouped in units of 16 to 64.

**World Wide Web**  The most widely used Internet service. Used to search and access information available on the Internet.

**Worm**  Program that is able to reproduce itself over a network.

1.  a) Describe a situation where a desktop computer might be preferred over a notebook computer.
    b) List three advantages of purchasing a notebook computer instead of desktop computer.
    c) Describe a situation or user that would prefer a tablet PC over a notebook computer.
    d) Describe two occupations where it would be useful to have a hand-held computer.
    e) Describe how wearable computers are used in the health care industry.

2.  a) List and compare three input devices.
    b) List and compare three output devices.
    c) List and describe two peripheral devices.
    d) List three types of ports.

3.  List and describe five components found on the motherboard.

4.  Describe the flow of data between the components of a computer, starting with input.

5.  What is cache memory used for?

6.  a) Describe one difference between operating system software and applications software.
    b) List three different operating systems.
    c) What does environment refer to?
    d) What is another word for environment?

7.  What is a utility program? Give an example.

8.  Why is cross-platform connectivity important to many computer users?

9.  a) What is the difference between low and high level programming languages?
    b) List three high-level programming languages.
    c) What is the difference between a compiler and an interpreter?
    d) List an advantage of using an object-oriented programming language.

10. List four benefits of using a network.

11. a) What are the two common size classifications for networks?
    b) What size classification is used to connect devices over large geographical distances?

12. a) What is a network operating system?
    b) What does a network environment refer to?

13. Describe two common network architecture models.

14. a) What does physical topology refer to?
    b) What is a node?
    c) Which topology uses a hub?
    d) Which topology connects each node to form a closed loop?
    e) What is the difference between physical and logical topology?

15. Which netiquette rules apply in your classroom?

16. Explain why the binary number system was adopted for use in computers.

17. a) What is the decimal equivalent of $1011_2$?
    b) What is the decimal equivalent of $2A_{16}$?

18. What is Unicode?

19. a) How many bytes of data can 2 GB of RAM store?
    b) How many bytes of data can a 500 GB hard drive store?

20. a) When would an overflow error occur?
    b) What are real numbers?
    c) When would a roundoff error occur?

21. a) What is the difference between a text file and a binary file?
    b) Explain how an extension distinguishes file types.
    c) Describe how organizing your files into folders would help keep you organized.

22. List two ways storage devices can be classified and give an example of a storage device in each category.

23. List four rules that should be followed to avoid damaging files stored on disks or CD/DVDs.

24. a) What is the difference between an intranet and an extranet?
    b) Who controls the Internet?

25. a) What problem is associated with using a conventional modem?
    b) Describe the differences between a DSL modem and a cable modem.

26. a) What is the most widely used Internet service?
    b) List one benefit of e-mail over standard mail.
    c) Write your e-mail address and label the parts of the address.
    d) What are the two requirements for sending and receiving e-mail messages?
    e) List one example of a browser-based e-mail site.

27. a) Explain why sending an e-mail message should be thought of the same as sending a postcard.
    b) Discuss with a partner and then summarize issues that could occur if e-mail etiquette is not followed in the workplace.

28. a) List three commonly used search engines.
    b) Which search engine do you prefer to use, and why?
    c) Describe the importance of using effective search criteria.

29. Write search criteria to locate web pages that contain the following information:
    a) restaurants in Miami
    b) art museums in Montreal, Canada
    c) clothing stores in your city
    d) alligators, but not crocodiles
    e) the author James Patterson
    f) the phrase *garbage in garbage out*
    g) George Washington and John Adams, but not Thomas Jefferson
    h) travel to Florida, but not Orlando

30. Why should files only be downloaded from authentic sites?

31. a) List four questions to answer when evaluating a website source.
    b) Why is it necessary to cite sources?
    c) On August 2, 2012 you accessed a posting on the Clewiston Kite Surfing discussion list at http://www.lpdatafiles.com/kitesurf/color.txt. The posting was made by Tara Perez on the topic of kite colors. Write a citation for a research paper that quotes Tara's posting.

32. a) What is online profiling?
    b) What is a cookie?

c) What is a web beacon?
d) Who usually monitors the information collected by web beacons?

33. Locate a website's privacy policy and document its contents.

34. Name and briefly describe one law that helps protect the privacy of an individual.

35. List three reasons why many schools have developed an Acceptable Use Policy.

36. What can you do if you are turned down for credit at a bank and believe that the data used to deny credit is inaccurate?

37. a) What is necessary for a federal government authority to access an individual's financial records?
    b) What must a financial institution do after releasing an individual's records?

38. a) What is copyright infringement?
    b) Why is computer piracy such a concern to software developers?
    c) What is a computer virus?
    d) Describe phishing.

39. What ethical responsibilities does an IT professional have?

**True/False**

40. Determine if each of the following are true or false. If false, explain why.
    a) You must install the JDK to develop Java applications.
    b) Linux is an operating system.
    c) A utility program has one clearly defined task.
    d) Java applications are platform-dependent.
    e) A WAN connects devices over large geographical distances.
    f) A peer-to-peer network has a server.
    g) The binary number system uses only 1s and 0s.
    h) A conventional modem transmits data faster than a cable modem.
    i) An e-mail address is required to send e-mail messages.
    j) The present time is referred to as the industrial age.
    k) Ergonomics is the science that studies safe work environments.

## Exercise 1

In this exercise you will research the cost of purchasing a desktop computer.

a) Use computer websites, such as www.dell.com, www.apple.com or newspaper advertisements to research the costs of two comparable desktop computers.

b) Summarize the specifications and costs associated with each computer. Be sure to include the costs associated with any needed peripherals including auxiliary storage devices.

c) Decide which computer is a better choice. This may require additional research on company reliability and so forth. Be sure to assess the computer's warranty when making a decision.

d) Present your research and conclusion in a report or prepare a posting to the course wiki site that summarizes your research.

## Exercise 2

In this exercise you will research the capabilities and costs of mobile computers.

a) Assume you are a travelling salesman. You travel all over the country selling car parts. Keeping in mind the need to travel light, keep in contact with the main office, and have all price lists, inventory, and product information at your fingertips, research mobile computing devices and document what devices you think would be essential for this occupation. Include approximate costs in your documentation.

b) Assume you are a software engineer. You design software applications for the health services/medical industry. You work long hours both in the office and at home. You also need to travel frequently to provide on-site technical support to customers. Research and document what mobile computing devices you think would be essential for this occupation. Include approximate costs in your documentation.

## Exercise 3

Processor manufacturers include Intel and AMD. Select one of these manufacturers and use the company's website (www.intel.com or www.amd.com) to research the features and specifications of one of their processors. Present your research in a report or prepare a posting to the course wiki site that summarizes your research, citing the source of information.

# Exercise 4

In this exercise you will analyze your classroom computer network by answering the following questions:

a) Is your computer network a LAN or a WAN?

b) List three advantages of having your classroom computers set up on a network.

c) Are there any disadvantages of having your classroom computers set up on a network?

d) List the input devices accessible on the classroom network. List advantages and disadvantages associated with each accessible input device.

e) List the output devices accessible on the classroom network. List advantages and disadvantages associated with each accessible output device.

f) What type of physical topology is used?

g) What type of transmission media is used?

h) What network protocol is used?

i) What operating system is used? Describe three computer maintenance tasks that can be performed using operating system utilities (i.e., emptying the Recycle Bin, defragmenting a hard drive)

j) Describe your workstation's environment.

k) What telecommunication option is used?

l) List advantages to having a wireless network in your classroom?

m) Does the school have an intranet?

n) List four rules on the school's Internet Use Agreement.

o) List five applications software programs available on your network. Describe tasks each application is designed to perform.

p) Use the Internet, magazines, and books to research tips additional for keeping your computer in good condition (i.e., dusting, using a surge protector). Describe at least three additional tips.

q) What storage devices are available to backup your files or to bring your files home? Comment on any cross platform connectivity issues you may encounter with using your classroom files on your home computer or on another computer in the school.

r) Does your computer network allow for resource sharing through a public drive or other means? If yes, explain the process.

s) Describe measures that are in place to protect the classroom network, such as a firewall and antivirus software.

# Exercise 5

Repetitive stress injuries are caused by repeated movement of a particular part of the body and are often seen in workers whose physical routine is unvaried. The rise in computer usage is correlated to a substantial increase in the occurrences of repetitive stress injuries.

a) Conduct a search on the Internet using at least two search engines to find three web pages that have information about repetitive stress injuries.

b) Summarize your research in a report or prepare a posting to the course wiki site that summarizes your research. Be sure to include information on preventative measures and possible treatments.

c) Write a citation for each source.

# Exercise 6

Expand on the information presented in this chapter by researching one of the following topics:

- Network Protocols
- Operating Systems
- The History of the Internet
- Evolution of Programming Languages
- Identity Theft
- Number Systems
- Mobile Computing
- Wireless Networks
- Telecommunications
- Internet Services

a) Use the Internet, magazines, and books to find at least three sources of information.

b) Prepare a report or presentation that summarizes your research.

c) Write a citation for each source.

# Exercise 7

In this exercise you will research and compare the advantages and cost of obtaining Internet access through three different telecommunication options.

a) Use the Internet and newspapers to find information about Internet service providers (ISPs).

b) Compare the costs and the advantages of at least three different telecommunication options.

c) Write a one paragraph conclusion that explains what telecommunication option would be the best choice.

d) Write a citation for each source.

# Exercise 8

In this exercise you will further research emerging technologies and find real-life examples of how these technologies have impacted individuals and businesses.

    a)  Use the Internet, magazines, and books to learn more about at least three emerging technologies. Look specifically for information on how these emerging technologies impact individuals and businesses. For example, speech recognition technology greatly impacts those individuals who must rely on voice input rather than keyboard input for a PC.

    b)  Write a two-page report that summarizes the impact of and lists several functions of the emerging technologies you have researched.

    c)  Write a citation for each source.

# Exercise 9

Many computer viruses have been associated with e-mail attachments.

    a)  Conduct a search on the Internet to find information about a virus associated with an e-mail attachments.

    b)  Write a one-paragraph description of the virus. Include details, such as the damage caused by the virus and steps necessary to remove the virus. Be sure to document prevention methods for similar viruses as well.

    c)  Write a citation for each source.

# Exercise 10

You have decided to investigate computer-related careers.

    a)  Read about possible computer-related careers at www.emcschool.net/java3e or www.paradigmcollege.net/java3e.

    b)  Select one of the computer-related occupations and research the current job market for this occupation.

    c)  If possible, interview a professional in your chosen field to learn more about the occupation.

# Exercise 11

Environmental issues associated with computers include:

- significant energy use
- disposal of old computers
- health risks
- recycling

Select one of these topics to research further. Prepare a presentation that summarizes your research.

# Exercise 12

Ergonomics is the science that studies safe work environments. Using the correct type and configuration of mouse, keyboard, monitor, chair, and desk can help users work comfortably and efficiently while protecting their health.

a) Research tips for an ergonomically designed workstation (i.e, adjustable height chair with 5 legs for stability).

b) Analyze your school workstation. Comment on whether the workstation is ergonomically correct.

c) **Homework:** Analyze your home workstation. Comment on whether the workstation is ergonomically correct.

# Exercise 13

Prepare a poster or document that outlines tips for safe computing. You may want to include tips on creating safe passwords, avoiding spyware, using anti-virus software effectively, backing up files, using screen saver passwords, wireless precautions, and so forth.

*Chapter 1 Computer Technology*

# Chapter 2
# Introducing Java

## Key Concepts

Object-oriented terminology
Creating and executing Java applications
Displaying output
Formatting program output
Adding comments to program code
Applying code conventions
Using algorithm design as a problem-solving strategy

## Why Program in Java?

Java is an object-oriented programming language. *Object-oriented programming* (OOP) evolved out of the need to develop complex programs in a systematic, modular approach. OOP programmers create modules, called classes, that can be used over and over again in a variety of programs. A class groups related data and the instructions for performing actions on that data. Properly designed classes encapsulate data to hide implementation details, are versatile enough to be extended through inheritance, and give the programmer options through polymorphism. *Encapsulation, inheritance,* and *polymorphism* are features of every object-oriented language.

Java is more than just a programming language, it is a platform. A platform can be a combination of hardware and software, but the Java platform is software only and is used to run Java applications. The Java platform runs on all major operating systems allowing Java applications to run on just about any computer. Java applications are therefore referred to as *platform-independent applications*.

### Java Versions

Java SE (Standard Edition) 6 was released in December, 2006 and Java SE 7 was released in July, 2011.

## Objects, Classes, and Packages

Object-oriented program development involves selecting objects to perform the tasks outlined in a program specification. An *object* consists of related data and the instructions for performing actions on that data. The design for an object is called a class. A *class* defines the type of data and actions that will be associated with an object of that class, but not the actual data for an individual object. Classes are required to create objects. Many objects of the same class may be needed in an application.

### Program Specification

A program specification is a definition or outline of what a program is expected to do. In industry, a program specification can serve as a contract between the programmer and the client.

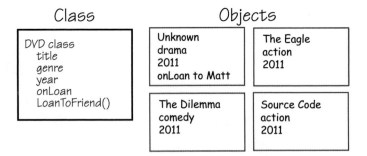

**TIP** *Reusability* is a feature that reduces development time and decreases the likelihood of bugs.

*A class can be used to create many objects—each object will have the same type of data and possible actions, but each object maintains its own set of data.*

*package, library*

A *package*, sometimes called a *library*, is a group of related classes. For example, classes related to a particular task, such as input and output, can be grouped together in a package. A media package containing a DVD class and a CD class can be illustrated as:

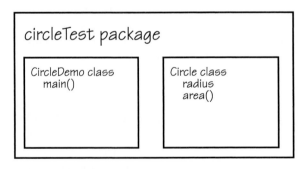

*A package contains related classes.*

**TIP** The Java platform includes the Java Application Programming Interface (API) with numerous libraries.

An application is also contained in a package. It contains a controlling class and can contain other classes as well:

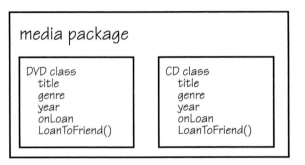

*An application is contained in a package.*

**TIP** Applications use, or import, packages to define objects.

Packages are *importable*, which means an application can use existing classes from another package.

# A Java Application

A *Java application* is a package with at least one class that contains a main() method. The following Greeting application is a simple, yet complete Java program:

```
/**
 * Greeting.java
 * A first Java application.
 * @author
 * Course
 * Date
 */

package firstApplication;

/**
 *The Greeting class displays a greeting.
 */

public class Greeting {                //start class definition

    public static void main(String[] args) {

        System.out.println("Hello World!");
    }
}                                       //end class definition
```

**TIP** The static void in the main() method means that it is a method of the class and does not generate a value.

Greeting generates output similar to:

```
Hello World!
```

*statements*    A program consists of a set of instructions called *statements*. A semi-colon is required to indicate the end of a statement. Related statements are enclosed by curly braces ({ }) to begin and end the instructions. The statements in the Greeting application are:

- package firstApplication declares a package name. If a package name is not declared, then the application is given the package name Default by the compiler. Simple applications often do not have package statements.

- public class Greeting is a class declaration. The class is available to anyone (public) and is named Greeting. The Greeting class does not define any data or actions for objects. However, it contains the main() method making it the application's controlling class. The *controlling class*    *controlling class* is a program's starting point.

- public static void main(String[] args) defines the main() method. *method*    A *method* is a named set of statements that perform a single, well-defined task. The main() method is placed in the controlling class. Its statements are automatically run when the program is executed. The statement in this main() method uses the println() method to display "Hello, world!" to the system output (the screen).

*comments*    In addition to statements, programs contain *comments*, which provide information about the program to the reader of the code. Comments have no affect on the program, but they allow a reader of the program to quickly understand the purpose and logic behind segments of code. Because complex applications are often developed and maintained by more than one programer, properly commented code allows for easier modifications and can decrease the number of mistakes.

Java programs can contain three types of comments:

- /*      */ are used to enclose single or multiline comments. These comments are appropriate at the beginning of a program to describe the application and where necessary to clarify a segment of code.

- // are used for adding a comment to the end of a statement or to create a single line comment. The // is also useful for debugging a program, which will be discussed in a later chapter.

- /**      */ are used for documentation. The javadoc tool copies these comments into a separate HTML document to create an instructional manual or external documentation. Documentation comments are appropriate for describing a class or method.

**TIP** The `main()` method does not typically have a comment block.

Multiline comments that describe a program, class, or method are sometimes referred to as a *comment block*. Tips throughout the text will provide additional pointers about commenting code.

## Executing a Java Application

Java code typed by a programmer is called *source code*. For source code to *execute*, or *run*, it must be translated to code the computer understands in a process called *compiling*. Many Java compilers provide an environment for entering the source code as well as for compiling and running an application. Source code files have the extension `.java`, while compiled files have the extension `.class`.

**TIP** *Virtual* means not real. A virtual machine is therefore conceptual, not made of hardware and other physical components.

Compiled Java source code is called *bytecode*. Executing a Java application means that its bytecode is interpreted with a *Java Virtual Machine* (Java VM). The *interpreter* runs each bytecode instruction as it is read. The Java VM can reside on any computer, regardless of operating system environment, making Java applications extremely portable, reliable, and platform-independent.

Although bytecode is versatile for porting applications to several different environments, programs compiled to machine code run faster. *Machine code* is comprised of just 1s and 0s and is different depending on the computer platform. A *just-in-time compiler* (JIT) converts bytecode to machine code before it is executed with the Java VM.

### Platform-Dependent

Programming languages such as Visual Basic are compiled directly to machine language. Although faster, these programs must be recompiled for every platform that will run the application.

A program containing syntax errors will not compile. A *syntax error* occurs in a statement that violates the rules of Java. For example, all Java statements must end with a semicolon. A statement without a semicolon generates a syntax error when the program is compiled, preventing the compiler from generating bytecode for the application.

## Review: Greeting

Create a Greeting application similar to the one shown in the "A Java Application" section. Refer to Appendix B or the online materials at www.emcschool.net/Java3e (hardcover) or www.paradigmcollege.net/Java3e (softcover) for guidance with your Java compiler. Your instructor may also have specific information regarding your compiler. The goal of this review is to write the source code for a simple application and then compile and run the code.

# Displaying Output

*output stream*

*print() println()*

**TIP** The System class is in the `java.lang` package.

An *output stream* sends data to an output device. To process data for the output stream, Java provides the System class with methods for displaying output. For displaying data to the standard output stream, which is typically the computer screen, use `System.out`. out contains print() and println() methods. The difference between these methods is how they control output. The print() method displays data and leaves the insertion point at the end of the output, while println() moves the insertion point to the next line after displaying output. The following application uses both methods:

```
/**
 * Displays a welcome message.
 */

public class MulticulturalGreeting {

    public static void main(String[] args) {

        System.out.print("Hello");
        System.out.print("Buenos Dias");
        System.out.println("Bounjour");
        System.out.println("How do you greet another?");
    }
}
```

*argument*

*string*

The print() and println() methods require arguments. An *argument* is data passed to a method for processing. In this case, the print() and println() arguments are strings. A *string* is a set of characters, which are enclosed by quotation marks.

MulticulturalGreeting produces output similar to:

```
HelloBuenos DiasBounjour
How do you greet another?
```

*escape sequence*

An *escape sequence* is a backslash (\) followed by a symbol that together represent a character. Escape sequences are used to display special characters. Common escape sequences include:

\n    newline
\t    tab
\\    backslash
\"    double quotation mark

The modified MulticulturalGreeting illustrates the use of escape sequences:

```
public class MulticulturalGreeting {

    public static void main(String[] args) {

        System.out.print("Hello\t");
        System.out.print("Buenos Dias\t\t");
        System.out.println("Bounjour");
        System.out.println("How do you greet another?");
    }
}


Hello   Buenos Dias     Bounjour
How do you greet another?
```

Create an AboutMe application that displays your first name and last initial, your instructor's name, and your school name on three separate lines. Below the personal information, display a phrase that encourages your school team. For example, "Go Bears!" Be sure the phrase is displayed with quotation marks.

## Formatting Output

**Numeric Output**

The NumberFormat class, discussed in Chapter 3, can also be used to format numeric data.

The format() method can be used in place of the print() or println() methods to control the way output is displayed. The format() method arguments include a format string and an argument list. The format string contains specifiers that indicate how the corresponding strings in the argument list should be displayed. The following code demonstrates the format() method:

```
System.out.format("%-10s %8s %8s", "Team", "Wins", "Losses\n");
System.out.format("%-10s %8s %8s", "Jaguars", "10", "5\n");
System.out.format("%-10s %8s %8s", "Cheetahs", "14", "1\n");
System.out.format("%-10s %8s %8s", "Panthers", "8", "7\n");
System.out.format("%-10s %8s %8s", "Penguins", "4", "11\n");
```

When executed, the statements display:

```
Team          Wins  Losses
Jaguars         10       5
Cheetahs        14       1
Panthers         8       7
Penguins         4      11
```

A format string specifier takes the form:

```
%[alignment][width]s
```

| | |
|---|---|
| % | indicates the start of a specifier |
| [alignment] | skip for right alignment. Include a minus sign (–) for left alignment |
| [width] | the number of characters to use for output |
| s | indicates that the corresponding argument is a string |

If [width] is greater than the number of characters in the corresponding string argument, then spaces pad the output. A string longer than [width] characters is displayed, but any strings to the right are moved over.

Text may also be included within the format string. For example, the statement:

```
System.out.format("The final game score: %-8s %8s", "10", "5");
```

displays:

```
The final game score: 10            5
```

Modify the AboutMe application to include your class schedule, the days of the week that your class meets, and the start and end time of each class. Include code to properly align the data into three columns with the weekdays left aligned and the class start and end times right-aligned.

## Code Conventions

*Code conventions* are a set of guidelines for writing an application. These guidelines provide details about commenting, rules for naming methods, classes, and packages, and statement formatting. Just as comments inform a reader about a segment of code, a program that follows specific code conventions is easier to read and understand.

A company or organization that employs programmers will typically adhere to specific code conventions. A programmer familiar with the code conventions will more quickly become familiar with code written by another programmer in the company. Code conventions can make modifying and maintaining code faster, easier, and less expensive. Because of these benefits, organizations often not only encourage the use of code conventions, but require it.

**TIP** Code conventions are important. About 80% of the lifetime cost of a piece of software goes to maintenance. Rarely is software maintained for its whole life by the original author.

The code conventions introduced in this chapter are:

- An introductory comment should begin a program. This comment should include information such as your name, class name, the date, and a brief statement about the program.

- Package names should begin with a lowercase letter and then an uppercase letter should begin each word within the name. Package names may not contain spaces.

- Class names should be nouns and begin with an uppercase letter and an uppercase letter should begin each word within the name. Class names may not contain spaces.

- A comment block should be included before each class and method. A comment block is not typically placed before the main() method.

- Comments should not reiterate what is clear from the code.

- Statements in a method should be indented.

- An open curly brace ({) should be placed on the same line as the class or method declaration, and the closing curly brace (}) should be on a separate line and aligned with the class or method declaration.

# Algorithm Design

Programs are created to solve problems. However, problems of any complexity require outlining, or designing, a solution before typing any source code. One method of design is called an algorithm. An *algorithm* is a set of steps that outline how to solve a problem.

*pseudocode*

Algorithms can be created in several ways. Steps written out in plain English is one approach. *Pseudocode*, which is a mix of English and program code is another approach. A visual representation of a solution can also be created using a UML (Unified Modeling Language) diagram, sequence diagram, or flowchart.

A description of the problem to be solved is used in developing an algorithm. For example, a program specification may state "The Triangle application displays a right triangle made up of the asterisk (*) symbol. The triangle should be 4 asterisks high by 4 asterisks wide." Triangle appears to be a very simple application. From the description, we conclude that Triangle should display an image of a right triangle.

The next step is to produce the algorithm:

1. Print an asterisk to the screen.

2. Print two asterisks to the screen.

3. Print an asterisk followed by a space and an asterisk to the screen.

4. Print four asterisks to the screen.

# Chapter Summary

This chapter introduced Java, which is an object-oriented programming language. OOP languages evolved out of the need to better develop complex programs. In addition to being object-oriented, Java is platform independent. Platform-independent applications can run on any computer, regardless of the operating system or hardware configuration.

Object-oriented languages use classes to define objects. A class defines the type of data and actions associated with an object, but not the actual data for an object. A package groups related classes.

A Java application is a package with at least one class. Statements in an application provide instructions. Methods are a named set of statements that perform a single, well-defined task. Comments in an application provide details about the code to the reader. Comments can be single or multiline and can also be extracted for documentation.

The code typed by a programmer is called source code. The source code is translated to bytecode with a compiler. Program execution occurs when the bytecode is interpreted with a Java Virtual Machine (Java VM). The Java VM can reside on any computer. A just-in-time (JIT) compiler converts bytecode to machine code before execution by the Java VM. Although less portable, machine code is faster. If a program contains errors, it will not compile. One type of error is the syntax error, which results when a statement violates the rules of Java.

Program output is through the output stream. The standard output stream is typically the computer screen and requires the `System.out` methods print() and println(). These methods require a string argument. Escape sequences are used to display special characters. Output can be formatted with the format() method.

Code conventions are a set of guidelines for writing an application. The code conventions introduced in this chapter are:

- An introductory comment should begin a program. This comment should include information such as your name, class name, the date, and a brief statement about the program.

- Package names should begin with a lowercase letter and then an uppercase letter should begin each word within the name. Package names may not contain spaces.

- Class names should be nouns and begin with an uppercase letter and then an uppercase letter should begin each word within the name. Class names may not contain spaces.

- A comment block should be included before each class and method. A comment block is not typically placed before the main() method.

- Comments should not reiterate what is clear from the code.

- Statements in a method should be indented.

- An open curly brace ({) should be placed on the same line as the class or method declaration, and the closing curly brace (}) should be on a separate line and aligned with the class or method declaration.

Programs are created to solve problems. However, problems of any complexity require outlining, or designing, a solution before typing any source code. One method of design is called an algorithm. An algorithm can be implemented through steps written in plain English, steps written in a mixture of code and English called pseudocode, or steps presented visually.

**Algorithm**   A set of steps that outline how to solve a problem.

**Argument**   Data passed to a method for processing.

**Bytecode**   Compiled Java source code.

**Class**   The description of an object.

**Code conventions**   A set of guidelines for writing an application.

**Comment**   Text that provides information to the reader of program code.

**Comment block**   Multiline comments that describe a program, class, or method.

**Compiling**   The process where source code is converted to code the computer understands.

**Controlling class**   The class in an application that contains the main() method.

**Encapsulation**   An object-oriented language feature.

**Escape Sequence**   A backslash followed by a symbol that together represent a character.

**Execute**   To run a program.

**Importable**   Package code that can be used by an application.

**Inheritance**   An object-oriented language feature.

**Interpreter**   Software that runs each bytecode instruction of a compiled Java program.

**Java application**   A package with a controlling class and possibly other classes.

**Java Virtual Machine (Java VM)**   The Java bytecode interpreter.

**Just-in-time compiler (JIT)**   Software that converts bytecode to specific machine code.

**Library**   *see* Package.

**Machine code**   The most basic computer language, which is comprised of just 1s and 0s.

**Method**   A named set of statements that perform a single, well-defined task. A method is always a member of a class.

**Object**   A named entity that consists of related data and instructions for performing actions on that data.

**Object-oriented programming (OOP)**   A systematic, modular approach to developing complex programs.

**OOP**   *see* Object-oriented programming.

**Output Stream**   Sends data to an output device, typically the computer screen.

**Package**   A group of related classes. Also called a library.

**Platform-independent application**   A program that can be run on any computer regardless of operating system or hardware configuration.

**Polymorphism**   An object-oriented language feature.

**Pseudocode**   An algorithm written in a mix of English and program code.

**Run**   *see* Execute.

**Source code**   The code typed by a programmer.

**Statement**   An instruction in a program.

**String**   A set of characters.

**Syntax error**   A statement that violates the rules of Java.

`/* */` Used to enclose single or multiline comments.

`/** */` Used to enclose documentation comments.

`//` Used to begin a single line comment.

`{ }` Used to begin and end a set of related statements.

`;` Required at the end of each program statement.

`\\` Escape sequence for displaying a backslash.

`\"` Escape sequence for displaying a double quotation mark.

`\n` Escape sequence for displaying a newline.

`\t` Escape sequence for displaying a tab.

`class` Used to declare a class.

**format()** Method that displays more precisely formatted output to the screen.

**java.lang.System** The class that contains the `out` member.

**main()** The method in the controlling class that is automatically executed when a Java application is run.

`out` The java.lang.System member that represents the standard output stream.

`package` Statement used to declare a package.

**print()** Method that displays output to the screen.

**println()** Method that displays output to the screen and then moves the insertion point to the next line.

`public` An access modifier that declares a class or method as available to any code.

`static` A declaration used for class methods.

`void` Indicates a method will not return a value.

1. a) List three features of every object-oriented programming language.
   b) Explain, what you think the meaning is of each of the three features listed in part (a).

2. Draw a sketch that shows the relationship, and/or hierarchy, of object, class, and package for the package File, class FileReader, and the object fileInput.

3. Write an appropriate comment block for the beginning of a program to describe an application that is intended to calculate test averages.

4. Write an appropriate comment for describing a class that displays the average of a set of scores.

5. Write a statement that declares a package with the name gradeCalculator.

6. Write a statement that declares a class named AverageScore that is available to any code.

7. Explain the difference between source code and bytecode.

8. Describe machine code.

9. Explain the difference between a Java compiler and the Java VM.

10. What is the advantage of compiling Java source code using a JIT?

11. The following application has seven syntax errors. What are they?

```
//
 * Test.java
 * What's wrong application.
 * Student Name
 */

package testMyKnowledge;

/**
 * The Test class should display a string,
 */
public class Test {

    private static int main(string[] args) {
            System.out.println("Testing...)
    }
```

12. Explain the difference between the print() and println() methods.

13. Explain the advantages of using the format() method in place of the print()and println() methods.

14. There are five places in which the application below does not follow the code conventions outlined in this chapter. Where are they?

```
/*
 * getGreeting.java
 * What's wrong application.
 * Student Name
 */

package notSoGood;

/**
 * Good Morning is displayed.
 */
public class getGreeting {

    public static void main(String[] args) {
    //Output Good Morning to the screen
    System.out.println("Good Morning");
    } }
```

## True/False

15. Determine if each of the following are true or false. If false, explain why.
    a) Java applications can run only on the Windows platform.
    b) Statements must end with a semicolon.
    c) Comments have no effect on program execution.
    d) The main() method is placed in the controlling class.
    e) Related statements are enclosed with brackets ([]).
    f) A file containing only source code can be executed on a computer.
    g) Compiled source code is called machine code.
    h) A program containing syntax errors will compile.
    i) An algorithm is a set of steps that outline how to solve a problem.
    j) Pseudocode cannot be used to implement an algorithm.

## Exercise 1 ──────────────────────────────────────── BingoCard

Create a BingoCard application that displays a traditional bingo card with five columns of five unique numbers. The column labels are B, I, N, G, and O. Column B contains numbers ranging from 1 through 15, column I has numbers ranging from 16 through 30, column N has four numbers ranging from 31 through 45 and a Free Space in the middle of the column, column G has numbers ranging from 46 through 60, and column O has numbers ranging from 61 through 75. The application output should look similar to:

```
B       I       N       G       O
2      20      42      60      64
14      25      32      55      70
5      18     FREE     53      67
12      16      31      46      75
10      22      39      59      71
```

## Exercise 2 ──────────────────────────────────────── BingoRules

Create a BingoRules application that displays the rules for playing bingo. Place each rule on a separate line and place a blank line between rules. The application output should look similar to:

```
Bingo Card

1. The caller randomly pulls a numbered bingo ball.

2. The number is placed on the bingo board and called out.

3. Players look for the called number on their bingo card.

4. If the number is located, it is marked off.

5. Steps 1 to 4 are repeated until a player matches the BINGO pattern.

6. The winning player yells BINGO.
```

## Exercise 3 ──────────────────────────────────────── Rectangle

Create a Rectangle application that displays a rectangle of asterisks (*). The rectangle should be 15 asterisks wide and 7 asterisks high. The application output should look similar to:

```
***************
*             *
*             *
*             *
*             *
*             *
***************
```

## Exercise 4 ——————————————— RockPaperScissorsRules

Create a RockPaperScissorsRules application that displays the rules for playing Rock Paper Scissors. Place each rule on a separate line and place a blank line between rules. The application output should look similar to:

```
Rock Paper Scissors Rules

Players decide on different hand signals to represent
rock, paper, and scissors.

Players make a throw at the same time.

The hand signals thrown by the players are then compared
to the rules of the game to determine the winner:

        Rock dulls Scissors (Rock wins).

        Scissors cuts Paper (Scissors wins).

        Paper covers Rock (Paper wins).
```

## Exercise 5 ——————————————— TicTacToeBoard

Create a TicTacToeBoard application that displays a tic-tac-toe board with an X in the center. The application output should look similar to:

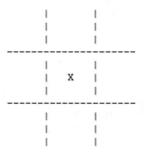

## Exercise 6 ——————————————— TicTacToeRules

Create a TicTacToeRules application that displays the rules for playing tic-tac-toe. Place each rule on a separate line and place a blank line between rules. The application output should look similar to:

```
Tic Tac Toe Rules

Tic Tac Toe is a game for 2 players.

1. A grid of 9 squares is drawn.

2. The first player draws an X in an empty square.

3. The second player draws an O in an empty square.

4. Steps 2 and 3 are repeated until a Tic Tac Pattern is created:

     Patterns can be diagonal, horizontal, or vertical.

5. A winning pattern is completed by drawing a line through the pattern.
```

*Chapter 2 Introducing Java*

## Exercise 7 ──────────────────── JavaTerminology

Create a JavaTerminology application that displays at least five words from the vocabulary list in this chapter and the corresponding definition. Place each word on a separate line followed by the definition. Place a blank line between entries.

## Exercise 8 ──────────────────── CompilerDocumentation

Create a CompilerDocumentation application that creates compiler-specific documentation for the compiler you will be using in your class.

    a) Add the compiler name to the right of "Compiler" and then explain how to create a new project, enter source code, compile, and run a Java application using a format similar to:

```
Compiler:                      -

Steps to create a new project:

A list of compiler-specific steps to create a new project.


Compile a project:

A list of compiler-specific steps to compile a project.


Run a project:

A list of compiler-specific steps to run a project.
```

    b) Explore the compiler's help features. Add documentation that explains how to use the compiler's Help features.

# Exercise 9 ———————————————————— BinaryNumbers

As discussed in Chapter 1, computers are digital and they recognize two states: on and off. Therefore, the binary number system (base 2), which uses only two digits (0 and 1), was adopted for use in computers. Our most familiar number system is the decimal, or base 10, system. It uses ten digits: 0 through 9.

a) Create a BinaryNumbers application that illustrates the binary numbers 1 through 20 and their decimal equivalents. Refer to Chapter 1 for the conversion formula or if you have the Windows operating system, use the Calculator in the Start → All Programs → Accessories menu to convert the numbers. In the Calculator, select View → Programmer and then enter the number and select Bin to convert the decimal (Dec) number:

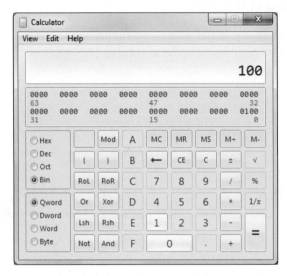

The application output should look similar to:

| Decimal | Binary |
|---------|--------|
| 1 | 1 |
| 2 | 10 |
| 3 | 11 |
| 4 | 100 |
| 5 | 101 |
| 6 | 110 |
| 7 | 111 |
| 8 | 1000 |

b) The hexadecimal, or base 16, system is based on 16 digits: 0 through 9, and the letters A through F representing 10 through 15 respectively. Modify the BinaryNumbers application to include a Hexadecimal column that contains the corresponding hexadecimal numbers.

*Chapter 2 Introducing Java*

# Chapter 3
# Variables and Constants

## Key Concepts

Declaring and initializing variables and constants
Obtaining user input
Differentiating between data types
Accessing Java packages
Writing numeric expressions
Formatting numeric output
Identifying Java keywords
Recognizing syntax and logic errors
Understanding run-time exceptions
Problem-solving using a case study approach

## Case Study

Birthday Game application

## Declaring Variables

A *variable* is a name for a value stored in memory. Variables are used in programs so that values can be represented with meaningful names. For example, when a variable named `length` is used in a program, it is clear that its value is a distance. Variables should be used to represent values because they make code easier to read, understand, and modify.

*declaration*

A variable must be declared before it is used. A *declaration* takes the form:

```
<type> <name>
```

*data type*

*identifier*

The declaration includes two parts. The first is the *data type*, which determines the type of data the variable will store. The second part of a declaration is the variable name, called the *identifier*. For example

```
int length;
```

`int` is the data type and `length` is the identifier. An `int` stores an integer value, which is a positive or negative whole number. When an integer variable is declared it stores the value 0.

An identifier must begin with a letter and contain only letters, numbers, and some special characters. Typically variable identifiers begin with a lowercase letter. Any word after the first in a variable identifier should begin with an uppercase letter. For example, `rectangleLength`.

Multiple variables with the same data type can be declared in a single statement, similar to:

```
int length, width;
```

Grouping variables together in a single statement is good programming style when the variables represent related items. Declarations should not be grouped together in the same statement just because the variables are all the same type.

## Using Variables

Applications typically contain many variables, as in RectangleArea:

```
/**
 * Calculates and displays the area of a rectangle
 */
public class RectangleArea {

    public static void main(String[] args) {
        int length = 10;    //longer side of rectangle
        int width = 2;      //shorter side of rectangle
        int area;           //calculated area of rectangle

        area = length * width;
        System.out.println("Area of rectangle: " + area);
    }
}
```

RectangleArea produces output similar to:

```
Area of rectangle: 20
```

Variable declarations should be grouped at the beginning of a method. A blank line after the declarations makes it easy to determine where the declarations end.

*assignment*  The value of a variable is changed through assignment. An *assignment statement* is formed with the variable name on the left side of an equal sign and the value it is to receive on the right side of the equal sign. The *equal sign* (=) is an operator that indicates that the variable on the left is to *literal* receive the value on the right. The value on the right can be a *literal*, which is any actual value. It could also be another variable or an expression. For example, `area` was assigned the value of the length multiplied by the width (`length * width`). Note that the * symbol indicates multiplication.

*initialize*  An assignment statement can be part of a variable declaration. In addition to being declared, the variable is *initialized*. For example, in RectangleArea, variables `length` and `width` were assigned values when declared.

*concatenation*  A `System.out.println()` statement can be used to output the value of a variable. Variable identifiers are not enclosed by quotation marks. To append, or *concatenate*, the value of a variable to a string, the + operator is used. The + operator converts the value of the variable to a string and then concatenates the strings before output.

It is important to realize that a variable can store only one value at any one time. For example, after the following statements execute

```
int x;
x = 5;
x = 10;
```

x
☐

x
5

x
10

the value of x is 10 because this was the last value assigned to x.

## Review: RectanglePerimeter

Create a RectanglePerimeter application that calculates and displays the perimeter of a rectangle with width 4 and length 13. The perimeter of a rectangle is calculated as 2w + 2l. Use variables as appropriate.

## Primitive Data Types

### String Data

Strings are comprised of a set of characters and therefore cannot be represented by a primitive data type. The String class in the java.lang package is used to create string variables. Strings are discussed in more detail in Chapter 5.

The `int` data type is called a primitive data type. A variable that is defined with a *primitive data type* stores a single piece of data. Java supports several primitive data types, including:

| Type | Bytes | Data Range |
|------|-------|------------|
| int | 4 | a positive or negative integer from –2,147,483,648 to 2,147,483,647 |
| double | 8 | a positive or negative number that may contain a decimal portion in the range –1.7E+308 to 1.7E+308 |
| char | 2 | a single character |
| boolean | | `true` or `false` |

An `int` variable uses 4 bytes of memory to store its value and is used for representing whole numbers.

*floating point*

Values that are represented by the `double` data type are sometimes referred to as *floating point*, meaning that the values contain numbers after the decimal point. Because of the many digits that are possible in a `double`, a variable of this type uses 8 bytes of memory.

**TIP** Java also supports the `byte`, `short`, `long`, and `float` primitive data types.

A `char` variable requires 2 bytes of memory because Java uses the 16-bit Unicode character encoding. Assignment to a `char` variable requires enclosing a single character in single quotation marks, as in `'a'`.

Variables that are type `boolean` can have only one of two values—`true` or `false`. Boolean variables are particularly useful for representing yes/no or on/off values.

**TIP** Primitive data types are also called built-in data types.

When choosing a data type, it is important to choose the most appropriate type for the quantity being represented. If a value could possibly have a decimal portion, then `double` is the best choice. If a variable will represent only whole numbers, then `int` is the best choice even though `double` will work. Using the most appropriate data types for variables has two benefits. First, both the compiler and the reader will understand the possible values for a variable. Second, the compiler allocates the appropriate memory for the variable.

## Review: Distance – part 1 of 2

Create a Distance application that calculates and displays the total distance of a race with three segments. The first segment is 12.2 km, the second is 10.6 km, and the third is 5.8 km. Use variables of the appropriate type.

## Abstract Data Types

In addition to primitive data types, a variable can be declared using an abstract data type. One kind of *abstract data type* is the class. Many classes are provided in Java, and many more classes will be created throughout this text. Each class defines not just a single piece of data like a primitive data type, but a set of data along with methods for performing actions on that data.

*object*

A variable declared with a class is called an *object*. The variable itself actually stores a reference to the area in memory where the object's data and methods are stored:

*instantiation*

Creating a new object is called *instantiation*. In addition to declaring a variable to refer to the object, the object must be created and initialized in a statement that takes the form:

```
<class> <variable name> = new <class>(<arguments>);
```

The `new` operator allocates memory for the object and returns a reference to the object. `<arguments>` are used to initialize the data for the object.

The code below creates a new object using a class named Circle:

```
Circle spot = new Circle(4);   //spot with radius 4
```

In this statement, the variable `spot` refers to a Circle object that has been initialized with a radius of 4.

To access a member of a class, such as a method, use the object name followed by a dot (.) and then the member name. For example, the code below executes method members getRadius() and area():

```
Circle spot = new Circle(4);
System.out.println("Radius of spot is " + spot.getRadius());
System.out.println("Area of spot is " + spot.area());
```

These statements produce output similar to:

```
Radius of spot is 4.0
Area of spot is 50.24
```

The Circle class will be developed later in this text.

## Java Packages

Java SE includes numerous packages as part of the JDK. End-users will have the packages as part of the Java Runtime Environment (JRE). These packages contain general use classes, utility classes, or special purpose classes. The most fundamental package is java.lang with classes that define the language itself. Other packages such as java.util have classes for reading input and storing data. These packages will be explained and used throughout this text.

**TIP** Companies sometimes use their reversed Internet domain in package names. For example, com.mycompany.util names a package with utility classes.

Packages follow a certain naming convention. Java packages start with `java` followed by a dot (.) and then the package name. Companies and other organizations will often name a package with the organization name followed by a dot and then the package name.

The `import` statement is used to make the members of a package accessible to an application. To make a single class from a package accessible, a statement similar to the following is used:

```
import java.util.Scanner;
```

The class name starts with an uppercase letter, following the appropriate naming convention for class names. If several classes in a package are to be accessible, then a statement that imports the entire package may be used:

```
import java.util.*;
```

*java.lang*

The asterisk (*) indicates that all members of the util package are to be accessible. `import` statements must appear after a package statement and before any class definitions. Java applications automatically import the entire java.lang package.

## Obtaining a Value from the User

*input stream*

An application is more flexible when values can be read from an input stream. An *input stream* is the sequence of characters received from an input device, such as a keyboard. For example, as a user types data, the data goes into the input stream. To process data in the input stream, Java includes the Scanner class with methods for reading integers, floating point numbers, and strings.

*Scanner*

A program that obtains a value from the user must instantiate a `Scanner` object that is initialized with an input stream. For data typed from a keyboard, initialize the object with `System.in` because it represents the standard input stream.

Scanner class methods include:

Class Scanner (java.util.Scanner)

Methods

| | |
|---|---|
| `next()` | returns a string from the input stream. |
| `nextLine()` | returns the string up to the end of line character from the input stream. |
| `nextInt()` | returns the `int` read from the input stream. |
| `nextDouble()` | returns the `double` read from the input stream. |
| `nextBoolean()` | returns the `boolean` read from the input stream. |
| `close()` | closes the input stream. |

*exception*

The next() method is used for reading a string that does not contain spaces. For example, "apple". Attempting to read the string "apple pie" generates a run-time exception called InputMismatchException. An *exception* is an error affecting program execution. Exceptions are discussed later in this chapter.

When reading in a combination of numeric and string data, the next() method should be used for reading string data after reading numeric data. Using the nextLine() method is ineffective. It reads the end-of-line character left by the numeric data entry, essentially reading an empty string. If a string with multiple words is expected from the user, the nextLine() can be used to read in the end-of-line character and then another nextLine() used to read the string.

The RectangleArea2 class below instantiates a Scanner object and reads values typed by the user:

```java
import java.util.Scanner;

/**
 * Calculates and displays the area of a rectangle
 * based on the width and length entered by the user.
 */

public class RectangleArea2 {

    public static void main(String[] args) {

        int length;     //longer side of rectangle
        int width;      //shorter side of rectangle
        int area;       //calculated area of rectangle
        Scanner input = new Scanner(System.in);

        System.out.print("Enter the length: ");
        length = input.nextInt();
        System.out.print("Enter the width: ");
        width = input.nextInt();
        input.close();

        area = length * width;
        System.out.println("Area of rectangle: " + area);
    }
}
```

Note that the `import` statement appears above the class. RectangleArea2 produces output similar to the following when values 6 and 2 are typed by the user:

```
Enter the length: 6
Enter the width: 2
Area of rectangle: 12
```

*prompt*

In the RectangleArea2 code, a Scanner object is declared, instantiated, and initialized in the statement `Scanner input = new Scanner(System.in)`. The calls to the nextInt() method are used to obtain the values typed by the user. When a call to nextInt() occurs, the application waits until the user types a value and presses enter before the next statement is executed. The application also includes *prompts* that tell the user what kind of input is expected. For example, `System.out.print("Enter the length: ")` prompts the user for a length value. When a Scanner object is no longer needed, it should be closed with the close() method.

## Review: Distance – part 2 of 2

Modify the Distance application to first prompt the user for the distance of each race segment and then display the total distance to run.

*Chapter 3 Variables and Constants*

# Numeric Expressions

---

**Object Operators**

Objects typically cannot be manipulated with the built-in arithmetic operators. A class usually defines methods that are used to perform operations on objects.

---

Java includes built-in arithmetic operators for addition (+), subtraction (–), multiplication (*), division (/), and modulus division (%). These operators are for use with primitive data and can be used to form numeric expressions. A *numeric expression* contains at least one operand, which is a value or primitive variable, and may contain operators. For example, the numeric expression 6 + 5 contains two operands and one operator. Numeric expressions can be used in assignment statements, as in the statement `area = length * width`.

The / division operator performs differently depending on the data type of the operands. When both operands are type `int`, the / operator performs integer division. *Integer division* truncates the decimal portion of the quotient to result in an integer:

*Integer division*

$$\begin{array}{r} \overset{\displaystyle 20/7}{\underset{\displaystyle \begin{array}{r} 14 \\ \hline 6 \end{array}}{7)\overline{20}}} \\ \textcircled{2}\ r6 \end{array}$$

Real division returns the entire quotient, including the decimal portion, and is performed when one or both operators are type `double`.

*modulus division*

*Modulus division* returns the remainder resulting from division. The % operator truncates the operands, if necessary, to return an integer:

$$\begin{array}{r} \overset{\displaystyle 20\%7}{\underset{\displaystyle \begin{array}{r} 14 \\ \hline 6 \end{array}}{7)\overline{20}}} \\ 2\ \textcircled{r6} \end{array}$$

Modulus division is useful for retrieving digits of a number.

The statements below demonstrate the division operators:

```java
int num1 = 5;
int num2 = 3;
int result;
double doubleNum1 = 5;
double doubleNum2 = 3;
double doubleResult;

result = num1 / num2;
System.out.println("num1 / num2: " + result);

doubleResult = doubleNum1 / doubleNum2;
System.out.println("doubleNum1 / doubleNum2: " + doubleResult);

doubleResult = num1 / doubleNum2;
System.out.println("num1 / doubleNum2: " + doubleResult);

result = num1 % num2;
System.out.println("num1 % num2: " + result);

doubleResult = doubleNum1 % doubleNum2;
System.out.println("doubleNum1 % doubleNum2: " + doubleResult);
```

Executing the statements on the previous page produces the output:

```
num1 / num2: 1
doubleNum1 / doubleNum2: 1.6666666666666667
num1 / doubleNum2: 1.6666666666666667
num1 % num2: 2
doubleNum1 % doubleNum2: 2.0
```

*operator precedence*

Java evaluates an expression using a specific order of operations based on operator precedence. *Operator precedence* is the level assigned to an operator. Multiplication and division (including modulus division) have the highest precedence, followed by addition and subtraction. Two operators of the same precedence are evaluated in order from left to right.

The order of operations can be changed by including parentheses in a numeric expression. The operations within parentheses are evaluated first. For example, the expression 6 + 4 * 2 − 1 evaluates to 13, and the expression (6 + 4) * (2 − 1) evaluates to 10. It is also considered good programming style to include parentheses when there is any possibility of ambiguity or question about the expression.

## Review: Digits

Create a Digits application that prompts the user for a two-digit number and then displays the ones-place and tens-place digits.

## Type Casting

*Type casting* converts a number of one type to a number of a different, but compatible type. For example, a `double` can be cast as an `int`, as in the statements:

```
int i = 2;
double d = 3.7;
int x;
x = i * (int)d    //d is explicitly cast; x is assigned 2x3
```

Type casting is necessary in this case because one of the operands in the expression has less precision than the variable that will store the result. Explicit casting also makes it clear that the programmer intended for the calculation result to be an `int`.

*truncate*

Casting a `double` to an `int` *truncates*, or removes, the decimal portion of the number, as in the statements above. When decreasing the precision of a number, it is better to round the number. A number with a decimal portion greater than or equal to 0.5 should be rounded up to the next integer, and a number with a decimal portion less than 0.5 should be rounded down. For example, rounding 3.7 results in 4.

**TIP** Truncation is always toward 0.

*Chapter 3 Variables and Constants*

Rounding can be simulated when casting a `double` to an `int` by adding 0.5 to the number before casting, as in the statement:

```
x = i * (int)(d + 0.5)      //x is assigned 2x4
```

If casting a negative number, then 0.5 should be subtracted from the number before casting.

Casting is useful when real division with integers is preferred. The following statements demonstrate the difference between integer division and real division with integers:

```
int i = 5;
int j = 2;
double result;

result = i / j;                //integer division; result=2
result = (double)i / (double)j;   //real division; result=2.5
```

Java will implicitly type cast operands in a mixed expression to match the precision of the variable storing the result, as in the statements:

```
int i = 2;
double d = 3.7;
double y;

y = i * d      //i is implicitly cast; y is assigned 2.0x3.7
```

Although explicit type casting is not necessary in this case, it is better programming style to include casts. Casting makes a programmer's intentions clear and may make bugs easier to find. Therefore, the statements above should be written as:

```
int i = 2;
double d = 3.7;
double y;

y = (double)i * d      //better code; y is assigned 2.0x3.7
```

## Review: GradeAvg – part 1 of 2

Create a GradeAvg application that prompts the user for five grades and then displays the average of the grades. Assume the grades are integer values (for example, 89, 97, and so on). Real division should be performed when calculating the average.

## Review: TempConverter

Create a TempConverter application that converts a Fahrenheit temperature to the corresponding Celsius temperature. The formula for converting Fahrenheit to Celsius is C = 5/9(F – 32). The application should prompt the user for the Fahrenheit temperature. Be sure to carefully form the expression. Parentheses will be needed to specify the order of operations.

# Formatting Numeric Output

*java.text*

The NumberFormat class, which is part of the java.text package, is used to create objects that format numbers. NumberFormat objects return a string that contains a formatted number. The formatting of the number depends on which NumberFormat object is used. The NumberFormatExample application creates four different NumberFormat objects:

```java
import java.text.NumberFormat;

public class NumberFormatExample {

    public static void main(String[] args) {
        double dollars = 21.5;
        int num = 1234;
        double numWithDecimal = 2.0 / 3.0;
        double sale = .15;
        NumberFormat money = NumberFormat.getCurrencyInstance();
        NumberFormat number = NumberFormat.getIntegerInstance();
        NumberFormat decimal = NumberFormat.getNumberInstance();
        NumberFormat percent = NumberFormat.getPercentInstance();

        System.out.println(money.format(dollars));
        System.out.println(number.format(num));
        System.out.println(decimal.format(numWithDecimal));
        System.out.println(percent.format(sale));
    }
}
```

When executed, the application produces the following output:

```
$21.50
1,234
0.667
15%
```

## The DecimalFormat Class

The DecimalFormat class offers additional options for formatting numbers to a specified decimal place. Refer to Java online documentation for more information.

## The format() Method

The format() method, discussed in Chapter 2, can also be used to format numeric values. A specifier can take the form:

```
%[alignment][width][.decimal]f
```

where [.decimal] indicates the number of decimal places and f indicates a floating point number. For an integer, the specifier takes the form:

```
%[alignment][width]d
```

# Assignment Operators

In an assignment statement, the expression on the right side of the equal sign (=) is evaluated first and then that value is given to the variable on the left. Because the expression on the right is evaluated before an assignment is made, it is possible to use the current value of the variable in the expression itself. For example:

```
numPlayers = 12;            //numPlayers is assigned 12
numPlayers = numPlayers + 2;  //numPlayers is now 14
```

Changing the value of a variable based on its current value is often done in programming. Therefore, in addition to the = assignment operator, Java recognizes the +=, -=, *=, /=, and %= assignment operators. These operators perform an operation before making an assignment. For example, the previous assignment statement can be rewritten as:

```
numPlayers += 2;      //numPlayers is now 14
```

The -=, *=, /=, and %= operators work similarly, as in the statements:

```
numPlayers -= 3;      //same as: numPlayers = numPlayers - 3
numCopies *= 5;       //same as: numCopies = numCopies * 5
total /= 2;           //same as: total = total / 2
remainder %= 6;       //same as: remainder = remainder % 6
```

Modify the GradeAvg application to use the += operator to sum the grades as they are entered by the user. Format the average grade to display as a percentage.

## Using Named Constants

### When should a named constant be used?

Named constants should be used wherever they can add clarity to code. However, there are some values that should not be replaced with named constants. For example, in an expression that calculates the area of a triangle (½bh), the value 0.5 is best used instead of a named constant because the value does not have an obvious name.

A *constant* is a name for a memory location that stores a value that cannot be changed from its initial assignment. Constants, like variables, are used in programs so that values can be represented with meaningful names. A constant declaration is a variable declared final and takes the form:

```
final <type> <identifier>
```

The declaration begins with final, which indicates that the value will not change, followed by the type of data the constant will store and the constant identifier. For example, the following declaration represents π:

```
final double PI = 3.14;
```

double declares a numeric value possibly containing a decimal portion. Constant identifiers are typically all uppercase, and may include underscore (_) characters to separate words. For example, MAX _ PRICE.

The following class uses a constant in the main() method:

```
/**
 * Calculates and displays the area of a circle
 */

public class CircleArea {

    public static void main(String[] args) {

        final double PI = 3.14;
        double radius = 5;       //radius of circle
        double area;

        area = PI * radius * radius;
        System.out.println("Area of circle: " + area);
    }
}
```

CircleArea produces output similar to:

```
Area of circle: 78.5
```

A constant can be assigned a value only once. Trying to change the value of a constant after the initial assignment generates an error. Constant declarations should be grouped at the beginning of a method before any variable declarations.

## Identifiers and Keywords

*case sensitivity*

Identifiers in Java must begin with a letter and may contain letters, numbers, and some special symbols. Periods and spaces are not allowed. Identifiers are also *case sensitive*, which means that an uppercase letter is different from the same letter in lowercase. For example, identifiers `Count` and `count` are viewed by Java as two different identifiers.

The Java language contains *keywords*, which have special meaning to the Java compiler and therefore cannot be used for a variable or constant identifier. The Java keywords are:

| | | | |
|---|---|---|---|
| abstract | double | int | strictfp |
| boolean | else | interface | super |
| break | extends | long | switch |
| byte | final | native | synchronized |
| case | finally | new | this |
| catch | float | package | throw |
| char | for | private | throws |
| class | goto | protected | transient |
| const | if | public | try |
| continue | implements | return | void |
| default | import | short | volatile |
| do | instanceof | static | while |

Although not keywords, `true`, `false`, and `null` are reserved and not for use as identifiers.

## Review: CircleCircumference – part 1 of 2

Create a CircleCircumference application that calculates and displays the circumference of a circle. The application should prompt the user for the value of the radius. The circumference of a circle is calculated as $2\pi r$. Use variables and constants as appropriate.

## Programming Errors

There are many types of errors that can occur in a program. Some errors are found by the compiler. Others occur at run time. A program that has been carefully designed will have fewer errors. Code reuse can also lead to fewer errors because packages that have been carefully tested and properly documented produce cleaner and more robust code.

*syntax error*

Errors that violate the rules of Java are called *syntax errors*. For example, forgetting a semicolon at the end of a statement generates a syntax error. Syntax errors are found by the compiler. An application with syntax errors will not run because it will not compile.

*logic error, semantic error*

A *logic error*, also called a *semantic error*, is more difficult to detect. Logic errors occur in statements that are syntactically correct, but produce undesired or unexpected results, as in the following example:

```
int length;
int area;

length = 3.2;          //3 is actually assigned
area = length * length;   //expected value is 10.24
```

The statements assign the value 9 to `area` rather than the expected 10.24. Although, it is possible that the programmer intended for the value to be truncated, it is more likely that variables `length` and `area` were supposed to be declared as `double`.

Logic errors must be found by the programmer through testing and by carefully examining the source code. Accurate and careful commenting, proper indentation, and descriptive identifiers can help in finding and preventing logic errors.

*run-time error, exception*

Errors that are not detected by the compiler may generate a *run-time error*. A run-time error, also called an *exception*, halts program execution at the statement that cannot be executed. For example, although the statements below are syntactically correct, they will generate a run-time error because division by 0 is undefined:

```
int totalScores = 40;
int totalTests = 0;
double avgScore;
avgScores = totalScores / totalTests;
```

*ArithmeticException*

This code generates an ArithmeticException exception.

*InputMismatchException*

Exceptions can also be generated when user input is not as expected. For example, the application run below generates an InputMismatchException exception because the user typed a string when a numeric was expected:

```
Enter the length: h
Exception in thread "main" java.util.InputMismatchException
    at java.util.Scanner.throwFor(Scanner.java:909)
    at java.util.Scanner.next(Scanner.java:1530)
    at java.util.Scanner.nextInt(Scanner.java:2160)
    at java.util.Scanner.nextInt(Scanner.java:2119)
    at RectangleArea2.main(RectangleArea2.java:27)
```

The program only had code to handle numeric user input. When a letter, rather than a number was typed, an exception was "thrown." Writing code to handle exceptions is discussed in Chapter 11.

This and all subsequent chapters end with a case study. Case studies are used to learn problem-solving techniques. Each case study will include a description, program specification, code design, program implementation, and a discussion about testing and debugging.

In this case study, a Birthday game will be created. The BirthdayGame guesses a player's birthday by having the player perform mathematics with the month and day of their birthday. The number computed by the player is then entered and the program displays the month and day of the player's birthday.

## BirthdayGame Specification

BirthdayGame is played with one player. The player is given directions for computing a number that uses the player's birth month and birth day in the calculations:

1. Determine your birth month (January=1, February=2, and so on).

2. Multiply that number by 5.

3. Add 6 to that number.

4. Multiply the number by 4.

5. Add 9 to the number.

6. Multiply that number by 5.

7. Add your birth day to the number (10 if born on the 10th and so on).

BirthdayGame prompts the player for the calculated number and then displays the player's birthday. To determine the player's birthday, 165 is subtracted from the number entered by the player. This number is then divided by 100. The decimal portion of the quotient represents the birth month. The remainder of the division is the birth day.

The BirthdayGame interface should consist of steps that tell the user how to calculate the number that needs to be entered. The player should then be prompted for their number. Finally, the application displays the player's birthday.

A sketch of a program run:

```
Using paper and pencil, perform the following calculations:

1. Determine your birth month (January=1, February=2 and so on).
2. Multiply that number by 5.
3. Add 6 to that number.
4. Multiply the number by 4.
5. Add 9 to the number.
6. Multiply that number by 5.
7. Add your birth day to the number (10 if the 10th and so on).

Enter your number: 393
Your birthday is 2/28
```

An algorithm for BirthdayGame:

1. Display the directions for the player to calculate the number.

2. Prompt the player for the calculated number.

3. Subtract 165 from the number.

4. Use integer division to divide the number by 100. Store the quotient as the birth month.

5. Use modulus division to divide the number by 100. Store the remainder as the birth day.

6. Display a message containing the player's birthday.

## BirthdayGame Code Design

The code design describes how to accomplish the specification. Included in the code design are a description of the input, output, data generated, and additional algorithms, and pseudocode.

The input for BirthdayGame is a number calculated by the user. An integer variable to store the user's input will be needed.

The output for BirthdayGame is a message with the user's birthday.

Data generated by BirthdayGame is the birth month and the birth day. Integer variables to store the birth month and birth day will be needed.

Based on the algorithm, the code design for the BirthdayGame application will include statements for input and output. Calculations will require both integer and modulus division. A pseudocode algorithm for BirthdayGame follows:

```
Display directions (7 steps)
Prompt the user for the calculated number
playerNum -= 165
birthMonth = playerNum / 100
birthDay = playerNum % 100
Display player's birthday
```

## BirthdayGame Implementation

Based on the code design, the BirthdayGame implementation follows:

```java
/*
 * BirthdayGame.java
 */

import java.util.Scanner;

/**
 * Plays a birthday guessing game with one player.
 */
public class BirthdayGame {

    public static void main(String[] args) {
        int playerNum;
        int birthMonth, birthDay;
        Scanner input = new Scanner(System.in);

        /* Give the player directions for calculating the number */
        System.out.println("Using paper and pencil, perform the following
            calculations:\n");
```

```
System.out.println("1. Determine your birth month (January=1, February=2
    and so on).");
System.out.println("2. Multiply that number by 5.");
System.out.println("3. Add 6 to that number.");
System.out.println("4. Multiply the number by 4.");
System.out.println("5. Add 9 to the number.");
System.out.println("6. Multiply that number by 5.");
System.out.println("7. Add your birth day to the number (10 if the 10th
    and so on).\n");
System.out.print("Enter your number:  ");
playerNum = input.nextInt();
input.close();

/* Calculate birth day and month and display result. */
playerNum -= 165;
birthMonth = playerNum / 100;
birthDay = playerNum % 100;

System.out.println("Your birthday is " + birthMonth + "/" + birthDay);
    }
}
```

A run of BirthdayGame looks similar to:

```
Using paper and pencil, perform the following calculations:

1. Determine your birth month (January=1, February=2 and so on).
2. Multiply that number by 5.
3. Add 6 to that number.
4. Multiply the number by 4.
5. Add 9 to the number.
6. Multiply that number by 5.
7. Add your birth day to the number (10 if the 10th and so on).

Enter your number: 1179
Your birthday is 10/14
```

### BirthdayGame Testing and Debugging

This case study performs minimal calculations and the algorithm is simple and straight forward. Simply testing it with your birthday is one method of verifying results.

## Chapter Summary

Variables and constants are used in programs so that values can be represented with meaningful names. Variables and constants should be used because they make code easier to read, understand, and modify.

Both variables and constants are created with a declaration statement. A variable declaration includes the data type and identifier. A constant declaration also includes the keyword `final`. Identifiers are case sensitive and cannot be the same as a Java keyword. The value of a variable can be changed throughout program execution with assignment statements. The value of a constant cannot be changed from its initial assignment.

*Chapter 3 Variables and Constants*

A primitive data type stores a single piece of data and can include `int`, `double`, `char`, and `boolean`. Abstract data types include classes. Each class defines not just a single piece of data like a primitive data type, but a set of data along with methods for performing actions on that data. Variables declared with an abstract data type are called objects. An object declaration is called instantiation. An object is instantiated with the keyword `new`.

Data can be read from the user at run time by using the Scanner class. This class processes data from the input stream. Objects that read data from the keyboard are initialized with `System.in`. When obtaining data from the user, a prompt should be included so that the user knows what information is expected.

Java includes many packages. Package members are accessible with an `import` statement. The Scanner class is in the java.util package. The NumberFormat class is in the java.text class. The NumberFormat class is used for formatting numbers.

Java includes built-in operators that are used to form numeric expressions. Arithmetic operators include `+`, `-`, `*`, `/`, and `%`. The / operator performs integer division when both operands are type `int`, and real division when at least one operand is a `double`. Modulus division is performed with the % operator. An expression is evaluated according to operator precedence. The order of operations can be changed with parentheses. Assignment operators include `+=`, `-=`, `*=`, `/=`, and `%=`. Each of these operators perform an operation before making an assignment.

Type casting converts a number of one type to a number of a different type. Casting is useful when real division with integers is preferred. A `double` can be rounded by first adding 0.5 before casting to an `int`.

Programming errors occur for many reasons. A syntax error violates the rules of Java. A logic error is also called a semantic error and is more difficult to detect because statements are syntactically correct, but produce unexpected results. A run-time error is also called an exception. An exception halts program execution.

Code conventions introduced in this chapter are:

- Variable identifiers begin with a lowercase letter and any word after the first within the identifier should begin with an uppercase letter.

- Constant identifiers are all uppercase. Multiple words in an identifier can be separated with an underscore (_) character.

- Variable and constant declarations should be grouped at the beginning of a method.

- Each line of a program should contain only one statement.

**Abstract data type** A class. A data type that can store data and methods.

**ArithmeticException exception** An exception thrown when division by 0 occurs.

**Assignment statement** A statement that gives the variable or constant on the left of an assignment operator the value of the expression on the right side of the assignment operator.

**Case sensitive** An uppercase letter is different from the same letter in lowercase.

**Class** *see* Abstract data type.

**Concatenate** To join two or more strings to form one larger string.

**Constant** A name for a memory location that stores a value than cannot be changed from its initial assignment.

**Data type** The kind of information a variable stores.

**Declaration** A statement that creates a variable or constant.

**Equal sign (=)** An assignment operator that indicates the variable or constant on the left is to receive the value of the expression on the right.

**Exception** *see* Run-time error.

**Floating point** Values that are represented by the `double` data type. Values that contain numbers after the decimal point.

**Identifier** A name for a variable or constant. An identifier must begin with a letter and can include any number of letters, numbers, and some special characters.

**Initialize** To assign a variable a value in a declaration statement.

**InputMismatchException exception** An exception thrown when user input is not as expected.

**Input stream** The sequence of characters received from an input device.

**Instantiation** To create a new object.

**Integer division** Division that truncates the decimal portion.

**Keyword** A word that has special meaning to the Java compiler and therefore cannot be used as a variable or constant identifier.

**Literal** An actual value.

**Logic error** An error caused by a statement that is syntactically correct, but produces unexpected or undesired results. Also called a semantic error.

**Modulus division** Division that returns the remainder.

**Numeric expression** At least one operand and possibly one or more operators that evaluate to a single value.

**Object** A variable declared with a class.

**Operator precedence** The level assigned to an operator so that a specific order of operations is maintained.

**Primitive data type** A data type that can store only a single piece of data. Primitive data types are also called built-in data types.

**Prompt** A string that informs the user of the kind of data expected to be typed.

**Run-time error** An error affecting program execution. Also called an exception.

**Semantic error** *see* Logic error.

**Syntax error** An error caused by a statement that violates the rules of Java.

**Truncate** Removing the decimal portion of a number when casting a `double` to an `int`.

**Type casting** Converting a number from one type to a different type.

**Variable** A name for a memory location that stores a value.

+ Operator used for concatenating strings.

+ The arithmetic addition operator.

− The arithmetic subtraction operator.

* The arithmetic multiplication operator.

/ The arithmetic division operator.

% The arithmetic modulus division operator.

() Used to change the order of operations in an expression. Also used for type casting.

= An assignment operator that gives the variable on the left the value on the right.

+= An assignment operator that adds the value on the right to the variable on the left and then assigns that value to the variable on the left.

−= An assignment operator that subtracts the value on the right from the variable on the left and then assigns that value to the variable on the left.

*= An assignment operator that multiplies the value on the right by the value of the variable on the left and then assigns that value to the variable on the left.

/= An assignment operator that divides the value of the variable on the left by the value on the right and then assigns that value to the variable on the left.

%= An assignment operator that divides the value of the variable on the left by the value on the right and then assigns the remainder of that division to the variable on the left.

boolean A data type that represents true or false.

char A data type that represents a single character.

double A data type that represents positive or negative floating point numbers.

final Keyword used to declare an identifier a constant.

import Statement used to make a package or classes from a package accessible to an application.

in The java.lang.System member that represents the standard input stream.

int A data type that represents positive or negative integers.

**java.lang** The most fundamental Java package. It contains classes that define the Java language.

**java.text** A Java package with the NumberFormat class for formatting numbers.

**java.util** A Java package with the Scanner class for reading input.

new An operator that allocates memory for an object.

**NumberFormat** A java.text class with methods for formatting numbers.

**Scanner** A java.util class with methods for reading input from the user.

System.in The input stream for reading from the keyboard.

1. a) List four legal identifier names.
   b) List four illegal identifier names and explain why each is illegal.

2. a) In two statements, declare a variable named `numBeads` and assign it the value 5.
   b) In one statement, declare a variable named `numBeads` and assign it the value 5.

3. a) What is the final value of `yourNumber` after the last statement executes?
   ```
   int myNumber = 5;
   int yourNumber = 4;
   myNumber = yourNumber * 2;
   yourNumber = myNumber + 5;
   ```
   b) What is the final value of `yourNumber` after the last statement executes?
   ```
   int myNumber;
   int yourNumber = 4;
   myNumber = yourNumber + 7;
   yourNumber = myNumber;
   ```

4. Determine the appropriate data type for each of the following values:
   a) the number of basketballs in a department store.
   b) the price of a basketball.
   c) the number of players on a basketball team.
   d) the average age of the players on a basketball team.
   e) whether a basketball player has received a jersey or not.
   f) the first initial of a basketball player's first name.

5. a) What is the difference between a primitive data type and an abstract data type?
   b) What is the difference between a class and an object?

6. Assume a class named Team defines a sports team.
   a) Methods define the actions in a class and typically include action words in their name. For example, getTeamName is a method name that returns the name of the team. List three more possible method names for the Team class.
   b) List three possible object names of type Team.

7. The java.util package contains a class named `ArrayList`. Write a statement that makes the ArrayList class accessible to an application.

8. What is the value of each of the following expressions?
   a) $5 + 7 - 3$
   b) $10 * 2 - 3$
   c) $10 * (2 - 3)$
   d) $8 - 3 * 2$
   e) $10 / 5 * 4$
   f) $10 / 2 + 3$
   g) $6 \% 3 + 4$
   h) $12 \% 5 * 3$
   i) $12 \% (5 * 3)$

9. What is the result of the following expression when x is 2005? When x is 1776? When x is 39?

   `(x/10)%10`

10. Write each equation as a valid Java expression:

    a) $A = lw$ (geometry)

    b) $P = \dfrac{R - C}{N}$ (business)

    c) $A = \dfrac{h(b_1 + b_2)}{N}$ (geometry)

    d) $V = \dfrac{4}{3}\pi r^3$ (geometry)

    e) $A = \dfrac{F + S + T}{3}$ (algebra)

    f) $P = \dfrac{5F}{4d^2}$ (physics)

    g) $A = P + Prt$ (business)

11. Using the following declarations, rewrite the statements to include the appropriate type casting, rounding where necessary. If type casting is not necessary, explain why:
    ```
    int j = 5;
    double k = 1.6;
    int y;
    double z;
    ```
    a) `y = j * k;`
    b) `z = j * k;`

c) `z = k * k;`

d) `j = k;`

e) `k = j;`

f) `y = j + 3;`

12. Compare the way the / and % operators perform to the effects of type casting.

13. Rewrite the statements below using the appropriate assignment operator:

    a) `total = total + 10;`

    b) `numStones = numStones - 1;`

    c) `days = days % 24;`

    d) `price = price * 1.2;`

14. Determine if each of the following are better represented by a variable or a constant and then write declarations using appropriate data types and descriptive identifiers:

    a) the number of votes received by an election candidate

    b) the percentage of votes won by a candidate

    c) the first, middle, and last initials of an election candidate

    d) the year of the election

15. Determine if each of the following segments of code contain a syntax error, logic error, or runtime error. Explain.

    a) `duble salary;`

    b) `int numHats`

    c) `length == 12;`

    d) `int test1 = 90;`

       `int test2 = 85;`

       `double avg;`

       `avg = test1 + test2 / 2;`

    e) `double x = 12;`

       `double y = 0;`

       `double z;`

       `z = x / y;`

    f) `double payCheck = 120.00;`

       `NumberFormat money =`

               `NumberFormat.getPercentInstance();`

       `System.out.println(money.format(payCheck);`

d) Values typed by the user cannot be used in an application.

e) The Scanner class is part of a Java package.

f) The + operator has higher precedence than the – operator.

g) The – operator has lower precedence than the % operator.

h) `byte` is a keyword.

i) The identifiers apple and Apple are considered the same in Java.

j) Errors that violate the rules of Java are called semantic errors.

## True/False

16. Determine if each of the following are true or false. If false, explain why.

    a) An identifier can contain spaces.

    b) Data of type `double` is sometimes referred to as floating point.

    c) An abstract data type is also called a primitive data type.

## Exercise 1 ——————————————————————————————ObjectHeight

The height of an object at any given time dropped from a starting height of 100 meters is given by the equation h=100−4.9*t$^2$ where t is the time in seconds. Create an ObjectHeight application that prompts the user for a time less than 4.5 seconds and then displays the height of the object at that time. The application output should look similar to:

```
Enter a time less than 4.5 seconds: 2
The height of the object is: 80.4 meters
```

## Exercise 2 ——————————————————————————————— PizzaCost

The cost of making a pizza at a local shop is as follows:

- Labor cost is $0.75 per pizza, regardless of size

- Rent cost is $1.00 per pizza, regardless of size

- Materials is $0.05*diameter*diameter (diameter is measured in inches)

Create a PizzaCost application that prompts the user for the size of a pizza and then displays the cost of making the pizza. The application output should look similar to:

```
Enter the diameter of the pizza in inches: 10
The cost of making the pizza is: $6.75
```

## Exercise 3 ——————————————————————————————— CollegeCalculator

In small groups brainstorm all the expenses involved in attending a college or university (rent, tutition, books, etc) and possible offset costs (scholarships, etc). Create a CollegeCalculator application that prompts the user for the amount of each expense and offset cost. If the cost is not applicable the user should enter a value of 0. Add the expenses and subtract the offset costs to determine how much money an individual will need for their school year. College websites can be used as a guide to determine relevant and appropriate expenses.

## Exercise 4 ———————————————————— Energy

Einstein's famous formula, e=mc², gives the amount of energy released by the complete conversion of matter of mass m into energy e. If m represents the mass in kilograms and c represents the speed of light in meters per second (3.0 ∗ 10⁸ m/s), then the result is in the energy units Joules. It takes 360000 Joules to light a 100-watt light bulb for an hour. Create an Energy application that prompts the user for a mass in kilograms and then displays the energy and the number of light bulbs that could be powered. The application output should look similar to:

```
Enter the mass in kilograms: 1
The energy produced in Joules is = 9.0E16
The number of 100-watt light bulbs powered = 2.5E11
```

## Exercise 5 ———————————————————— Change

Create a Change application that prompts the user for an amount less than $1.00 and then displays the minimum number of coins necessary to make the change. The change can be made up of quarters, dimes, nickels, and pennies. The application output should look similar to:

```
Enter the change in cents: 212
The minimum number of coins is:
Quarters: 8
Dimes: 1
Nickels: 0
Pennies: 2
```

## Exercise 6 ⚙ ———————————————————— Digits

Modify the Digits application created in a review earlier in this chapter to show the hundreds-place digit of a three digit number. The application output should look similar to:

```
Enter a three-digit number: 256
The hundreds place digit is: 2
The tens place digit is: 5
The ones place digit is: 6
```

## Exercise 7 ———————————————————— DivAndMod

Create a DivAndMod application that prompts the user for two integers and then displays the result of integer and modulus division in either order. The application output should look similar to:

```
Enter an integer: 14
Enter a second integer: 4

14 / 4 = 3
14 % 4 = 2

4 / 14 = 0
4 % 14 = 4
```

## Exercise 8 ——————————————————————— TimeConversion

Create a TimeConversion application that prompts the user for a time in minutes and then displays the time in hours and minutes. Be sure to consider times whether the number of minutes left over is less than 10. For example, 184 minutes in hour:minute format is 3:04 (Hint: use the modulus operator). The application output should look similar to:

```
Enter the time in minutes: 135
The time is: 2:15
```

## Exercise 9 ————————————————————————————— Sleep

Create a Sleep application that calculates the number of hours of your life that you have spent sleeping. Assume that you sleep 8 hours each night. To simplify the problem, assume that there are 30 days in each month and 365 days in each year. The application output should look similar to:

```
Enter your birthdate:
Year: 1997
Month: 2
Day: 12
Enter today's date:
Year: 2012
Month: 08
Day: 03
You have been alive for 5,646 days.
You have slept 45,168 hours.
```

## Exercise 10 ————————————————————————————— Order

A fast food restaurant charges $1.69 for burgers, $1.09 for fries, and $0.99 for sodas.

a) Create an Order application that prompts the employee for the number of burgers, fries, and sodas and then displays the total, the tax (6.5%), and the final cost. The application output should look similar to:

```
Enter the number of burgers: 2
Enter the number of fries: 5
Enter the number of sodas: 5
Total before tax: $13.78
Tax: $0.90
Final total: $14.68
```

b) Modify Order to prompt the employee for the amount tendered and then display the change due. Application output should look similar to:

```
Enter amount tendered: $20.00
Change: $5.32
```

# Exercise 11 ———————————————————————————————Project

Create a Project application to help analyze the time taken for a Java project. The application should prompt you for the time spent designing, coding, debugging, and testing, and then displays a table showing the percentage of time taken for each part. The application output should look similar to:

```
Designing: 120
Coding: 240
Debugging: 30
Testing: 30

Task        % Time
Designing   28.57 %
Coding      57.14 %
Debugging    7.14 %
Testing      7.14 %
```

# Exercise 12 ——————————————————————————— Spending

Create a Spending application to help examine the spending patterns of a user. The application should prompt the user for the amount spent last month on food, clothing, entertainment, and rent, and then displays a table showing the percentage of expenditures in each category. The application output should look similar to:

```
Enter the amount spent last month on the following items:

Food: $350
Clothing: $300
Entertainment: $200
Rent: $1250

Category       Budget
Food           16.67 %
Clothing       14.29 %
Entertainment   9.52 %
Rent           59.52 %
```

# Exercise 13 ———————————————————— SimpleInterest

There are two kinds of interest: simple and compound. With simple interest, the amount of the deposit remains the same, and the amount of interest is paid at the end of a time interval. For example, if $1,000 is deposited for 7 years at an interest rate of 6% per year, $60 will be deposited at the end of each year, for a total of $1,420 after 7 years.

a) The value of the amount after the term is calculated using the formula:

```
Amount = Principal * (1 + years * interest rate)
```

Create a SimpleInterest application that prompts the user for the principal, number of years, and the interest rate (as a fraction) and then calculates the amount of interest. The application should display output similar to:

```
Enter the principal: 5000
Enter the number of years: 5
Enter the interest rate: .06
The value after the term is: $6,500.00
```

b) The formula in part (a) can be adjusted to calculate what principal will need to be invested in order to have a certain amount of money after a specified term and interest rate:

```
Principal = Amount / (1 + years * interest rate).
```

Modify SimpleInterest to prompt the user for the desired amount, number of years, and interest rate and then calculate the principal that will need to be invested.

# Exercise 14 ———————————————————————— Election

The results of a primary election between two candidates in three states are:

|             | Awbrey | Martinez |
|-------------|--------|----------|
| New York    | 314159 | 271860   |
| New Jersey  | 89008  | 121032   |
| Connecticut | 213451 | 231034   |

Write a program that prompts the user for the election results, and then displays output similar to:

```
Election Results for New York:
Awbrey: 314159
Martinez: 271860

Election Results for New Jersey:
Awbrey: 89008
Martinez: 121032

Election Results for Connecticut:
Awbrey: 213451
Martinez: 231034

Candidate        Votes Percentage
Awbrey          616618    49.71 %
Martinez        623926    50.29 %
TOTAL VOTES:    1240544
```

# Chapter 4
# Conditional Control Structures

## Key Concepts

Controlling the flow of a program
Generating random numbers
Writing compound Boolean expressions
Accessing methods in the Math class
Modifying existing code
Selecting appropriate test data
Creating and modifying problem solutions

## Case Study

Rock Paper Scissors game

## The if Statement

*conditional control structure*

The `if` statement is a *conditional control structure*, also called a *decision structure*, which executes a set of statements when a condition is true. Conditional control structures are used to change program flow. The `if` statement takes the form:

```
if (<condition>) {
    <statements>
}
```

For example, in the following `if` statement, `guess == SECRET_NUM` is the condition, and there is one statement that will be executed when this condition is true:

```
if (guess == SECRET_NUM) {
    System.out.println("You guessed it!");
}
```

The `==` relational operator determines if the value of `guess` is equal to the value of `SECRET_NUM`. If equal, the println() statement executes. If not, then program flow continues to the next statement after the closing brace of the `if` statement.

*Boolean expression*

The condition of an `if` statement is a *Boolean expression*, which evaluates to either `true` or `false`. *Relational operators* can be used to form Boolean expressions. There are six relational operators:

| Operator | Meaning |
|----------|---------|
| == | equal |
| < | less than |
| <= | less than or equal |
| > | greater than |
| >= | greater than or equal |
| != | not equal |

> **TIP** The condition of an `if` statement should never make an equality comparison between floating point numbers because of the possibility of roundoff error.

> **TIP** Using = instead of == in an if statement condition generates an error.

### Comparing Objects

Because objects point to a location in memory, rather than directly storing a value, they cannot be compared using built-in relational operators. A class defines methods that are used to compare objects.

A `boolean` variable may also be used as the condition of an `if` statement because its value is `true` or `false`. For example, in the following statements, the message is displayed:

```
boolean gameOver = true;
if (gameOver) {
    System.out.println("Thanks for playing!");
}
```

## Review: SurfsUp – part 1 of 3

Create a SurfsUp application that prompts the user for the wave height and then displays "Great day for surfing!" when the waves are 6 feet and over.

## The if-else Statement

The `if` statement can include an optional `else` clause that is executed when the `if` condition evaluates to false. The `if-else` statement takes the following form:

```
if (<condition>) {
    <statements>
} else {
    <statements>
}
```

For example, in the following `if-else` statement, different messages are displayed for correct and incorrect guesses:

```
if (guess == SECRET_NUM) {
    System.out.println("You guessed it!");
} else {
    System.out.println("Try again.");
}
```

The indentation and organization of the `if-else` is important for readability. The structure shown is a code convention that clearly indicates the actions for a true condition and the actions for a false condition.

## Review: SurfsUp – part 2 of 3

Modify the SurfsUp application to display "Great day for surfing!" when the waves are 6 feet or over and "Go body boarding!" when the waves are less than 6 feet.

## Review: CircleCircumference – part 2 of 2

Modify the CircleCircumference application from Chapter 3 so that the message "Negative radii are illegal." is displayed if a negative number is entered by the user for the radius value. Otherwise the application should calculate and display the circumference of the circle.

## Nested Statements

An `if-else` statement can contain another `if-else` or `if` statement. Statements placed within the same type of statements are called *nested*. For example, the nested `if-else` gives a hint when the user does not guess the correct number:

```
if (guess == SECRET_NUM) {        //correct
   System.out.println("You guessed it!");
} else {
   if (guess < SECRET_NUM) {      //too low
      System.out.println("Too low.");
   } else {                       //too high
      System.out.println("Too high.");
   }
}
```

Carefully indenting the statements makes it clear which are nested.

## Review: Stages

Create a Stages application that prompts the user for an age. For an age over 18, `adult` is displayed. For an age less than or equal to 18, `toddler` is displayed when the age is less than or equal to 5, `child` when the age is less than or equal to 10, `preteen` when the age is less than or equal to 12, and `teen` when the age is over 12.

## The if-else if Statement

The `if-else if` statement is used to decide among three or more actions and takes the form:

```
if (<condition>) {
   <statements>
} else if (<condition>) {
   <statements>
} else {
   <statements>
}
```

**Commenting Complex Decision Structures**

Decision structures with many branches can quickly become difficult to understand. Brief inline comments can make code much more readable. This is especially important for the last branch of a decision structure, which usually does not include an explicit condition.

There can be multiple `else if` clauses, and the last `else` clause is optional. For example, there are three possible decisions in the `if-else if` statement below:

```
if (guess == SECRET_NUM) {          //correct
   System.out.println("You guessed it!");
} else if (guess < SECRET_NUM) {    //too low
   System.out.println("Too low.");
} else {                            //too high
   System.out.println("Too high.");
}
```

The logic used in developing an `if-else if` statement is important. For example, when testing a range of numbers, `if` conditions must be properly ordered because statements are executed for the first true condition only and then program flow continues to the next statement after the `if-else if`.

When choosing between nested if-else statements and a single if-else if statement, the if-else if allows only one branch to execute and the conditions show a clear sequence. In general, the if-else if statement is easier to read and understand.

## Review: SurfsUp – part 3 of 3

Modify the SurfsUp application to display "Great day for surfing!" when the waves are 6 feet or over, "Go body boarding!" when the waves are between 3 and 6 feet, "Go for a swim." when the waves are from 0 to 3 feet, and "Whoa! What kind of surf is that?" otherwise.

## Review: Discriminant

In mathematics, the quantity $b^2 - 4ac$ is called the "discriminant." Create a Discriminant application that prompts the user for the values of a, b, and c an then displays "No roots" if the discriminant is negative, "One root" is the discriminant is zero, and "Two roots" if the discriminant is positive. Application output should look similar to:

```
Enter the value for a: 7
Enter the value for b: -9
Enter the value for c: 2
Two roots
```

## The switch Statement

The switch statement is a conditional control structure that uses the result of an expression to determine which statements to execute. The switch statement is sometimes preferable to the if-else if statement because code may be easier to read. The switch statement takes the form:

```
switch (<integer expression>) {
   case x:
       <statement>;
       break;
   ...
   default:
       <statements>;
       break;
}
```

The expression must evaluate to an integer. There can be multiple case clauses. The break statement is necessary to move program control to the next statement after the switch statement. The default code is optional and is executed when none of the previous cases are met. For example, when score is 5, the case 5 statement executes and then program control moves to the next statement after the switch (skipping the case 10 statement):

```
switch (score) {
   case 0: System.out.println("Better luck next time."); break;
   case 5: System.out.println("Pretty good."); break;
   case 10: System.out.println("Great!"); break;
}
```

*Chapter 4 Conditional Control Structures*

If the `break` statement is not included in a `case` clause, execution continues on to the next statement within the `switch` statement. This can be useful when the same set of statements applies to more than one situation:

```
switch (score) {
    case 0: System.out.println("Better luck next time."); break;
    case 1:
    case 2:
    case 3:
    case 4:
    case 5: System.out.println("Pretty good."); break;
    case 6:
    case 7:
    case 8:
    case 9:
    case 10: System.out.println("Great!"); break;
}
```

In this statement, "Pretty good." is displayed when the score is 1, 2, 3, 4, or 5. Scores 6 though 10 display "Great".

## Review: Hurricane

The Saffir-Simpson Hurricane Scale provides a rating (a category) depending on the current intensity of a hurricane. Create a Hurricane application that displays the wind speed for the hurricane category entered by the user. Display the speed in miles per hour (mph), knots (kts), and kilometers per hour (km/hr). Refer to the Saffir-Simpson Hurricane Scale below for wind speeds:

Category 1: 74-95 mph or 64-82 kt or 119-153 km/hr

Category 2: 96-110 mph or 83-95 kt or 154-177 km/hr

Category 3: 111-130 mph or 96-113 kt or 178-209 km/hr

Category 4: 131-155 mph or 114-135 kt or 210-249 km/hr

Category 5: greater than 155 mph or 135 kt or 249 km/hr

## Generating Random Numbers

Games, simulators, screen savers, and many other types of applications make use of random numbers. A widely used method for generating random numbers is called the *Linear Congruential Method*. This method uses a formula to generate a sequence of numbers. Although the numbers in the sequence vary and for most applications can be considered random, the sequence will at some point repeat. Therefore, random numbers in a computer application are referred to as *pseudorandom* (like random).

*Linear Congruential Method*

*pseudorandom*

Java includes the Math class in the java.lang package for generating random numbers. This class includes the random() method, which uses the Linear Congruential Method:

Class Math (java.lang.Math)

Methods

`random()`      returns the next random double between 0 (inclusive) and 1.0.

The RandomNumberDemo class below uses the random() method to display five numbers between 0 and 1.0:

```java
import java.lang.Math;

public class RandomNumberDemo {

    public static void main(String[] args) {
        System.out.println("First number: " + Math.random());
        System.out.println("Second number: " + Math.random());
        System.out.println("Third number: " + Math.random());
        System.out.println("Fourth number: " + Math.random());
        System.out.println("Fifth number: " + Math.random());
    }
}
```

RandomNumberDemo produces output similar to the following:

```
First number: 0.704224453762737
Second number: 0.9828125227293675
Third number: 0.18495228518760576
Fourth number: 0.21394693270948373
Fifth number: 0.590769262147367
```

To generate a random number in a range the following expression is used:

```
(highNum - lowNum + 1) * Math.random() + lowNum
```

For example, the RandomNumberDemo2 class generates five numbers between 5 and 10:

```java
import java.lang.Math;

public class RandomNumberDemo2 {

    public static void main(String[] args) {
        System.out.println("First number: " +
            (6 * Math.random() + 5));
        System.out.println("Second number: " +
            (6 * Math.random() + 5));
        System.out.println("Third number: " +
            (6 * Math.random() + 5));
        System.out.println("Fourth number: " +
            (6 * Math.random() + 5));
        System.out.println("Fifth number: " +
            (6 * Math.random() + 5));
    }
}
```

RandomNumberDemo2 produces output similar to the following:

```
First number: 9.810719658756218
Second number: 7.485568749893893
Third number: 10.764334636863762
Fourth number: 5.903921379998897
Fifth number: 8.07746275565783
```

*Chapter 4 Conditional Control Structures*

Numbers generated by random() have a decimal portion. Casting can be used to produce random integers (whole numbers). Casting a `double` to an `int` truncates the decimal portion of the number. For example, the RandomIntDemo class generates an integer between 5 and 10:

```
import java.lang.Math;

public class RandomIntDemo {

    public static void main(String[] args) {
        System.out.println("Number: " +
        (int)(6 * Math.random() + 5));
    }
}
```

RandomIntDemo produces output similar to the following:

```
Number: 7
```

## Review: RandomNum

Create a RandomNum application that prompts the user for two numbers. The first number is a minimum value and the second is a maximum value. RandomNum then displays an integer between the min and max values entered by the user.

## Compound Boolean Expressions

*&& and ||*
*logical And*

*logical Or*

Conditions with complex criteria are formed using the `&&` and `||` operators. The `&&` operator is called the *logical And*. It is used to form an expression that evaluates to true only when both operands are also true. The `||` operator is called the *logical Or*. An expression formed with this operator evaluates to true when either operand is true. For example, the following statement tests for invalid guesses:

**TIP** The ¦ key is located above the Enter key on most standard keyboards.

```
if (guess < 1 || guess > 50) {     //invalid guess
    System.out.println("Invalid guess.");
} else if (guess == SECRET_NUM) {   //correct guess
    System.out.println("You guessed it!");
}
```

When a guess is either less than 1 *or* greater than 50, "Invalid guess." is displayed. The condition in the `if` statement is called a *compound Boolean expression* because more than one Boolean expression determines whether the condition is true or false.

*truth table*

How a compound Boolean expression evaluates with `&&` and `||` operators can be shown with truth tables. A *truth table* shows the possible outcomes of compound Boolean expressions:

| | And | | | | Or | |
|------|-------|--------|---|------|-------|--------|
| Exp1 | Exp2 | Result | | Exp1 | Exp2 | Result |
| True | True | True | | True | True | True |
| True | False | False | | True | False | True |
| False | True | False | | False | True | True |
| False | False | False | | False | False | False |

As another example, consider an application that computes a discount depending on the item and quantity purchased:

```
if (itemNum == 873 && quantity > 50) {    //more than 50 of 873
    discount = 1;                         //$1 discount
}
```

This `if` statement executes the `discount = 1` statement if item number is 873 *and* quantity is greater than 50.

A third operator is `!`. The `!` operator is called the *logical Not*. An expression including `!` is evaluated according to the following truth table:

Not

| Exp | Result |
|-----|--------|
| True | False |
| False | True |

For example, the following statements display a message when the item number is *not* 873:

```
if (!itemNum == 873) {          //any item EXCEPT 873
    System.out.println("No discount given.");
}
```

*short circuit evaluation*

Java uses short-circuit evaluation for determining the result of a compound Boolean expression that includes `&&` or `||`. In *short-circuit evaluation*, the left operand is evaluated first. If the result of the entire expression can be determined by the value of the left operand, then no other operands will be evaluated. For example, the expression `x < 0 || x > 5` evaluates to `true` if x is less than 0 regardless of the value of `x > 5`. Therefore, when x is less then 0, the second operand will not be evaluated. As another example, the expression `x > 5 && x < 20` evaluates to `false` if x is less than or equal to 5 regardless of the value of `x < 20`. Therefore, when x is less than or equal to 5, the second operand will not be evaluated.

In the order of operations, `!` is evaluated before `&&`. `||` is evaluated last. For example, the expression `!5 < 6 || 2 > 4 && 3 < 6` evaluates to false because `!5 < 6` is performed first, then `2 > 4 && 3 < 6`, and then `False ||` `False`. Use parentheses to change operator precedence and to make code more readable.

## Review: Delivery

Create a Delivery application that prompts the user for the length, width, and height of a package, and then displays "Reject" if any dimension is greater than 10, and "Accept" if all the dimensions are less than or equal to 10.

*Chapter 4 Conditional Control Structures*

# The Math Class

*java.lang*

Java includes the Math class in the java.lang package for performing math functions such as exponentiation and square root. The Math class contains numerous methods, which include:

## Class Math (java.lang.Math)

### Methods

abs(num)  returns the absolute value of num, which can be an int or a double value.

pow(double num1, double num2)

returns the num1 raised to the num2 power.

sqrt(double num)

returns the square root of num, where num is a positive number.

**TIP** The Math class also contains the double constant PI that approximates $\pi$.

Calling a Math method requires using the class name. For example, Math.abs(–3) returns 3. The application on the next page demonstrates the Math methods:

```java
import java.lang.Math;

public class TestMathMethods {

  public static void main(String[] args) {
    int posNum = 12, negNum = -12;
    int num1 = 2, num2 = 6;
    int square = 49;

    System.out.println("The absolute value of " + posNum
                    + " is " + Math.abs(posNum));
    System.out.println("The absolute value of " + negNum
                    + " is " + Math.abs(negNum));
    System.out.println(num1 + " raised to the " + num2
                    + " power is " + Math.pow(num1, num2));
    System.out.println("The square root of " + square
                    + " is " + Math.sqrt(square));
  }
}
```

The TestMathMethods produces the following output:

```
The absolute value of 12 is 12
The absolute value of -12 is 12
2 raised to the 6 power is 64.0
The square root of 49 is 7.0
```

# Review: PerfectSquare

Create a PerfectSquare application that prompts the user for an integer and then displays a message indicating whether or not the number is a perfect square. This can be determined by finding the square root of a number, truncating it (by casting the double result), and then squaring that result.

In this case study, a computerized version of the Rock Paper Scissors game will be created. Rock Paper Scissors is a popular game played between two individuals for decision making or just for competitive fun. The rules of the game are Rock dulls Scissors (Rock wins), Scissors cuts Paper (Scissors wins), and Paper covers Rock (Paper wins). The two players make a "throw" at the same time. The hand signals thrown by the players are then compared to the rules of the game to determine the winner. In the computerized version, the user plays against the computer.

## RPS Specification

RPS is played between the computer and a single player. The player is prompted for a throw where 1 corresponds to Rock, 2 to Paper, and 3 to Scissors. A random number between 1 and 3 is generated for the computer throw. The winner is determined based on the rules of Rock Paper Scissors.

The RPS interface should be simple. The user will be prompted to enter an integer between 1 and 3, where 1 represents Rock, 2 represents Paper, and 3 represents Scissors. The program then generates a random number between 1 and 3, displays the generated number and the player's number and determines a winner.

The RPS output sketch:

```
Enter your throw (1=Rock, 2=Paper, 3=Scissors): 3
Player throws SCISSORS.
Computer throws PAPER.
Player wins!
```

The RPS algorithm:

1. Prompt the user for a number between 1 and 3.

2. Generate a random number between 1 and 3.

3. Compare the generated number to the number typed by the user.

4. Determine a winner and display an appropriate message.

## RPS Code Design

The input for RPS is a number typed by the user. An integer variable to store the user's input will be needed.

The output for RPS is a message with the user's input, the generated number, and the winner.

Data generated by RPS is a random integer between 1 and 3, which represents the computer's "throw." An `int` variable to store the computer-generated number will be needed. Other data used in this application can be represented by `int` constants that represent Rock (1), Paper (2), and Scissors(3).

Based on the algorithm, the code design for the RPS application will include decision structures to compare the user's input to the number generated by the computer. This comparison can be done with either a `switch` statement or `if-else if` statements. For this implementation, an `if-else if` will be used. A pseudocode algorithm for RPS follows:

```
Prompt user for a number (1=Rock, 2=Paper, 3=Scissors)
Generate a random number between 1 and 3, inclusive
Display a message with player's number and computer's number
if (playerThrow == 1 and computerThrow == 1)
   Draw message
else if (playerThrow == 1 and computerThrow == 2)
   Computer wins message
else if (playerThrow == 1 and computerThrow == 3)
   Player wins message
if (playerThrow == 2 and computerThrow == 1)
   Player wins message
else if (playerThrow == 2 and computerThrow == 2)
   Draw message
else if (playerThrow == 2 and computerThrow == 3)
   Computer wins message
if (playerThrow == 3 and computerThrow == 1)
   Computer wins message
else if (playerThrow == 3 and computerThrow == 2)
   Player wins message
else if (playerThrow == 3 and computerThrow == 3)
   Draw message
```

### RPS Implementation

Based on the code design, the RPS implementation follows:

```java
/*
 * RPS.java
 */

import java.util.Scanner;
import java.util.Math;

/**
 * Plays Rock Paper Scissors against one player.
 */
public class RPS {

    public static void main(String[] args) {
        final int ROCK = 1, PAPER = 2, SCISSORS = 3;
        int playerThrow, computerThrow;
        Scanner input = new Scanner(System.in);

        /* prompt player for throw and read number typed */
        System.out.print("Enter your throw (1=Rock, 2=Paper, 3=Scissors): ");
        playerThrow = input.nextInt();
        input.close();
```

```
/* Generate computer throw */
computerThrow = (int)(3 * Math.random() + 1);

/* Inform player of throws */
System.out.print("Player throws ");
switch (playerThrow) {
    case ROCK: System.out.println("ROCK."); break;
    case PAPER: System.out.println("PAPER."); break;
    case SCISSORS: System.out.println("SCISSORS."); break;
}
System.out.print("Computer throws ");
switch (computerThrow) {
    case ROCK: System.out.println("ROCK."); break;
    case PAPER: System.out.println("PAPER."); break;
    case SCISSORS: System.out.println("SCISSORS."); break;
}

/* Determine winner */
if (playerThrow == ROCK && computerThrow == ROCK) {
    System.out.println("It's a draw!");
} else if (playerThrow == ROCK && computerThrow == PAPER) {
    System.out.println("Computer wins!");
} else if (playerThrow == ROCK && computerThrow == SCISSORS) {
    System.out.println("Player wins!");
}

if (playerThrow == PAPER && computerThrow == ROCK) {
    System.out.println("Player wins!");
} else if (playerThrow == PAPER && computerThrow == PAPER) {
    System.out.println("It's a draw!");
} else if (playerThrow == PAPER && computerThrow == SCISSORS) {
    System.out.println("Computer wins!");
}

if (playerThrow == SCISSORS && computerThrow == ROCK) {
    System.out.println("Computer wins!");
} else if (playerThrow == SCISSORS && computerThrow == PAPER) {
    System.out.println("Player wins!");
} else if (playerThrow == SCISSORS && computerThrow == SCISSORS) {
    System.out.println("It's a draw!");
}
    }
}
```

The RPS application output looks similar to:

```
Enter your throw (1=Rock, 2=Paper, 3=Scissors): 2
Player throws PAPER.
Computer throws SCISSORS.
Computer wins!
```

### RPS Testing and Debugging

This case study should test all possible throw combinations. For testing purposes, the random integer should be replaced with a constant. By varying only the player input from run to run, each of the combinations can be tested. The easiest way to change computerThrow to a constant is to set it to a value, such as 3 for Scissors, and then comment out the part of the statement that generates a random number:

```
/* Generate computer throw */
computerThrow = 3;      /* (int) (3 * Math.random() + 1) */
```

Running the application with a constant reduces the number of factors to consider when testing. Three runs using the constant look similar to:

```
Enter your throw (1=Rock, 2=Paper, 3=Scissors): 1
Player throws ROCK.
Computer throws SCISSORS.
Player wins!


Enter your throw (1=Rock, 2=Paper, 3=Scissors): 2
Player throws PAPER.
Computer throws SCISSORS.
Computer wins!


Enter your throw (1=Rock, 2=Paper, 3=Scissors): 3
Player throws SCISSORS.
Computer throws SCISSORS.
It's a draw!
```

Different constants can be used until all combinations are tested. Note that this application has a small and limited number of combinations to test. Other methods of testing will be discussed as applications become more complex.

Testing also involves considering user input and exception handling. What happens when the player enters 4? How should illegal input be handled? Preventing input errors and exception handling are discussed later in the text.

## Review: RPS – part 1 of 2

Modify the RPS Chapter 4 Case Study to use nested if-else statements rather than if-else if statements to determine the winner.

## Review: RPS – part 2 of 2

Modify the RPS Chapter 4 Case Study to use a switch statement to determine the winner. (Hint: You may need an if-else if statement within the case statements.)

## Chapter Summary

This chapter introduced conditional control structures, random numbers, and logical operators. Conditional control structures, also called decision structures, include the if and switch statements. The if uses the result of a Boolean expression to determine program flow, and the switch uses the result of an integer expression to determine program flow.

In the `if` statement, program flow branches to a set of statements when the condition evaluates to `true`. In the `if-else` statement, program flow branches to one set of statements for a `true` condition and a different set when the condition is `false`. Nested `if-else` statements can be used for even more control over program flow. The `if-else if` is used to decide among three or more actions.

Relational operators can be used to form a Boolean expression. They include the `==`, `<`, `<=`, `>`, `>=`, and `!=` operators. Two or more Boolean expressions can be joined with logical operators to form a compound Boolean expression. Logical operators include `&&` (logical And), `¦¦` (logical Or), and `!` (logical Not). A truth table shows how a compound Boolean expression evaluates.

Roundoff error occurs when a floating point number cannot be exactly represented in binary notation by the computer. Therefore equality comparisons between floating point numbers should not be made.

The `switch` statement contains multiple `case` clauses. A `break` statement is required to move program control out of the `switch` statement.

Java uses the Linear Congruential Method to generate a sequence of random numbers. Because the sequence eventually repeats, random number in a computer application are really pseudorandom. Java includes the Math.random() method in the java.lang package for generating random numbers.

The Math class, part of the java.lang package, contains many useful methods for performing math functions. Calling a Math method requires including the class name.

Code conventions introduced in this chapter are :

- The clauses of an `if` statement should be indented.

- nested `if` statements should be indented.

- The `case` clause of a `switch` statement should be indented.

**Boolean expression**   An expression that evaluates to true or false.

**Compound Boolean expression**  An expression that includes more than one Boolean expression.

**Conditional control structure**   A statement that branches program flow depending on a condition. Also called a decision structure.

**Decision structure**   *see* Conditional control structure.

**Linear Congruential Method**   A method that uses a formula to generate a sequence of pseudorandom numbers.

**Logical And**   The && operator used to form a compound Boolean expression.

**Logical Not**   The ! operator used to reverse the value of a Boolean expression.

**Logical Or**  The ¦¦ operator used to form a compound Boolean expression.

**Nested**   A statement placed within the same type of statement.

**Pseudorandom**   Not truly random, but like random.

**Relational operator**   Operators (==, <, <=, >, >=, !=) that can be used to form a Boolean expression.

**Short circuit evaluation**  A process for determining the result of a Boolean expression where the left operand is evaluated first. If the result of the entire expression can be determined by the left operand, no other operands are evaluated.

**Truth table**  A table that shows the possible outcomes of two expressions joined by a logical operator.

## Java

==   The equality relational operator.

<   The less than relational operator.

<=   The less than or equal relational operator.

>   The greater than relational operator.

>=   The greater than or equal relational operator.

!=   The not equal relational operator.

&&   The logical And operator.

¦¦   The logical Or operator.

!   The logical Not operator.

break   A statement that moves program control to the next statement after the current structure.

case   A clause in the switch statement that contains statements to be executed when the case condition matches the result of the switch expression.

if   A decision structure that executes a set of statements when a condition is true.

if-else   A decision structure that executes one set of statements when a condition is true and another set of statements when the condition is false.

if-else if   A decision structure used to decide among three or more actions.

**Math**   A java.lang class with methods for generating random numbers and performing math functions.

switch   A decision structure that uses the result of an expression to determine which set of statements to execute.

1. Use a decision structure to write an appropriate statement for each of the following:
   a) Display `Great job!` when `grade` is `90` or higher.
   b) Display `Error` when `number` is less than `20` or greater than `50`.
   c) Add `2` to the value of `y` when `y` is less than `100`.

2. Assume `num1` and `num2` contain integer values. Write an `if-else if` statement that displays one of the following messages as appropriate:

   ```
   First number is larger.
   Second number is larger.
   Numbers are equal.
   ```

3. a) Which is the appropriate word, `odd` or `even` for the blanks below?

   ```
   if (num % 2 == 0) {
       System.out.println("___ number");
   } else {
       System.out.println("___ number");
   }
   ```

   b) Rewrite the `if-else` as a `switch` statement.

4. Write statements that use Math.random() to generate random numbers for each of the following situations:
   a) Generate a random integer between 1 and 50.
   b) Generate a random integer between 20 and 100.
   c) Generate a random double between 10 and 20, inclusive.

5. Identify the logic errors in the statements below, which should display a single appropriate message for any value of age:

   ```
   if (age < 18) {
       System.out.println("child");
   } else if (age > 18 && age < 65) {
       System.out.println("adult");
   } else if (age > 65) {
       System.out.println("senior");
   }
   ```

6. Given the following assignments, determine if each of the following expressions evaluates to true or false:

   ```
   size = 100      weight = 50      value = 75
   ```
   a) `size > 50 && weight == 50`
   b) `value < 100 && !(weight == 50)`
   c) `size >= 100 || value >= 100`
   d) `weight < 50 || size > 50`
   e) `!(value < 75)`
   f) `!(size > 100 && weight >50 && value > 75)`
   g) `(value < 125 || weight < 76) && size ==100`

7. a) Write a statement that will calculate $y^x$.
   b) Write a statement that will calculate the absolute value of y.
   c) Write a statement that will calculate the square root of y.

## True/False

8. Determine if each of the following are true or false. If false, explain why.
   a) The condition of an `if` statement must be a Boolean expression.
   b) A nested `if` statement and an `if-else if` statement are the same.
   c) The expression in a `switch` statement must evaluate to a `double`.
   d) Numbers generated by a computer program are actually pseudorandom.
   e) The `(double)` cast is needed to generate a random integer.
   f) A compound Boolean expression can contain more than two Boolean expressions.
   g) In a logical And expression, both operands must be true for the expression to evaluate to true.
   h) In logical expressions, && is evaluated before !.
   i) The pow() method in the Math class is used for exponentiation.
   j) The statement `x = abs(-3);` will return the value 3.

## Exercise 1 ———————————————————————— Printing

Printing prices are typically based on the number of copies to be printed. For example:

| | |
|---|---|
| 0 – 99 | $0.30 per copy |
| 100 – 499 | $0.28 per copy |
| 500 – 749 | $0.27 per copy |
| 750 – 1000 | $0.26 per copy |
| over 1000 | $0.25 per copy |

Create a Printing application that prompts the user for the number of copies to print and then displays the price per copy and the total price for the job. Application output should look similar to:

```
Enter the number of copies to be printed: 1001
Price per copy is: $0.25
Total cost is: $250.25
```

## Exercise 2 ———————————————————————— PackageCheck

A delivery service does not accept packages heavier than 27 kilograms or larger than 0.1 cubic meters (100,000 cubic centimeters). Create a PackageCheck application that prompts the user for the weight of a package and its dimensions (length, width, and height), and then displays an appropriate message if the package does not meet the requirements. Messages should include:

```
Too heavy.
Too large.
Too heavy and too large.
```

The application output should look similar to:

```
Enter package weight in kilograms: 32
Enter package length in centimeters: 10
Enter package width in centimeters: 25
Enter package height in centimeters: 38
Too heavy.
```

## Exercise 3 ———————————————————————— Eggs

A wholesale egg company bases their prices on the number of eggs purchased:

| | |
|---|---|
| 0 up to but not including 4 dozen | $0.50 per dozen |
| 4 up to but not including 6 dozen | $0.45 per dozen |
| 6 up to but not including 11 dozen | $0.40 per dozen |
| 11 or more dozen | $0.35 per dozen |

Extra eggs are priced at $1/12$ the per dozen price.

Create an Eggs application that prompts the user for the number of eggs, and then calculates the bill. The application output should look similar to:

```
Enter the number of eggs purchased: 18
The bill is equal to: $0.75
```

## Exercise 4 ———————————————————————— CarRecall

An auto company produced some models of cars that may be difficult to drive because the car wheels are not exactly round. Cars with model numbers 119, 179, 189 through 195, 221, and 780 have been found to have this defect. Create a CarRecall application that prompts a customer for the model number of their car to find out if it is defective and then displays "Your car is not defective." when the user typed a model number without a defect. Otherwise, the message "Your car is defective. It must be repaired." should be displayed. Application output should look similar to:

```
Enter the car's model number: 191
Your car is defective. It must be repaired.
```

## Exercise 5 ———————————————————————— Grade

Create a Grade application that prompts the user for the percentage earned on a test or other graded work and then displays the corresponding letter grade. The application should use the grading scale at your school or the following grading scale:

| | |
|---|---|
| 90 – 100 | A |
| 80 – 89 | B |
| 70 – 79 | C |
| 60 – 69 | D |
| below 60 | F |

The application output should look similar to:

```
Enter the percentage: 75
The corresponding letter grade is: C
```

## Exercise 6 ———————————————————————— MathTutor

Create a MathTutor application that displays math problems by randomly generating two numbers, 1 through 10 and an operator (*, +, –, /), and then prompts the user for an answer. The application should check the answer, display a message, and the correct answer, if necessary. The application output should look similar to:

```
What is 2 * 9? 18
Correct!
```

# Exercise 7 ——————————————— EquivalentFractions

Create an EquivalentFractions application that quizzes the user on equivalent fractions.

    a)  Display eight fractions and prompt the user to match pairs of equivalent fractions. Application output should look similar to:

```
Equivalent Fractions Quiz

    1. 21/3
    2. 2/3
    3. 4/3
    4. 28/4
    5. 8/12
    6. 1 1/3
    7. 5/1
    8. 125/5

Which fraction number is equivalent to fraction #1? #4
Correct!
```

    b)  Modify the EquivalentFractions application to display the user's score.

    c)  Modify the EquivalentFractions application to have the user select a beginner or advanced mathematical level and based on their choice display a different set of fractions.

# Exercise 8 ——————————————— RandomGenerator

Create a RandomGenerator application that implements the Linear Congruential Method. The formula used by this method is:

$$X_{n-1} = (aX_n + c) \% m$$

Use constant integers for a, c, and m. Choose a seed integer value for $X_0$. Show 10 numbers from the sequence. Application output should look similar to:

```
Seed = 12, a = 1246, c = 200, m = 50


(1246*12 + 200) % 50=2
(1246*2 + 200) % 50=42
(1246*42 + 200) % 50=32
(1246*32 + 200) % 50=22
(1246*22 + 200) % 50=12
(1246*12 + 200) % 50=2
(1246*2 + 200) % 50=42
(1246*42 + 200) % 50=32
(1246*32 + 200) % 50=22
(1246*22 + 200) % 50=12
```

Note the sequence shown in the output repeats after five numbers. Experiment by changing the values for a, c, m, and $X_0$ (the seed) to see which values create the most "random" sequence of numbers (the largest set of nonrepeating numbers).

# Exercise 9 ———————————————————— GuessingGame

The GuessingGame is a number guessing game played between the computer and one player. The GuessingGame algorithm follows:

    1. Determine a secret number between 1 and 20.

    2. Prompt the player for a number between 1 and 20.

    3. Compare the player's number to the secret number.

    4. Display the secret number and the player's number.

    5. If the player's number matches the secret number, then display a "You won!" message. Otherwise display a "Better luck next time." message.

a) Create the GuessingGame application. The application output should look similar to:

```
Enter a number between 1 and 20: 14
Computer's Number: 6
Player's Number: 14
Better luck next time.
```

b) Write down how the application was tested and list any debugging techniques used.

# Exercise 10 ———————————————————————— Volumes

The volume of objects are calculated differently depending on the shape of the object.

a) The volume of rectangular prism is calculated using the formula:

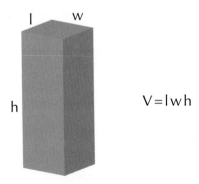

$$V = lwh$$

Create a Volumes application that prompts the user for the length, width, and height of a rectangular prism and then calculates the volume.

b) The volume of a sphere is calculated using the formula:

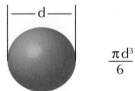

$$\frac{\pi d^3}{6}$$

Modify the Volumes application to prompt the user for the radius (d = 2*r) of a sphere after displaying the volume of the rectangular prism. The application should then display the volume of the sphere.

c)  The volume of a cube is calculated using the formula:

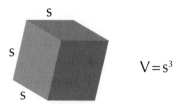

$$V = s^3$$

Modify the Volumes application to prompt the user for the length of each side of a cube after displaying the volume of the rectangular prism and the sphere. The application should then display the volume of the cube.

The application output should look similar to:

```
Rectangular Prism
Enter the length: 3
Enter the width: 4
Enter the height: 5
The volume is: 60

Sphere
Enter the radius: 3
The volume is: 113.097

Cube
Enter the length of each side: 4
The volume is: 64
```

## Exercise 11 ———————————————————————— QuadraticEquation

Create a QuadraticEquation application that gives the solution to any quadratic equation. The application should prompt the user for values for a, b, and c ($ax^2 + bx + c = 0$) and then display the roots, if any. The quadratic equation takes the form:

$$\frac{-b \pm \sqrt{b^2 - 4ac}}{2a}$$

Application output should look similar to:

```
Enter value for a: 2
Enter value for b: 4
Enter value for c: -30
The roots are 3.0 and -5.0
```

# Exercise 12 ——————————————————————— MyPow

Create a MyPow application that uses the formula $e^{(Y*\log(X))}$ to calculate $X^Y$. The MyPow application should prompt the user for two numbers and then display the result from the formula and, for comparison, show the same result using the Math pow() method. The application should display output similar to:

```
Enter a value for X: 7
Enter a value for Y: 5

The result from using the formula is: 16806.99999999998

The result from using the Math pow() method is: 16807.0
```

The Math library provides methods for calculating base 10 and base $e$ (natural) logarithms. The exp() method raises $e$ to a given power:

### Class Math (java.lang.Math)

### Methods

| | |
|---|---|
| `log(double num)` | returns the natural logarithm of `num`. |
| `log10(double num)` | returns the base 10 logarithm of `num`. |
| `exp(double num)` | returns $e$ raised to the power of `num`. |

# Exercise 13 ——————————————————————— CarPayment

Create a CarPayment application that calculates a monthly car payment after prompting the user for the principal owing (P), the interest rate (r) and the number of monthly payments (m). The monthly car payment is calculated using the formula:

$$\frac{P(r/12)}{(1-(1+r/12)^{-m})}$$

Application output should be similar to:

```
Principal: 20000
Interest Rate: .06
Number of monthly payments: 48
The monthly payment is $469.70
```

# Exercise 14 ————————————————————————— BacteriaGrowth

The formula $y = ne^{kt}$ can be used for estimating growth where:

    y  is the final amount

    n  is the initial amount

    k  is a constant

    t  is the time

For example, this formula could be used for estimating population growth in a region or for estimating cell growth in a lab experiment. Create a BacteriaGrowth application that calculates how many bacteria will be present based on this formula. The application should prompt the user initial bacteria, the constant k, and the time. Refer to Exercise 12 for documentation for the Math methods for this exercise. Application output should look similar to:

```
Enter initial bacteria amount: 5
Enter a constant value for k: .8
Enter the growth time period in hours: 8

3,009 bacteria will be present after 8.0 hours.
```

# Exercise 15 ————————————————————————————— Decay

The formula used in Exercise 14 for growth problems can also be used in decay problems. In decay problems, k is negative. Create an application that allows the user to select from the following options:

- calculate the final amount: $ne^{-kt}$

- calculate the initial amount: $y / e^{-kt}$

- calculate the constant (called the half-life): $(\log (y/n)) / t$

  (where $\log e = 0.4343$)

The application should prompt the user to select one of the three choices and based on the selected option prompts the user to enter the appropriate known information. For example, a radioactive mass of 200 grams will reduce to 100 grams in 10 years. Based on this information, the half-life is calculated to be −0.06931. Refer to Exercise 12 for documentation for the Math methods for this exercise. Application output should look similar to:

```
1. Final Amount
2. Initial Amount
3. Constant (half-life)
Find: 3
Enter the initial mass: 200
Enter the final mass: 100
Enter the elapsed time in years: 10
Constant (half-life): -0.069
```

# Exercise 16 ────────────────────────────── TrigFunctions

Create a TrigFunctions application that prompts the user for an angle in degrees and then displays the sine, cosine, and tangent of the angle. The application should display output similar to:

```
Enter an angle in degrees: 30
Sine: 0.5
Cosine: 0.866
Tangent: 0.577
```

The Math library provides methods for performing trigonometric functions:

### Class Math (java.lang.Math)

### Methods

`sin(double angle)`   returns the sine of `angle`, where `angle` is in radians.

`cos(double angle)`   returns the cosine of `angle`, where `angle` is in radians.

`tan(double angle)`   returns the sine of `angle`, where `angle` is in radians.

`toRadians(double deg)`
      converts degrees to radians.


# Exercise 17 ────────────────────────── InverseTrigFunctions

Create an InverseTrigFunctions application that prompts the user for an angle in degrees and then displays the arcsin, arccos, and arctan of the angle. The application should display output similar to:

```
Enter an angle in degrees: 30
Arcsin: 0.551
Arccos: 1.02
Arctan: 0.482
```

The Math library provides methods for performing trigonometric functions:

### Class Math (java.lang.Math)

### Methods

`asin(double s)`   returns the angle, in radians, that has the sine `s`.

`acos(double s)`   returns the angle, in radians, that has the cosine `s`.

`atan(double s)`   returns the angle, in radians, that has the tangent `s`.

`toDegrees(double rad)`
      converts radians to degrees.

*Chapter 4 Conditional Control Structures*

# Chapter 5
# Loop Structures and Strings

**Key Concepts**

Using repetition control structures
Debugging infinite loops
Using counters and accumulators
Using tools and techniques to debug an application
Manipulating and comparing strings
Applying problem solving strategies

**Case Study**

Word Guess application

## The while Statement

*loop structure*

The while statement is a *loop structure*, which executes a set of statements over and over again based on a condition. Loop structures are used to perform tasks such as summing a set of numbers as they are entered by the user or repeatedly prompting the user for a value until valid data is entered. The while statement takes the form:

```
while (<condition>) {
    <statements>
}
```

The condition of the while loop is a Boolean expression, which is evaluated before the statements are executed. When the condition is true the s tatements are executed, when the condition is false program flow continues to the next statement after the closing curly brace of the while. Each execution

*iteration*

of the loop is called an *iteration*. Note that a while loop may never execute if the condition initially evaluates to false.

> ### Nested Loops
>
> A loop structure can contain another loop structure. Loops placed within a loop are called *nested loops*. Each time the outer loop iterates, the inner loop iterates until its condition is met.

The following while statement executes five times:

```
int num = 0;
while (num < 5) {
    num += 1;
}
```

After the fifth execution, num is equal to 5, making the condition false.

## The do-while Statement

The do-while statement is an alternative form of the while statement. In the do-while statement the condition is not evaluated until after the first execution of the loop. Therefore, the do-while executes at least once.

The do-while takes the following form:

```
do {
    <statements>
} while (<condition>);
```

The following `do-while` example prompts the user until a valid number is entered:

```
do {
    System.out.print("Enter a number less than 4:");
    playerNum = input.nextInt();
} while (playerNum >= 4);
```

## Infinite Loops

The condition of a loop is used to determine when the loop should stop executing. A `while` continues until its condition is false. What happens, though, if the condition never becomes false? The result is an *infinite loop*—one which continues forever. For example, the following generates an infinite loop. Can you see why?

```
int num = -1;
while (num < 0) {
    num = -1;
}
```

The code causes the application to simply stop responding or just "hang." When this happens, close the output window to end the application. Note that some compilers may require a different procedure to end an infinite loop.

Syntax errors are a common cause of infinite loops. For example, a semicolon after the condition causes the statement to check the condition, do nothing, check the condition, do nothing, and on and on:

```
while (num < 0); {     //an infinite loop here--added semicolon
    num += 1;
}
```

Another example of a syntax error that can lead to an infinite loop is omitting the curly braces:

```
while (num < 0)        //an infinite loop here--no braces
    System.out.print("Enter a value: ");
    num = input.nextInt();
```

In this case, only the first statement is executed and `num` is never assigned the input. Although properly done, the indentation makes it difficult to find the syntax error.

A logic error can also lead to an infinite loop condition. For example, in the code below `num` is initialized to 1 and never decremented to a number less than 0 in the loop, making the condition of the loop structure always true:

```
int num = 1;
do {
    num += 1;
} while (num >= 0);
```

*overflow*

In this case, the loop isn't infinite because `num` is eventually assigned a number so large that an overflow results. An *overflow* occurs when there are not enough bits to store a number. This may generate a run-time error or, in the case of the code above, actually cause the condition to become false. An overflow changes the sign of the number stored.

## Review: Prompter

Create a Prompter application that prompts the user for two numbers. The first number is a min value and the second is a max value. Prompter then prompts the user for a number between the min and max numbers entered. The user should be continually prompted until a number within the range is entered. Be sure to include the min and max numbers in the prompt.

## Counters and Accumulators

Many algorithms require counting and summing values. For example, an application that calculates the average of a set of numbers must sum the numbers and then divide the total by the count. The AverageValue application performs counting and summing. A run of the application looks similar to:

```
Enter a value (0 to quit): 14
1Enter a value (0 to quit): 8
Enter a value (0 to quit): 33
Enter a value (0 to quit): 40
Enter a value (0 to quit): 0
Average is 24.0
```

The AverageValue application is based on the pseudocode:

```
Prompt user for a value
while (value != 0)
    count value
    add value to sum of values
    prompt user for another value
Display average of values (sum/count)
```

A program that counts the number of values entered by the user is actually counting the number of loop iterations. To count loop iterations, a statement similar to the following is used within the loop:

```
numValues += 1;
```

Each time the statement executes, one is added to the current value of the variable. This type of variable is called a *counter* because it is incremented by a constant value. Counters are useful for keeping track of the number of times a user enters a value, makes a guess, or types a password. A counter should be initialized when it is declared and then incremented by a fixed amount.

A similar assignment statement is used to sum values as they are entered by the user:

```
sumOfValues += newValue;
```

Each time the statement executes, the value of `newValue` is added to the current value of the variable. This type of variable is called an *accumulator* because its value "accumulates." As with a counter, an accumulator should be initialized when it is declared.

The AverageValue code includes both a counter (numValues) and an accumulator (sumOfValues):

```
/* AverageValue application. */

import java.util.Scanner;

/**
 * Displays the average of a set of numbers
 */
public class AverageValue {

  public static void main(String[] args) {
    final int SENTINEL = 0;
    int newValue;
    int numValues = 0;
    int sumOfValues = 0;
    double avg;
    Scanner input = new Scanner(System.in);

    /* Get a set of numbers from user */
    System.out.println("Calculate Average Program");
    System.out.print("Enter a value (" + SENTINEL + " to quit): ");
    newValue = input.nextInt();
    while (newValue != SENTINEL) {
      numValues += 1;
      sumOfValues += newValue;
      System.out.print("Enter a value(" + SENTINEL + " to quit): ");
      newValue = input.nextInt();
    }
    input.close();

    /*Calculate average of numbers entered by user */
    avg = (double)sumOfValues / (double)numValues;
    System.out.println("Average is " + avg);
  }
}
```

*flag, sentinel*

The AverageValue code uses a constant named SENTINEL. This constant stores a value to act as a *flag*, or *sentinel*, to signify that the loop should stop iterating. AverageValue defines the sentinel with a constant. Another approach is to use a variable and prompt the user for the sentinel value.

## Review: Evens

Create an Evens application that displays the even numbers between 1 and 20, inclusive.

## Review: NumbersSum

Create a NumbersSum application that prompts the user for a number and then displays the numbers 1 through the number entered, each on a separate line. Below the numbers, the sum is displayed.

## Review: PercentPassing

Create a PercentPassing application that prompts the user for a set of scores and then calculates the percentage of scores above 70%. The user should have the option to enter as many scores as needed.

*Chapter 5 Loop Structures and Strings*

# The for Statement

The `for` statement is a loop structure that executes a set of statements a fixed number of times. The `for` statement takes the form:

```
for (<initialization>; <condition>; <increment>) {
    <statements>
}
```

The initialization is performed only once when a `for` statement is executed. The condition is a Boolean expression, which is evaluated before each loop iteration. When the condition is true the statements are executed, when false, program flow continues to the next statement after the closing curly brace of the `for`. After each loop iteration, the increment is executed.

*loop control variable*

The following statement uses a counter to control the iterations of a `for` statement. The counter `i` is the *loop control variable*. When `i` is greater than 10, looping terminates:

```
for (int i = 1; i <= 10; i++) {
    System.out.println(i);
}
```

**TIP** Counter variables in a `for` loop are often named i, j, or k.

*scope*

Note that the counter is declared in the initialization of the `for` statement (`int i = 1`). With a declaration in this location, the *scope* of the counter is from the initialization to the closing curly brace of the `for` statement. The application will not recognize the variable outside of that statement. Declaring variables so that their scope is limited to where they are needed is good programming style because it produces cleaner code and helps eliminate the possibility of errors.

*increment operator*

The statement above uses the ++ operator in the increment part of the `for` statement (`i++`). The ++ operator is called the *increment operator* because it increases the value of a variable by 1. The ++ operator is a good choice in the increment of a `for` statement because the effect is to increase the operand by 1. However, ++ should not be used within an expression, such as `i++ <= 10`, because the value returned by the operator is used in the expression, not the final value of the operand.

## Expressions Using ++ or --

If the ++ or -- operator appears before the operand, it is called *prefix* (i.e. ++i). An operator after the operand is called *postfix* (i.e. i++). Either operator location has the same effect on the final value of the operand. However, in an expression, the prefix version uses the value of the operand *after* the operation. For example, when x is 12, the statement ++x returns 13. In the postfix version, x++, 12 is returned. Therefore, a statement such as x++ >= 13 is false and could be ambiguous. Using the ++ and -- operators in an expression is poor programming style.

Any combination of components can be left out of a `for` statement. This can be useful when a counter is declared and initialized outside the statement, as in the following code:

```
int num;
System.out.print("Enter the starting number: ");
num = input.nextInt();
for (; num <= 10; num++) {
    System.out.println(num);
}
```

A `for` statement may also count down from a start value to an end value using the *decrement operator*, --:

```
for (int countDown = 10; countDown <= 0; countDown--) {
    System.out.println(countDown);
}
```

While it is possible to modify a loop control variable from within a `for` loop or to terminate a loop prematurely, this is considered poor programming style. Good programming style dictates that changes to the loop control variable occur in the increment portion of the loop only and that the loop end only when the condition is false.

## Review: Factorial

Create a Factorial application that prompts the user for a number and then displays its factorial. The factorial of a number is the product of all the positive integers from 1 to the number. For example, 5! = 5*4*3*2*1.

## Review: OddSum

Create an OddSum application that prompts the user for a number and then sums the odd numbers from 1 to the number entered.

## Debugging Techniques

TIP A "bug" is an error in a program.

The source of bugs, which are often logic errors, can be hard to determine without tools for debugging an application. *Debugging* is the process of getting an application to work correctly. One tool included with many compilers is called a debugger.

*debugger*
*breakpoints*

A *debugger* is used to select statements where execution will be suspended. These statements are called *breakpoints*. Application output goes to a Debug Window and statements can be executed one at a time between breakpoints by using a Step command. When stepping through an application, selected variables are displayed in a Watch window along with their value. When a watch variable is assigned a new value, the Watch window is updated. Stepping through code and watching variables can be an effective way to determine logic errors.

*variable trace*

Another debugging tool is called a variable trace. A *variable trace* is a table listing the values of variables at the points of assignment. For the following code, num1 and num2 would be included in a variable trace:

```
int num1 = 0;
int num2 = 0;
while (num1 < 10) {
  if (num1 % 3 == 0) {
     num2 += num1;
     System.out.print(num2 + " ");
  }
  num1 += 1;
}
```

TIP A common error with loops is an off-by-one error. This occurs when a loop iterates one too many or one too few times due to a Boolean expression error.

The variables are listed in the order that assignment occurs within the loop. Output is also listed to better understand the code:

| num2 | output | num1 |
|---|---|---|
| 0 | 0 | 1 |
|  |  | 2 |
|  |  | 3 |
| 3 | 3 | 4 |
|  |  | 5 |
|  |  | 6 |
| 9 | 9 | 7 |
|  |  | 8 |
|  |  | 9 |
| 18 | 18 | 10 |

A third debugging technique involves adding additional println() statements to an application. Adding println() statements just after a variable is assigned a new value or before and after a condition is evaluated can help detect the source of a logic error. For example, the code segment below includes additional statements for debugging:

```
int num1 = 0;
int num2 = 0;
System.out.println("num1 before while:  " + num1);      //debug
while (num1 < 10) {
   System.out.println("num1 in while:  " + num1);       //debug
   if (num1 % 3 == 0) {
      num2 += num1;
      System.out.println("num2:" + num2);               //debug
      System.out.println(num2 + "  ");
   }
   num1 += 1;
}
```

When run, the code above displays the following output, which can be compared to the values expected. Note the similarity to a variable trace:

```
num1 before while: 0
num1 in while: 0
num2:0
0
num1 in while: 1
num1 in while: 2
num1 in while: 3
num2:3
3
num1 in while: 4
num1 in while: 5
num1 in while: 6
num2:9
9
num1 in while: 7
num1 in while: 8
num1 in while: 9
num2:18
18
```

*commenting out code*     Commenting out statements can be an effective way to locate a bug through process of elimination. Typically the // characters are easiest to type at the beginning of a statement to "comment it out."

## Review: Variable Trace

Using paper and pencil, create a variable trace for the following code, tracing the values of num1, num2, i, and any output:

```
int num1 = 0;
int num2 = 0;
for (int i = 0; i <= 4; i++) {
    num1 = i * i;
    num2 += num1;
    System.out.print(num1 + "  ");
}
System.out.println(num2);
```

# The String Class

Primitive data types such as `int` and `double` are used for storing numeric data. However, when data is comprised of a sequence of characters, a data type for storing strings is needed. Java includes the String class in the java.lang package for storing and manipulating strings. The String class is large, with numerous methods for string manipulation. Some of the String class methods include:

## Class String (java.lang.String)

### Methods

`length()`     returns an integer corresponding to the number of characters in the string.

`substring(int start, int end)`

returns a substring of the string, which starts at `start` position and ends one character before the `end` position.

`substring(int start)`

returns a substring of the string, which starts at `start` position and extends to the end of the string.

`toLowerCase()`    returns a copy of the string with all lowercase letters.

`toUpperCase()`    returns a copy of the string with all uppercase letters.

`trim()`      returns a copy of the string with all leading and trailing spaces removed.

`replaceFirst(String str, String str2)`

returns a string with the first occurrence of `str` replaced by `str2`.

`replaceAll(String str, String str2)`

returns a string with all occurrences of `str` replaced by `str2`.

*index*    The position of a character in a string is called its *index*. The first character of a string is at index 0. The last character of a string is at index length() – 1. The MiddleThree class below displays the three letters in the middle of a string:

```java
public class MiddleThree {

    public static void main(String[] args) {
        String phrase, threeLetters;
        int phraseLength;
        int mid;
        Scanner input = new Scanner(System.in);

        /* get string from user */
        System.out.print("Enter text that contains at least
            three characters: ");
        phrase = input.nextLine();
        input.close();

        /* determine middle of phrase */
        phraseLength = phrase.length();
        mid = phraseLength / 2;
```

---

**More on Concatenation**

As introduced in Chapter 3, concatenation appends one string to another. When the + operator is used to join a string and a numeric, the compiler first converts any non-String data to a String object before joining the strings. The String class also contains the concat() method for joining two strings.

---

*Chapter 5 Loop Structures and Strings*

```
                    /* display middle three characters */
                    threeLetters = phrase.substring(mid - 1, mid + 2);
                    System.out.println("Middle three characters are: "
                                        + threeLetters);
            }
        }
```

Note that the String objects (phrase, threeLetters) can be declared in the same way primitives are declared—the data type followed by the variable name. With the String class, the following two statements perform the same task:

```
String alpha = new String("abc");  //these assignments are
String alpha = "abc";              //efffectively the same
```

The MiddleThree application produces output similar to:

```
Enter text (at least three characters): abcde
Middle three characters are: bcd
```

*immutable*     A string is said to be *immutable* because it cannot be changed. Methods that manipulate the original string, for example toLowerCase(), create a new string in memory because the original string cannot be changed. Assigning a new string to a String object simply changes the object reference to point to the new string in memory. For example, the following code generates a new string. Assigning the string to the text object changes the object's reference:

```
String text;
text = "heLl0";
text = text.toLowerCase();
System.out.println(text);
```

The code produces the output:

```
hello
```

*null*     Until a String object is assigned a value, it refers to null. Calling a method
*NullPointerException*     from a null String object generates the exception NullPointerException.

## Review: AccountSetup

Create an AccountSetup application that prompts the user for a user name and a password. The application should prompt the user until a password with at least eight characters is entered. The user name and password should be converted to all lowercase letters and then an appropriate message displayed. Application output should look similar to:

```
Enter a user name: MattD
Enter a password that is at least 8 characters: Programmer7
Your user name is mattd and your password is programmer7
```

## Comparing Strings

Strings are compared when determining equality or alphabetical order. In chapter 4, relational operators, including == and >, were used to compare primitive types. When objects need to be compared, methods from their class are used. Some of the String class methods for comparing strings include:

### Class String (java.lang.String)

### Methods

equals(String str)

> returns true when the string is the same as str. Returns false otherwise.

equalsIgnoreCase(String str)

> same as equals() except that uppercase and lowercase differences between the strings are ignored.

compareTo(String str)

> returns 0 when str is the same as the string, a negative integer is returned when str comes alphabetically after the string, and a positive integer is returned when str comes alphabetically before the string. Note that uppercase and lowercase letters are considered different.

compareToIgnoreCase(String str)

> same as compareTo() except that uppercase and lowercase differences between the strings are ignored.

indexOf(String str)

> returns the integer corresponding to the location of the first occurrence of str in the string. Otherwise –1 is returned.

lastIndexOf(String str)

> returns the integer corresponding to the location of the last occurrence of str in the string. Otherwise –1 is returned.

startsWith(String str)

> returns true when the string begins with str. Returns false otherwise.

endsWith(String str)

> returns true when the string ends with str. Returns false otherwise.

<aside>

### Unicode

The *Unicode Standard* is a 16-bit encoding system that assigns a value for each character and symbol of every language. Java uses this standard when defining strings, and String class methods use the character values when comparing strings.

</aside>

The AlphaOrder class compares two strings and then displays them in alphabetical order:

```
public class AlphaOrder {

    public static void main(String[] args) {
        String word1, word2;
        Scanner input = new Scanner (System.in);
```

```
System.out.print("Enter a word: ");
word1 = input.nextLine();
System.out.print("Enter a second word: ");
word2 = input.nextLine();
input.close();

if (word1.compareToIgnoreCase(word2) == 0) {
    System.out.println("Words are equal.");
} else if (word1.compareToIgnoreCase(word2) < 0) {
    System.out.println("In alphabetical order: " + word1
        + " " + word2);
} else {
    System.out.println("In alphabetical order: " + word2
        + " " + word1);
}
    }
}
```

AlphaOrder produces output similar to the following:

```
Enter a word: unicode
Enter a second word: hexadecimal
In alphabetical order: hexadecimal unicode
```

## Review: FormalGreeting

Create a FormalGreeting application that prompts the user for his or her name, including title. The application should display "Hello, sir." if the string starts with Mr., "Hello, ma'am." if the string starts with Ms., Mrs., or Miss, and "Hello, *name*." otherwise where *name* is the user's name.

## Chapter 5 Case Study

In this case study, a word guessing game will be created. The word guessing game allows the player to guess the letters of a secret word. At the start of the game, the player is shown only how many letters the word contains through a set of dashes. When a letter matching one in the word is guessed, it replaces the appropriate dash. Play continues until the entire word is guessed letter-by-letter or when the player chooses to guess the entire word.

### WordGuess Specification

WordGuess is played between the computer and a single player. The secret word is BRAIN. At the start of the game, five dashes are displayed (–––––), one for each letter of the word. The player is repeatedly prompted for a letter guess. When a letter matching one in the word is guessed, the letter replaces the corresponding dash. Letters may be entered as uppercase or lowercase. However, only uppercase letters should be displayed. If the player enters an exclamation point (!), the player is prompted to guess the word. At that point the player either wins (a correct guess) or loses (an incorrect guess). Alternatively, the player can continue to guess letters until the entire word is revealed. The games ends by showing the player the total number of guesses.

The WordGuess interface should display a row of dashes, one dash for each letter in the word. Prompts should be used to get letter guesses from the player. As corresponding letters are guessed, the letter is displayed instead of the dash. At the end of the game, the user should be shown the word along with the number of guesses.

The WordGuess output sketch:

```
WordGuess game.
-----
Enter a letter (! to guess entire word): a
--A--
Enter a letter (! to guess entire word): v
--A--
Enter a letter (! to guess entire word): !
--A--

What is your guess?
brain
You won!
The secret word is BRAIN
You made 3 guesses.
```

The WordGuess algorithm:

1. Display a row of dashes to represent the word.

2. Prompt the user for a letter guess.

3. If the letter guessed is part of the word, then display that letter in place of the corresponding dash.

4. Repeat steps 2 and 3 until all the letters have been guessed or an exclamation point has been entered by the user.

5. If an exclamation point has been entered, prompt the user to guess the entire word.

6. If the player correctly guesses the entire word or all the letters have been guessed, then display a message indicating that the player has won, otherwise the message should indicate that the player has lost.

7. Display the secret word and the number of guesses.

# WordGuess Code Design

The input for WordGuess are letters typed by the user. A String variable to store the player's letter guess will be needed. The player may also choose to guess the entire word, so another String variable to store a word guess will be needed.

The output for WordGuess is the secret word displayed as dashes and then redisplayed whenever a dash should be replaced by a letter, a prompt for the user's guess, a message indicating a win or loss, and a message indicating the secret word and the number of guesses made.

Data generated by WordGuess is a count of the number of guesses made by the user. A counter variable to store the number of guesses will be needed. Other data used in this application can be represented by String constants to represent the secret word (SECRET_WORD) and to use as a loop sentinel (FLAG). A String variable will also be needed to "build" a new string that contains any correctly guessed letters.

Based on the algorithm, the code design for the WordGuess application will include a loop structure to compare the user's input to the letters in the secret word. The best loop structure will be a `do-while` because under any condition the loop statements should iterate at least once. It also unknown how many times the loop statements should iterate, so a type of `while` statement, not a `for` statement, should be used. This comparison will be done with an `if` statement. A pseudocode algorithm for WordGuess follows:

```
Generate and display a set of dashes that represent the word
do
   update guesses counter
   Prompt user for a letter
   Convert to all uppercase
   Determine if letter is in word
   if letter is in word
      Create new string that contains the guessed letter
while (all letters haven't been guessed and user hasn't chosen
to guess the entire word)
if (! has been entered)
   get a word guess from player
   convert word to all uppercase
if (word guessed equals secret word OR all the letters have
been guessed)
   display message that player has won
else
   display message that player has lost
Display secret word
Display number of guesses
```

## WordGuess Implementation

Based on the code design, the WordGuess implementation follows:

```java
/*
 * WordGuess.java
 */

import java.util.Scanner;

/**
 * Plays a word guessing game with one player.
 */
public class WordGuess {

    public static void main(String[] args) {
        final String SECRET_WORD = "BRAIN";
        final String FLAG = "!";
        String wordSoFar = "", updatedWord = "";
        String letterGuess, wordGuess = "";
        int numGuesses = 0;
        Scanner input = new Scanner(System.in);

        /* begin game */
        System.out.println("WordGuess game.\n");
        for (int i = 0; i < SECRET_WORD.length(); i++) {
            wordSoFar += "-";                             //word as dashes
        }
        System.out.println(wordSoFar + "\n");        //display dashes

        /* allow player to make guesses */
        do {
            System.out.print("Enter a letter (" + FLAG + " to guess entire word): ");
            letterGuess = input.nextLine();
            letterGuess = letterGuess.toUpperCase();

            /* increment number of guesses */
            numGuesses += 1;

            /* player correctly guessed a letter--extract string in wordSoFar
             * up to the letter guessed and then append guessed letter to that
             * string Next, extract rest of wordSoFar and append after the guessed
             * letter
             */
            if (SECRET_WORD.indexOf(letterGuess) >= 0) {
                updatedWord = wordSoFar.substring(0, SECRET_WORD.indexOf(letterGuess));
                updatedWord += letterGuess;
                updatedWord += wordSoFar.substring(SECRET_WORD.indexOf(letterGuess)+1,
                    wordSoFar.length());
                wordSoFar = updatedWord;
            }

            /* display guessed letter instead of dash */
            System.out.println(wordSoFar + "\n");
        } while (!letterGuess.equals(FLAG) && !wordSoFar.equals(SECRET_WORD));

        /* finish game and display message and number of guesses */
        if (letterGuess.equals(FLAG)) {
            System.out.println("What is your guess? ");
            wordGuess = input.nextLine();
            wordGuess = wordGuess.toUpperCase();
        }
        if (wordGuess.equals(SECRET_WORD) || wordSoFar.equals(SECRET_WORD)) {
```

```
        System.out.println("You won!");
    } else {
        System.out.println("Sorry.  You lose.");
    }
    System.out.println("The secret word is " + SECRET_WORD);
    System.out.println("You made " + numGuesses + " guesses.");
    }

}
```

A run of WordGuess looks similar to:

```
WordGuess game.

-----

Enter a letter (! to guess entire word): a
--A--

Enter a letter (! to guess entire word): b
B-A--

Enter a letter (! to guess entire word): i
B-AI-

Enter a letter (! to guess entire word): !
B-AI-

What is your guess?
brain
You won!
The secret word is BRAIN
You made 4 guesses.
```

### WordGuess Testing and Debugging

This case study should test all possible guess combinations. For example, the player may enter an exclamation point on the first guess. Testing should also include incorrect word guesses.

## Review: WordGuess

Modify the WordGuess Chapter 5 Case Study to display a score at the end of each game. The player should start with 100 points and have 10 points taken off for each guess. The score should be updated and displayed as the game is played. Display a player loses message if the score gets down to 0.

# Chapter Summary

This chapter introduced loop structures and the String class. The `while` statement and `do-while` statement are loop structures that iterate a set of statements repeatedly based on a condition. The difference between the loops is when the condition is evaluated. The `while` statement evaluates the condition before any iterations are performed. The `do-while` does not evaluate the condition until after the first iteration.

Some syntax errors and logic errors can lead to an infinite loop, which executes forever causing the application to just hang. A logic error can also cause an overflow, which occurs when there are not enough bits to store a number.

Counters are used for keeping track of loop iterations and are used in applications that keep track of the number of guesses or the number of values entered. An accumulator is increased by varying amounts. Accumulators are often used to sum values.

A flag, also called a sentinel, is used to signify that a loop should stop iterating. Flags are usually a constant that is declared in the application, but may also be determined by prompting the user for a value.

The `for` statement is another loop structure. This loop structure executes a set of statements a fixed number of times. A loop control variable is used to determine loop iterations and can be declared in the `for` statement itself. When a variable is declared in a statement, its scope is limited to the opening and closing curly braces of that statement. The increment operator (++) and decrement operator (--) are used to increase or decrease the value of a `for` loop control variable.

Debugging techniques include using a debugger, often included with a compiler, and a variable trace, which is a manual technique. Debuggers have the advantage of being able to display the actual value of a variable as it changes. Other techniques include adding println statements before and after variable assignment. Commenting out statements can also locate an error through process of elimination.

The String class is used to declare string variables. It contains numerous methods for determining the length of a string, converting a string to lowercase or uppercase characters, extracting substrings, and for comparing strings. A string is immutable, which means it cannot be changed from its original value. However, a String object can be assigned a new string in memory.

Code conventions introduced in this chapter are :

* The statements of an `while` statement should be indented.

* The statements of a `do-while` statement should be indented.

* The statements of a `for` statement should be indented.

* Declare variables so that their scope is limited to where they are needed.

* Changes to a loop control variable should occur in the increment portion of the loop only, and the loop should end only when the condition is false.

*Chapter 5 Loop Structures and Strings*

# Vocabulary

**Accumulator** A variable that is incremented by varying amounts.

**Breakpoint** A statement selected where execution will be suspended.

**Counter** A variable that is incremented by a fixed value.

**Debugger** A tool included with some compilers for debugging.

**Debugging** The process of getting an application to work correctly.

**Decrement operator** The -- operator, which decreases the value of a variable by 1.

**Flag** *see* Sentinel.

**Immutable** Unable to change.

**Increment operator** The ++ operator, which increases the value of a variable by 1.

**Index** The position of a character in a string.

**Infinite loop** A loop that continues forever.

**Iteration** The execution of a loop.

**Loop control variable** A counter that is used to control the number of `for` loop iterations.

**Loop structure** A statement that executes a set of statements repeatedly based on a condition.

**NullPointerException exception** An exception thrown when operations on a null String are attempted.

**Overflow** A condition that occurs when a number is too large to be stored in a specified number of bits.

**Sentinel** A constant that stores a value that is used to signify that a loop should stop iterating. Also called a flag.

**Scope** The set of statements that are able to access a declared variable.

**Variable trace** A table listing the values of variables at the points of assignment. Used for manually debugging an application.

# Java

`++` The increment operator.

`--` The decrement operator.

`do-while` A loop structure that executes a set of statements over and over again based on a condition, which is evaluated after an iteration.

`for` A loop structure that executes a set of statements a fixed number of times.

`while` A loop structure that executes a set of statements over and over again based on a condition, which is evaluated before any iterations.

**String** A java.lang class with methods for manipulating and comparing strings.

1. What is the purpose of a loop structure?

2. Explain the difference between a `while` statement and a `do-while` statement.

3. An input validation loop is a loop that checks user input for valid data. If valid data is not entered, the loop iterates until valid data is entered. In which review of this chapter did you write code for an input validation loop?

4. a) What is an infinite loop?
   b) List two types of errors that can lead to an infinite loop.
   c) What is meant by overflow?

5. How many times will the `do-while` loop execute?

```
int x = 0;
do {
    x = x + 2;
} while (x < 120);
```

6. What initial value of x would make the loop infinite?

```
do {
    x = x - 3;
} while (x < 120);
```

7. Compare and contrast counters and accumulators. List two uses for each.

8. Write a `for` statement that sums the integers from 3 to 10, inclusive.

9. List two factors that should be considered when determining which loop structure to choose.

10. a) List two methods for debugging an application.
    b) Which method listed in part (a) would be best for debugging an application that generates random numbers that are used for determining the condition of an `if` statement? Why?

11. Consider the following assignment:
    `String x = "my string.";`

    Determine the value returned by each of the following methods:
    a) `x.length()`
    b) `x.substring(0, 3)`

    c) `x.toLowerCase()`
    d) `x.toUpperCase`
    e) `x.trim()`

12. Consider the following statements:
    ```
    String x = "lots of words.";
    String y = "Lots of Words.";
    String z = "Two words.";
    ```

    Determine the value returned by each of the following methods:
    a) `x.equals(y)`
    b) `x.equalsIgnoreCase(y)`
    c) `x.compareTo(z)`
    d) `x.compareToIgnoreCase(y)`
    e) `x.compareToIgnoreCase(z)`
    f) `x.IndexOf("or")`
    g) `x.lastIndexOf("o")`
    h) `z.startsWith("Tw")`
    i) `x.endsWith("ds")`

13. a) Write an algorithm to count the number of words in a sentence.
    b) Write an algorithm to count the number of letters in a sentence.

**True/False**

14. Determine if each of the following are true or false. If false, explain why.
    a) A `while` statement iterates once before evaluating the condition.
    b) A counter is incremented by a constant amount.
    c) An accumulator signifies that a loop should stop iterating.
    d) Sentinel values must always be the value –1.
    e) A variable declared in a `for` statement can be used again anywhere in the program code.
    f) String variables are primitive data types.
    g) The first character of a string has index position 1.
    h) Strings are compared using relational operators such as >.
    i) The String class includes a method for determining the location of a substring within a string.

## Exercise 1 ———————————————————————— PrimeNumber

a) A prime number is an integer greater than 1 that is evenly divisible by only 1 and itself. For example, 2, 3, 5, and 7 are prime numbers, but 4, 6, 8, and 9 are not. Create a PrimeNumber application that prompts the user for a number and then displays a message indicating whether the number is prime or not. Hint: The % operator can be used to determine if one number is evenly divisible by another.

b) Modify the application to prompt the user for two numbers and then display the prime numbers between those numbers.

## Exercise 2 ——————————————————————————PrimeFactors

The Fundamental Theorem of Arithmetic states that every positive integer is the product of a set of prime numbers. This set is called the prime factors. For example, the prime factors for 140 are 2, 2, 5, and 7 (2*2*5*7 = 140). Create a PrimeFactors application that prompts the user for a positive integer and then displays that integer's prime factors. Use the following pseudocode when implementing the PrimeFactors code:

```
Initialize a counter to 2
while the counter is less than or equal to the number
    if the counter divides the number evenly
        display the counter
        divide the number by the counter to get a new number
    else increment counter by 1
```

## Exercise 3 ——————————————————————————Investment

Create an Investment application that calculates how many years it will take for a $2,500 investment to be worth at least $5,000 if compounded annually at 7.5%

## Exercise 4  ———————————————————————— CarRecall

Modify the CarRecall application created in Chapter 4 Exercise 4 to allow the user to input as many model numbers as needed. Use 0 as a sentinel to end user input. The application output should look similar to:

```
Enter the car's model number or 0 to quit: 221
Your car is defective. It must be repaired.
Enter the car's model number or 0 to quit: 123
Your car is not defective.
Enter the car's model number or 0 to quit: 780
Your car is defective. It must be repaired.
Enter the car's model number or 0 to quit: 0
```

# Exercise 5 ———————————————————— DigitsDisplay

Create a DigitsDisplay application that prompts the user for a non-negative integer and then displays each digit on a separate line. Application output should look similar to:

```
Enter a positive integer: 546
5
4
6
```

# Exercise 6 ———————————————————————— DigitsSum

Create a DigitsSum application that prompts the user for a non-negative integer and then displays the sum of the digits. Application output should look similar to:

```
Enter a positive integer: 892
The sum of the digits is: 19
```

# Exercise 7 ——————————————————————CubesSum

a)  Create a CubesSum application that prompts the user for a non-negative integer and then displays the sum of the cubes of the digits. Application output should look similar to:

```
Enter a positive integer: 223
The sum of the cubes of the digits is: 43
```

b)  Modify the application to determine what integers of two, three, and four digits are equal to the sum of the cubes of their digits.

# Exercise 8  ——————————————————— GuessingGame

The GuessingGame application created in Chapter 4 Exercise 9 would be more fun if users could make as many guesses as necessary to guess the secret number. Modify the GuessingGame application as follows:

a)  Modify the algorithm to allow for as many guesses as needed.

b)  Modify the GuessingGame code. Application output should look similar to:

```
Enter a number between 1 and 20: 12
Try again.
Enter a number between 1 and 20: 10
Try again.
Enter a number between 1 and 20: 8
Try again.
Enter a number between 1 and 20: 7
Try again.
Enter a number between 1 and 20: 15
You won!
```

c) A binary search is a divide-and-conquer technique for efficiently searching a list of numbers that are sorted from lowest to highest. A strategy that incorporates the binary search technique can be used by the Guessing Game player when making guesses about the secret number:

1. Guess the number halfway between the lowest and highest numbers.

2. If the number guessed matches the secret number, then the player wins.

3. If the number guessed is too high, then take the number guessed minus one and make this the highest number and go back to Step 1.

4. If the number guessed is too low, then take the number guessed plus one and make this the lowest number and go back to Step 1.

   For example, assuming 15 is the random number generated in the Guessing Game application, the game would play out as follows when the player uses a divide-and-conquer technique:

| Current Low | Current High | Player Types | Message Displayed |
|---|---|---|---|
| 1 | 50 | 26 (i.e., (1+50)/2=25.5) | Too high. |
| 1 | 25 | 13 (i.e., (1+25)/2=13) | Too low. |
| 14 | 25 | 20 (i.e., (14+25)/2=19.5) | Too high. |
| 14 | 19 | 16 (i.e., (14+19)/2=16.5) | Too high. |
| 14 | 15 | 14 (i.e., (14+15)/2=14.5) | Too low. |
| 15 | 15 | 15 (i.e., (15+15)/2=15) | You guessed it! |

In another program run, assuming the random number generated is 20, the game would play out as follows using the same divide-and-conquer technique:

| Current Low | Current High | Player Types | Message Displayed |
|---|---|---|---|
| 1 | 50 | 26 (i.e., (1+50)/2=25.5) | Too high. |
| 1 | 25 | 13 (i.e., (1+25)/2=13) | Too low. |
| 14 | 25 | 20 (i.e., (14+25)/2=19.5) | You guessed it! |

When this approach is taken, it has been proven that a player will not be required to make more than $Log_2 n$ guesses, in this case $Log_2 50$, or at most 6 guesses. Try this technique yourself. Explain in your own words why this works. Would this strategy be possible if hints were not given after each guess?

## Exercise 9 ———————————————————————— PowersTable

Create a PowersTable application that displays a table of of powers similar to:

```
x^1      x^2      x^3      x^4      x^5
  1        1        1        1        1
  2        4        8       16       32
  3        9       27       81      243
  4       16       64      256     1024
  5       25      125      625     3125
  6       36      216     1296     7776
```

# Exercise 10 ———————————————————————— GCD

Create a GCD application that prompts the user for two non-negative integers and then displays the greatest common divisor (GCD) of the two numbers. The GCD is the largest integer that divides into both numbers evenly. An algorithm for finding the GCD is called Euclid's Algorithm. Use the following pseudocode when implementing the GCD code:

```
while (num2 > 0) {
    temp = num1 % num2;
    num1 = num2;
    num2 = temp;
}
```

Application output should look similar to:

```
Enter a number: 32
Enter a second number: 40
The GCD is 8
```

# Exercise 11 ———————————————————— ElapsedTimeCalculator

What comes 13 hours after 4 o'clock? Create an ElaspedTimeCalculator application that prompts the user for a starting hour, whether it is am or pm, and the number of elapsed hours. The application then displays the time after that many hours have passed. Application output should look similar to:

```
Enter the starting hour: 7
Enter am or pm: pm
Enter the number of elapsed hours: 10
The time is: 5:00am
```

# Exercise 12 ———————————————————————— Necklace

An interesting problem in number theory is sometimes called the "necklace problem." This problem begins with two single-digit numbers. The next number is obtained by adding the first two numbers together and saving only the ones digit. This process is repeated until the "necklace" closes by returning to the original two numbers. For example, if the starting two numbers are 1 and 8, twelve steps are required to close the necklace: 1 8 9 7 6 3 9 2 1 3 4 7 1 8

Create a Necklace application that prompts the user for two single-digit integers and then displays the sequence and the number of steps taken. The application output should look similar to:

```
Enter the first starting number: 1
Enter the second starting number: 8
1 8 9 7 6 3 9 2 1 3 4 7 1 8
```

## Exercise 13 ——————————————— Hailstone

An interesting (yet unsolved) question in mathematics is called "hailstone numbers." This series is produced by taking an initial integer, and if the number is even, dividing it by 2. If the number is odd, multiply it by 3 and add 1. This process is then repeated. For example, an initial number of 10 produces:

10, 5, 16, 8, 4, 2, 1, 4, 2, 1 …

An initial value of 23 produces:

23, 70, 35, 106, 53, 160, 80, 40, 20, 10, 5, 16, 8, 4, 2, 1, 4, 2, 1 …

Note that both numbers eventually reach the 4, 2, 1, 4, 2, 1 … cycle. Create two applications (Hailstone1 and Hailstone2) that answer the following questions for initial values of 1 to 200:

a)  Do all integers from 1 to 200 eventually reach this cycle?

b)  What is the maximum number of iterations to reach the cycle and which starting number produces this maximum?

## Exercise 14 ——————————————— DiceRolls

Create a DiceRolls application that displays five rolls of two dice where each die is numbered from 1 to 6. The application should also show the total of each roll:

| Dice 1 | Dice 2 | Total |
|--------|--------|-------|
| 3 | 3 | 6 |
| 2 | 1 | 3 |
| 1 | 3 | 4 |
| 4 | 3 | 7 |
| 3 | 1 | 4 |

## Exercise 15 ——————————————— Chaos

"Chaos theory" is a subfield of mathematics which relies heavily on the computer. A simple chaos experiment is:

Start with any real number x between 0 and 1. Generate a new number using the "logistic equation:"

x = 2*x(1 - x)

Display this new x and repeat the process 50 times.

a)  Create a Chaos application that prompts the user for a starting value and then performs this experiment. Make a prediction about what happens for different starting values.

b)  Modify the application so that the 2 in the logistic equation can be replaced with a value specified by the user in the range 2 to 4, but the starting value of x is always 0.5. Note any interesting behavior.

# Exercise 16 ————————————————————RandomWalk

In the "random walk" problem, a person is placed at the center of a 7 meter long bridge. Each step the person moves 1 meter either forward or backward at random.

Create a RandomWalk application that determines how many steps the person will walk before taking a step off the bridge. Have the application average 50 trials, and display the average and the greatest number of steps. (Hint: Generate a random number between 0 and 1, with 0 meaning to go forward and 1 meaning to go backward.)

# Exercise 17 ———————————————————— Password

Create a Password application that stores a secret password of your choice. The Password application should prompt the user for the password and then display "Welcome" if the correct password is typed. If after three tries the correct password has not been entered, the message "Access denied." should be displayed. Application output should look similar to:

```
Enter the password: programmer7
The password you typed is incorrect.
Enter the password: R*@!ST
The password you typed is incorrect.
Enter the password: WXT78
Access denied.
```

# Exercise 18 ————————————————————Monogram

Create a Monogram application that prompts the user for his or her first name, middle name, and last name and then displays a monogram with the first and middle initials in lowercase and the last initial in uppercase. Application output should look similar to:

```
Enter your first name: Alonso
Enter your middle initial: H
Enter your last name: Eloy

Your monogram is: aEh
```

# Exercise 19 ———————————————————— RemoveString

Create a RemoveString application that prompts the user for a sentence and a string. The application should then remove every occurrence of the string from the sentence. The application should look similar to:

```
Enter a sentence: I really hope you get an interview.
Enter a string: really
I hope you get an interview.
```

# Exercise 20 ———————————————————CountVowels

Create a CountVowels application that prompts the user for a string and then displays a count of the number of vowels in the string. Application output should look similar to:

```
Enter text: Java Programming Assignment
The number of vowels in Java Programming Assignment is 8.
```

# Exercise 21 ——————————————————— GroupAssignment

Create a GroupAssignment application that prompts the user for his or her name and then displays a group assignment. The group assignment depends on the first letter of the student's last name. Last names beginning with A through I are assigned to Group 1, J through S are assigned to Group 2, T through Z are assigned to Group 3. Application output should look similar to:

```
Enter your first name: Christina
Enter your last name: Briglio
Christina Briglio is assigned to Group 1
```

*Chapter 5 Loop Structures and Strings*

# Chapter 6
# Methods

## Key Concepts

Using top-down development and procedural abstraction to develop problem solutions
Writing methods
Using method parameters
Method overloading
Writing method documentation
Generating test data
Applying code conventions to methods

## Case Study

Grade Converter application

## Program Development Using Methods

**TIP** Top-down development is also called top-down design or step-wise refinement.

*top-down development*

*procedural abstraction*

The solution to a task can be developed by breaking the task down into smaller subtasks. These subtasks can then be reduced to yet simpler tasks. This process can be continued until the original task is broken down into units that each describe a specific goal. As the task is broken down into smaller subtasks and then further into units, more detail for achieving the specific goal is added. This problem-solving approach describes a software development process called *top-down development*.

In top-down development, the first level of subtasks translates into the main() method. Levels of tasks below main() are developed into a series of additional methods. Using methods to define tasks is called *procedural abstraction*. For example, consider the following program specification:

> TempConverter allows the user to convert a temperature from either Fahrenheit to Celsius or Celsius to Fahrenheit.

The algorithm for this application breaks the program specification down into the first level of subtasks:

1. Determine the type of conversion to be done.

2. Convert the temperature using the appropriate formula.

Step 2 can then be broken down into another level of subtasks:

2a. Prompt the user for a Celsius temperature.
Convert the temperature to Fahrenheit using the formula:
$F = 9/5C + 32$.
Display the temperature.

2b. Prompt the user for a Fahrenheit temperature.
Convert the temperature to Celsius using the formula:
$C = 5/9(F - 32)$.
Display the temperature.

Top-down development and procedural abstraction were used to break the program specification down into levels of subtasks, as shown on the previous page. Outlining the levels of subtasks in pseudocode defines a main() method and two other methods:

```
main()
Prompt the user for the conversion type.
Execute the appropriate method to convert the temperature.

fahrenheitToCelsius()
Prompt the user for a temperature in degrees Fahrenheit
Convert the temperature to degrees Celsius
Display the temperature

celsiusToFahrenheit()
Prompt the user for a temperature in degrees Celsius
Convert the temperature to degrees Fahrenheit
Display the temperature
```

The TempConverter application implements the pseudocode above:

```java
import java.util.Scanner;

public class TempConverter {

  public static void fahrenheitToCelsius() {
     double fTemp, cTemp;
     Scanner input = new Scanner(System.in);

     System.out.print("Enter a Fahrenheit temperature: ");
     fTemp = input.nextDouble();
     input.close();

     cTemp = (double)5/(double)9*(fTemp - 32);
     System.out.println("The Celsius temperature is " + cTemp);
  }

  public static void celsiusToFahrenheit() {
     double cTemp, fTemp;
     Scanner input = new Scanner(System.in);

     System.out.print("Enter a Celsius temperature: ");
     cTemp = input.nextDouble();
     input.close();

     fTemp = (double)9/(double)5*cTemp + 32;
     System.out.println("The Fahrenheit temperature is "
         + fTemp);
  }

  public static void main(String[] args) {
     int choice;
     Scanner input = new Scanner(System.in);

     /* Prompt user for type of conversion */
     System.out.println("1. Fahrenheit to Celsius conversion.");
     System.out.println("2. Celsius to Fahrenheit conversion.");
     System.out.print("Enter your choice: ");
     choice = input.nextInt();
     if (choice == 1) {
        fahrenheitToCelsius();
     } else {
        celsiusToFahrenheit();
     }
     input.close();
  }
}
```

**TIP** Methods must be part of a class.

The TempConverter controlling class contains two methods as well as a main() method. The methods are executed when they are called. A *call* method *call* consists of the method name followed by parentheses. The `if` statement in the main() method on the previous page contains two method calls, `fahrenheitToCelsius()` and `celsiusToFahrenheit()`.

TempConverter produces output similar to:

```
1. Fahrenheit to Celsius conversion.
2. Celsius to Fahrenheit conversion.
Enter your choice: 1
Enter a Fahrenheit temperature: 32
The Celsius temperature is 0.0
```

In this run of the application, the user entered 1 and therefore the fahrenheitToCelsius() method was called.

## Writing Methods

*method declaration*  A method consists of a declaration and a body. The *method declaration* *method body* includes access level, return type, name, and parameters, if any. The *method body* contains the statements that implement the method. A method takes the form:

```
<access_level> <return_type> <name>(<parameters>) {
   <statements>
}
```

For example, consider the fahrenheitToCelsius() method from the TempConverter application:

```
public static void fahrenheitToCelsius() {
   double fTemp, cTemp;
   Scanner input = new Scanner(System.in);

   System.out.print("Enter a Fahrenheit temperature: ");
   fTemp = input.nextDouble();
   input.close();

   cTemp = (double)5/(double)9*(fTemp - 32);
   System.out.println("The Celsius temperature is " + cTemp);
}
```

*access level*  The method above is a class method with access level `public`, return type `void`, name fahrenheitToCelsius, and no parameters. The *access level* of a method determines if other classes can call the method. The keyword *access modifier* `public` is an *access modifier*. A public method can be called by any other *visibility* method. The access level of a method can also be thought of as its *visibility*. Access levels are discussed further in Chapter 7.

*class method*  The keyword `static` declares the method a class method. A *class method* can be called from the class itself. Methods that are not class methods must be called from an instantiated object of that class.

*void*  The return type `void` means that the method will not return a value, and parameters are specified when a method needs values to perform its task. The body of the method starts with the first opening brace ({) and ends with the closing brace (}).

*naming conventions*

Method names should indicate an action. Verbs make good method names. A method name should also begin with a lowercase letter and then an uppercase letter should begin each word within the name. Method names may not contain spaces.

*local scope*

Methods can also have their own set of variables, constants, and objects. Variable, constant, and object declarations in the body of a method have a scope that extends from the declaration to the end of the method body. These variables, constants, and objects are said to be *local* to the method because their scope is limited to that method. For example, the fahrenheitToCelsius() method contains local variables fTemp and cTemp and a local object named input.

## Review: TimeConverter

Create a TimeConverter application that allows the user to choose among converting hours to minutes, days to hours, minutes to hours, or hours to days. Use methods as appropriate.

## Method Parameters

A method declaration can include *method parameters*, which accept values from the method call. The data passed to the method can then be used inside the method to perform its task. For example, the drawBar() method includes an int parameter named length:

**TIP** The terms "parameter" and "argument" are often used synonymously.

```
public static void drawBar(int length) {

    for (int i = 0; i < length; i++) {
        System.out.print("*");
    }
    System.out.println();
}
```

*passing data*

*argument*

Data is given, or *passed*, to a method by enclosing the data in parentheses in the method call. The value or variable passed to a method is called the *argument*. For example, the RightTriangle application makes six calls to drawBar(). Each call passes a different variable argument:

**TIP** The term "formal parameter" is sometimes used to refer to a parameter in the method declaration, and the term "actual parameter" is used to refer to the argument being passed to the method.

```
public class RightTriangle {

    public static void drawBar(int length) {

        for (int i = 1; i <= length; i++) {
            System.out.print("*");
        }
        System.out.println();
    }

    public static void main(String[] args) {

        /* draw a right triangle with base size 6 */
        for (int i = 1; i <= 6; i++) {
            drawBar(i);
        }
    }
}
```

The RightTriangle application produces the output:

```
*
**
***
****
*****
******
```

*pass by value*    In Java, arguments are *passed by value*, which means that the data stored in an argument is passed. An argument that is a primitive data type gives the method a copy of its value. An argument that is an object gives the method a copy of its reference that points to methods for changing object data. Therefore, a method can change the data stored in an object because it has access to the object's methods, but it cannot change the data stored in a primitive variable because the method does not have access to the actual location of the primitive data.

When a method declaration includes more than one parameter, the parameters are separated by commas. For example, a modified drawBar() has an `int` parameter for the length of the bar and a String parameter for the character to use to draw the bar:

```
public static void drawBar(int length, String mark) {

    for (int i = 1; i <= length; i++) {
        System.out.print(mark);
    }
    System.out.println();
}
```

**TIP** Passing an argument of a type that is not expected by a method generates the exception IllegalArgumentException.

A call to the modified drawBar() method includes two arguments separated by commas:

```
drawBar(6, "$");
```

This call produces the following output:

```
$$$$$$
```

The order of the arguments in a method call is important because the first argument corresponds to the first parameter in the method declaration, the second argument corresponds to the second parameter, and so on. Note that argument names do not necessarily match parameter names. Descriptive variable names should be used throughout a program without regard to matching parameter names in a method declaration.

## Review: SpanishNumbers

Create a SpanishNumbers application that displays numbers 1 through 10 in Spanish. A method with an `int` parameter should display the Spanish word for the number passed. A loop structure in the main() method should be used to call the method ten times. The Spanish word equivalents for numbers 1 through 10 are:

| | | | |
|---|---|---|---|
| 1 | uno | 6 | seis |
| 2 | dos | 7 | siete |
| 3 | tres | 8 | ocho |
| 4 | cuatro | 9 | nueve |
| 5 | cinco | 10 | diez |

Create a DisplayBox application that prompts the user for a height and width and then displays a box of that size. The DisplayBox application should include a method named drawBox() that has two parameters and makes calls to the drawBar() method.

## Method Overloading

The method declaration is used by the compiler to determine which method to execute. Therefore, method names do not have to be unique as long as the parameters are different for methods with the same name. *Method overloading* is when more than one method of the same name is included in a class. For example, the following application contains two drawBar() methods:

```java
public class MethodOverloadingExample {

    public static void drawBar(int length) {

        for (int i = 1; i <= length; i++) {
            System.out.print("*");
        }
        System.out.println();
    }

    public static void drawBar(int length, String mark) {

        for (int i = 1; i <= length; i++) {
            System.out.print(mark);
        }
        System.out.println();
    }

    public static void main(String[] args) {

        drawBar(10);
        drawBar(5, "@");
    }
}
```

The MethodOverloading application produces the output:

```
**********
@@@@@
```

Note that the first call in main() executes the drawBar() method containing only one parameter. The second call executes the drawBar() method that contains two parameters. The compiler uses the types, order, and number of parameters to determine which method to execute.

Modify the DrawBox application to ask the user if a specific character should be used for the display. For example, the prompt could be "Do you want to enter a character to use to display the box? (enter y for yes):" If the user types y, then prompt the user for the character. Otherwise, the default character should be used. The modified application should contain overloaded drawBox() and drawBar() methods.

## The return Statement

A method can return a value. For example, the cubeOf() method returns the cube of its parameter:

```
public static double cubeOf(double x) {
   double xCubed;

   xCubed = x * x * x;
   return(xCubed);
}
```

The return statement is used to send a value back to the calling statement. A return statement can return only one value.

A method that returns a value must include the return type in the method declaration. For example, the cubeOf() method declaration declares a return type double. Return types can be primitive types, such as int, double, and boolean, or abstract types, such as the String class. The return type void is used when there will be no return value. A method declared as void does not contain a return statement.

A method that returns a value is called from a statement that will make use of the returned value, such as an expression or an assignment statement. For example, the following application calls cubeOf() from an assignment statement:

```
public class CubeCalculator {

   public static double cubeOf(double x) {
      double xCubed;

      xCubed = x * x * x;
      return(xCubed);

   }

   public static void main(String[] args) {
      double num = 2.0;
      double cube;

      cube = cubeOf(num);
      System.out.println(cube);
   }
}
```

The CubeCalculator application produces the following output:

```
8.0
```

## Review: Exponentiation

Create an Exponentiation application that prompts the user for two numbers and then displays the first number raised to the power of the second number. The application should include a method named powerOf() that returns its first parameter raised to the power of its second parameter.

## Documenting Methods

Methods should be carefully commented so that a reader of the program understands what task the method is performing and what data, if any, will be returned by the method. Method documentation is in the form of documentation comments (/**    */) that appear just above the method declaration. For example, the drawBar() method with documentation:

```
/**
 * Print a bar of asterisks across the screen.
 * pre: length > 0
 * post: Bar drawn of length characters, insertion
 * point moved to next line.
 */
public static void drawBar(int length) {

    for (int i = 0; i < length; i++) {
        System.out.print("*");
    }
    System.out.println();
}
```

*precondition*

The assumptions, or initial requirements, of a method are stated in the documentation in a section called the *precondition*, or just `pre`. Note that the pre for drawBar() states that `length` must be greater than 0, but not that `length` must be an `int`. Information that the compiler will verify, such as data types, should not be stated in method documentation.

*postcondition*

The *postcondition* section of the documentation, or `post`, states what must be true after the method has been executed. However, the post should not state how the method accomplished its task.

A method may not have a precondition, but every method must have a postcondition. For example, below is the cubeOf() method with documentation:

```
/**
 * Calculates the cube of a number.
 * pre: none
 * post: x cubed returned
 */
public static double cubeOf(double x) {
    double xCubed;

    xCubed = x * x * x;
    return(xCubed);
}
```

To summarize, the guidelines for writing pre and post conditions are:

- The precondition states what must be true at the beginning of a method for the method to work properly.

- The postcondition states what must be true after the method has executed if the method has worked properly.

- Preconditions and postconditions should not state facts that the compiler will verify. They should also not refer to variables or information outside the method.

- The postcondition should not state how the method accomplished its task.

## Review

Modify each of the Reviews in this chapter so that the methods are properly documented.

## Chapter 6 Case Study

This case study will focus on top-down development and procedural abstraction. Testing and debugging methods in isolation will also be demonstrated.

An application for generating a letter grade based on a numeric grade will be created. The GradeConverter application allows the user to enter a numeric grade and then a letter grade is displayed. The user may then choose to enter another grade or quit.

### GradeConverter Specification

The GradeConverter application prompts the user for a numeric grade in the range 0 to 100 or a –1 to end the application. When a valid numeric grade is entered, the corresponding letter grade is then displayed. Grades from 90 to 100 are an A, grades from 80 to 89 are a B, grades from 70 to 79 are a C, grades from 60 to 69 are a D, and grades below 60 are an F. After displaying the corresponding letter grade, the user is prompted to enter another letter grade or can choose to quit the application.

The GradeConverter interface should include a prompt asking for the numeric grade. The prompt should give the option of quitting the application. After displaying the letter grade, the user should be prompted to enter another numeric grade or quit the application.

The GradeConverter output sketch:

```
Enter a numeric grade (–1 to quit): 88
The grade 88 is a(n) B.
Enter a numeric grade (–1 to quit): 90
The grade 90 is a(n) A.
Enter a numeric grade (–1 to quit): –1
```

The GradeConverter algorithm:

1. Prompt the user for a number.

2. Determine the letter grade that corresponds to the entered numeric grade and display the result.

3. Repeat steps 1 and 2 until the user chooses to quit.

Using the top-down development approach, the algorithm is further refined:

Step 1 of the algorithm can be broken down further:

1a. Display a prompt that gives the user the option to quit.

Check that the number entered is valid. It should correspond to either a sentinel value that indicates the user wants to quit or a number in the range 0 through 100.

Step 2 of the algorithm can be broken down further:

2a. Determine if the numeric grade is between 90 to 100, 80 to 89, 70 to 79, 60 to 69, or 0 to 59.

Assign the letter A to a grade from 90 to 100, a letter B to a grade from 80 to 89, the letter C to a grade from 70 to 79, the letter D to a grade from 60 to 69, and the letter F to a grade from 0 to 59.

Using the algorithm and procedural abstraction, the pseudocode for the GradeConverter application can be created. The code will include a loop structure to get the user's input and two additional methods. One method will determine if the input is valid and another determines which letter corresponds to the numeric grade:

```
main()
Prompt the user for a number
while (number != -1) {
    if (isValidNumber(number)) {
        getLetterGrade(number)
        Display message with letter grade
    }
    Prompt the user for a number
}

isValidNumber(userNum, maxNum, minNum)
if (minNum <= userNum <= maxNum) {
    return (true);
} else {
    return(false);
}

getLetterGrade(numericGrade)
if (numericGrade < 60) {
    return ("F");
} else if (numericGrade < 70) {
    return ("D");
} else if (numericGrade < 80) {
    return ("C");
} else if (numericGrade < 90) {
    return ("B");
} else {
    return ("A");
}
```

*Chapter 6 Methods*

## GradeConverter Implementation

Testing methods in isolation is important to ensure that the program as a whole will run without error. When testing a method, statements in main() should call the method using test data. The main() method should not call any other method or perform any other task except test the current method.

Rather than writing code for the entire application, one method will be added at a time and then tested. When testing the methods is complete, the main() method will be rewritten to implement the pseudocode.

The isValidNumber() method is the first method written and tested:

```
public class GradeConverter {

    /**
     * Determines if a numeric entry is valid.
     * pre: none
     * post: true return if minNum <= userNum <= maxNum;
     * false returned otherwise
     */
    public static boolean isValidNumber(int userNum, int minNum, int maxNum) {
        if (minNum <= userNum && userNum <= maxNum) {
            return(true);
        } else {
            return(false);
        }
    }

    public static void main(String[] args) {
        final int minValue = 0;
        final int maxValue = 100;
        int numericGrade;

        numericGrade = 0;
        if (isValidNumber(numericGrade, minValue, maxValue)) {
            System.out.println(numericGrade + " is valid.");
        } else {
            System.out.println(numericGrade + " is NOT valid.");
        }

        numericGrade = 100;
        if (isValidNumber(numericGrade, minValue, maxValue)) {
            System.out.println(numericGrade + " is valid.");
        } else {
            System.out.println(numericGrade + " is NOT valid.");
        }

        numericGrade = -1;
        if (isValidNumber(numericGrade, minValue, maxValue)) {
            System.out.println(numericGrade + " is valid.");
        } else {
            System.out.println(numericGrade + " is NOT valid.");
        }

        numericGrade = 101;
        if (isValidNumber(numericGrade, minValue, maxValue)) {
            System.out.println(numericGrade + " is valid.");
        } else {
            System.out.println(numericGrade + " is NOT valid.");
        }
    }
}
```

The statements in main() test the isValidNumber() method with data that includes boundary values. A *boundary value* is data that is just inside or just outside the range of valid values. For example, the value 100 lies just inside the high end of the range of valid grades. Testing the method with this data verifies that the <= operator was used rather than the < operator. The GradeConverter application produces the following output:

```
0 is valid.
100 is valid.
-1 is NOT valid.
101 is NOT valid.
```

Next, the getLetterGrade() method is added and the main() statements are changed to test that method:

```java
public class GradeConverter {

    /**
     * Determines if a numeric entry is valid.
     * pre: none
     * post: true has been returned if minNum <= userNum <= maxNum;
     * false has been returned otherwise
     */
    public static boolean isValidNumber(int userNum, int minNum, int maxNum) {
        if (minNum <= userNum && userNum <= maxNum) {
            return(true);
        } else {
            return(false);
        }
    }


    /**
     * Determines the letter grade that corresponds to the numeric grade.
     * pre:  0 <= numGrade <= 100
     * post: The letter grade A, B, C, D, or F has been returned.
     */
    public static String getLetterGrade(int numGrade) {
        if (numGrade < 60) {
            return("F");
        } else if (numGrade < 70){
            return("D");
        } else if (numGrade < 80) {
            return("C");
        } else if (numGrade < 90) {
            return("B");
        } else {
            return("A");
        }
    }

    public static void main(String[] args) {
        int numericGrade;

        numericGrade = 90;
        System.out.println(numericGrade + " is " + getLetterGrade(numericGrade));
        numericGrade = 89;
        System.out.println(numericGrade + " is " + getLetterGrade(numericGrade));
        numericGrade = 80;
        System.out.println(numericGrade + " is " + getLetterGrade(numericGrade));
        numericGrade = 79;
        System.out.println(numericGrade + " is " + getLetterGrade(numericGrade));
```

```
        numericGrade = 70;
        System.out.println(numericGrade + " is " + getLetterGrade(numericGrade));
        numericGrade = 69;
        System.out.println(numericGrade + " is " + getLetterGrade(numericGrade));
        numericGrade = 60;
        System.out.println(numericGrade + " is " + getLetterGrade(numericGrade));
        numericGrade = 59;
        System.out.println(numericGrade + " is " + getLetterGrade(numericGrade));
    }

}
```

Boundary values for getLetterGrade() are tested with statements in main(). Running GradeConverter displays the output:

```
90  is  A
89  is  B
80  is  B
79  is  C
70  is  C
69  is  D
60  is  D
59  is  F
```

After verifying that the methods are working as expected, the final GradeConverter application can be completed:

```
/*
 * GradeConverter.java
 */


import java.util.Scanner;


/**
 * Display the letter grade that corresponds to the numeric
 * grade entered by the user.
 */
public class GradeConverter {

    /**
     * Determines if a numeric entry is valid.
     * pre: none
     * post: true has been returned if minNum <= userNum <= maxNum;
     * false has been returned otherwise
     */
    public static boolean isValidNumber(int userNum, int minNum, int maxNum) {
        if (minNum <= userNum && userNum <= maxNum) {
            return(true);
        } else {
            return(false);
        }
    }
    /**
     * Determines the letter grade that corresponds to the numeric grade.
     * pre: 0 <= numGrade <= 100
     * post: The letter grade A, B, C, D, or F has been returned.
     */
    public static String getLetterGrade(int numGrade) {
        if (numGrade < 60) {
            return("F");
        } else if (numGrade < 70){
            return("D");
        } else if (numGrade < 80) {
            return("C");
        } else if (numGrade < 90) {
```

```
                return("B");
        } else {
                return("A");
        }
    }

    public static void main(String[] args) {
        final int FLAG = -1;
        final int minValue = 0;
        final int maxValue = 100;
        int numericGrade;
        String letterGrade;
        Scanner input = new Scanner(System.in);

        System.out.print("Enter a numeric grade (-1 to quit): ");
        numericGrade = input.nextInt();
        while (numericGrade != FLAG) {
            if (isValidNumber(numericGrade, minValue, maxValue)) {
                letterGrade = getLetterGrade(numericGrade);
                System.out.println("The grade " + numericGrade + " is a(n) " +
                    letterGrade + ".");
            } else {
                System.out.println("Grade entered is not valid.");
            }
            System.out.print("Enter a numeric grade (-1 to quit): ");
            numericGrade = input.nextInt();
        }
    }
}
```

The GradeConverter application produces output similar to:

```
Enter a numeric grade (-1 to quit): 88
The grade 88 is a(n) B.
Enter a numeric grade (-1 to quit): 90
The grade 90 is a(n) A.
Enter a numeric grade (-1 to quit): -1
```

### GradeConverter Testing and Debugging

Testing done at this point should test the logic in main() because the other methods have already been verified. The logic in main() is simple. Therefore, testing need only include verifying that the loop control variable is working as expected, the user is able to enter grades as expected, and that letter grades are returned for values entered by the user in the range 0 though 100.

## Review: GradeConverter

Modify the GradeConverter Case Study to display an A+ for a grade of 100, a B+ for a grade of 89, a C+ for a grade of 79, and a D+ for a grade of 69.

This chapter introduced a new level of software development that included writing methods to perform tasks. In the software development process, top-down development is a problem-solving approach that breaks a task down into smaller subtasks and then further into units.

Methods are executed in a statement by including the method name followed by parentheses. A statement that executes a method is said to call the method. When a method requires data to perform its tasks, the data is included inside the parentheses in the method call.

A method includes a declaration and a body. The method declaration includes the access level, return type, if any, method name, and parameters for receiving data, if necessary. The access level of a method can be declared `public`, which means that the method can be called from a statement in any other method. The keyword `public` is called an access modifier. A method declaration that includes the keyword `static` is a class method, which can be called from the class itself.

The return type of a method declares what type of value will be given back to the calling statement. The return type `void` indicates that the method will not return a value at all. Return types can be primitive types, such as `int` and `double`, or abstract data types, such as String. Methods that return a value must include a `return` statement in the method body.

A method can have multiple parameters. Arguments in a method call must be passed to a method in the same order as the parameter declarations. Methods with the same name, but with different parameters are said to be overloaded.

Primitive arguments are passed by value, which means that the data stored in the argument is passed, not a reference to the argument location. A method can only use the argument values in the task it performs. A method cannot change the data stored in an argument.

The body of a method can include variable, constant, and object declarations. These declarations are said to be local because they have a scope that extends just from the declaration to the end of the method body.

Careful documentation is important for the reader of a program to understand a method. Method documentation is enclosed by /** */ and includes a brief description of the method, a precondition, and a postcondition. Every method must have a postcondition, but not every method requires a precondition.

Code conventions introduced in this chapter are:

- Method names should indicate an action and begin with a lower-case letter and then an uppercase letter should begin each word within the name.

- Method documentation should be enclosed in /** */ comment blocks.

- Method documentation should include a brief description of the task the method performs, a precondition, and a postcondition.

# Vocabulary

**Access level** The part of a method declaration that determines if the method can be called by other classes.

**Access modifier** A keyword in the declaration of a method that determines the access level of a method.

**Argument** The value or variable passed to a method.

**Boundary value** A value that lies just inside or just outside the range of valid values.

**Call** A statement that contains a method name followed by parentheses.

**Class method** A method that can be called from the class itself.

**Local** Variables, constants, and objects that are declared within a method and therefore have a scope limited to that method.

**Method body** The statements that implement a method.

**Method declaration** The first line of a method, which contains the method name, access level, return type, and parameters, if any.

**Method overloading** Writing more than one method of the same name in a class.

**Method parameters** The part of a method declaration that accepts values from the method call.

**Pass** Giving data to a method by enclosing the data in parentheses in the method call.

**Pass by value** Passing the value of an argument to a method. The type of data passed depends on whether the argument is a primitive or an object.

**Postcondition** The part of a method's documentation that states what must be true after the method has been executed. Also called *post*.

**Precondition** The part of a method's documentation that states the assumptions, or initial requirements, of the method. Also called *pre*.

**Procedural abstraction** Breaking a task down into methods.

**Top-down development** A problem-solving approach where a task is broken down into subtasks and then the subtasks are reduced to yet simpler tasks.

**Visibility** The access level of a method.

# Java

`/** */` Used to enclose documentation comments for a method.

`public` An access modifier used in the declaration of a method to indicate that the method is visible to any other class.

`return` Statement used to send a value from a method back to the calling statement.

`static` A keyword used in the declaration of a method to indicate that the method is a class method.

`void` A keyword used in the declaration of a method to indicate that the method will not return a value.

1. Use top-down development and procedural abstraction to write pseudocode for the following specification:

   The Pizza application allows the user to choose to display the instructions for making a pizza in either English or Spanish.

2. Explain the difference between method declaration and method body.

3. What type of keyword is used to change the access level of a method?

4. What is another word used for describing the access level of a method?

5. Explain the scope of each of the variables in the code below:

```
public class ScopeExample {

  public static void method1() {
    int var3;
    for (int var4 = 0; var4 < 2; var4++) {
      var3 += 1;
    }
  }

  public static void main(String[] args) {
    int var1;
    for (int var2 = 0; var2 < 5; var2++) {
      method1();
    }
  }
}
```

6. Write a method declaration for each of the following descriptions:
   a) A class method named getVowels that can be called by any other method, requires a String parameter, and returns an integer value.
   b) A class method named extractDigit that can be called by any other method, requires an integer parameter, and returns an integer value.
   c) A class method named insertString that can be called by any other method, requires a String parameter and an integer parameter, and returns a String parameter.

7. a) How does the compiler distinguish one method from another?
   b) Can two methods in the same class have the same name? Explain.

8. a) What is the return statement used for?
   b) How many values can a return statement send back to the calling statement?
   c) How is the declaration of a method returning a value different from the declaration of a method that does not return a value?

9. Find and explain the error in the code below:

```
public class MethodCallExample {

  public static int doSomething() {
    return(5);
  }
}

  public static void main(String[] args) {
    int num;
    doSomething();
    num = doSomething();
  }
}
```

10. a) What type of comments should be used for describing a method?
    b) What three things should the comments for a method describe?

**True/False**

11. Determine if each of the following are true or false. If false, explain why.
    a) Breaking a task down into methods is called procedural abstraction.
    b) A method call consists of the method declaration in an assignment statement.
    c) A void method must return a value.
    d) An access modifier declares the return type of a method.
    e) The keyword static declares a method is a class method.
    f) Method parameters are enclosed by braces ({}).
    g) Local variables can be used by any method in a class.
    h) The value of an argument passed to a method can be changed in an assignment statement in the method.
    i) Method overloading means that an application contains more than 10 methods.
    j) The return statement is used to send a value back to the calling statement.
    k) The precondition of a method states the data types of the method's parameters.
    l) The postcondition of a method describes the way the method accomplishes its task.

## Exercise 1 ——————————————————————————— House

Create a House application that calls methods addRoof(), addBase(), and addWalk() to display the following:

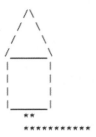

## Exercise 2 ——————————————————————— MetricConversion

The following formulas can be used to convert English units of measurements to metric units:

$$inches * 2.54 = centimeters$$

$$feet * 30 = centimeters$$

$$yards * 0.91 = meters$$

$$miles * 1.6 = kilometers$$

Create a MetricConversion application that displays a menu of conversion choices and then prompts the user to choose a conversion. Conversion choices should include inches to centimeters, feet to centimeters, yards to meters, miles to kilometers, and vice versa. The application should include separate methods for doing each of the conversions. Application output should look similar to:

```
Enter a number: 10

Convert:
1. Inches to Centimeters    5. Centimeters to Inches
2. Feet to Centimeters      6. Centimeters to Feet
3. Yards to Meters          7. Meters to Yards
4. Miles to Kilometers      8. Kilometers to Miles

Enter your choice: 1

10 inches equals 25.4 centimeters.
```

## Exercise 3  ——————————————————————— PrimeNumber

Modify the PrimeNumber application created in Chapter 5 Exercise 1 to include a method named isPrime(). The isPrime() method should require one parameter and return a Boolean value.

# Exercise 4 —————————————————————— IsoTriangle

Create an IsoTriangle application that prompts the user for the size of an isosceles triangle and then displays the triangle with that many lines. The IsoTriangle application code should include:

- the drawBar() method from the chapter.

- An addSpaces() method which "prints" spaces.

Application output should look similar to:

```
Enter the size: 4
   *
  ***
 *****
*******
```

# Exercise 5 —————————————————————— AddCoins

Create an AddCoins application that prompts the user for the number of pennies, nickels, dimes, and quarters, and then displays their total dollar amount. The AddCoins application should include a getDollarAmount() method that has four int parameters corresponding to the number of pennies, nickels, dimes, and quarters, and returns a String that corresponds to the dollar value of the coins. Note that the String returned should include the currency sign ($). Application output should look similar to:

```
Enter your total coins:

Quarters: 3
Dimes: 2
Nickels: 1
Pennies: 8

Total: $1.08
```

# Exercise 6 —————————————————————— PythagoreanTriple

Create a PythagoreanTriple application that displays all pythagorean triples with values of A and B less than 100. A pythagorean triple is a set of three integers that make the equation $a^2 + b^2 = c^2$ true. The application should include a PerfectSquare() method that uses the solution from the PerfectSquare review in Chapter 4. (*Hint*: You will need to generate all possible combinations of A and B and display just those that work.)

# Exercise 7 ————————————————————————PerfectIntegers

Create a PerfectIntegers application that displays all perfect integers up to 100. A perfect integer is a number which is equal to the sum of all its factors except itself. For example, 6 is a perfect number because 1 + 2 + 3 = 6. The application should include a `boolean` method isPerfect().

# Exercise 8 ————————————————————————————HiLo

a) In the Hi-Lo game, the player begins with a score of 1000. The player is prompted for the number of points to risk and a second prompt asks the player to choose either High or Low. The player's choice of either High or Low is compared to random number between 1 and 13, inclusive. If the number is between 1 and 6 inclusive, then it is considered "low". A number between 8 and 13 inclusive is "high". The number 7 is neither high nor low, and the player loses the points at risk. If the player had guessed correctly, the points at risk are doubled and added to the total points. For a wrong choice, the player loses the points at risk. Create a HiLo application based on this specification. Application output should look similar to:

```
High Low Game

Numbers 1 through 6 are low.
Numbers 7 through 13 are high.
You have 1000 points.

Enter points to risk: 500

Predict (1=High, 0=Low): 0
Number is 8
You lose.
Play again? y

You have 500 points.
```

b) Modify the application to allow the player to continue until there are 0 points left. At the end of the game, display the number of guesses the user took before running out of points.

# Exercise 9 ——————————————————————————————— Nim

The game of Nim starts with a random number of stones between 15 and 30. Two players alternate turns and on each turn may take either 1, 2, or 3 stones from the pile. The player forced to take the last stone loses. Create a Nim application that allows the user to play against the computer. In this version of the game, the application generates the number of stones to begin with, the number of stones the computer takes, and the user goes first. The Nim application code should:

- prevent the user and the computer from taking an illegal number of stones. For example, neither should be allowed to take three stones when there are only 1 or 2 left.

- include an isValidEntry() method to check user input.

- include a drawStones() method that generates a random number from 1 to 3 for the number of stones the computer draws.

- include separate methods to handle the user's turn and the computer's turn.

Application output should look similar to that shown on the next page:

```
There are 22 stones. How many would you like? 3
There are 19 stones. The computer takes 3 stones.
There are 16 stones. How many would you like? 3
There are 13 stones. The computer takes 1 stones.
There are 12 stones. How many would you like? 3
There are 9 stones. The computer takes 1 stones.
There are 8 stones. How many would you like? 3
There are 5 stones. The computer takes 3 stones.
There are 2 stones. How many would you like? 2
The computer beats the player!
```

# Exercise 10 ◈ ——————————————————————————— GuessingGame

The GuessingGame application modified in Chapter 5 Exercise 8 should include a separate method for displaying a hint to the user. Modify the GuessingGame application as follows:

a) Modify the algorithm to include a call to a method named giveHint(), which displays a hint, but does not return a value.

b) Modify the GuessingGame code. Application output should look similar to:

```
Enter a number between 1 and 20: 15
Hint: try a lower number
Enter a number between 1 and 20: 12
Hint: try a lower number
Enter a number between 1 and 20: 8
Hint: try a lower number
Enter a number between 1 and 20: 6
Hint: try a lower number
Enter a number between 1 and 20: 4
You won!
```

# Chapter 7
# Classes and Object-Oriented Development

### Key Concepts

Designing and implementing a class
Applying functional decomposition
Accessor, modifier, and helper methods
Writing constructors
Applying encapsulation
The Object class
Identifying reusable code

### Case Study

Rock Paper Scissors 2 game

## What is an Object?

*state*
*behavior*

In object-oriented programming, an *object* stores data and can perform actions and provide communication. The *state* of an object refers to the data it stores. The *behavior* of an object is defined by the action and communication it provides.

Objects often model, or simulate, real-world things. For example, consider a circle shape. To create a Circle object modeled after the circle shape, we analyze the state and behavior of the shape. A circle is defined by its radius, so this will make up the state of the object. A circle shape doesn't do much in the way of actions, but a Circle object could change its radius, calculate its area, and tell us what its radius is. These actions will make up the behavior of a Circle object.

**TIP** A class is an abstract data type, which was discussed in Chapter 3.

An object is an *instance* of a class. A *class* is a data type that defines variables for the state of an object and methods for an object's behavior. Good programming style dictates that the state of an object can only be changed through its behavior. For example, to change the radius of a Circle object, a method for changing the radius variable must be called. Protecting an object's data is called *encapsulation*. Encapsulation is also called *information hiding* because the object hides certain data from code outside the class. For example, a Circle object declared in client code can be visualized as:

*encapsulation*
*information hiding*

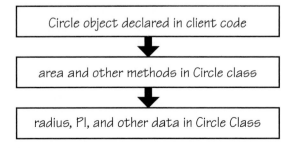

Circle object declared in client code

↓

area and other methods in Circle class

↓

radius, PI, and other data in Circle Class

*Client code* refers to an application that uses one or more classes. The client can access the methods of the class, but cannot directly access the data defined in the class. This reinforces that the state of an object can only be changed through its behavior.

**TIP** In Java, the controlling class is the client code.

TestCircle is client code. It uses the Circle class:

```
public class TestCircle {

    public static void main(String[] args) {
        Circle spot = new Circle();

        spot.setRadius(5);

        System.out.println("Circle radius:" + spot.getRadius());
        System.out.println("Circle area:  " + spot.area());
    }
}
```

In the TestCircle application, a Circle object named `spot` is instantiated. The object `spot` uses behavior setRadius() to change the state of the object, making the radius of the circle 5. Two other behaviors are implemented to produce the application output:

```
Circle radius: 5.0
Circle area: 78.5
```

## Designing and Writing a Class

> ### *Functional Decomposition*
>
> The process of creating clearly defined functions, or behavior, for a class is sometimes called *functional decomposition*. A well-written class has been functionally decomposed into a set of methods that cannot be simplified further.

Designing a class requires choosing the data the object will store and determining the actions and communication the object will provide. The design should include variable names and method names along with a description of the method and any required parameters. For example, the Circle class design appears similar to:

Circle

variables: radius, PI

methods:
    setRadius – changes the radius. Requires one
                parameter for radius.
    getRadius – returns the circle radius.
    area – returns the area of the circle based on
            the current radius.

*class declaration, body*

*constructor*

*member*

A class is written in a separate file and consists of a declaration and a body. The *class declaration* includes the access level, the keyword `class`, and the class name. The *class body* contains variables, constructors, and methods. *Constructors* are used to initialize variables in a class. Variables and methods are called the *members* of a class. A class takes the form:

```
<access_level> class <name> {
    <variables>
    <constructors>
    <methods>
}
```

The Circle class code is based on the design on the previous page:

```
/**
 * Circle class.
 */
public class Circle {
    private static final double PI = 3.14;
    private double radius;

    /**
     * constructor
     * pre: none
     * post: A Circle object created. Radius initialized to 1.
     */
    public Circle() {
        radius = 1;           //default radius
    }


    /**
     * Changes the radius of the circle.
     * pre: none
     * post: Radius has been changed.
     */
    public void setRadius(double newRadius) {
        radius = newRadius;
    }


    /**
     * Calculates the area of the circle.
     * pre: none
     * post: The area of the circle has been returned.
     */
    public double area() {
        double circleArea;

        circleArea = PI * radius * radius;
        return(circleArea);
    }


    /**
     * Returns the radius of the circle.
     * pre: none
     * post: The radius of the circle has been returned.
     */
    public double getRadius() {
        return(radius);
    }
}
```

The Circle class has access level `public` which means that it is visible to other classes and can be used to instantiate objects in those classes. The class name is `Circle`. A class name should be a noun, begin with an uppercase letter, and each word within the name should also begin with an uppercase letter. Class names may not contain spaces.

The body of a class starts with an opening brace (`{`) and ends with a closing brace (`}`). Member variables are declared after the opening brace, and outside of any methods. Variable declarations in the body of a class have a local scope that extends from the opening brace of the class body to the closing. Note that the Circle class also has a member variable that is a constant.

**TIP** Access modifiers and visibility were introduced in Chapter 6.

The visibility of a member variable is controlled with an access modifier. Declaring a variable as `private` makes it visible to the class, but not to client code. This encapsulates the data and provides information hiding. For example, the Circle class contains a `private` variable `radius` that can be used by any of the methods of the class, but cannot be directly accessed by statements in the client code where the Circle object was created.

A constructor is automatically called when an object is created. The constructor is where variables are initialized. Variables that are not initialized may contain data that could generate a run-time error when a method of the class is executed.

*accessor method*

*modifier method*

The methods in a class are accessor methods, modifier methods, or helper methods. *Accessor methods* are called to determine the value of a variable. For example, in the Circle class, getRadius() is an accessor method. It returns the value of the variable `radius`. A *modifier method* is called to change the value of a variable. In the Circle class, setRadius() is a modifier method. It assigns a value passed in a parameter to the variable `radius`. Accessor and modifier methods have access level `public` so that they may be called from the class where the Circle object was created.

*helper method*

*Helper methods* are called from within a class by other methods. They are used to help complete a task and have access level `private`.

An application that includes Circle objects can include statements that call the `public` methods, but statements that refer to the `private` members will generate a compiler error.

## Review: Circle – part 1 of 4

Modify the Circle class to include a member method named `circumference`. The circumference() method should return the circumference of the circle (2πr). Test the class with the following client code:

```
public static void main(String[] args) {
    Circle spot = new Circle();

    spot.setRadius(3);
    System.out.println("Circle radius: " + spot.getRadius());
    System.out.println("Circle circumference: " + spot.circumference());
}
```

## Review: Coin – part 1 of 2

Create a Coin class that includes a variable `faceUp` that stores either a 0 for heads up or 1 for tails up, an accessor method named showFace() that returns a 0 if the coin is heads up or a 1 if the coin is tails up, and a modifier method named flipCoin() that assigns a random integer between 0 and 1, inclusive, to the variable `faceUp`. Test the class with the following client code:

```
public static void main(String[] args) {
    Coin nickel = new Coin();

    nickel.flipCoin()
    if (nickel.flipCoin() == 0) {
        System.out.println("Heads up!");
    } else {
        System.out.println("Tails up!");
    }
}
```

# Writing Constructors

The constructor of a class is automatically executed when an object is instantiated. Once an object is instantiated, the method members of the class can be called in any order. Unexpected results may occur if an accessor method is called before a member variable has been set to a valid value. To prevent this, variables should be initialized in the constructor.

A constructor takes the form:

```
public <class name>(<parameters>) {
    <statements>
}
```

The constructor of a class does not have a return type and always has the same name as the class. When a constructor contains parameters, they are separated by commas.

*overloading constructors*

Constructors can be overloaded to provide more options for instantiating an object. For example, if the radius of the circle object is known when the Circle object is created, it would be more efficient to assign the value to radius when the object is created:

```
Circle spot = new Circle(5);
```

A constructor can be added to the Circle class to handle creating an object with a parameter that contains the circle radius:

```
/**
 * Circle class.
 */
public class Circle {
    private static final double PI = 3.14;
    private double radius;


    /**
     * constructor
     * pre: none
     * post: A Circle object created. Radius initialized to 1.
     */
    public Circle() {
        radius = 1;          //default radius
    }


    /**
     * constructor
     * pre: none
     * post: A Circle object created with radius r.
     */
    public Circle(double r) {
        radius = r;
    }
```

*…rest of Circle class*

When a class contains more than one constructor, the compiler uses the number and types of parameters to determine which constructor to execute.

## Review: Circle – part 2 of 4

Modify the Circle class to include an overloaded constructor that accepts the radius of the Circle object, as shown in the previous section.

## Review: Rectangle – part 1 of 5

Design and then create a Rectangle class that has overloaded constructors. The first constructor requires no parameters. The second has two parameters, one for length and a second for width. Member variables store the length and width of the rectangle, and member methods assign and retrieve the length and width and return the area and perimeter of the rectangle. Test the class by writing appropriate client code.

## Instance and Class Members

*instance variable*
*class variable*

Each object, or instance, of a class has its own copy of variables called *instance variables*. For example, the Circle class contains the instance variable radius. A class may also contain class variables. A *class variable* is declared with the keyword static and only one copy is maintained for all objects to refer to. For example, the Circle class contains the class variable PI. Note that because PI is a constant, it also includes the keyword final:

```
/**
 * Circle class.
 */
public class Circle {
    private static final double PI = 3.14;  //class constant
    private double radius;                   //instance variable
```

...*rest of Circle class*

In the statements below, two Circle objects are instantiated. Each instance has its own copy of the instance variable radius, but both objects refer to the same copy of the class constant PI:

```
Circle spot1 = new Circle(2);    radius  2   PI ──▶ 3.14
Circle spot2 = new Circle(5);    radius  5   PI ╱
```

*instance methods*

*class methods*

Methods can be either instance methods or class methods. Accessor and modifier methods are *instance methods* because they change the state of an object. They must be called from an instance of a class. Chapter 6 introduced *class methods* that are declared with the keyword static. Class methods can be called from the class itself, rather than an object of the class, to perform a task. For example, consider the Circle class with the following class method added:

```
/**
 * Displays the formula for the area of a circle.
 * pre: none
 * post: The formula for area of a circle has been displayed.
 */
public static void displayAreaFormula() {
    System.out.println("The formula for the area of a
        circle is a=Pi*r*r");
}
```

The following client code calls the displayAreaFormula() class method:

```
public class TestCircle {

    public static void main(String[] args) {
        Circle spot = new Circle(5);

        System.out.println("Circle radius:" + spot.getRadius());
        System.out.println("Circle area:  " + spot.area());
        Circle.displayAreaFormula();
    }
}
```

**TIP** Class methods cannot be used to change the value of an instance variable.

The class method is called from the class itself (Circle) rather than an object of the class. The TestCircle application displays the following output:

```
Circle radius: 5.0
Circle area: 78.5
The formula for the area of a circle is a=Pi*r*r
```

To summarize the differences between instance and class members:

- Instance variables are created each time an object is declared.

- Class variables and constants are created once for the class and then objects of the class refer to this copy.

- Instance methods can only be called from an object of the class.

- Class methods can be called from the class itself.

## Review: Circle – part 3 of 4

Modify the Circle class to include a class method named displayAreaFormula, as shown in the previous section. Modify existing client code to test the new method.

## Review: Rectangle – part 2 of 5

Modify the Rectangle class to include a class method named displayAreaFormula. Modify existing client code to test the new method.

## The Object Class

*superclass*
*subclass*

The Object class is the *superclass* of all other classes. Classes, such as Circle and String, are *subclasses* of Object:

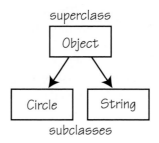

Subclasses *inherit*, or receive, the methods of its superclass. The Object class includes methods for comparing objects and representing an object as a string:

### Class Object (java.lang.Object)

### Method

```
equals(Object obj)
```

returns `true` if `obj` is equal to the object.

`toString()`     returns a String that represents the object.

> **TIP** If a subclass does not override the equals() and toString() methods, then the Object class methods are used.

A subclass typically contains its own version of the equals() and toString() superclass methods to better suit the object of the subclass. For example, two Circle objects are equal when they both have the same radius, and two String objects are equal when they consist of the same set of characters.

*override*  When a subclass redefines a superclass method, the subclass method is said to *override* the superclass method. The Circle class should contain an equals() method that compares the state of the object to another Circle object and a toString() method that returns a String describing the object:

---

### equals() vs. ==

Objects compared using the == operator are equal only if they refer to the same object. The == operator compares the references of the objects, not the data stored by the objects as the equals() methods does.

---

```
/**
 * Determines if the object is equal to another
 * Circle object.
 * pre: c is a Circle object.
 * post: true has been returned if the objects have
 * the same radii. false has been returned otherwise.
 */
public boolean equals(Object c) {
    Circle testObj = (Circle)c;

    if (testObj.getRadius() == radius) {
        return(true);
    } else {
        return(false);
    }
}


/**
 * Returns a String that represents the Circle object.
 * pre: none
 * post: A string representing the Circle object has
 * been returned.
 */
public String toString() {
    String circleString;

    circleString = "Circle has radius " + radius;
    return(circleString);
}
```

The equals() method requires an Object parameter. In the body of the method, the `obj` parameter must be cast as the appropriate type, in this case Circle, and then assigned to an object of the appropriate type. If an Object variable is cast with an incompatible class, then the exception
*ClassCastException*  ClassCastException will be generated. To convert an object to its superclass Object, no class casting is required.

The code below creates two Circle objects, compares them, and displays information about the objects. An object's toString() method is invoked when an object is passed to the println() method:

```java
public static void main(String[] args) {
    Circle spot1 = new Circle(3);
    Circle spot2 = new Circle(4);

    if (spot1.equals(spot2)) {
        System.out.println("Objects are equal.");
    } else {
        System.out.println("Objects are not equal.");
    }
    System.out.println(spot1);
    System.out.println(spot2);
}
```

**TIP** The concatenation operator + also invokes the toString() method of an object.

The code above displays the output:

```
Objects are not equal.
Circle has radius 3.0
Circle has radius 4.0
```

## Review: Circle – part 4 of 4

Modify the Circle class to override the equals() and toString() methods, as shown in the previous section. Modify existing client code to test the new methods.

## Review: Rectangle – part 3 of 5

Modify the Rectangle class to override the equals() and toString() methods. Two rectangles are equal when they both have the same length and width. Modify the existing client code to test the new method.

## Review: Coin – part 2 of 2

Modify the Coin class to override the toString() method so that it indicates whether the coin is face up or face down. For example, "The coin is face up." Modify existing client code to test the new method.

## Classes Using Classes

*has-a relationship*

A class may contain member variables that are class data types. Complex data can be easily represented in this way. A class that contains class member variables demonstrates a *has-a relationship*. The class "has a" class. For example, a class with a String member variable demonstrates a has-a relationship.

The Bank program specification is best implemented with two classes. One class (Account) has a member variable (Customer) for representing the customers that hold the accounts:

A bank maintains accounts where account holders can deposit money and withdraw money. The account holders are customers with a first and last name and complete address.

A model of Bank includes an Account object that stores customer data and a current balance. Account methods should return a balance, perform deposits, and perform withdrawals. If an Account object is passed to the println() method, customer data and their balance should be displayed.

The designs for the Bank classes are:

Account

variables: balance, Customer cust

methods:
getBalance – returns the current balance.
deposit – increases the balance. Requires parameter for amount.
withdrawal – decreases the balance. Requires parameter for amount. If balance is less than withdrawal, then balance left unchanged.
toString – returns a string with customer information and current balance.


Customer

variables: firstName, lastName, street, city, state, zip

methods:
toString() – returns a string with customer information.


The Bank client code uses the class designs and looks similar to:

```
import java.util.Scanner;
import java.text.NumberFormat;

public class Bank {

  public static void main(String[] args) {
    Account munozAccount = new Account(250, "Maria", "Munoz", "110 Glades Road",
                                  "Mytown", "FL", "33445");
    Scanner input = new Scanner(System.in);
    double data;
    NumberFormat money = NumberFormat.getCurrencyInstance();

    System.out.println(munozAccount);

    System.out.print("Enter deposit amount: ");
    data = input.nextDouble();
    munozAccount.deposit(data);
    System.out.println("Balance is: " + money.format(munozAccount.getBalance()));

    System.out.print("Enter withdrawal amount: ");
    data = input.nextDouble();
    munozAccount.withdrawal(data);
    System.out.println("Balance is: " + money.format(munozAccount.getBalance()));
  }
}
```

The Account class is implemented below:

```java
import java.text.NumberFormat;

public class Account {
  private double balance;
  private Customer cust;


  /**
   * constructor
   * pre: none
   * post: An account created. Balance and
   * customer data initialized with parameters.
   */
  public Account(double bal, String fName, String lName,
                 String str, String city, String st, String zip) {
    balance = bal;
    cust = new Customer(fName, lName, str, city, st, zip);
  }


  /**
   * Returns the current balance.
   * pre: none
   * post: The account balance has been returned.
   */
  public double getBalance() {
    return(balance);
  }


  /**
   * A deposit is made to the account.
   * pre: none
   * post: The balance has been increased by the amount of the deposit.
   */
  public void deposit(double amt) {
    balance += amt;
  }


  /**
   * A withdrawal is made from the account if there is enough money.
   * pre: none
   * post: The balance has been decreased by the amount withdrawn.
   */
  public void withdrawal(double amt) {
    if (amt <= balance) {
      balance -= amt;
    } else {
      System.out.println("Not enough money in account.");
    }
  }
```

**this**

The keyword this can be used to distinguish between a parameter and a member variable. For example, it can be convenient to use the same name for both a method parameter and a member variable in a class, in which case, the member variable is preceded by this. If in the Account class, the constructor used double balance as a parameter, then the statement in the body must be written as: this.balance = balance;

```
/**
 * Returns a String that represents the Account object.
 * pre: none
 * post: A string representing the Account object has
 * been returned.
 */
public String toString() {
  String accountString;
  NumberFormat money = NumberFormat.getCurrencyInstance();

  accountString = cust.toString();
  accountString += "Current balance is " + money.format(balance);
  return(accountString);
}
}
```

The Customer class is implemented below:

```
public class Customer {
    private String firstName, lastName, street, city,
                   state, zip;


    /**
     * constructor
     * pre: none
     * post: A Customer object has been created.
     * Customer data has been initialized with parameters.
     */
    public Customer(String fName, String lName, String str,
                    String c, String s, String z) {
        firstName = fName;
        lastName = lName;
        street = str;
        city = c;
        state = s;
        zip = z;
    }


    /**
     * Returns a String that represents the Customer object.
     * pre: none
     * post: A string representing the Account object has
     * been returned.
     */
    public String toString() {
        String custString;

        custString = firstName + " " + lastName + "\n";
        custString += street + "\n";
        custString += city + ", " + state + "  " + zip + "\n";
        return(custString);
    }
}
```

Running the Bank application produces output similar to:

```
Maria Munoz
110 Glades Road
Mytown, FL  33445
Current balance is $250.00
Enter deposit amount: 500
Balance is: $750.00
Enter withdrawal amount: 800
Not enough money in account.
Balance is: $750.00
```

## Review: Bank

Modify the Customer class to include changeStreet(), changeCity(), changeState(), and changeZip() methods. Modify the Account class to include a changeAddress() method that has street, city, state, and zip parameters. Modify the Bank application to test the changeAddress() method.

## Object-Oriented Development

Object-oriented programming requires that the solution to a task be implemented as a system of objects. In this system, objects communicate with other objects to provide a solution to the task. This approach to creating software is called *object-oriented development*.

In object-oriented development, the programmer reads the specification and selects objects to model the specification. Some of these objects will require new classes designed and written by the programmer. Other objects can be created from existing classes previously written by the programmer or by other programmers. For example, the JRE contains *reusability* numerous classes for use in a Java application. *Reusability* is an important feature of object-oriented programming because it reduces development time and decreases the likelihood of bugs.

To demonstrate object-oriented development, consider the following Carnival program specification:

A carnival has many games that are similar in nature. These games allow the player three tries, and the player who is successful all three times is a winner. For example, the Balloon Dart Toss game allows the player to throw three darts at a wall of balloons. If each dart pops a balloon, then the player is a winner. The Ring Toss and Break A Plate games work similarly.

Every player gets a prize. There are winning prizes and consolation prizes. The Balloon Dart Toss prizes are tiger plush and sticker. The Ring Toss prizes are bear key chain and pencil, and the Break A Plate prizes are pig plush and plastic dinosaur. The Balloon Dart Toss and Ring Toss games are $2 to play. The Break A Plate game costs $1.50.

The player comes to the carnival with some spending money and can play games until the money runs out. The player also holds onto all the prizes won.

The Carnival application should produce output similar to the following when Shonda has $5 spending money and Luis has $3:

```
Shonda goes to Balloon Dart Toss. prize won: tiger plush
Luis goes to Ring Toss. prize won: bear keychain
Shonda goes to Ring Toss. prize won: pencil
Luis goes to Break a Plate. Sorry, not enough money to play.
Shonda won: pencil, tiger plush
Luis won: bear keychain
```

In the first step of object-oriented development, objects are selected to model the specification. In this case, the carnival can be modeled with game booth objects and player objects. A game booth object should store data about the cost of playing the game, the winning prize, and the consolation prize. Game booth methods should start the game and give the cost to play. A player object should store data about the spending money of the player and the prizes won. Player methods should play the game and show the list of prizes won.

*designing objects*      The designs for the Carnival classes are:

```
GameBooth

variables: cost, firstPrize, consolationPrize

methods:
    start – plays the game and returns the prize won.
    getCost – returns the cost of playing the game.


Player

variables: spendingMoney, prizesWon

methods:
    play – determines if player has enough money to
            play the game, decreases money by cost of
            game,  and adds prize won to prizes list.
    showPrizes – returns the prize list.
```

The Carnival client code uses the class designs and looks similar to:

```
GameBooth balloonDartToss = new GameBooth(2,"tiger plush", "sticker");
GameBooth ringToss = new GameBooth(2,"bear keychain", "pencil");
GameBooth breakAPlate = new GameBooth(1.5, "pig plush", "plastic dinosaur");
Player shonda = new Player(5);      //$5 spending money
Player luis = new Player(3);        //$3 spending money

System.out.print("Shonda goes to Balloon Dart Toss. ");
System.out.println(shonda.play(balloonDartToss));

System.out.print("Luis goes to Ring Toss. ");
System.out.println(luis.play(ringToss));

System.out.print("Shonda goes to Ring Toss. ");
System.out.println(shonda.play(ringToss));

System.out.print("Luis goes to Break A Plate. ");
System.out.println(luis.play(breakAPlate));

System.out.println("Shonda won: " + shonda.showPrizes());
System.out.println("Luis won: " + luis.showPrizes());
```

*modular*

Note how simple the application appears. All the work is being done by the objects, rather than with individual statements in the main() method. The Carnival application, like other object-oriented applications, is *modular*. It uses components that are separately written and maintained.

*message*

Another aspect of object-oriented development is that objects send information to other objects to perform a task. When information is passed from one object to another, the object is said to be passing a *message*. For example, in the pseudocode above, the Player objects are passed a message that includes the cost of game and the prize the player won.

***implementing the classes***

The GameBooth class is implemented below. Note that in the start() method, the player's throws are simulated with random numbers. The player is said to win if three ones are generated:

```
import java.util.Math;

public class GameBooth {
    private double cost;
    private String firstPrize, consolationPrize;


    /**
     * constructor
     * pre: none
     * post: A GameBooth object created.
     * The cost and prizes are set.
     */
    public GameBooth(double charge, String p1, String p2) {
        cost = charge;
        firstPrize = p1;
        consolationPrize = p2;
    }
```

```
/**
 * Game is played and prize awarded.
 * pre: none
 * post: Player had three tries. Player successful all
 * three times received the first prize. A consolation
 * prize has been awarded otherwise.
 */
public String start() {
    int toss;
    int successes = 0;

    /* play game */
    for (int i = 0; i < 3; i++) {   //player gets three tries
        toss = (int)(Math.random() + 0.5);   //0 or 1
        if (toss == 1) {
            successes += 1;          //1 is a successful toss
        }
    }

    /* award prize */
    if (successes == 3) {
        return(firstPrize);
    } else {
        return(consolationPrize);
    }
}


/**
 * Returns the cost to play the game.
 * pre: none
 * post: Cost of the game has been returned.
 */
public double getCost() {
    return(cost);
}
}
```

**TIP** Both casting and rounding are used to produce an integer that is either a 0 or a 1.

The Player class is implemented below:

```
public class Player {
    private double spendingMoney;
    private String prizesWon;


    /**
     * constructor
     * pre: none
     * post: A Player object created. Spending money given to
     * player. The prizes won set to none.
     */
    public Player(double money) {
        spendingMoney = money;
        prizesWon = "";
    }
```

*Chapter 7 Classes and Object-Oriented Development*

```
/**
 * Player pays for and then plays a game.
 * pre: none
 * post: Player's spending money decreased by cost of game.
 * The player has a new prize added to existing prizes.
 */
public String play(GameBooth game) {
    String newPrize;

    if (game.getCost() > spendingMoney) {
        return("Sorry, not enough money to play.");
    } else {
        spendingMoney -= game.getCost();        //pay for game
        newPrize = game.start();                //play game
        prizesWon = newPrize + ", " + prizesWon;
        return("prize won: " + newPrize);
    }
}


/**
 * Returns the list of prizes won.
 * pre: none
 * post: The list of prizes has been returned.
 */
public String showPrizes() {
    return(prizesWon);
}
}
```

Running the Carnival application produces output similar to:

```
Shonda goes to Balloon Dart Toss. prize won: sticker
Luis goes to Ring Toss. prize won: pencil
Shonda goes to Ring Toss. prize won: pencil
Luis goes to Break A Plate. Sorry, not enough money to play.
Shonda won: pencil, sticker,
Luis won: pencil,
```

Although the classes may look long, once written they are available for many different implementations of a Carnival or another application that involves games.

## Review: Carnival

Modify the Player class to override the toString() method. When a Player object is passed to the println() method, a message should display how much money the player has left and the prizes won so far.

Modify the GameBooth class to keep track of the number of prizes awarded. There should be separate totals for the first prizes awarded and the consolation prizes awarded. Add a method to the GameBooth class named prizesAwarded() that displays the number of first prizes and the number of consolation prizes given away.

Modify the Carnival client code to pass the Player objects to println() in the last two statements, and in separate statements, display how many prizes were given away by each booth.

In this case study, a Rock Paper Scissors game will be created using object-oriented development. Rock Paper Scissors is a popular game played between two individuals for decision making or just for competitive fun. The rules of the game are Rock dulls Scissors (Rock wins), Scissors cuts Paper (Scissors wins), and Paper covers Rock (Paper wins). The two players make a "throw" at the same time. The hand signals thrown by the players are then compared to the rules of the game to determine the winner. In the computerized version, the user plays against the computer.

**TIP** An RPS application was also developed for the Chapter 4 Case Study.

## RPS2 Specification

The computerized version of the Rock Paper Scissors game is played by one user that "throws" either rock, paper, or scissors. The game then randomly selects either rock, paper, or scissors for the computer's "throw" and the winner is determined by comparing the two choices. Rock wins over scissors, scissors wins over paper, and rock wins over scissors. The player can initially choose to play multiple rounds. At the end of the rounds, an overall winner is declared.

The RPS2 interface should show the result of each round and the overall winner. The RPS2 output sketch:

```
How many rounds? 3
Enter your throw (1=Rock, 2=Paper, 3=Scissors): 3
You throw SCISSORS.
Computer throws PAPER.
You win!
Enter your throw (1=Rock, 2=Paper, 3=Scissors): 3
You throw SCISSORS.
Computer throws ROCK.
Computer wins!
Enter your throw (1=Rock, 2=Paper, 3=Scissors): 3
You throw PAPER.
Computer throws ROCK.
You win!
Computer wins 1. You win 2.
You win!
```

The RPS2 algorithm:

1. Prompt the player for the number of rounds.

2. For each round:

> Prompt for the player's throw.
> Generate the computer's throw.
> Announce the winner of the round.

3. Announce an overall winner.

## RPS2 Code Design

The RPS2 application can be modeled with a player object and a game object. The player object should store the player's throw (either rock, paper, or scissors) and contain methods that make and return the player's throw. The game object should store the computer's throw, the number of computer wins, and the number of player wins and contain methods that make and return the computer's throw, determine the winner of each round, and determine an overall winner.

The designs for the RPS2 classes are:

RPSPlayer

variables: playerName, playerThrow

methods:
    makeThrow – prompts player for throw.
    getThrow – returns the player's throw.


RPSGame

variable: compThrow, playerWins, playerThrow

methods:
    makeCompThrow – generates the computer's throw.
    getCompThrow – returns the computer's throw.
    announceWinner – displays a message indicating the throws
                       and the winner. Requires parameters for
                       player throw and player name.
    bigWinner – determine overall winner.


Based on the algorithm and the class designs, the RPS2 code design will include two objects and a loop. The pseudocode for the RPS2 client code follows:

```
declare game object
declare player object

prompt player for number of rounds
for (i = 0; i < rounds; i++) {
    prompt player for throw
    player.makeThrow(playerThrow);
    gameObject.makeThrow();
    gameObject.announceWinner(playerObject.getThrow);
}
gameObject.bigWinner
```

## RPS2 Implementation

The RPS2 implementation involves creating three files. One file contains the client code and the other two files are the classes.

The RPS2Player class is implemented below:

```
/**
 * models the player in a game of RPS
 */
public class RPSPlayer {
    private int playerThrow;    //ROCK=1, PAPER=2, SCISSORS=3

    /**
     * constructor
     * pre: none
     * post: RPSPlayer object created. The player is given a
     * default throw.
     */
    public RPSPlayer() {
        playerThrow = 1;    //default throw
    }


    /**
     * Sets the player's throw.
     * pre: newThrow is the integer 1, 2, or 3.
     * post: Player's throw has been made.
     */
    public void makeThrow(int newThrow){
        playerThrow = newThrow;
    }


    /**
     * Returns the player's throw.
     * pre: none
     * post: Player's throw has been returned.
     */
    public int getThrow() {
        return(playerThrow);
    }

}
```

The RPSGame class is implemented below:

```java
/**
 * Models a game of RPS
 */

import java.util.Math;

public class RPSGame {
    public static final int ROCK = 1, PAPER = 2, SCISSORS = 3;
    private int compThrow;
    private int playerWins = 0, computerWins = 0;

    /**
     * constructor
     * pre: none
     * post: RPSGame object created. Computer throw generated.
     */
    public RPSGame() {
        compThrow = (int)(3 * Math.random() + 1);        //1, 2, or 3
        playerWins = 0;
        computerWins = 0;
    }


    /**
     * Computer's throw is generated (ROCK, PAPER, or SCISSORS)
     * pre: none
     * post: Computer's throw has been made.
     */
    public void makeCompThrow(){
        compThrow = (int)(3 * Math.random() + 1);        //1, 2, or 3
    }


    /**
     * Returns the computer's throw.
     * pre: none
     * post: Computer's throw has been returned.
     */
    public int getCompThrow() {
        return(compThrow);
    }


    /**
     * Determines the winner of the round.
     * pre: playerThrow is the integer 1, 2, or 3.
     * post: Displays a message indicating throws. Compares player's
     * throw to computer's throw and displays a message indicating
     * the winner.
     */
    public void announceWinner(int playerThrow) {

        /* Inform player of throws */
        System.out.print("You throw ");
        switch (playerThrow) {
            case ROCK: System.out.println("ROCK."); break;
            case PAPER: System.out.println("PAPER."); break;
            case SCISSORS: System.out.println("SCISSORS."); break;
        }
```

```java
            System.out.print("Computer throws ");
            switch (compThrow) {
                case ROCK: System.out.println("ROCK."); break;
                case PAPER: System.out.println("PAPER."); break;
                case SCISSORS: System.out.println("SCISSORS."); break;
            }

            /* Determine and annouce winner */
            if (playerThrow == ROCK && compThrow == ROCK) {
                System.out.println("It's a draw!");
            } else if (playerThrow == ROCK && compThrow == PAPER) {
                System.out.println("Computer wins!");
                computerWins += 1;
            } else if (playerThrow == ROCK && compThrow == SCISSORS) {
                System.out.println("You win!");
                playerWins += 1;
            }

            if (playerThrow == PAPER && compThrow == ROCK) {
                System.out.println("You win!");
                playerWins += 1;
            } else if (playerThrow == PAPER && compThrow == PAPER) {
                System.out.println("It's a draw!");
            } else if (playerThrow == PAPER && compThrow == SCISSORS) {
                System.out.println("Computer wins!");
                computerWins +=1;
            }

            if (playerThrow == SCISSORS && compThrow == ROCK) {
                System.out.println("Computer wins!");
                computerWins += 1;
            } else if (playerThrow == SCISSORS && compThrow == PAPER) {
                System.out.println("You win!");
                playerWins += 1;
            } else if (playerThrow == SCISSORS && compThrow == SCISSORS) {
                System.out.println("It's a draw!");
            }
        }


    /**
     * Displays the overall winner.
     * pre: none
     * post: Computer and player wins compared and
     * an overall winner announced.
     */
    public void bigWinner() {
        if (computerWins > playerWins){
            System.out.println("Computer wins!");
        } else if (playerWins > computerWins){
            System.out.println("You win!");
        } else {
            System.out.println("It's a draw!");
        }
    }

}
```

The RPS2 client code follows:

```
/*
 * RPS2.java
 */

import java.util.Scanner;

/**
 * Computer plays Rock Paper Scissors against one player.
 */
public class RPS2 {

  public static void main(String[] args) {
      RPSGame rps = new RPSGame();
      RPSPlayer rpsOpponent = new RPSPlayer();
      int rounds;
      int playerThrow;
      Scanner input = new Scanner(System.in);

      /* play RPS */
      System.out.print("How many rounds? ");
      rounds = input.nextInt();
      for (int i = 0; i < rounds; i++) {
          System.out.print("Enter your throw (ROCK=1,
              PAPER=2, SCISSORS=3): ");
          playerThrow = input.nextInt();
          rpsOpponent.makeThrow(playerThrow);

          rps.makeCompThrow();
          rps.announceWinner(rpsOpponent.getThrow());
      }
      rps.bigWinner();
  }
}
```

Note how concise the client code is. The RPS2 application uses objects to perform all the work.

Although the classes may look long, once written they are available for many different implementations of the RPS game. Client code can be written to use the classes in many different ways. For example, multiple players and games can be instantiated for tournaments.

### RPS2 Testing and Debugging

When a new class is written, client code should be written to test the class. For the RPSGame class, client code should test all the possible throw combinations, similar to the testing discussed in the Chapter 4 Case Study.

Modify the RPSPlayer class to include a `playerName` variable and methods named `assignName` and `getName`. The assignName() method has a String parameter `name` that is assigned to `playerName`. The getName() method returns the value of `playerName`. Modify the announceWinner() and bigWinner() methods in the RPSGame class to include a String parameter `name` that is the player's name. Change the messages displayed in the announceWinner() and bigWinner() methods to include the player's name rather than the word "You". Modifying the two classes should produce output similar to the sketch below:

```
Enter your name: Lucy
How many rounds? 3

Enter your throw (1=Rock, 2=Paper, 3=Scissors): 3
Lucy throws SCISSORS.
Computer throws PAPER.
Lucy wins!

Enter your throw (1=Rock, 2=Paper, 3=Scissors): 3
Lucy throws SCISSORS.
Computer throws ROCK.
Computer wins!

Enter your throw (1=Rock, 2=Paper, 3=Scissors): 3
Lucy throws PAPER.
Computer throws ROCK.
Lucy wins!

Computer wins 1. Lucy wins 2.
Lucy is the winner!
```

Modify the RPS2 client code to perform error checking on the player's input. Have the client code verify that the user has entered a 1, 2, or 3 for a throw before passing the entered value to the makeThrow() method.

# Chapter Summary

This chapter introduced writing and designing classes. Classes are the data types of objects. An object has a state (data) and behavior (actions and communication in the form of methods). An important aspect of object-oriented programming is encapsulation, also called information hiding. In OOP, classes are written to encasulate, or hide, data from outside code. Client code is code that uses one or more classes.

A class includes a class declaration, variables, constructors, and methods. The class declaration includes the access level, the keyword `class`, and a name. Variables and methods are the members of a class. Variables are the data members and should be declared `private`. Accessor and modifier methods are declared `public`, while helper methods are declared `private`. Constructors are used to initialize variables and can be overloaded so that objects can be declared with vaying numbers of parameters.

The variables and methods of a class are either instance or class members. Instance members are copied for each instance of a class. Only one copy of a class member exists for the class. Every object of a class refers to the same class member. The keyword `static` is used for a class member declaration. Class methods can be called from the class itself. An object of the class can call either instance or class members.

Every class is a subclass of the Object class. The Object class could also be called the superclass of all other classes. The equals() and toString() methods in the Object class are inherited by all other classes. In most cases, these methods should be redefined in subclasses.

An object that contains an object is said to demonstrate a has-a relationship. Any class that contains a String data member demonstrates a has-a relationship.

Object-oriented development requires the solution to a task be implemented as a system of objects. In this system, objects pass messages back and forth to provide a solution to the task.

This chapter discussed several important aspects of the object-oriented paradigm, including encapsulation, reusability, and modularity.

The code convention introduced in this chapter is:

- Class names should be a noun, begin with an uppercase letter, and each word within the name should also begin with an uppercase letter.

**Accessor method** A method of a class that is used to determine the value of a variable member. Accessor methods have access level `public`.

**Behavior** The action and communication an object provides.

**Class** A data type that defines variables for the state of an object and methods for an object's behavior.

**Class body** The variables, constructors, and methods that implement a class.

**ClassCastException** An exception thrown when an object variable is cast with an incompatible class.

**Class declaration** The first line of a class, which contains the access level, the keyword `class`, and the class name.

**Class method** A method of a class that can be called from the class itself. It cannot change the state of an object. Class methods include the keyword `static`.

**Class variable** A variable of a class that exists as one copy that all instances of a class refer to. Class variables include the keyword `static`.

**Client code** An application that uses one or more classes.

**Constructor** The part of a class that is used to initialize the variable members of a class.

**Encapsulation** Protecting an object's data from code outside the class.

**Has-a relationship** The relationship demonstrated by a class that contains another class.

**Helper method** A method of a class that is used by other methods in a class to help complete a task. Helper methods have access level `private`.

**Information hiding** Also called encapsulation.

**Inherit** To receive the methods of a superclass.

**Instance** An object of a class.

**Instance method** A method of a class that changes the state of a class. It must be called from an instance of the class.

**Instance variable** A variable of a class that is copied for each instance of the class.

**Member** A variable or method of a class.

**Message** Information passed from one object to another.

**Modifier method** A method of a class that is used to change the value of a variable member. Modifier methods have access level `public`.

**Modular** An application that uses components that are separately written and maintained.

**Object** An instance of a class. An object stores data and can perform actions and provide communication.

**Object casting** To cast an object as the appropriate class.

**Object-oriented development** The solution to a task that is implemented as a system of objects.

**Override** To redefine a method from a superclass in a subclass.

**Reusability** A feature of object-oriented programming that reduces development time and decreases the likelihood of bugs.

**State** The data an object stores.

**Subclass** A class below another class in a class hierarchy. A class that inherits another class.

**Superclass** The upper-most class in a class hierarchy. A class that has subclasses.

**Visibility** The access level of a method.

`class` The keyword used to declare a class.

`public` An access modifier used in the declaration of a class to indicate that the class is visible to client code. Also used in the declaration of class methods to indicate that the method is visible to client code.

`private` A keyword used in the declaration of class members when those members should be visible to the class but not to client code.

`static` The keyword used in the declaration of a variable or method in a class to indicate that the member is a class method.

1. Which members of the Circle class are encapsulated?

2. What name must the constructor of a class have?

3. Explain the difference between the `private` and `public` access modifiers.

4. Consider the following code. Is the last statement valid or invalid? Explain.

```
Circle dot = new Circle(2);
dot.radius = 5;
```

5. Use the following class to answer the questions below:

```
public class Roo {

  private int x;

  public Roo {
    x = 1;
  }

  public void setX(int z) {
    x = z;
  }

  public int getX() {
    return(x);
  }

  public int calculate() {
    x = x * factor();
    return(x);
  }

  private int factor() {
    return(0.12);
  }
}
```

a) What is the name of the class?
b) What is the name of the data member?
c) List the accessor method.
d) List the modifier method.
e) List the helper method.
f) What is the name of the constructor?
g) How many method members are there?

6. What is the difference between a class and an object?

7. Imagine a band festival where there are many bands playing—the TwoToos, the EggRolls, and Goop. Each band can TuneUp, PlayMusic, and TakeABow. A set list can be read or created. If this was simulated in an object-oriented program, what would appropriate names be for:
a) the class
b) the objects
c) a data member
d) the method members

8. Assume a class for a sports team named Team.
a) List three possible object names.
b) List three possible method members.
c) List three possible data members.

9. Use the following class data member definitions to answer the questions below:

```
public class Moo {

  private double y;
  private static int x;
  private static final z;

  ...
```

a) Which data member is a constant?
b) Which data members are variables?
c) Which data member(s) are instance members?
d) Which data member(s) are class members?

10. Explain the difference between calling an instance method member and a class method member.

11. Compare and contrast overriding methods to overloading methods.

12. The Customer class in the Bank application also demonstrates a has-a relationship. Explain.

13. How can reusing code decrease the likelihood of bugs in an application?

14. Explain what is meant by passing a message.

## True/False

15. Determine if each of the following are true or false. If false, explain why.
    a) The state of an object is described by its methods.
    b) The behavior of an object is described by its variables.
    c) An instance of a class is called an object.
    d) Client code is an application that uses a class.
    e) Encapsulation means that all the variables in a class are available to client code.
    f) A constructor is a member of a class.
    g) A variable that is visible to a class, but not to client code is declared with the keyword `private`.
    h) An accessor method is called to change the value of a data member.
    i) A modifier method returns the value of a data member.
    j) A constructor of a class is automatically called when an object of the class is instantiated.
    k) A class can contain multiple constructors.
    l) An instance variable is copied for each instance of a class.
    m) A class variable is declared with the keyword `public`.
    n) A class method must be called from an object of the class.
    o) A class constant is declared with only the keyword `final`.
    p) The Object class is a subclass of all other classes.
    q) The toString() method can be redefined in subclasses.
    r) Object-oriented development requires that only one object be used in an application.

## Exercise 1 ———————————————————————————————MySavings

Create a MySavings application that displays a menu of choices for entering pennies, nickels, dimes, and quarters into a piggy bank and then prompts the user to make a selection. The MySavings application should include a PiggyBank object that can add coins to the piggy bank, remove coins, and return the total amount in the bank. Application output should look similar to:

```
1. Show total in bank.
2. Add a penny.
3. Add a nickel.
4. Add a dime.
5. Add a quarter.
6. Take money out of bank.
Enter 0 to quit
Enter you choice: 5
```

## Exercise 2 ——————————————————————————————— DigitExtractor

Create a DigitExtractor application that prompts the user for an integer and then displays the ones, tens, and hundreds digit of the number. The DigitExtractor application should include a Num object that can return the ones digit, tens digit, hundreds digit, and the whole number. Application output should look similar to:

```
Enter an integer: 123
show (W)hole number.
show (O)nes place number.
show (T)ens place number.
show (H)undreds place number.
(Q)uit
Enter you choice: h
The hundreds place digit is: 1

show (W)hole number.
show (O)nes place number.
show (T)ens place number.
show (H)undreds place number.
(Q)uit
Enter you choice: q
```

# Exercise 3 ——————————————————————— LunchOrder

Create a LunchOrder application that prompts the user for the number of hamburgers, salads, french fries, and sodas and then displays the total for the order. The LunchOrder application should include a Food object with a constructor that accepts the price, fat, carbs, and fiber for an item. Food methods should return the price of the item and return the fat, carbohydrates, and fiber. Use the chart below for food prices and nutrition information:

| Item | Price | Fat(g) | Carbohydrates(g) | Fiber(g) |
|------|-------|--------|------------------|----------|
| hamburger | $1.85 | 9 | 33 | 1 |
| salad | $2.00 | 1 | 11 | 5 |
| french fries | $1.30 | 11 | 36 | 4 |
| soda | $0.95 | 0 | 38 | 0 |

Application output should look similar to:

```
Enter number of hamburgers: 3
Each hamburger has 9.0g of fat, 33.0g of carbs, and 1.0g of fiber.

Enter number of salads: 4
Each salad has 1.0g of fat, 11.0g of carbs, and 5.0g of fiber.

Enter number of fries: 2
French fries have 11.0g of fat, 36.0g of carbs, and 4.0g of fiber.

Enter number of sodas: 5
Each soda has 0.0g of fat, 38.0g of carbs, and 0.0g of fiber.

Your order comes to: $20.90
```

# Exercise 4 ——————————————————————— DiceRollGame

In the Dice Roll game, the player begins with a score of 1000. The player is prompted for the number of points to risk and a second prompt asks the player to choose either high or low. The player rolls two dice and the outcome is compared to the player's choice of high or low. If the dice total is between 2 and 6 inclusive, then it is considered "low". A total between 8 and 12 inclusive is "high". A total of 7 is neither high nor low, and the player loses the points at risk. If the player had called correctly, the points at risk are doubled and added to the total points. For a wrong call, the player loses the points at risk. Create a DiceRollGame application that uses a DRPlayer object based on this specification. The DRPlayer object should have two Die member variables that represent the dice. The Die class should use a random number generator to determine the outcome in a roll() method. Application output should look similar to:

```
You have 1000 points.
How many points do you want to risk? (-1 to quit) 100
Make a call (0 for low, 1 for high): 1
You rolled: 3
You now have 900 points.
How many points do you want to risk? (-1 to quit) 100
Make a call (0 for low, 1 for high): 0
You rolled: 5
You now have 1100 points.
How many points do you want to risk? (-1 to quit) 100
Make a call (0 for low, 1 for high): 1
You rolled: 8
You now have 1300 points.
How many points do you want to risk? (-1 to quit) -1
```

*Chapter 7 Classes and Object-Oriented Development*

## Exercise 5 ——————————————————— Nim2

The game of Nim starts with a random number of stones between 15 and 30. Two players alternate turns and on each turn may take either 1, 2, or 3 stones from the pile. The player forced to take the last stone loses. Use object-oriented development to create a Nim2 application that allows the user to play Nim against the computer. The Nim2 application and its objects should:

- Generate the number of stones to begin with.

- Allow the player to go first.

- Use a random number generator to determine the number of stones the computer takes.

- Prevent the player and the computer from taking an illegal number of stones. For example, neither should be allowed to take three stones when there are only 1 or 2 left.

## Exercise 6 ——————————————————— GameOf21

In the Game of 21, a player is dealt two cards from a deck of playing cards and then optionally given a third card. The player closest to 21 points without going over is the winner. Use object-oriented development to create a Game of 21 application that allows the user to play the Game of 21 against the computer. The Game of 21 application and its objects should:

- Deal a card from a deck of playing cards by generating a random number between 1 and 13. A 1 corresponds to an Ace, numbers 2 through 10 correspond to those cards, and 11 through 13 correspond to Jack, Queen, and King. The Jack, Queen, and King have a value of 10 in the Game of 21. An Ace can have a value of either 1 or 11.

- Allow the player to stay with two cards or be given a third card.

- Announce the winner.

- Play rounds until the player says to stop.

## Exercise 7 ——————————————————— Bowling

In bowling, a ball is rolled down a lane, also called an alley, at a set of ten pins. A game consists of a bowler bowling for ten frames, where each frame consists of two chances (throws) to knock over all ten pins. Bowling centers often use computers to electronically keep scores for bowlers. Use object-oriented development to create a Bowling application that simulates a simplified game of bowling. The Bowling application and its objects should:

- Allow a bowler to bowl ten frames. Each frame consists of two throws, unless a strike is thrown.

- Award 20 points to the bowler when all ten pins are knocked over on the first throw of a frame.

- Award 15 points to the bowler when all ten pins are knocked over within the two throws of a frame.

- Award one point for each pin knocked over in the two throws of a frame when all ten pins are not knocked over.

- If there is more than one bowler in a game, then the bowlers take turns until each has bowled ten frames.

- Use a random number generator to determine how many pins a bowler has knocked over with each throw.

- Display an updated score after each frame.

# Exercise 8 ———————————————————— Adder

The Adder game prompts a player for the answer to an addition problem. The Adder game creates a problem from two randomly selected integers between 0 and 20. Adder allows the player three tries to enter a correct answer. If the correct answer is entered on the first try, the player is awarded 5 points. If the correct answer is entered on the second try, 3 points are awarded. The correct answer on the third try earns 1 point. If after three tries, the correct answer is still not entered, the player receives no points and the correct answer is displayed. The game continues until 999 is entered as an answer. At the end of the game, Adder displays the player's score. Application output should look similar to:

```
14 + 7 = 21
17 + 7 = 24
0 + 15 = 15
5 + 18 = 22
Wrong answer. Enter another answer: 23
3 + 9 = 12
12 + 13 = 25
5 + 1 = 6
19 + 8 = 27
4 + 4 = 8
20 + 13 = 33
14 + 8 = 22
18 + 12 = 30
7 + 7 = 14
17 + 18 = 36
Wrong answer. Enter another answer: 35
3 + 19 = 22
20 + 8 = 999
Your score is: 71
```

# Chapter 8
# Inheritance and Polymorphism

## Key Concepts

Extending a class using inheritance
Understanding an is-a relationship
Implementing a subclass
Polymorphism
Abstract classes
Extending existing code using inheritance

## Case Study

Sales Center application

## Extending a Class

Often times there is an existing class that provides a basis for an object that models a specification. However, the existing class may need additional methods or different implementations of existing methods to more closely represent the object for the model. For example, consider a disk, which has circular shape. It is similar to a circle. However, a disk is three-dimensional and also has a thickness. Rather than create a whole new class to represent a disk, a class named Disk could extend the Circle class.

*inheritance*

Making one class an extension of another involves inheritance. *Inheritance* allows a class to define a specialized type of an already existing class. In this case, a disk is a solid circle with a thickness. Classes that are derived from existing classes demonstrate an *is-a relationship*. A class "is a" type of another class. In this case, a disk is a circle with a thickness.

*is-a relationship*

A class can have many levels of inheritance. For example, consider the following class hierarchy:

**TIP** The Object class is the superclass of all other classes.

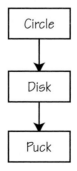

The Puck class inherits the Disk class, which inherits the Circle class. The Circle class is the superclass of Disk. Disk is the subclass of Circle and the superclass of Puck. Puck is the subclass of Disk.

# Implementing a Subclass

*extends*

A class that inherits another class includes the keyword `extends` in the class declaration and takes the form:

```
public class <name> extends <class _ name> {
  <class definition>
}
```

*base class*

Designing a subclass requires selecting the superclass, or *base class*, and then defining any additional variable and method members for the subclass. In many cases, existing methods in the base class will also be overridden by new definitions in the subclass, also called the *derived class*. For example, the Disk class design appears similar to:

*derived class*

Disk inherits Circle

variable: thickness

methods:
    setThickness – changes the thickness.
    getThickness – returns the thickness.
    volume – returns the volume of the disk.
    equals – overrides the equals() method in Circle.
    toString – overrides the toString() method in Circle.

The Disk class implementation, based on the design above, is:

```
/**
 * Disk class.
 */
public class Disk extends Circle {
  private double thickness;

  /**
   * constructor
   * pre: none
   * post: A Disk object has been created with radius r
   * and thickness t.
   */
  public Disk(double r, double t) {
    super(r);
    thickness = t;
  }


  /**
   * Changes the thickness of the disk.
   * pre: none
   * post: Thickness has been changed.
   */
  public void setThickness(double newThickness) {
    thickness = newThickness;
  }
```

*Chapter 8 Inheritance and Polymorphism*

```
/**
 * Returns the thickness of the disk.
 * pre: none
 * post: The thickness of the disk has been returned.
 */
public double getThickness() {
  return(thickness);
}



/**
 * Returns the volume of the disk.
 * pre: none
 * post: The volume of the disk has been returned.
 */
public double volume() {
  double v;

  v = super.area() * thickness;
  return(v);
}



/**
 * Determines if the object is equal to another
 * Disk object.
 * pre: d is a Disk object.
 * post: true has been returned if objects have the same
 * radii and thickness. false has been returned otherwise.
 */
public boolean equals(Object d) {
  Disk testObj = (Disk)d;

  if (testObj.getRadius() == super.getRadius()
      && testObj.getThickness() == thickness) {
    return(true);
  } else {
    return(false);
  }
}



/**
 * Returns a String that represents the Disk object.
 * pre: none
 * post: A string representing the Disk object has
 * been returned.
 */
public String toString() {
  String diskString;

  diskString = "The disk has radius " + super.getRadius()
               + " and thickness " + thickness + ".";
  return(diskString);
}
}
```

**TIP** The equals() and toString() methods override the methods by the same name in the Circle class.

*super*

*visibility*

In a subclass, the keyword super is used to access methods of the base class. For example, the statement super(r) calls the constructor of the superclass, Circle, and passes an argument for setting the radius value. Members that are declared private are not accessible to derived classes. Therefore, accessor methods are used to get inherited member variable values. For example, the equals() method in the Disk class calls getRadius().

Inherited methods are called directly from an object, just as any method of the class is called. Whether a method is original to the Disk class or inherited from the Circle class is transparent to client code, as demonstrated in the TestDisk application:

```java
public class TestDisk {

  public static void main(String[] args) {
    Disk saucer = new Disk(10, 0.02);

    System.out.println("Disk radius: " + saucer.getRadius());
    System.out.println("Disk surface area: " + saucer.area());
    System.out.println("Disk volume: " + saucer.volume());

    Disk plate1 = new Disk(12, 0.05);
    Disk plate2 = new Disk(12, 0.07);
    if (plate1.equals(plate2)) {
      System.out.println("Objects are equal.");
    } else {
      System.out.println("Objects are not equal.");
    }
    System.out.println(plate1);
    System.out.println(plate2);
  }
}
```

The TestDisk application displays the following output:

```
Disk radius: 10.0
Disk surface area: 314.0
Disk volume: 6.28
Objects are not equal.
The disk has radius 12.0 and thickness 0.05.
The disk has radius 12.0 and thickness 0.07.
```

# Review: Puck – part 1 of 2

Create a Puck class that inherits the Disk class. The Puck class should include member variables weight, standard, and youth. The standard and youth variables should be boolean variables that are set to either true or false depending on the weight of the puck. A standard puck weighs between 5 and 5.5 ounces. A youth puck weighs between 4 and 4.5 ounces. Official hockey pucks, regardless of weight, are one inch-thick with a three-inch diameter. The Puck class should also contain member methods getWeight(), getDivision(), which returns a string stating whether the puck is standard or youth, and equals() and toString(), which overrride the same methods in the Disk class. The Puck constructor should require an argument for weight. Be sure that the constructor initializes other variables to appropriate values as necessary.

Create a Hockey application that tests the Puck class.

# Polymorphism

*Polymorphism* is an OOP property in which objects have the ability to assume different types. In object-oriented programming, polymorphism is based on inheritance. Because a subclass is derived from a superclass, a superclass object can reference an object of the subclass. For example, the following statements are valid because Disk inherits Circle:

```
Circle wafer;
Disk cookie = new Disk(2, 0.5);
wafer = cookie;    //wafer now references cookie
```

The wafer object, declared a Circle, is polymorphic, as demonstrated in the statement wafer = cookie where wafer assumes the form of cookie, a Disk object.

Polymorphism is further demonstrated when the referenced object determines which method to execute. This is possible when a subclass overrides a superclass method. In this case, the Disk class has overridden the equals() and toString() methods. Because of this, the following statement executes the Disk toString() method even though wafer was declared a Circle object:

```
/* displays: The disk has radius 2.0 and thickness 0.5. */
System.out.println(wafer);
```

To further demonstrate polymorphism, the Music application will be developed in this section. The Music application allows the user to assemble a small band. The user can assign a band member either vocals (voice) or a woodwind instrument (piccolo or clarinet). The user can then select to hear either a solo, duet, or trio performance from this band.

The Instrument class, its subclasses, and the Performance class are used to model the objects for the Music application. The diagram below illustrates the client code and classes for the Music application. Note the hierarchy of the Instrument class and its subclasses:

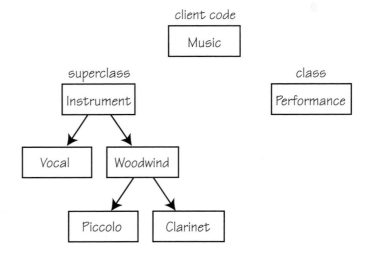

The Music client code is shown below:

```
/*
 * Music.java
 */
import java.util.Scanner;

public class Music {

  /* Returns a selected instrument.
   * pre: none
   * post: An instrument object has been returned.
   */
  public static Instrument assignInstrument() {
    String instrumentChoice;
    Scanner input = new Scanner(System.in);

    System.out.println("Select an instrument for the
                        band member. ");
    System.out.print("Vocals, Piccolo, or Clarinet: ");
    instrumentChoice = input.nextLine();
    System.out.print("Enter the band member's name: ");
    name = input.nextLine();
    if (instrumentChoice.equalsIgnoreCase("V")) {
      return(new Vocal(name));
    } else if (instrumentChoice.equalsIgnoreCase("P")) {
      return(new Piccolo(name));
    } else {   //default to clarinet
      return(new Clarinet(name));
    }
  }

  public static void main(String[] args) {
    Performance band;
    Instrument bandMember1, bandMember2, bandMember3;
    Scanner input = new Scanner(System.in);
    String performanceChoice;

    /* assign instruments */
    bandMember1 = assignInstrument();
    bandMember2 = assignInstrument();
    bandMember3 = assignInstrument();
    System.out.println(bandMember1 + " " + bandMember2 + " "
                       + bandMember3 + "\n");

    System.out.print("Would you like to hear a Solo, a Duet,
                      a Trio, or Leave? ");
    performanceChoice = input.nextLine();
    while (!performanceChoice.equalsIgnoreCase("L")) {
      if (performanceChoice.equalsIgnoreCase("S")) {
        band = new Performance(bandMember1);
      } else if (performanceChoice.equalsIgnoreCase("D")) {
        band = new Performance(bandMember1, bandMember2);
      } else {     //default to trio
        band = new Performance(bandMember1, bandMember2,
                               bandMember3);
      }
      band.begin();

      System.out.print("\nWould you like to hear a Solo,
                        a Duet, a Trio, or Leave? ");;
      performanceChoice = input.nextLine();
    }
  }
}
```

*Chapter 8 Inheritance and Polymorphism*

The assignInstrument() method declares an Instrument return type, but the individual `return` statements return Vocal, Piccola, and Clarinet types. The Instrument object returned by the method is polymorphic, changing to whichever subclass is actually returned.

The Music application produces output similar to:

```
Select an instrument for the band member.
Vocals, Piccolo, or Clarinet: c
Enter the band member's name: Anthony
Select an instrument for the band member.
Vocals, Piccolo, or Clarinet: v
Enter the band member's name: Emily
Select an instrument for the band member.
Vocals, Piccolo, or Clarinet: p
Enter the band member's name: Dana
Anthony plays squawk. Emily sings LaLaLa. Dana plays peep.

Would you like to hear a Solo, a Duet, a Trio, or Leave? d
squawkLaLaLa

Would you like to hear a Solo, a Duet, a Trio, or Leave? t
squawkLaLaLapeep

Would you like to hear a Solo, a Duet, a Trio, or Leave? l
```

The Music application allows the user numerous combinations for selecting a band and hearing performances. The code for such an application would be more complicated and less flexible without the object-oriented principles of inheritance and polymorphism. Music is versatile because it takes advantage of inheritance and polymorphism.

The documentation for the Instrument, Vocal, Woodwind, Piccolo, and Clarinet classes is below. Note that the makeSound() method in the Instrument class is a method that must be implemented (written) in a subclass. This is discussed further in the next section. The code for the classes is also shown in the next section where abstract classes are discussed.

### Class Instrument

### Constructor/Methods

`Instrument(String name)`
>
> creates an instrument object with musician `name`.

`getMusician()`     returns a string that is the musician's name.

`makeSound()`     an abstract method that should return a String representing the instrument's sound.

### Class Vocal (inherits Instrument)

**Constructor/Methods**

`Vocal(String name)`
               creates a singer object with singer `name`.

`makeSound()`       returns the String `LaLaLa`.

`toString()`         returns a String that represents the singer.


### Class Woodwind (inherits Instrument)

**Constructor/Method**

`Woodwind(String name)`
               creates a woodwind instrument object with musician `name`.

`makeSound()`       returns the String `toot`.


### Class Piccolo (inherits Woodwind)

**Constructor/Methods**

`Piccolo(String name)`
               creates a piccoloist object with musician `name`.

`makeSound()`       returns the String `peep`.

`toString()`         returns a String that represents the object.


### Class Clarinet (inherits Woodwind)

**Constructor/Methods**

`Clarinet(String name)`
               creates a clarinetist object with musician `name`.

`makeSound()`       returns the String `squawk`.

`toString()`         returns a String that represents the object.


The Performance class creates an arrangement of Instrument objects. The constructors require Instrument arguments, but polymorphism enables objects of Instructor subclasses to be passed:

```
/**
 * Performance class.
 */
public class Performance {
  private String arrangement;
  private Instrument solo;
  private Instrument duet _ 1, duet _ 2;
  private Instrument trio _ 1, trio _ 2, trio _ 3;


  /**
   * constructor
   * pre: none
   * post: A soloist has been selected.
   */
  public Performance(Instrument s) {
    solo = s;
    arrangement = solo.makeSound();
  }
```

```
/**
 * constructor
 * pre: none
 * post: The members of a duet have been selected.
 */
public Performance(Instrument d1, Instrument d2) {
  duet_1 = d1;
  duet_2 = d2;
  arrangement = duet_1.makeSound() + duet_2.makeSound();
}


/**
 * constructor
 * pre: none
 * post: The members of a trio have been selected.
 */
public Performance(Instrument t1, Instrument t2,
                      Instrument t3) {
  trio_1 = t1;
  trio_2 = t2;
  trio_3 = t3;
  arrangement = trio_1.makeSound() + trio_2.makeSound()
              + trio_3.makeSound();
}


/**
 * Begins the performance.
 * pre: none
 * post: The performance has been played.
 */
public void begin() {
  System.out.println(arrangement);
}


/**
 * Returns a String that represents the performers.
 * pre: none
 * post: A string representing the performers has
 * been returned.
 */
public String toString() {
  String program = "The performance includes ";
  program += arrangement;
  return(program);
}
}
```

## Review: Music – part 1 of 2

Modify the Music application to allow the user to select a quartet (four band members) in addition to the other performances. Changes to the Performance class will also be required to provide the option of creating a quartet.

An *abstract class* models an abstract concept. For example, a musical instrument is an abstract concept. An instrument is something that can be played, but there is no such thing an "instrument" instrument. There are however, flutes, piccolos, drums, and cymbals.

Abstract classes cannot be instantiated because they should not represent objects. They instead describe the more general details and actions of a type of object. For example, the Instrument class describes the very basics of an instrument—it can make a sound. The Woodwind class is also an abstract class because it describes a group of instruments. It includes a general sound that woodwind instruments make.

*abstract*

Abstract classes are declared with the keyword `abstract` in the class declaraction. They are intended to be inherited. The public members of the abstract class are visible to derived objects. However, an abstract class *abstract method* can also contain an abstract method. An *abstract method* is declared with the keyword `abstract` and contains a method declaration, but no body. The abstract class must be implemented in its subclass.

The Instrument class is an abstract class with an abstract method. The makeSound() method must be implemented in an Instrument subclass:

```
/**
 * Instrument class.
 */
abstract class Instrument {
  String musician;

  /**
   * constructor
   * pre: none
   * post: A musician has been assigned to the instrument.
   */
  public Instrument(String name) {
    musician = name;
  }


  /**
   * Returns the name of the musician
   * pre: none
   * post: The name of the musician playing the instrument
   * has been returned.
   */
  public String getMusician() {
    return(musician);
  }


  /**
   * Should return the sound of the instrument.
   * pre: none
   * post: The sound made by the instrument is returned.
   */
  abstract String makeSound();
}
```

The Vocal class is a subclass of Instrument. It provides the body for the makeSound() method:

```
/**
 * Vocal class.
 */
public class Vocal extends Instrument {

  /**
   * constructor
   * pre: none
   * post: A singer has been created.
   */
  public Vocal(String singerName) {
    super(singerName);
  }


  /**
   * Returns the sound of the instrument.
   * pre: none
   * post: The sound made by the singer.
   */
  public String makeSound() {
    return("LaLaLa");
  }


  /**
   * Returns a String that represents the instrument.
   * pre: none
   * post: A string representing the singer.
   */
  public String toString() {
    return(super.getMusician() + " sings " + makeSound() + ".");
  }
}
```

The Woodwind class is also an Instrument subclass. It too implements the makeSound() method. However, Woodwind describes a group of instruments so it has also been declared abstract:

```
/**
 * Woodwind class.
 */
abstract class Woodwind extends Instrument {

  /**
   * constructor
   * pre: none
   * post: A woodwind instrument has been created.
   */
  public Woodwind(String player) {
    super(player);
  }


  /**
   * Returns the sound of the instrument.
   * pre: none
   * post: The sound made by the instrument is returned.
   */
  public String makeSound() {
    return("toot");
  }
}
```

The Piccolo class is a subclass of Woodwind. It overrides the makeSound() method:

```java
/**
 * Piccolo class.
 */
public class Piccolo extends Woodwind {

  /**
   * constructor
   * pre: none
   * post: A piccolo has been created.
   */
  public Piccolo(String piccoloist) {
    super(piccoloist);
  }


  /**
   * Returns the sound of the instrument.
   * pre: none
   * post: The sound made by the instrument is returned.
   */
  public String makeSound() {
    return("peep");
  }


  /**
   * Returns a String that represents the instrument.
   * pre: none
   * post: A string representing the instrument has
   * been returned.
   */
  public String toString() {
    return(super.getMusician() + " plays " + makeSound() + ".");
  }
}
```

The Clarinet class is also a Woodwind subclass. It too overrides the makeSound() method:

```java
/**
 * Clarinet class.
 */
public class Clarinet extends Woodwind {

  /**
   * constructor
   * pre: none
   * post: A clarinet has been created.
   */
  public Clarinet(String clarinetist) {
    super(clarinetist);
  }


  /**
   * Returns the sound of the instrument.
   * pre: none
   * post: The sound made by the instrument is returned.
   */
  public String makeSound() {
    return("squawk");
  }
}
```

*Chapter 8 Inheritance and Polymorphism*

```
/**
 * Returns a String that represents the instrument.
 * pre: none
 * post: A string representing the instrument has
 * been returned.
 */
public String toString() {
  return(super.getMusician() + " plays " + makeSound() + ".");
}
}
```

Through inheritance and abstraction, a hierarchy of classes can be created that begin with a general abstraction and lead to a specific object.

## Review: Music – part 2 of 2

Modify the Music application to allow the user to select a cymbal or drum in addition to the other instruments for the band members. The Music application changes will require that Percussion, Cymbal, and Drum classes be created. The Percussion class should be an abstract class that inherits the Instrument class. The Cymbal and Drum classes should inherit the Percussion class.

## Interfaces

An *interface* is a class with method declarations that have no implementations. Although an interface may seem similar to an abstract class, it is very different. An interface cannot be inherited. It may only be implemented in a class. An interface can add behavior to a class, but it does not provide a hierarchy for the class.

An interface takes the form:

```
<access_level> interface <name> {
  <return_type> <method_name> (<method_param>);
  ...additional methods
}
```

The methods defined in an interface are by default public and abstract. Therefore, the methods in an interface are only declarations followed by a semicolon.

*Comparable interface*    The Comparable interface is part of the java.lang package. It contains one method:

### Interface Comparable (java.lang.Comparable)

### Method
compareTo(Object obj)

> returns 0 when obj is the same as the object, a negative integer is returned when obj is less than the object, and a positive integer is returned when obj is greater than the object.

When an interface is implemented in a class, the class must implement each method defined in the interface. In this case, the Comparable interface contains just one method. The Circle class shown on the next page has been modified to implement the Comparable interface.

```
/**
 * Circle class.
 */
public class Circle implements Comparable {
  private static final double PI = 3.14;
  private double radius;

  /**
   * constructor
   * pre: none
   * post: A Circle object created. Radius initialized to 1.
   */
  public Circle() {
    radius = 1;              //default radius
  }
```

*...getRadius(), setRadius(), and other Circle class methods*

```
  /**
   * Determines if object c is smaller, the same,
   * or larger than this Circle object.
   * pre: c is a Circle object
   * post: -1 has been returned if c is larger than
   * this Circle, 0 has been returned if they are the
   * same size, and 1 has been returned if c is smaller
   * then this Circle.
   */
  public int compareTo(Object c) {
    Circle testCircle = (Circle)c;

    if (radius < testCircle.getRadius()) {
      return(-1);
    } else if (radius == testCircle.getRadius()) {
      return(0);
    } else {
      return(1);
    }
  }
}
```

The TestCircle client code tests the compareTo() method:

```
/**
 * The Circle class is tested.
 */
public class TestCircle {

  public static void main(String[] args) {
    Circle spot1 = new Circle(3);
    Circle spot2 = new Circle(4);
    if (spot1.compareTo(spot2) == 0) {
      System.out.println("Objects are equal.");
    } else if (spot1.compareTo(spot2) < 0) {
      System.out.println("spot1 is smaller than spot2.");
    } else {
      System.out.println("spot1 is larger than spot2.");
    }
    System.out.println(spot1);
    System.out.println(spot2);
  }
}
```

*Chapter 8 Inheritance and Polymorphism*

The TestCircle application produces the output:

```
spot1 is smaller than spot2.
Circle has radius 3.0
Circle has radius 4.0
```

*multiple interfaces*   A class can implement multiple interfaces. When more than one interface is implemented, the interface names are separated by commas in the class declaration.

## Review: Disk

Modify the Disk class to implement the Comparable interface. Two disks are equal when they have the same thickness and same radius. Modify the existing client code to test the new method.

## Review: Puck – part 2 of 2

Modify the Puck class to implement the Comparable interface. Two pucks are the equal when they have the same weight. Modify the existing client code to test the new method.

## Review: Rectangle – part 4 of 5

Modify the Rectangle class to implement the Comparable interface. Two rectangles are the equal when they have the same width and length. Modify the existing client code to test the new method.

## Review: Rectangle – part 5 of 5

Create an interface named ComparableArea that contains one method named compareToArea(). This method should return 0 when the object has the same area as another object, –1 should be returned when the object has an area less than another object, and 1 returned otherwise.

Modify the Rectangle class to implement the ComparableArea interface as well as the Comparable interface implemented in the previous review. Modify the existing client code to test the new method.

## Chapter 8 Case Study

In this case study, a sales center application will be created. The sales center has three employees, which include a manager and two associates. The manager earns a salary and the associates are paid by the hour. The owner of the sales center wants a computer application to display employee information and calculate payroll.

## SalesCenter Specification

The SalesCenter application stores information about three employees. There is one manager (Diego Martin, salary $55,000), and two associates (Kylie Walter earning $18.50 per hour and Michael Rose earning $16.75 per hour). SalesCenter should be able to display the name and title for a specified employee. Additionally, the SalesCenter application should calculate and display the pay for a specified employee based on the pay argument entered by the user. The pay argument should correlate to hours worked if the pay for an associate is to be calculated. The pay argument for a manager should correlate to the number of weeks the manager is to be paid for.

The SalesCenter interface should provide a menu of options. Depending on the option selected, additional input may be needed. The SalesCenter output sketch:

```
Employee\Pay\Quit
Enter choice: E
Enter employee number (1, 2, or 3): 2 Kylie Walter, associate

Employee\Pay\Quit
Enter choice: P
Enter employee number (1, 2, or 3): 2
Enter the hours for associate or pay period for manager: 40
Kylie Walter, associate
$740.00

Employee\Pay\Quit
Enter choice: Q
```

The SalesCenter algorithm:

1. Display a menu of options.

2. Prompt the user for a menu choice.

3. If the user has not selected to quit, prompt the user to specify employee 1, 2, or 3.

4. Perform the action requested by the user.

5. Repeat steps 1 through 4 until the user has selected the option to quit.

## SalesCenter Code Design

The SalesCenter application can be modeled with objects for a manager and two associates. The manager and associate objects are both employee objects. Therefore, an Employee abstract class should be used for subclasses Manager and Associate. The Employee class should define an emplyee's first and last name and include an abstract class for calculating pay. A manager's pay is based on a pay period specified in weeks. Associates are paid by the hour. The `abstract` pay() method in Employee will have different implementations in Manager and Associate.

The SalesCenter class designs are:

Employee

variables: firstName, lastName

methods:
- pay – abstract class. Should return an employee's pay for a specified period.
- toString – returns a string with employee first and last names.


Manager extends Employee

variable: yearlySalary

methods:
- getSalary – returns the yearly salary.
- pay – returns amount earned based on the yearly salary and the specified period. Requires a parameter for the weeks in the pay period.
- toString – returns a string with employee name and title.


Associate extends Employee

variable: hourlyPayRate

methods:
- getRate – returns the hourly pay rate.
- pay – returns amount earned based on the hourly pay rate and the specified hours. Requires a parameter for hours worked.
- toString – returns a string with employee name and title.

Based on the algorithm and the class designs, the SalesCenter code design will include a loop. The pseudocode for the SalesCenter client code follows:

```
import java.util.Scanner;
import java.text.NumberFormat;

public class SalesCenter {

    payEmployee(emp, payArg) {
        System.out.println(emp);
        pay = emp.pay(payArg);
        System.out.println(pay);
    }


    public static void main(String[] args) {
        Manager emp1 = new Manager("Diego","Martin", 55000);
        Associate emp2 = new Associate("Kylie", "Walter", 18.50);
        Associate emp3 = new Associate("Michael", "Rose", 16.75);
        Employee emp = emp1;     //default employee choice

        /* display menu of choices */
        do {
          prompt user for employee/pay/quit
          get user choice;

          if (not quit) {
            prompt user for employee number 1, 2, or 3
            get empNum
            switch (empNum) {
              case 1: emp = emp1; break;
              case 2: emp = emp2; break;
              case 3: emp = emp3; break;
            }
            if (choice == employee) {
              display employee name and title;
            } else if (choice == pay) {
              prompt user for hours or pay period;
              payEmployee(emp, payArg);
            }
          }
        } while (not quit);
    }
}
```

## SalesCenter Implementation

The SalesCenter implementation involves creating four files. Three files are the classes and one file is the client code.

The Employee class is implemented below:

```java
/**
 * Employee class.
 */
abstract class Employee {
  String firstName, lastName;

  /**
   * constructor
   * pre: none
   * post: An employee has been created.
   */
  public Employee(String fName, String lName) {
    firstName = fName;
    lastName = lName;
  }


  /**
   * Returns the employee name.
   * pre: none
   * post: The employee name has been returned.
   */
  public String toString() {
    return(firstName + " " + lastName);
  }


  /**
   * Returns the employee pay.
   * pre: none
   * post: The employee pay has been returned.
   */
  abstract double pay(double period);
}
```

The Manager class is implemented below:

```java
/**
 * Manager class.
 */
class Manager extends Employee {
  double yearlySalary;

  /**
   * constructor
   * pre: none
   * post: A manager has been created.
   */
  public Manager(String fName, String lName, double sal) {
    super(fName, lName);
    yearlySalary = sal;
  }


  /**
   * Returns the manager salary.
   * pre: none
   * post: The manager salary has been returned.
   */
  public double getSalary() {
    return(yearlySalary);
  }
```

```
/**
 * Returns the manager pay for a specified period.
 * pre: none
 * post: The manager pay for the specified period
 * has been returned.
 */
public double pay(double weeks) {
  double payEarned;

  payEarned = (yearlySalary / 52) * weeks;
  return(payEarned);
}


/**
 * Returns the employee name and title.
 * pre: none
 * post: The employee name and title has been returned.
 */
public String toString() {
  return(super.toString() + ", manager");
}
}
```

The Associate class is implemented below:

```
/**
 * Associate class.
 */
class Associate extends Employee {
  double hourlyPayRate;

  /**
   * constructor
   * pre: none
   * post: An associate has been created.
   */
  public Associate(String fName, String lName, double rate) {
    super(fName, lName);
    hourlyPayRate = rate;
  }


  /**
   * Returns the associate pay rate.
   * pre: none
   * post: The associate pay rate has been returned.
   */
  public double getRate() {
    return(hourlyPayRate);
  }


  /**
   * Returns the associate pay for the hours worked.
   * pre: none
   * post: The associate pay for the hours worked
   * has been returned.
   */
  public double pay(double hours) {
    double payEarned;

    payEarned = hourlyPayRate * hours;
    return(payEarned);
  }
```

```
        /**
         * Returns the employee name and title.
         * pre: none
         * post: The employee name and title has been returned.
         */
        public String toString() {
          return(super.toString() + ", associate");
        }
      }
```

The SalesCenter client code is implemented below:

```java
import java.util.Scanner;
import java.text.NumberFormat;

public class SalesCenter {

    /**
     * Displays employee name and pay.
     * pre: none
     * post: Employee name and pay has been displayed
     */
    public static void payEmployee(Employee emp, double payArg) {
        NumberFormat money = NumberFormat.getCurrencyInstance();
        double pay;

        System.out.println(emp);
        pay = emp.pay(payArg);
        System.out.println(money.format(pay));
    }

    public static void main(String[] args) {
        Manager emp1 = new Manager("Diego","Martin", 55000);
        Associate emp2 = new Associate("Kylie", "Walter", 18.50);
        Associate emp3 = new Associate("Michael", "Rose", 16.75);
        Scanner input = new Scanner(System.in);
        String action;
        int empNum;
        double payArg;
        Employee emp = emp1;     //set to default emp1

        do {
            System.out.println("\nEmployee\\Pay\\Quit");
            System.out.print("Enter choice: ");
            action = input.next();

            if (!action.equalsIgnoreCase("Q")) {
                System.out.print("Enter employee number (1, 2, or 3):");
                empNum = input.nextInt();
                switch (empNum) {
                    case 1: emp = emp1; break;
                    case 2: emp = emp2; break;
                    case 3: emp = emp3; break;
                }
                if (action.equalsIgnoreCase("E")) {
                    System.out.println(emp);
                } else if (action.equalsIgnoreCase("P")) {
                    System.out.print("Enter the hours for associate or
                                      pay period for manager: ");
                    payArg = input.nextDouble();
                    payEmployee(emp, payArg);
                }
            }
        } while (!action.equalsIgnoreCase("Q"));
    }
}
```

The SalesCenter application generates output similar to:

```
Employee\Pay\Quit
Enter choice: e
Enter employee number (1, 2, or 3):1
Diego Martin, manager

Employee\Pay\Quit
Enter choice: p
Enter employee number (1, 2, or 3):1
Enter the hours for associate or pay period for manager: 2
Diego Martin, manager
$2,115.38

Employee\Pay\Quit
Enter choice: q
```

### SalesCenter Testing and Debugging

Client code should first be written to test each class. Testing should be done for the client code.

## Review: SalesCenter

Modify the SalesCenter application to compensate associates when they have worked more than 40 hours. Associates should be paid their hourly wage when 40 or fewer hours are worked. However, associates earn time and a half for hours over 40. For example, an associate paid $10 per hour will earn $300 for 30 hours of work. However, an associate working 42 hours will earn $400 + $30, or $430. The overtime pay is calculated as (hours over 40) * (1.5 * base hourly rate).

## Chapter Summary

This chapter discussed inheritance and polymorphism, two key aspects of object-oriented programming. Inheritance allows classes to be derived from existing classes. By extending an existing class, there is less development and debugging necessary. A class derived from an existing class demonstrates an is-a relationship.

A superclass is also called a base class, and a subclass is called a derived class. The keyword `extends` is used to create a derived class from a base class. The keyword `super` is used to access members of a base class from the derived class.

Polymorphism is the ability of an object to assume different types. In OOP, polymorphism is based on inheritance. An object can assume the type of any of its subclasses.

Abstract classes model abstract concepts. They cannot be instantiated because they should not represent objects. An abstract class is intended to be inherited.

Abstract classes may or may not contain abstract methods. An abstract method is a method declaration with no implementation. If a class contains one or more abstract methods, it must be declared abstract. Abstract methods must be implemented in a class that inherits the abstract class.

*Chapter 8 Inheritance and Polymorphism*

An interface is a class that contains only abstract methods. An interface can be implemented by a class, but it is not inherited. A class that implements an interface must implement each method in the interface. The Comparable interface is part of the java.lang package and is used to add a compareTo() method to classes that implement the interface.

# Vocabulary

**Abstract class** A class that models an abstract concept. A class that contains one or more abstract methods must be declared abstract.

**Abstract method** A method that has been declared, but not implemented. Abstract methods appear in abstract classes. They are implemented in a subclass that inherits the abstract class.

**Base class** A superclass.

**Derived class** A subclass.

**Inheritance** The OOP property in which a class can define a specialized type of an already existing class.

**Interface** A class with abstract methods. An interface cannot be inherited, but it can be implemented by any number of classes.

**Is-a relationship** The relationship demonstrated by a class derived from an existing class.

**Polymorphism** The OOP property in which objects have the ability to assume different types.

# Java

`abstract` The keyword used for declaring a class or a method as abstract.

**Comparable** A java.lang interface with the compareTo() method that can be implemented in classes to provide a means for an object to be compared to another object of the same type.

`extends` The keyword used in a class declaration to inherit another class.

`interface` The keyword used in a class declaration to declare it an interface.

`super` The keyword used to call a superclass constructor or method.

1. Explain the difference between a has-a and is-a relationship among classes.

2. If a base class has a public method go() and a derived class has a public method stop(), which methods will be available to an object of the derived class?

3. Compare and contrast implementing an abstract method to overriding a method.

4. Compare and contrast an abstract class to an interface.

5. List the method(s) contained in the Comparable interface.

6. Use the following classes to answer the questions below:

```
interface Wo {
   public int doThat();
}

public class Bo {
   private int x;

   public Bo(int z) {
     x = z;
   }

   public int doThis() {
     return(2);
   }

   public int doNow() {
     return(15);
   }
}

public class Roo extends Bo implements Wo {

   public Roo {
     super(1);
   }

   public int doThis() {
     return(10);
   }

   private int doThat() {
     return(20);
   }
}
```

a) What type of method is doThat() in Wo?
b) What is Wo?
c) Why is doThat() implemented in Roo?
d) List the methods available to a Roo object.

e) How does the implementation of doThis() in Roo affect the implementation of doThis() in Bo?
f) What action does the statement super(1) in Roo perform?
g) Can the doThis() method in Bo be called from a Roo object? If so, how?
h) Can a method in Roo call the doThis() method in Bo? If so, how?

**True/False**

7. Determine if each of the following are true or false. If false, explain why.
   a) Inheritance allows a class to define a specialized type of an already existing class.
   b) Classes that are derived from existing classes demonstrate a has-a relationship.
   c) A class can have only one level of inheritance.
   d) A class that inherits another class includes the keyword `inheritance` in the class declaration.
   e) When implementing a subclass, existing methods in the base class can be overridden.
   f) Members of a base class that are declared private are accessible to derived classes.
   g) Inherited methods are called directly from an object.
   h) Polymorphism is an OOP property in which objects have the ability to assume different types.
   i) Abstract classes can be instantiated.
   j) An abstract class must be implemented in its subclass.
   k) An abstract method contains a method declaration and a body.
   l) Inheritance and abstraction allow a hierarchy of classes to be created.
   m) An interface can be inherited.
   n) An interface can add behavior to a class.
   o) The methods defined in an interface are private by default.
   p) The Comparable interface contains three methods.

## Exercise 1 ——————————————————— UEmployee, Faculty, Staff

Create a UEmployee class that contains member variables for the university employee name and salary. The UEmployee class should contain member methods for returning the employee name and salary. Create Faculty and Staff classes that inherit the UEmployee class. The Faculty class should include members for storing and returning the department name. The Staff class should include members for storing and returning the job title.

## Exercise 2 ————————————— Account, PersonalAcct, BusinessAcct

Create PersonalAcct and BusinessAcct classes that inherit the Account class presented in Chapter 7. A personal account requires a minimum balance of $100. If the balance falls below this amount, then $2.00 is charged (withdrawn) to the account. A business account requires a minimum balance of $500, otherwise the account is charged $10. Create client code to test the classes.

## Exercise 3 ——————————————————— Vehicle, Car, Truck, Minivan

Create a Vehicle class that is an abstract class defining the general details and actions associated with a vehicle. Create Car, Truck, and Minivan classes that inherit the Vehicle class. The Car, Truck, and Minivan classes should include additional members specific to the type of vehicle being represented. Create client code to test the classes.

# Chapter 9
# Arrays

## Key Concepts

Creating one and two dimensional arrays
Using array parameters
Arrays with meaningful indexes
Manipulating characters in a string
Understanding Unicode
Applying search algorithms
The Wrapper class
Autoboxing and auto-unboxing

## Case Study

Local Bank application

## Declaring Arrays

An *array* is a structure that can store many of the same kind of data together at once. For example, an array can store 20 integers, another array can store 50 doubles, and a third array can store 100 objects, such as Strings. Arrays are an important and useful programming concept because they allow a collection of related values to be stored together with a single descriptive name.

An array has a fixed length and can contain only as many data items as its length allows:

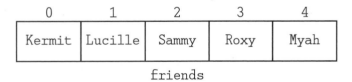

friends

*array element*
*index*

An array *element* is one of the data items in an array. For example, in the array of Strings above, Roxy is an element. Each element has an *index* value, with 0 being the index of the first item, 1 the index of the second item, and so on. In the array above, Roxy is the fourth element in the array and has the index value 3.

*declaring and allocating*
*space for an array*

An array must be declared and then space allocated for the elements of the array. The statements for declaring an array and allocating space for its elements take the form:

```
<type>[] <name>;             //declare array
<name> = new <type>[<num>];  //allocate space for elements
```

**TIP** The [] brackets are operators used for declaring and creating arrays and for accessing array elements.

The declaration includes the type followed by brackets ([]) to indicate an array. The array name can be any valid identifier. The new operator allocates space for the number of elements indicated in brackets. The statements on the next page declare an array and then prompt the user for the number of elements:

```
Scanner input = new Scanner(System.in);
int numFriends;
String[] friends;                 //declare array

System.out.print("How many friends? ");
numfriends = input.nextInt();
friends = new String[numFriends];    //allocate space
```

If the size of the array is known when the application is written, then the array can be created and space allocated for elements in one statement, similar to:

```
String[] friends = new String[5];    //5 friends
```

*initial array values*

When space has been allocated for the elements of an array, the array is initialized to the default values for that element type. For example, each element of an `int` array is automatically initialized to 0. An array of objects, such as a String array, contains `null` for each element.

*declaring and initializing*

A third way to create an array is to initialize it in the declaration. Initializing an array means that a value is given for each element. In this case, the length of the array is determined by the number of elements between the curly braces:

```
String[] friends = {"Kermit", "Lucille", "Sammy", "Roxy", "Myah"};
```

## Using Arrays

*accessing an element*

An array element is accessed by including its index in brackets after the array name. For example, the following statement displays the third element:

```
System.out.println(friends[2]);    //displays Sammy
```

*changing an element*

An array element is changed through assignment. For example, the assignment statement below changes the third element to "Sunshine":

```
friends[2] = "Sunshine";
```

*ArrayIndexOutOfBounds*

A run-time error is generated when an invalid index is used. For example, the exception ArrayIndexOutOfBoundsException is thrown when the following statement tries to execute:

```
friends[5] = "Wilbur";    //ERROR! Generates an exception.
```

The Array structure includes the length attribute, which can be used at run time to determine the length of an array:

```
numElements = friends.length;    //5
```

A `for` statement is often used to access the elements of an array because the loop control variable can be used as the array index. Accessing each element of an array is called *traversing* an array. For example, the following statement displays each element of the `friends` array:

*traversing*

```
for (int i = 0; i < friends.length; i++) {
    System.out.println(friends[i]);
}
```

Note that the loop iterates from 0 to one less than the length of the array because length is a count of the elements, not the greatest index value.

for-each statement

Java also provides a type of `for` loop just for traversing an array. Sometimes referred to as a `for-each` statement, the following statement displays each element in the array:

```
for (String element : friends) {
    System.out.println(element);
}
```

The statement above is read "for each String element in friends." It displays the names in the array one after the other. Using a `for-each` loop to traverse an array does not require a loop control variable. This type of `for` statement helps prevent the exception ArrayIndexOutOfBoundsException.

Although convenient at times, the modified `for` statement above cannot be used in situations where the array index value is needed. One example, is when the elements of an array are to be accessed in reverse order.

## Review: StudentRoster

Create a StudentRoster application that prompts the user for the number of students in the class and then prompts the user for each student's name and stores the names in an array. After all the names have been entered, the application should display the title "Student Roster" and then list the names in the array.

## Review: Squares

Create a Squares application that stores the square of an element's index in an integer array of 5 elements. For example, the third element, which has index 2, should store 4. The application should then display the value of each element in the array.

## Review: Reverse

Create a Reverse application that stores the number corresponding to the the element's index in an integer array of 10 elements. For example, the second element, which has index 1, should store 1. The application should then display the title "Countdown" and then list numbers stored in the array in reverse order.

## Array Parameters

A method declaration can include array parameters. The array passed to a method can be either an entire array or an element of the array. The method below includes an array parameter. A second parameter, an `int` parameter, corresponds to an element of the array:

```
public static void tryChanging(int[] numbers, int aNum) {
    numbers[1] = 123;
    aNum = 456;
}
```

Note that the data type followed by brackets indicates an array parameter, similar to an array declaration.

The statements below call the tryChanging() method shown on the previous page:

```
int[] myNums = {5, 8, 3};
System.out.println(myNums[1] + " " + myNums[0]);
tryChanging(myNums, myNums[0]);
System.out.println(myNums[1] + " " + myNums[0]);
```

The statements produce the output:

```
8 5
123 5
```

An array is a reference data type similar to a class. Therefore, passing a whole array to a method passes the reference to the elements, allowing the method to access an element of the array and change its value. However, because the elements of the array are a primitve data type, passing a single element passes only the data stored, not a reference to the data location.

## Arrays with Meaningful Indexes

Many algorithms make use of the index value of an array element for simplifying the storage and retrievel of data. For example, a testScores array with 101 elements indexed from 0 to 100 could store a count of all the scores of 90 in the element with index 90, the count of scores 82 in element 82, and so on.

The DiceRolls application counts the frequency of dice roll outcomes. A roll is simulated by generating two random numbers between 1 and 6. The outcome of each roll is then used to increment the counter in the element at the index corresponding to the outcome. For example, if a 4 is rolled, then the value at index 4 is incremented:

```
import java.util.Scanner;
import java.util.Math;

public class DiceRolls {

  public static void main(String[] args) {
    int[] outcomes = new int[13];
    Scanner input = new Scanner(System.in);
    int numRolls;
    int outcome;

    /* prompt user for number of rolls */
    System.out.print("How many rolls? ");
    numRolls = input.nextInt();

    /* roll dice and add to outcomes */
    for (int roll = 0; roll < numRolls; roll++) {
      outcome = (int)(6 * Math.random() + 1) +
        (int)(6 * Math.random() + 1);
      outcomes[outcome] += 1;
    }

    /* show counts of outcomes */
    for (int i = 2; i <= 12; i++) {
      System.out.println(i + ": " + outcomes[i]);
    }
  }
}
```

The DiceRolls application displays output similar to:

```
How many rolls? 1000
2: 24
3: 49
4: 93
5: 128
6: 132
7: 161
8: 125
9: 113
10: 87
11: 59
12: 29
```

In the DiceRolls application, the outcomes ranged from 2 through 12 making it possible to store counters at array indexes directly corresponding to the outcomes. However, this approach for a range of years 1900 through 2000 would require an array of 2001 elements with only the last 100 elements in use. For ranges such as these, the solution is to store counters at offset array indexes. For example, for an outcome of 1900, a counter at index 0 would be incremented. for an outcome of 1901, a counter at index 1 would be incremented, and so on.

To determine the array size when offset array indexes will be used, subtract the low value from the high and add 1:

```
int[] counts;
counts = new int[HIGH - LOW + 1];
```

The following statement increments a counter stored at an offset index:

```
counts[value - LOW] += 1;
```

## Review: DiceRolls – part 1 of 2

Modify the DiceRolls application to roll three dice.

## Review: DiceRolls – part 2 of 2

The DiceRolls application is not written generically. The application has "hard-coded" data, including the maximum random number in the nextInt() method and the initial and final values for i in the show counts for loop. Modify the DiceRolls application to prompt the user for the number of sides on each die, the number of dice to be rolled, and the number of rolls to make. For example, a ten-sided die will show a number between a 1 and a 10 on a roll. Rolling three ten-sided dice has the possible outcomes of 3 through 30.

## Review: NumberCounts

Create a NumberCounts application that prompts the user for a number and then counts the occurrences of each digit in that number.

# Characters and Arrays

**TIP** The char data type was introduced in Chapter 3.

Although strings are comprised of characters, a String object cannot be manipulated as a set of characters. However, the string stored in a String object can be converted to a char array. Additionally, an individual character of the String object can be converted to a char. The String class methods for working with the characters in a string include:

### Class String (java.lang.String)

### Method

charAt(int index)

returns a char value that corresponds to the letter at position index.

toCharArray()  returns the String object converted to a char array.

*charAt()*

*toCharArray()*

The value returned by the charAt() method is a char data type. A char data type represents a single character, such as a letter or symbol. The toCharArray() method converts each character in the string to a char and then assigns it to the appropriate element in an existing char array.

*Unicode*

Letters of every alphabet and symbols of every culture have been given a representation in a digital code called Unicode. *Unicode* uses a set of sixteen 1s and 0s to form a sixteen-bit binary code for each symbol. For example, the uppercase letter V is Unicode 00000000 01010110, which translates to the base 10 number 86. Lowercase v has a separate code that translates to the base 10 number 118.

**TIP** Refer to the appendix in this text for more Unicode symbols and their values.

When a letter is assigned to a char variable, the variable actually stores the Unicode representation of the letter. Uppercase letters from A to Z have values from 65 through 90. Lowercase letters from a to z have values from 97 through 122. Because char is a primitive data type, char values can be compared with relational operators, as the code below demonstrates:

```
char letter1, letter2;
letter1 = 'a';
letter2 = 'A'
if (letter1 > letter2) {
  System.out.println("greater than")  //greater than displayed
} else {
  System.out.println("less than")
}
```

The CountLetters application counts the frequency of letters in a string. Each letter in the string is first converted to uppercase and then the counter at the appropriate index is incremented. Since uppercase letters have a range from 65 to 90 in Unicode, offset array indexes are used to determine which element to update:

**TIP** Assignment to a char variable requires single quotation marks around the character.

```
import java.util.Scanner;

public class CountLetters {

  public static void main(String[] args) {
    final int LOW = 'A';       //smallest possible value
    final int HIGH = 'Z';      //highest possible value
    int[] letterCounts = new int[HIGH - LOW + 1];
    Scanner input = new Scanner(System.in);
    String word;
    char[] wordLetters;
    int offset;                //array index
```

```
/* prompt user for a word */
System.out.print("Enter a word: ");
word = input.nextLine();

/* convert word to char array and count letter occurrences */
word = word.toUpperCase();
wordLetters = word.toCharArray();
for (int letter = 0; letter < wordLetters.length; letter++) {
  offset = wordLetters[letter] - LOW;
  letterCounts[offset] += 1;
}

/* show letter occurrences */
for (int i = LOW; i <= HIGH; i++) {
  System.out.println((char)i + ": " + letterCounts[i - LOW]);
}
    }
  }
```

Note the statements for creating a char array from a String object. First, the char array wordLetters was declared. Later, wordLetters was initialized using the toCharArray() method in the statement:

```
wordLetters = word.toCharArray();
```

The number of characters in the string determined the number of array elements.

*type casting*    Type casting was used in the last statement of the CountLetters application ((char)i) to produce labels for the contents of the array. Casting the int to a char produces the Unicode equivalent character for that number.

The CountLetters application produces output similar to:

```
Enter a word: algorithm
A: 1
B: 0
C: 0
D: 0
E: 0
F: 0
G: 1
H: 1
I: 1
J: 0
K: 0
L: 1
M: 1
N: 0
O: 1
P: 0
Q: 0
R: 1
S: 0
T: 1
U: 0
V: 0
W: 0
X: 0
Y: 0
Z: 0
```

## Review: CountLetters

The CountLetters application is limited to counting letters in a single word. Modify the CountLetters application to count the letters in an entire phrase, which contains spaces. Care must be taken to ignore the spaces and any other nonalphabetic character found in the phrase. Be sure to change comments and variable names appropriately so that the reader of the application code understands that the letters in a phrase are counted.

## Review: NameBackwards

Create a NameBackwards application that prompts the user for his or her name and then displays the name backwards.

## Searching an Array

*linear search*

There are many ways to search an array for a specific value. The simpliest searching algorithm is called *linear search* and works by proceeding from one array element to the next until the specified value is found or until the entire array has been searched. The Search class below contains a linear() method that returns the index of a specified `int` element. If the element is not found, then –1 is returned:

```java
public class Search {

    /**
     * Returns the index of the element numToFind.
     * -1 returned if element not found.
     * pre: none
     * post: index of numToFind has been returned. -1 has been
     * returned if element not found.
     */
    public static int linear(int[] array, int numToFind) {
        int index = 0;

        while ((array[index] != numToFind) &&
                (index < array.length - 1)) {
            index += 1;
        }

        if (array[index] == numToFind) {
            return(index);
        } else {
            return(-1);
        }
    }
}
```

> ### *Algorithm Analysis*
>
> Algorithm analysis includes measuring how efficiently an algorithm performs its task. A linear search sequentially checks each element of an array for a specified element. For an array with *n* objects, finding an element could take as many as *n* checks. This measure can be written as O(n). This notation is called Big Oh notation and is a theoretical measure of an algorithm's efficiency.

The condition of the `while` statement checks all but the last element of the array, unless the search element is found earlier. If the `while` statement completes without finding the element, the index value has been incremented to the last index of the array The `if` statement then checks the last element of the array.

The application below uses the linear() method to find an element in the array:

```java
import java.util.Scanner;
import java.util.Math;

public class FindNum {

  public static void main(String[] args) {
    final int MAX = 20;
    int[] numArray = new int[MAX];
    Scanner input = new Scanner(System.in);
    int num, location;

    /* fill array with random numbers */
    for (int i = 0; i < numArray.length;i ++) {
      numArray[i] = (int)(MAX+1) * Math.random());
    }

    /* prompt user for a number to search for */
    System.out.print("Enter a number between 0 and " + MAX
                                    + ": ");
    num = input.nextInt();

    /* Search for number and notify user of num location */
    location = Search.linear(numArray, num);
    if (location == -1) {
      System.out.println("Sorry, number not found in array.");
    } else {
      System.out.println("First occurrence is element "
                                      + location);
    }
  }
}
```

The FindNum application output looks similar to:

```
Enter a number between 0 and 20: 7
First occurrence is element 11
```

## Review: FindName

Add a `static` method to the Search class that performs a linear search on a String array. The linear() method should overload the existing method, have parameters for accepting a String array and a String variable, and return an `int` indicating the position of the String. Create a FindName application that uses the Search class. FindName should prompt the user for names to fill an array and then prompt the user for the name to find.

## Two-Dimensional Arrays

An array with two dimensions can be used to represent data that corresponds to a grid. For example, a checkerboard, the streets in a city, and seats in a theater can all be represented with a grid. A tic-tac-toe board represented in a two-dimensional array can be visualized as shown on the next page.

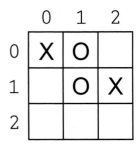

*A two-dimensional array with three rows (0, 1, and 2) and three columns (0, 1, and 2) represents a tic-tac-toe board*

**declaration**    A two-dimensional array must be declared and then space allocated for the elements of the array in statements that take the form:

```
<type>[][] <name>;
<name> = new <type>[<num>][<num>];
```

The declaration includes the type followed by two sets of brackets ([][]). The array name can be any valid identifier. The new operator allocates space for the number of elements indicated in brackets. For example, a tic-tac-toe board could be created with the statement:

```
String[][] tttBoard = new String[3][3];
```

**length**    The length property can be used to determine the number of rows and columns in a two-dimensional array with two separate statements:

```
rows = tttBoard.length;
cols = tttBoard[0].length;
```

Note that the number of columns is determined by checking the length of the first row.

**accessing elements**    An element of a two-dimensional array is accessed by including the indexes of the row and column in brackets after the array name. For example, the following statement assigns the element in the second row, third column the letter "X":

```
tttBoard[1][2] = "X";
```

**nested for statements**    Nested for statements are often used to access the elements of a two-dimensional array because one loop counter indicates the row and the second counter indicates the column. For example, the following statements display the contents of a two-dimensional array:

```
for(int row = 0; row < tttBoard.length; row++) {
    for (int col = 0; col < tttBoard[0].length; col++) {
        System.out.print(tttBoard[row][col]);
    }
    System.out.println();
}
```

**array parameter**    A method that requires a two-dimensional array parameter includes the array data type followed by two sets of brackets ([][]).

The TicTacToe application allows two players to play a computerized game of tic-tac-toe. The TTT class performs most of the work with private methods. The client code simply instantiates a TTT object and then calls the TTT object's play() method. The client code implementation is shown first and then the TTT class implementation:

```java
/**
 * Tic-tac-toe is played.
 */

public class TicTacToe {

  public static void main(String[] args) {
      TTT TTTGame = new TTT();
      TTTGame.play();
  }
}


/**
 * TTT class.
 */

import java.util.Scanner;

public class TTT {
   private String[][] tttBoard;
   private String player1, player2;


   /**
    * constructor
    * pre: none
    * post: tttBoard has been initialized.
    * player1 is X and player2 is 0.
    */
   public TTT() {
     player1 = "X";
     player2 = "0";
     tttBoard = new String[3][3];
     for(int row = 0; row < tttBoard.length; row++) {
       for (int col = 0; col < tttBoard[0].length; col++) {
         tttBoard[row][col] = " ";
       }
     }
   }


   /**
    * Plays a game of tic-tac-toe with two users,
    * keeping track of player (X or 0) turns.
    * player1 goes first.
    * pre: none
    * post: A game of tic-tac-toe has been played.
    */
   public void play() {
     String currPlayer = player1;
     int movesMade = 0;

     do {
       displayBoard();
       makeMove(currPlayer);
       movesMade += 1;
       if (currPlayer == player1){
         currPlayer = player2;
       } else {
         currPlayer = player1;
       }
     } while (movesMade <= 9 && winner() == " ");
     displayBoard();
     System.out.println("Winner is " + winner());
   }
```

```
/**
 * Displays the board.
 * pre:  none
 * post: The tic-tac-toe board has been displayed.
 */
private void displayBoard() {
  for(int row = 0; row < tttBoard.length; row++) {
    for (int col = 0; col < tttBoard[0].length; col++) {
      System.out.print("[" + tttBoard[row][col] + "]");
    }
    System.out.println();
  }
}


/**
 * Prompt user for a move until a valid move has been made.
 * pre:  none
 * post: A mark has been made in an empty tic-tac-toe
 * board square.
 */
private void makeMove(String player) {
  Scanner input = new Scanner(System.in);
  boolean validMove = false;
  int row, col;

  do {
    System.out.print("Enter row number (0, 1, 2): ");
    row = input.nextInt();
    System.out.print("Enter column number (0, 1, 2): ");
    col = input.nextInt();
    if ((row >= 0 && row < tttBoard.length &&
      col >= 0 && col < tttBoard[0].length) &&
      tttBoard[row][col].equals(" ")) {
      tttBoard[row][col] = player;
      validMove = true;
      } else {
        System.out.println("Invalid move.  Try again.");
      }
  } while (!validMove);
}


/**
 * Determine winner. Return " " if no winner.
 * pre:  none
 * post: X, O, or " " has been returned as the winner.
 */
private String winner() {

  /* test rows */
  for (int row = 0; row < tttBoard.length; row++) {
    if (tttBoard[row][0].equals(tttBoard[row][1]) &&
        tttBoard[row][1].equals(tttBoard[row][2]) &&
        !(tttBoard[row][0].equals(" "))) {
        return(tttBoard[row][0]);
    }
  }
```

```
/* test columns */
for (int col = 0; col < tttBoard[0].length; col++) {
  if (tttBoard[0][col].equals(tttBoard[1][col]) &&
      tttBoard[1][col].equals(tttBoard[2][col]) &&
      !(tttBoard[0][col].equals(" "))) {
      return(tttBoard[0][col]);
  }
}

/* test diagonal */
if (tttBoard[0][0].equals(tttBoard[1][1]) &&
    tttBoard[1][1].equals(tttBoard[2][2]) &&
    !(tttBoard[0][0].equals(" "))) {
  return(tttBoard[0][0]);
}

/* test other diagonal */
if (tttBoard[0][2].equals(tttBoard[1][1]) &&
    tttBoard[1][1].equals(tttBoard[2][0]) &&
    !(tttBoard[0][2].equals(" "))) {
  return(tttBoard[0][2]);
}
return(" ");
  }
}
```

The TicTacToe application displays output similar to:

```
[ ][ ][ ]
[ ][ ][ ]
[ ][ ][ ]
Enter row number (0, 1, 2): 0
Enter column number (0, 1, 2): 1
[ ][X][ ]
[ ][ ][ ]
[ ][ ][ ]
Enter row number (0, 1, 2): 5
Enter column number (0, 1, 2): 5
Invalid move.  Try again.
Enter row number (0, 1, 2): 2
Enter column number (0, 1, 2): 2
[ ][X][ ]
[ ][ ][ ]
[ ][ ][O]
Enter row number (0, 1, 2): 1
Enter column number (0, 1, 2): 0
[ ][X][ ]
[X][ ][ ]
[ ][ ][O]
Enter row number (0, 1, 2): 2
Enter column number (0, 1, 2): 0
[ ][X][ ]
[X][ ][ ]
[O][ ][O]
Enter row number (0, 1, 2): 0
Enter column number (0, 1, 2): 0
[X][X][ ]
[X][ ][ ]
[O][ ][O]
Enter row number (0, 1, 2): 2
Enter column number (0, 1, 2): 1
[X][X][ ]
[X][ ][ ]
[O][O][O]
Winner is O
```

# The ArrayList Class

*collection*

*collections framework*

**TIP** The ArrayList class is a data structure. Data structures are discussed further in Chapter 13.

### Data Structure Analysis

Data structure analysis includes measuring the efficiency of a data structure's operations. For example, adding an object to the end of an ArrayList data structure requires a single operation, which can be written as O(1). However, adding an object to the beginning of the array requires all the existing objects first be moved up one position. For an array with *n* objects, adding an object to the front of the array requires *n* operations, which can be written as O(n). This is a much less efficient operation.

*dynamic array*

A *collection* is a group of related objects, or elements, that are stored together as a single unit. An array is an example of a collection. Java also contains a *collections framework,* which provides classes for implementing collections. One such class is the ArrayList class, which includes methods for adding and deleting elements and finding an element.

### Class ArrayList (java.util.ArrayList)

### Method

`add(int index, Object element)`

inserts `element` at `index` position of the array. Existing elements are shifted to the next position up in the array.

`add(Object element)`

adds `element` to the end of the array.

`get(int index)`

returns the `element` at `index` position in the array.

`indexOf(Object obj)`

returns the `index` of the first element matching `obj` using the equals() method of the object's class to determine equality between the element and the object.

`remove(int index)`

removes the element at `index` position in the array.

`set(int index, Object element)`

replaces the element at `index` position with `element`.

`size()` returns the number of elements in the array.

The ArrayList class implements a dynamic array. A *dynamic array* varies in size during run time and is used in applications where the size of an array may need to grow or shrink. An ArrayList object shifts elements up one position when a new element is added at a specific index. Elements added to the end of the ArrayList do not move existing elements. Removing an element from an ArrayList also shifts elements as necessary to close the gap left by the removed element.

When using an ArrayList object, it is important to understand that only objects, not primitive types, can be stored. Because the indexOf() method compares its object parameter to each element of the array, it is important that the object's class has an appropriately overridden equals() method.

Collections, such as ArrayList, make use of *generics* for communicating to the compiler the type of data stored. For example, to declare an ArrayList of String objects, a statement using generics appears similar to:

```
ArrayList<String> myStrings = new ArrayList<String>();
```

The `<String>` part of the statement is a type parameter informing the compiler of what type of objects the ArrayList can contain. The type parameter is read "of Type" or in this case "of String."

The following application creates an ArrayList object, adds elements, removes an element, and then displays the remaining elements:

```
import java.util.ArrayList;

public class TestArrayList {

    public static void main(String[] args) {
        ArrayList<String> myStrings = new ArrayList<String>();

        myStrings.add("Kermit");
        myStrings.add("Lucille");
        myStrings.add("Sammy");
        myStrings.add("Roxy");
        myStrings.add("Myah");

        myStrings.remove(3);

        for (String name : myStrings) {
            System.out.println(name);
        }
    }
}
```

**TIP** The `for-each` statement is not a safe structure for finding and removing elements from an ArrayList.

The ArrayList declaration does not require an array size. An ArrayList object grows and shrinks automatically as elements are added and removed. The `for-each` statement traverses the ArrayList. An ArrayList converts elements to their superclass Object, which is why `name` is type Object, rather than String.

The TestArrayList application displays the output:

```
Kermit
Lucille
Sammy
Myah
```

# Wrapper Classes

**TIP** Java also includes the Character, Boolean, Byte, Short, Long, and Float wrapper classes.

Primitive data types cannot be directly stored in an ArrayList because the elements in an ArrayList must be objects. The Integer and Double classes, provided with Java, are used to "wrap" primitive values in an object. The Integer and Double *wrapper classes* include methods for comparing objects and for returning, or "unwrapping", the primitive value stored by the object:

### Class Integer (java.lang.Integer)

### Method

`compareTo(Integer intObject)`

returns 0 when the Integer object value is the same as `intObject`. A negative `int` is returned when the Integer object is less than `intObject`, and a positive `int` is returned when the Integer object is greater than `intObject`.

`intValue()`        returns the `int` value of the Integer object.

`compareTo(Double doubleObject)`

returns 0 when the Double object value is the same as `doubleObject`. A negative `int` is returned when the Double object is less than `doubleObject`, and a positive `int` is returned when the Double object is greater than `doubleObject`.

`doubleValue()`    returns the `double` value of the Double object.

The Integer and Double wrapper classes are in the java.lang package. An `import` statement is not required to use the wrapper classes.

The DataArrayList application creates an ArrayList of Integer values, compares the values, and then sums the elements:

```
import java.util.ArrayList;

public class DataArrayList {

 public static void main(String[] args) {
    ArrayList<Integer> numbers = new ArrayList<Integer>();
    Integer element, element1, element2;
    int sum = 0;

    numbers.add(new Integer(5));
    numbers.add(new Integer(2));

    /* compare values */
    element1 = numbers.get(0);
    element2 = numbers.get(1);
    if (element1.compareTo(element2) == 0) {
      System.out.println("The elements have the same value.");
    } else if (element1.compareTo(element2) < 0) {
      System.out.println("element1 value is less than element2.");
    } else {
      System.out.println("element1 value is greater than element2.");
    }
    /* sum values */
    for (Integer num : numbers) {
      element = num;
      sum += element.intValue(); //use int value for sum
    }
    System.out.println("Sum of the elements is: " + sum);
  }
}
```

In the first `numbers.add()` statement above, the `new` operator allocates memory and returns a reference to the Integer object that stores the value 5. A second statement performs the same type of action to add another Integer object to the ArrayList.

The values stored in the elements are compared using the compareTo() method. Note that the elements are first assigned to Integer objects `element1` and `element2`. Finally, the `for-each` statement traverses the ArrayList elements and sums their values. Each element must be "unwrapped" so that the `int` value of each Integer object is used to update sum.

The DataArrayList displays the output:

```
element1 value is greater than element2.
Sum of the elements is: 7
```

## Review: HighestGrade

Create a HighestGrade application that prompts the user for five grades between 0 and 100 points and stores the grades in an ArrayList. HighestGrade then traverses the grades to determine the highest grade and then displays the grade along with an appropriate message.

## Autoboxing and Auto-Unboxing

The use of primitives in an ArrayList requires additional code for wrapping and unwrapping values. The extra code can quickly "clutter" an application making it harder to read. Remembering the syntax for wrapping and unwrapping could also lead to longer development times. *Autoboxing* and *auto-unboxing* automatically wraps and unwraps primitives, eliminating the need for the extra code. The DataArrayList2 application creates an ArrayList of Integer values, compares the values, and then sums the elements without the extra wrapper class code:

```java
import java.util.ArrayList;

public class DataArrayList2 {

public static void main(String[] args) {
    ArrayList<Integer> numbers = new ArrayList<Integer>();
    int element1, element2;
    int sum = 0;

    numbers.add(5);  //autoboxing converts int 5 to Integer
    numbers.add(2);  //autoboxing converts int 2 to Integer

    /* compare values */
    element1 = numbers.get(0);    //auto-unboxing converts to int
    element2 = numbers.get(1);    //auto-unboxing converts to int
    if (element1 == element2) {   //primitives will be compared
      System.out.println("The elements have the same value.");
    } else if (element1 < element2) {
      System.out.println("element1 value is less than element2.");
    } else {
      System.out.println("element1 value is greater than element2.");
    }

    /* sum values */
    for (Integer num : numbers) {
        sum += num;     //uses int value for sum
    }
    System.out.println("Sum of the elements is:  " + sum);
  }
}
```

The code above is cleaner and easier to understand. Autoboxing wraps, or boxes, a number in its appropriate wrapper class. Auto-unboxing calls the appropriate wrapper class method to unwrap, or unbox, the value stored in a wrapper class object.

In this case study, a bank application will be created. A bank can open new accounts, modify existing accounts, and close accounts. An account has a number associated with it, and transactions, such as deposits and withdrawals, require the account number.

**TIP** A Bank application was also developed in Chapter 7.

### LocalBank Specification

The LocalBank application allows accounts to be opened, modified, and closed. Each account has a unique account number, which is required for all transactions. Transactions include deposits and withdrawals. An account balance can also be checked.

The LocalBank interface should provide a menu of options. Depending on the option selected, additional input may be needed. When a transaction is performed, updated account information should be displayed. The LocalBank output sketch:

```
Deposit\Withdrawal\Check balance
Add an account\Remove an account
Quit

Enter choice: a
First name: Adriana
Last name: Lee
Beginning balance: 100
Account created. Account ID is: ALee

Deposit\Withdrawal\Check balance
Add an account\Remove an account
Quit

Enter choice: D
Enter account ID: ALee
Deposit amount: 22
ALee
Adriana Lee
Current balance is $122

Deposit\Withdrawal\Check balance
Add an account\Remove an account
Quit

Enter choice:
```

The LocalBank algorithm:

1. Display a menu of options.

2. Prompt the user for a menu choice.

3. For all options except the option to add an account, prompt the user for an account number.

4. Perform the action requested by the user on the account with the number entered. If the user requested to create a new account, then add an account and display the new account's number.

5. Repeat steps 1 through 4 until the user has selected the option to quit.

## LocalBank Code Design

The LocalBank application can be modeled with a Bank object, Account objects, and Customer objects. The Bank object should store the accounts, add and remove accounts, and perform transactions that also display updated account information. A transaction requires finding the correct account. The Account objects should store the current balance, make deposits, make withdrawals, and return the current balance and account ID. An Account object must also have an equals() method for the Bank object to use when finding an account. The Customer objects should store the account holder's name. The Bank object will display account information, therefore, the Account and Customer objects will override the toString() methods.

The LocalBank class designs are:

Bank

variables: accounts

methods:
    addAccount – prompts the user for new account
                information. Displays the account number.
    deleteAccount – removes an account. Requires a
                parameter for the account number.
    transaction – performs a deposit or withdrawal. Requires
                parameters for the transaction code,
                account ID, and amount.
    checkBalance – Displays account information, including
                current balance. Requires a parameter for
                the account ID.


Account

variables: balance, Customer cust

methods:
    getID – returns the account ID.
    getBalance – returns the current balance.
    deposit – increases the balance. Requires
            parameter for amount.
    withdrawal – decreases the balance. Requires parameter
              for amount. If balance is less than withdrawal,
              then balance left unchanged.
    equals – returns true when another Account object has
             the same ID as the object, returns false otherwise.
             Requires a parameter for the other object.
    toString – returns string with customer information
            and current balance.

Customer

variables: firstName, lastName

methods:
toString() – returns a string with customer information.

The Account and Customer class designs are similar to the classes developed in Chapter 7. In the real world, the existing classes would probably be reused for the LocalBank application. The modularity of OOP makes programming more efficient and less error-prone. For this case study, simplified classes will be developed and used for the application.

Based on the algorithm and the class designs, the LocalBank code design will include a loop. The pseudocode for the LocalBank client code follows:

```
Bank easySave = new Bank();
do {
    prompt user for transaction type

    if (add account) {
        easySave.addAccount();
    } else if (not Quit) {
        prompt user for account ID;
        if (deposit) {
          prompt user for deposit amount
          easySave.transaction(make deposit, acctID, amt);
        } else if (withdrawal) {
          prompt user for withdrawal amount
          easySave.transaction(make withdrawal, acctID, amt);
        } else if (check balance) {
          easySave.checkBalance(acctID);
        } else if (remove account) {
          easySave.deleteAccount(acctID);
        }
    }
} while (not quit);
```

### LocalBank Implementation

The LocalBank implementation involves creating four files. Three files are the classes and one file is the client code.

The Bank class is implemented below:

```
/**
 * Bank class.
 */

import java.util.ArrayList;
import java.util.Scanner;
```

```java
public class Bank {
    private ArrayList accounts;


    /**
     * constructor
     * pre:  none
     * post: accounts has been initialized.
     */
    public Bank() {
        accounts = new ArrayList();
    }


    /**
     * Adds a new account to the bank accounts.
     * pre:  none
     * post: An account has been added to the bank's accounts.
     */
    public void addAccount() {
        Account newAcct;
        double bal;
        String fName, lName;
        Scanner input = new Scanner(System.in);

        System.out.print("First name: ");
        fName = input.nextLine();
        System.out.print("Last name: ");
        lName = input.nextLine();
        System.out.print("Beginning balance: ");
        bal = input.nextDouble();

        newAcct = new Account(bal, fName, lName);    //create acct object
        accounts.add(newAcct);                       //add account to bank accounts

        System.out.println("Account created. Account ID is: " + newAcct.getID());
    }


    /**
     * Deletes an existing account.
     * pre:  none
     * post: An existing account has been deleted.
     */
    public void deleteAccount(String acctID) {
        int acctIndex;
        Account acctToMatch;

        acctToMatch = new Account(acctID);
        acctIndex = accounts.indexOf(acctToMatch);         //retrieve location of account
        if (acctIndex > -1) {
            accounts.remove(acctIndex);                    //remove account
            System.out.println("Account removed.");
        } else {
            System.out.println("Account does not exist.");
        }
    }
```

```
/**
 * Performs a transaction on an existing account. A transCode of 1 is for deposits
 * and a transCode of 2 is for withdrawals.
 * pre: transCode is 1 or 2.
 * post: A transaction has occurred for an existing account.
 */
public void transaction(int transCode, String acctID, double amt) {
    int acctIndex;
    Account acctToMatch, acct;

    acctToMatch = new Account(acctID);
    acctIndex = accounts.indexOf(acctToMatch);        //retrieve location of account
    if (acctIndex > -1) {
        acct = (Account)accounts.get(acctIndex); //retrieve object to modify
        if (transCode == 1) {
            acct.deposit(amt);
            accounts.set(acctIndex, acct);        //replace object with updated object
            System.out.println(acct);
        } else if (transCode == 2) {
            acct.withdrawal(amt);
            accounts.set(acctIndex, acct);        //replace object with updated object
            System.out.println(acct);
        }
    } else {
        System.out.println("Account does not exist.");
    }
}


/**
 * Displays the account information, including the current balance,
 * for an existing account.
 * pre: none
 * post: Account information, including balance, has been displayed.
 */
public void checkBalance(String acctID) {
    int acctIndex;
    Account acctToMatch, acct;

    acctToMatch = new Account(acctID);
    acctIndex = accounts.indexOf(acctToMatch);        //retrieve location of account
    if (acctIndex > -1) {
        acct = (Account)accounts.get(acctIndex); //retrieve object to display
        System.out.println(acct);
    } else {
        System.out.println("Account does not exist.");
    }
}
}
```

In the deleteAccount() and transaction() methods, a new Account object is created for the purposes of finding the account to delete or modify. The new Account object is instantiated with just the acctID and then this object is passed to the indexOf() method of the ArrayList class. The indexOf() method searches the ArrayList and automatically invokes the equals() method of the Account class to determine equality. The Account class is implemented below. Note that the equals() method requires only that the account numbers of two object match to be considered equal:

```
/**
 * Account class.
 */

import java.text.NumberFormat;

public class Account {
    private double balance;
    private Customer cust;
    private String acctID;


    /**
     * constructor
     * pre: none
     * post: An account has been created. Balance and
     * customer data has been initialized with parameters.
     */
    public Account(double bal, String fName, String lName) {
        balance = bal;
        cust = new Customer(fName, lName);
        acctID = fName.substring(0,1) + lName;
    }


    /**
     * constructor
     * pre: none
     * post: An empty account has been created with the specified account ID.
     */
    public Account(String ID) {
        balance = 0;
        cust = new Customer("", "");
        acctID = ID;
    }


    /**
     * Returns the account ID.
     * pre: none
     * post: The account ID has been returned.
     */
    public String getID() {
        return(acctID);
    }


    /**
     * Returns the current balance.
     * pre: none
     * post: The account balance has been returned.
     */
    public double getBalance() {
        return(balance);
    }


    /**
     * A deposit is made to the account.
     * pre: none
     * post: The balance has been increased by the amount of the deposit.
     */
    public void deposit(double amt) {
        balance += amt;
    }
```

```
/**
 * A withdrawal is made from the account if there is enough money.
 * pre: none
 * post: The balance has been decreased by the amount withdrawn.
 */
public void withdrawal(double amt) {
    if (amt <= balance) {
        balance -= amt;
    } else {
        System.out.println("Not enough money in account.");
    }
}


/**
 * Returns a true when objects have matching account IDs.
 * pre: none
 * post: true has been returned when the objects are equal,
 * false returned otherwise.
 */
public boolean equals(Object acct) {
    Account testAcct = (Account)acct;
    if (acctID.equals(testAcct.acctID)) {
            return(true);
        } else {
            return(false);
        }
}


/**
 * Returns a String that represents the Account object.
 * pre: none
 * post: A string representing the Account object has been returned.
 */
public String toString() {
    String accountString;
    NumberFormat money = NumberFormat.getCurrencyInstance();

    accountString = acctID + "\n";
    accountString += cust.toString();
    accountString += "Current balance is " + money.format(balance);
    return(accountString);
}
}
```

The Account class has two constructors. The second constructor is used in the deleteAccount() and transaction() methods of the Bank class for the purposes of finding the index of the account matching the given account ID.

The Customer class is implemented on the next page:

```
/**
 * Customer class.
 */

public class Customer {
    private String firstName, lastName;


    /**
     * constructor
     * pre: none
     * post: A Customer object has been created.
     * Customer data has been initialized with parameters.
     */
    public Customer(String fName, String lName) {
        firstName = fName;
        lastName = lName;
    }



    /**
     * Returns a String that represents the Customer object.
     * pre: none
     * post: A string representing the Customer object has
     * been returned.
     */
    public String toString() {
        String custString;

        custString = firstName() + " " + lastName() + "\n";
        return(custString);
    }
}
```

The LocalBank client code is implemented below:

```
/**
 * A bank where accounts can be opened or closed and customers can
 * make transactions.
 */

import java.util.Scanner;

public class LocalBank {

    public static void main(String[] args) {
        Bank easySave = new Bank();
        Scanner input = new Scanner(System.in);
        String action, acctID;
        Double amt;

        /* display menu of choices */
        do {
            System.out.println("\nDeposit\\Withdrawal\\Check balance");
            System.out.println("Add an account\\Remove an account");
            System.out.println("Quit\n");
            System.out.print("Enter choice: ");
            action = input.next();
```

```
        if (action.equalsIgnoreCase("A")) {
            easySave.addAccount();
        } else if (!action.equalsIgnoreCase("Q")) {
            System.out.print("Enter account ID: ");
            acctID = input.next();
            if (action.equalsIgnoreCase("D")) {
                System.out.print("Enter deposit amount: ");
                amt = input.nextDouble();
                easySave.transaction(1, acctID, amt);
            } else if (action.equalsIgnoreCase("W")) {
                System.out.print("Enter withdrawal amount: ");
                amt = input.nextDouble();
                easySave.transaction(2, acctID, amt);
            } else if (action.equalsIgnoreCase("C")) {
                easySave.checkBalance(acctID);
            } else if (action.equalsIgnoreCase("R")) {
                easySave.deleteAccount(acctID);
            }
        }
    } while (!action.equalsIgnoreCase("Q"));
}
}
```

Running the LocalBank application displays output similar to:

```
Deposit\Withdrawal\Check balance
Add an account\Remove an account
Quit

Enter choice: a
First name: Jake
Last name: White
Beginning balance: 1500
Account created. Account ID is: JWhite

Deposit\Withdrawal\Check balance
Add an account\Remove an account
Quit

Enter choice: d
Enter account ID: JWhite
Enter deposit amount: 478
JWhite
Jake White
Current balance is $1,978.00

Deposit\Withdrawal\Check balance
Add an account\Remove an account
Quit

Enter choice:
```

It was possible to create the LocalBank application with fewer classes. However, by breaking the application into discrete objects, it will be easier to later extend the classes to enhace the client code. For example, an account can easily be extended to include an account holder's address by modifying, or extending, the Customer class. Then, only the first constructor of the Account class will need to be modifed to handle additional parameters for creating a Customer object.

### LocalBank Testing and Debugging

When a new class is written, client code should be written to test the class. Each class should be tested first and then for the client code.

*Chapter 9 Arrays*

Modify the Bank class to prompt the user for a full address (street, city, state, and zip) when an account is opened. Modify the Customer class to include street, city, state, and zip variable members and changeStreet(), changeCity(), changeState(), and changeZip() method members. Modify the Customer toString() method to display complete customer information. Modify the Account class to include a changeAddress() method member. Modify the Bank class to include a modifyAccount() method member that requires a parameter for the account ID. modifyAccount() should prompt the user for the new street, city, state, and zip for the account, find the account with the matching account ID, and then overwrite the existing account object with the object containing the updated information.

## Chapter Summary

This chapter discussed arrays as a structure for storing many of the same kind of data together at once. A data item stored by an array is called an element. An element has an index value and is accessed by using the index inside of [] brackets along with the array name. A `for` statement and the `for-each` statement can be used to access all the elements of an array. Accessing the elements of an array is called traversing the array. When the index of an element is needed, the `for` statement should be used.

An array can be passed to a method as a parameter and is a reference data type. Passing a single element passes the data stored, not a reference to the data location.

Many algorithms make use of the index value for simplifying the storage and retrieval of data. Offset array indexes are used when a range should be shifted to correlate to a lower range of index values.

A String can be converted to an array of characters so that individual characters can be manipulated. Unicode is the standard for numeric representation of every letter and symbol in use.

The linear search is an algorithm for searching an array where each element is checked one after the other until the desired element is found.

Two-dimensional arrays represent data that corresponds to a grid. The number of rows in an existing two-dimensional array corresponds to the length of the array. The number of columns corresponds to the length of the first row. Elements in a two-dimensional array are accessed by using a double bracket ([][]) along with the array name.

The ArrayList class is used for storing a collection of objects. Methods are used for accessing and retrieving elements and for determining the number of elements in the collection. An ArrayList object is a dynamic array, which can vary in size at run time. Because an ArrayList can store only objects, wrapper classes are used to convert primitives to objects. Autoboxing and auto-unboxing reduces the clutter of wrapper classes.

# Vocabulary

**Array** A structure that can store many of the same kind of data together at once.

**ArrayOutOfBoundsException** An exception thrown when an invalid array index is used.

**Autoboxing** The process in which a primitive is automatically converted to a wrapper class object.

**Auto-unboxing** The process in which a primitive is automatically extracted from a wrapper class object.

**Collection** A group of related elements that are stored together as a single unit.

**Collections framework** Classes for implementing collections.

**Dynamic array** An array that varies in size at run time.

**Element** A data item in an array.

**Generics** Used for communicating to the compiler the type of data stored in an ArrayList.

**Index** The value associated with an element in an array. Index values begin at 0 and count up.

**Linear search** An algorithm for searching an array in which each element of the array is checked one after the other.

**Traversing** Iterating through element of an array.

**Type parameter** The part of an ArrayList statement that informs the compiler of what type of objects the ArrayList can contain, for example, `<String>`.

**Unicode** The sixteen-bit digital code used to represent every letter and symbol.

**Wrapper class** A class that wraps primitive values in an object.

# Java

`[]` The operators for accessing an array element.

**ArrayList** A java.util class with methods for implementing a dynamic array.

**Double** A java.lang class for wrapping `double` values in an object.

`for` A statement that can be used to traverse an array. In one form, it is referred to as a `for-each` statement and does not use a counter variable.

**Integer** A java.lang class for wrapping `int` values in an object.

`new` Operator that allocates space for the elements in an array.

**String** A java.lang class with methods for converting a string to a set of characters or for inspecting individual characters of a string.

1. What index value does the third element of an array have?

2. Write the declaration for an array named `quantities` that stores 20 integers.

3. Write a declaration for an array named `heights` storing the numbers 1.65, 2.15, and 4.95.

4. Write a `for-each` statement that displays the integer values stored in an array named `grades`.

5. a) Write an algorithm for inserting data into an array so that existing data is moved up one position to make room for the new data.
   b) Write an algorithm for deleting data from an array so that existing data is moved to close the gap made by the deleted data.

6. How does passing an entire array to a method differ from passing a single element of the array?

7. Why are offset array indexes required in some cases.

8. What output is displayed by the statements below?

   ```
   String name = "Elaine";
   System.out.println(name.charAt(3));
   ```

9. Compare and contrast an array to an ArrayList by describing the differences between the two for:
   a) accessing an element.
   b) adding an element.
   c) deleting an element.
   d) assigning a new value to an element.
   e) determining the size of the collection.

10. Give an example of when a dynamic array might be a better structure choice over an array.

11. How does the ArrayList indexOf() method determine equality between the object passed to the method and an element in the array?

12. How can the values of wrapper class objects be compared?

13. a) Explain the process of autoboxing and give an example.
    b) Explain the process of auto-unboxing and give an example.
    c) What are the advantages of autoboxing and auto-unboxing?

**True/False**

14. Determine if each of the following are true or false. If false, explain why.
    a) All data in an array has the same data type.
    b) Index values always begin at 0.
    c) The statement `int[] empNums = new int[10]` declares an array with 10 elements.
    d) In the statement `int[] empNums = new int[10]`, the elements are automatically initialized to 1.
    e) An entire array can be passed to a method.
    f) The method toCharArray() converts a String object to a char array.
    g) A linear search never searches an entire array.
    h) The statement `int[][] grid = new int[4][4]` declares a total of eight elements.
    i) In Unicode, uppercase letters have higher base 10 number values than lowercase letters.
    j) The size of an array can change during the execution of a program.
    k) The ArrayList class implements a dynamic array.
    l) Primitive data types can be stored directly in an ArrayList.

## Exercise 1 ———————————————— EvensAndOdds

Create an EvensAndOdds application that generates 25 random integers between 0 and 99 and then displays all the evens on one line and all the odds on the next line. Application output should look similar to:

```
ODD:
37 47 43 41 55 7 37 15 17 75 19 17 53 91 55 23 41
EVEN:
28 70 62 32 68 80 58 36
```

## Exercise 2 ———————————————— GeneratedNums

Create a GeneratedNums application that generates the number to store in an array element by summing its index and the individual digits of the index. For example, the element with index 17 should store 25 (17 + 1 + 7 = 25) and the element with index 2 should store 4 (2 + 0 + 2 = 4). GeneratedNums should use an array with 101 elements and then display the value at each element. Application output should look similar to:

```
Index     Generated Number
0         0
1         2
2         4
3         6
4         8
5         10
6         12
7         14
8         16
9         18
10        11
```

...

## Exercise 3 ———————————————— RandomStats

Create a RandomStats application that generates 500 random numbers between 0 and 9 and then displays the number of occurrences of each number. Application output should look similar to:

```
Number    Occurrences
0         45
1         42
2         55
3         44
4         51
5         54
6         52
7         47
8         61
9         49
```

# Exercise 4 ——————————————— Analysis

A program that analyzes a set of numbers can be very useful. Create an Analysis application that prompts the user for numbers in the range 1 through 50, terminated by a sentinel, and then performs the following analysis on the numbers:

- Determine the average number

- Determine the maximum number

- Determine the range (maximum – minimum)

- Determine the median (the number that occurs the most often)

- Displays a bar graph called a histogram that shows the numbers in each five-unit range (1–5, 6–10, 11-15, etc.). The histogram may look similar to:

```
Enter a number from 1 to 50 (99 to end): 46
Enter a number from 1 to 50 (99 to end): 48
Enter a number from 1 to 50 (99 to end): 8
Enter a number from 1 to 50 (99 to end): 7
Enter a number from 1 to 50 (99 to end): 28
Enter a number from 1 to 50 (99 to end): 28
Enter a number from 1 to 50 (99 to end): 99
The average of the numbers entered are: 27.5
The maximum number entered is: 48
The values have a range: 41
The median value is: 28
A histogram of the data appears like:
  1 -   5 :
  6 -  10 : **
 11 -  15 :
 16 -  20 :
 21 -  25 :
 26 -  30 : **
 31 -  35 :
 36 -  40 :
 41 -  45 :
 46 -  50 : **
```

# Exercise 5 ——————————————— Mastermind

The game of Mastermind is played as follows: One player (the code maker) chooses a secret arrangement of colored pegs and the other player (the code breaker) tries to guess it. For each guess, the code breaker puts forth an arrangement of colored pegs, and the code maker reports two numbers:

1. The number of pegs that are the correct color and in the correct position.

2. The number of pegs that are the correct color regardless of whether they are in the correct position.

Create a Mastermind application that plays the game of Mastermind with the computer as the code maker and the user as the code breaker. The application should use a MastermindGame class, which has a constructor with parameters for the number of pegs in the code (1 to 10) and the number of colors for the pegs (1 to 9). The secret code generated by a MastermindGame object can contain duplicate colors. For example, a 5-peg code could be 1 2 2 5 6. A guess with duplicates will require extra attention when counting the number of pegs of the correct color. For example, if the code is 1 2 3 4 5 6 and the guess is 2 1 1 2 2 2, then the MastermindGame object should only report two correct colors (a single 1 and a single 2). Application output should look similar to:

```
Enter the number of pegs to use (1-10): 3
Enter the number of colors to use (1-9): 3

Guess 1:
Color for peg 1:1
Color for peg 2:2
Color for peg 3:3
You have 1 peg(s) correct and 3 color(s) correct.

Guess 2:
Color for peg 1:2
Color for peg 2:2
Color for peg 3:1
You have 0 peg(s) correct and 2 color(s) correct.

Guess 3:
Color for peg 1:1
Color for peg 2:3
Color for peg 3:2
You have 3 peg(s) correct and 3 color(s) correct.

You have broken the code in 3 guesses.
```

# Exercise 6 ——————————————————————— Lockers

Create a Lockers application that simulates a progressive cycle of closing and opening every *n*th locker in a hall of 100 lockers, with *n* starting at the 2nd locker and continuing through to the 100th locker. The application should represent the locker status (*opened or closed*) as a `boolean` array with `true` representing opened. When the application first starts, all of the lockers should be opened - the array initialized to all `true` values. First, the status of every 2nd lockers should be switched (*if it is open then close it and if it is closed open it*). Then, the status of every 3rd locker should be switched. Continue this process for every 4th through 100th locker. Display the concluding locker statuses.

# Exercise 7 ——————————————————————— WordGuess

Modify the WordGuess case study from Chapter 5 to keep track of the letters guessed in an array with meaningfl indexes. Have WordGuess display a message to the user if a letter has already been guessed.

# Exercise 8 ——————————————————————— Palindrome

Create a Palindrome application that prompts the user for a string and then displays a message indicating whether or not the string is a palindrome. A palindrome is a word or phrase that is spelled the same backwards and forwards. For example, "mom" is a palindrome, as well as "kayak" and "Never odd or even".

# Exercise 9 ———————————————————— CountConsonants

Create a CountConsonants application that prompts the user for a string and then displays the number of consonants in the string. Application output should look similar to:

```
Enter text: java programming
The number of consonants in java programming is 10
```

# Exercise 10 ———————————————————— Coder

Create a Coder application that prompts the user for a string and then displays an encoded string. The encoding should add 2 to the Unicode value of each letter to create a new letter. The application should keep all spaces between the words in their original places and the letters y and z should be converted to a and b, respectively. Coder application output should look similar to:

```
Enter a string: password is RhYxtz
Encoded message: rcuuyqtf ku TjAzvb
```

# Exercise 11 ———————————————————— SortedArray

An array is said to be sorted if its elements are in either increasing or decreasing order. One way the selection sort algorithm works is by repeatedly taking the lowest element from an array and adding it to a new array, so that all the elements in the new array are sorted from lowest to highest.

Create a SelectionSort class with a constructor that has an `int` array parameter, member variables `originalArray` and `sortedArray`, `public` method display() that displays the contents of the sorted array, `private` methods sort() that populates a new array with the elements of the original array in order from lowest to highest, and findLowest() that returns the index of the element containing the lowest value. Hint: Since elements of an array cannot actually be "removed" an element can be set to a very high value after determining its value is the lowest.

Create client code SortedArray, which tests the SelectionSort class. Use the pseudocode below when implementing the SortedArray client code:

```
int[] myNums;
SelectionSort sortedArray;

prompt user for the number of values to populate array with
myNums = new int[values];
populate array with random integers between 0 and 100
display contents of original array

sortedArray = new SelectionSort(myNums);
sortedArray.display();
```

## Exercise 12 ──────────────────────────── CourseGrades

Create a CourseGrades application that simulates a grade book for a class with 12 students that each have 5 test scores. The CourseGrades application should use a GradeBook class that has member variables grades, which is a two-dimensional array or integers, and methods getGrades() for prompting the user for the test grades for each student, showGrades() that displays the grades for the class, studentAvg() that has a student number parameter and then returns the average grade for that student, and testAvg() that has a test number parameter and then returns the average grade for that test.

## Exercise 13 ──────────────────────────── PennyPitch

The Penny Pitch game is popular in amusement parks. Pennies are tossed onto a board that has certain areas marked with different prizes. For example:

| PUZZLE | | POSTER | | DOLL |
|--------|--------|--------|--------|------|
| | POSTER | | DOLL | BALL |
| | PUZZLE | GAME | | |
| PUZZLE | BALL | | POSTER | GAME |
| DOLL | GAME | | | BALL |

The prizes available on this board are puzzle, game, ball, poster, and doll. At the end of the game, if all of the squares that say BALL are covered by a penny, the player gets the ball. This is also true for the other prizes. The board is made up of 25 squares (5 x 5). Each prize appears on three randomly chosen squares so that 15 squares contain prizes.

Create a PennyPitch application that displays a Penny Pitch board (use [ and ] to indicate squares) with prizes randomly placed and then simulates ten pennies being randomly pitched onto the board. After the pennies have been pitched, the application should display a message indicating which prizes have been won, it any.

## Exercise 14 ──────────────────────────── Life

The Game of Life was devised by mathematician John Conway in 1970. It models a very simple world. The Life world is a two-dimensional plane of cells. Each cell may be empty or contain a single creature. Each day, creatures are born or die in each cell according to the number of neighboring creatures on the previous day. A neighbor is a cell that adjoins the cell either horizontally, vertically, or diagonally. The rules in pseudocode style are:

```
if (the cell is alive on the previous day) {
    if (the number of neighbors was 2 or 3) {
       the cell remains alive
    } else {
       the cell dies
    }
} else if (the cell is not alive on the previous day) {
    if (the number of neighbors was exactly 3) {
       the cell becomes alive
    } else {
       the cell remains dead
    }
}
```

For example, the world displayed as:

```
0000000000
0000000000
000XXX0000
0000000000
0000000000
0000000000
```

where X's indicate living cells, becomes:

```
0000000000
0000X00000
0000X00000
0000X00000
0000000000
0000000000
```

Create a Life application that has a 20 x 20 grid. To initialize the grid, the application should prompt the user for the coordinates of live cells on the first day. The application should then generate each day's world as long as the user wishes to continue or until there are no more live cells.

## Exercise 15 ———————————————————————— Manakala

The game of Mankala is played on a board like that illustrated below:

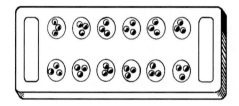

Players sit on opposite sides with the large bin to a player's right designated her home bin. On a turn, a player selects one of the six pits to remove the stones from and then "sows" the stones counterclockwise around the board, placing one stone in each pit including the player's home bin (but excluding the opponent's home bin). If the last stone lands in the player's home bin, the player gets another turn. If the last stone lands in an empty pit on the player's side of the board, the player takes all stones in the corresponding pit on the opponent's side and places them in the player's home bin. When a player cannot play, the game is over and all stones remaining in the opponent's pits go to the opponent's home bin. The winner is the player with the most stones in the player's home bin at the end of the game.

For example, if the bottom player plays first and chooses the fourth pit to play from, the board looks like:

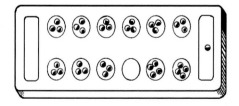

Since the last stone landed in the player's home bin, the player takes another turn. The player may choose the first pit this time in order to capture the opponent's stones:

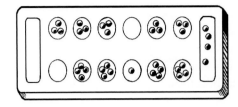

The player's turn is now over, and the opponent now has a turn.

Create a Mankala application. The application should use simple characters to illustrate the board, and letters to identify the pits, similar to that shown below:

```
      3  3  3  3  3  3
   0                    0
      3  3  3  3  3  3
      A  B  C  D  E  F
```

## Exercise 16 —————————————————————————— Inventory

Create an Inventory application that keeps track of the inventory for a sports store. Each item has a stock number, with the first item having a stock number of 1000. The second item has a stock number 1001, the third has stock number 1002, and so on. Along with a stock number, each item has an item name and an amount in stock. New items can be added to the inventory at any time. When added, the item stock number is generated and displayed to the user. Discontinued items should not be deleted from the inventory, but rather their item name should be changed to "discontinued" and the amount in stock should be decreased to 0. The Inventory application should use an ArrayList for maintaining the inventory and application output should display a menu of choices, which allow for adding an item, discontinuing an item, and displaying the amount in stock for an item.

# Chapter 10
# GUIs and Event-Driven Programming

**Key Concepts**

Designing graphical user interfaces
The Swing package
Creating event-driven applications
Controlling the layout of an interface
Using text fields and combo boxes
Applying color
Adding images

**Case Study**

Break a Plate game

## What is a GUI?

A *GUI* is a graphical user interface (sometimes pronounced "gooey"). An application written for the Microsoft Windows or Mac OS X operating system typically has a GUI. The GUI below includes a frame, also called a window, and a label:

Not only does a GUI use components such as frames, buttons, and text fields to communicate with the user, but GUIs are event-driven. An *event-driven application* executes code in response to events. An *event* is an interaction from the user, such as a button click. A GUI responds to an event by executing a method called an *event handler*. For example, when the user clicks a button, the application must be able to determine which button was clicked and then execute the code that relates to that button.

*event-driven application*

*event handler*

## The Swing Package

The Swing API is part of the Java Foundation Classes (JFC) and contains numerous components for creating GUIs. This chapter focuses on the javax.swing package. Two classes in this package are JFrame and JLabel. The JFrame class is used to instantiate a frame. A *frame* is a window with a border, title, and buttons for minimizing, maximizing, and closing the frame. A frame is a top-level *container* for a GUI, which holds and displays all the other components of an interface in a *content frame*. One of the most common components in a content frame is a label. *Labels,* created with the JLabel class, are used to display text that cannot be changed by the user.

*javax.swing*

*frame*

*container, content frame*

*labels*

The swing package includes the JFrame class with the following methods:

### Class JFrame (javax.swing.JFrame)

### Method

`setDefaultLookAndFeelDecorated(boolean)`

> sets the frames created after this class method is called to have Java Window decorations, such as borders and a title, when the `boolean` argument is `true`.

`setDefaultCloseOperation(class_constant)`

> sets the operation that occurs when the user clicks the Close button. The `class_constant` argument is usually `JFrame.EXIT_ON_CLOSE`.

`getContentPane()`

> returns a Container object corresponding to the content pane.

`setContentPane(Container contentPane)`

> sets the content pane to `contentPane`. The Container class is the superclass for the JPanel class, a class for creating content panes.

`pack()`  sizes the frame so that all of its contents are at or above their preferred sizes.

`setVisible(boolean)`

> displays the frame when the `boolean` argument is `true`.

*JPanel content pane*

A JFrame object uses a content pane to hold GUI components. A JPanel object is one choice for a simple content pane. The JPanel class includes the following methods for adding and removing components:

### Class JPanel (javax.swing.JPanel)

### Method

`add(Component GUIcomponent)`

> adds a `GUIcomponent` to the content pane. When added, components are given an index value, with the first component at index 0.

`remove(int index)`

> removes the component with index value `index`.

After adding components to the JPanel object, the content frame is added to the JFrame object using the JFrame setContentPane() method described above.

The swing package includes the JLabel class for creating labels that can be added to a content pane. JLabels have several constructors, two of which are described, in addition to the setText() method:

Class JLabel (javax.swing.JLabel)

**Constructor/Method**

```
JLabel(String str)
```

> creates a JLabel object with text `str`.

```
JLabel(String str, align _ constant)
```

> creates a JLabel object with text `str` and alignment `align _ constant` that can be set to JLabel class constants LEADING or TRAILING, which are left and right alignment, respectively.

```
setText(String str)
```

> sets the text of the JLabel object to `str`.

The HelloWorldWithGUI1 application creates a frame and a content pane, adds the content pane to the frame, and then displays the frame:

```java
import javax.swing.*;

public class HelloWorldWithGUI1 {
    final static String LABEL _ TEXT = "Hello, world!";
    JFrame frame;
    JPanel contentPane;
    JLabel label;

    public HelloWorldWithGUI1(){
        /* Create and set up the frame */
        frame = new JFrame("HelloWorldWithGUI");
        frame.setDefaultCloseOperation(JFrame.EXIT _ ON _ CLOSE);

        /* Create a content pane */
        contentPane = new JPanel();

        /* Create and add label */
        label = new JLabel(LABEL _ TEXT);
        contentPane.add(label);

        /* Add content pane to frame */
        frame.setContentPane(contentPane);

        /* Size and then display the frame. */
        frame.pack();
        frame.setVisible(true);
    }

    /**
     * Create and show the GUI.
     */
    private static void runGUI() {
        JFrame.setDefaultLookAndFeelDecorated(true);

        HelloWorldWithGUI1 greeting = new HelloWorldWithGUI1();
    }

    public static void main(String[] args) {
        /* Methods that create and show a GUI should be
           run from an event-dispatching thread */
        javax.swing.SwingUtilities.invokeLater(new Runnable() {
            public void run() {
                runGUI();
            }
        });
    }
}
```

**TIP** The HelloWorldWithGUI1 application output is shown on the first page of this Chapter.

*Chapter 10 GUIs and Event-Driven Programming*

The implementation of a Swing application is different from previous applications presented in this text. The controlling class contains a constructor and members in addition to the main() method. Therefore, the controlling class is actually used to instantiate an object, which implements the GUI.

*thread*

The statement in the main() method runs the GUI from an event-dispatching thread. A *thread* is simply a process that runs sequentially from start to finish. GUIs should be invoked from an event-dispatching thread to ensure that each event-handler finishes executing before the next one executes. Thorough coverage of this topic is beyond the scope of this text. However, the code shown is needed in every application that implements a Swing GUI.

## Review: Name – part 1 of 2

Create a Name application that displays your name in a label inside a JFrame.

## The JButton Class

A button is a commonly used GUI component. A *button* can be clicked by the user to communicate with the application. For example, the HelloWorldWithGUI2 application includes a button that when clicked either hides or displays text in the label:

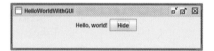

The swing package includes the JButton class for creating buttons:

Class JButton (javax.swing.JButton)

Method

JButton(String str)

> creates a JButton object displaying the text str.

setActionCommand(String cmd)

> sets the name of the action performed when the button is clicked to cmd .

getActionCommand()

> returns the name of the action that has been performed by the button.

addActionListener(Object)

> adds an object that listens for the user to click this component.

Unlike a JLabel, a JButton can respond to interaction from the user.

*Chapter 10 GUIs and Event-Driven Programming*

## Handling Events

*listener*

Swing components use listeners to determine if an event has occurred. A *listener* is an object that listens for action events. When an event is heard, the listener responds by executing an event handler named actionPerformed(). The actionPerformed() method has an ActionEvent parameter passed by the GUI when an event occurs. The ActionEvent object includes an action

*action command*

command. An *action command* is a string describing an event, or action.

The HelloWorldWithGUI2 application output is shown in the previous section. When the Hide button is clicked, the application GUI changes to display:

*this*

The HelloWorldWithGUI2 application code is below. For this GUI, a JButton is created, the JButton action command is set, and the current object is the listener for JButton action events. Note the use of the keyword this for the listener object to indicate the HelloWorldWithGUI2 object itself:

```
import javax.swing.*;
import java.awt.event.*

public class HelloWorldWithGUI2 implements ActionListener {
  final static String LABEL _ TEXT = "Hello, world!";
  JFrame frame;
  JPanel contentPane;
  JLabel label;
  JButton button;

  public HelloWorldWithGUI2(){
    /* Create and set up the frame */
    frame = new JFrame("HelloWorldWithGUI");
    frame.setDefaultCloseOperation(JFrame.EXIT _ ON _ CLOSE);

    /* Create a content pane */
    contentPane = new JPanel();

    /* Create and add label */
    label = new JLabel(LABEL _ TEXT);
    contentPane.add(label);

    /* Create and add button */
    button = new JButton("Hide");
    button.setActionCommand("Hide");
    button.addActionListener(this);
    contentPane.add(button);

    /* Add content pane to frame */
    frame.setContentPane(contentPane);

    /* Size and then display the frame. */
    frame.pack();
    frame.setVisible(true);
  }
```

```
/**
 * Handle button click action event
 * pre: Action event is Hide or Show
 * post: Clicked button has different text, and label
 * displays message depending on when the button was clicked.
 */
public void actionPerformed(ActionEvent event) {
  String eventName = event.getActionCommand();

  if (eventName.equals("Hide")) {
    label.setText(" ");
    button.setText("Show");
    button.setActionCommand("Show");
  } else {
    label.setText(LABEL _ TEXT);
    button.setText("Hide");
    button.setActionCommand("Hide");
  }
}


/**
 * Create and show the GUI.
 */
private static void runGUI() {
  JFrame.setDefaultLookAndFeelDecorated(true);

  HelloWorldWithGUI2 greeting = new HelloWorldWithGUI2();
}


public static void main(String[] args) {
  /* Methods that create and show a GUI should be
     run from an event-dispatching thread */
  javax.swing.SwingUtilities.invokeLater(new Runnable() {
    public void run() {
      runGUI();
    }
  });
}
}
```

**TIP** awt stands for Abstract Windows Toolkit.

A class that uses a listener must implement an ActionListener. This is done by adding implements ActionListener to the class declaration and then defining an actionPerformed() method, which is the only method in the ActionListener interface. An import java.awt.event statement is required to import the package containing the ActionListener interface.

The GUI is implemented in the constructor. The segment of code that creates and adds the button does four things. First, a button that displays Hide is created. Second, because the user will see a Hide button the action command associated with this button should be "Hide". Third, a listener is needed to determine when the user clicks the button. The listener is set to the HelloWorldWithGUI2 object itself (this). Fourth, the button is added to the content pane.

The actionPerformed() method is passed an ActionEvent argument by the GUI when the button is clicked. ActionEvent objects have a getActionCommand() method. This method returns the string assigned as the object's action command. For the Show/Hide button, the action command, as well as the button text, is changed each time the button is clicked.

*Chapter 10 GUIs and Event-Driven Programming*

## Review: Name – part 2 of 2

Modify the Name application to display or hide your name depending on the button clicked by the user, similar to the HelloWorldWithGUI2 application.

## Review: NumClicks

Create a NumClicks application that contains a button displaying how many times the user has clicked that button. The application interface should look similar to the following after the user has clicked the button 9 times:

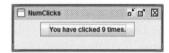

For this application it is not necessary to set the action command. A call to the getActionCommand() method in the actionPerformed() method is also not needed.

## Controlling Layout

*layout*

*Layout* refers to the arrangement of components. In a Swing GUI, the layout of a content pane can be controlled by adding borders, using a layout manager, and setting alignments.

A border can be added to most components, including the content pane. An invisible, or empty, border can be used to add "padding" around a component to give it distance from other components. Adding an empty border to the content pane adds space between the components and the edges of the frame. For example, the content pane in the GUI on the left has no border, but the content pane on the right has an empty border of 20 pixels on the top, left, bottom, and right:

**TIP** *Pixel* stands for picture element and the number of pixels in a surface depends on the screen resolution.

*An empty border in the content pane on the right provides padding between the components and the frame*

*layout manager*

*FlowLayout manager*

A *layout manager* determines the order of components on a content pane. There are many layout managers to choose from, including FlowLayout, BoxLayout, and GridLayout. The *FlowLayout manager* places components one next to the other in a row. When a row becomes too long, a new row is started. The FlowLayout manager is the default manager. The HelloWorldWithGUI applications use this manager.

*BoxLayout manager*

The *BoxLayout manager* places components one after the other in a column, with one component per line. For example, the GUI below uses the BoxLayout manager:

**TIP** The BoxLayout manager also includes methods for adding "glue" and "rigid areas" to a layout to control placement of components.

*The BoxLayout manager places components one after the other in a column*

*GridLayout manager*

The *GridLayout manager* places components into a grid of rows and columns. The intersection of a row and column is called a *cell*. There is one component per cell in a GridLayout. The GUI below uses a GridLayout. An additional button was added to illustrate the grid:

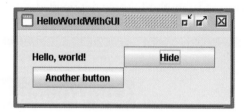

*The GridLayout manager places components into a grid of cells*

*alignment*

Another factor that affects layout is alignment. *Alignment* refers to the placement of a component within a layout. For example, both GUIs below use a BoxLayout, have an empty border of 20, 20, 20, and 20 in the content pane, and a 20, 50, 20, 50 empty border around the label. The GUI on the left specifies no aligment for the components, and the GUI on the right center aligns the label and the button:

*Alignment affects the placement of components within a layout*

The HelloWorldWithGUI2 application modified to use a layout manager, borders, and alignment:

```
import javax.swing.*;
import java.awt.event.*;

public class HelloWorldWithGUI2 implements ActionListener {
  final static String LABEL_TEXT = "Hello, world!";
  JFrame frame;
  JPanel contentPane;
  JLabel label;
  JButton button;

  public HelloWorldWithGUI2(){
    /* Create and set up the frame */
    frame = new JFrame("HelloWorldWithGUI");
    frame.setDefaultCloseOperation(JFrame.EXIT_ON_CLOSE);

    /* Create a content pane with a BoxLayout and
       empty borders */
    contentPane = new JPanel();
    contentPane.setLayout(new BoxLayout(contentPane,
                                     BoxLayout.PAGE_AXIS));
    contentPane.setBorder(BorderFactory.createEmptyBorder(20,20,20,20));

    /* Create and add label that is centered and
       has empty borders */
    label = new JLabel(LABEL_TEXT);
    label.setAlignmentX(JLabel.CENTER_ALIGNMENT);
    label.setBorder(BorderFactory.createEmptyBorder(20, 50, 20, 50));
    contentPane.add(label);

    /* Create and add button that is centered */
    button = new JButton("Hide");
    button.setAlignmentX(JButton.CENTER_ALIGNMENT);
    button.setActionCommand("Hide");
    button.addActionListener(this);
    contentPane.add(button);

    /* Add content pane to frame */
    frame.setContentPane(contentPane);

    /* Size and then display the frame. */
    frame.pack();
    frame.setVisible(true);
  }
```

*...rest of HelloWorldWithGUI2 code*

TIP Experiment with the numerous types of borders.

*setLayout() method*

The JPanel setLayout() method is used to specify a layout for the content pane. A BoxLayout object requires arguments for the content pane and the arrangement. To arrange components in a vertical line, the class constant PAGE_AXIS is specified.

*setBorder() method*

The JPanel setBorder() method is used to specify borders for the content pane. The BorderFactory class has many different kinds of borders to choose from. For invisible, or empty borders, the createEmptyBorder() method is used. The arguments specify the width of the top, left, bottom, and right of the border.

*setAlignment() method*

The JLabel and JButton setAlignmentX() methods are used to specify the vertical alignment of the components within the layout. Both classes include several alignment constants, including CENTER_ALIGNMENT.

The modified HelloWorldWithGUI2 application produces a GUI that looks similar to:

*GridLayout manager*

For GUIs with components that should be side by side in rows, the GridLayout manager may be a better choice. The GridLayout manager is specified in a statement similar to:

```
contentPane.setLayout(new GridLayout(0, 2, 10, 5))
```

**TIP** The GridLayout manager places components in rows from left to right in the order that they are added to the content pane.

The GridLayout object requires arguments for specifying the number of rows and columns and the space between columns and rows. If 0 is specified for either the rows or columns, the class creates an object with as many rows or columns as needed. However, only one argument can be 0. In the statement above, the GridLayout object will have as many rows as needed and 2 columns. There will be 10 pixels between columns and 5 pixels between rows. The GridLayout class is part of the java.awt package.

*java.awt*     Code using this manager requires an `import java.awt.*` statement.

## Review: Sunflower

Create a Sunflower application that displays the Latin name for the sunflower when Latin is clicked and the English name when English is clicked. The application GUI should use a BoxLayout manager and look similar to the following after Latin has been clicked:

## Review: Riddle

Create a Riddle application that displays a riddle and then solves it when Answer is clicked. The application GUI should use a GridLayout manager and look similar to the following after Answer has been clicked:

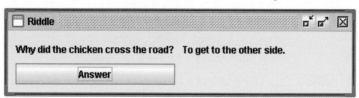

*Chapter 10 GUIs and Event-Driven Programming*

# Getting Input from the User

A *text field* allows a user to enter information at run time. Text fields are usually placed next to a label to prompt the user for the type of data expected in the text field. For example, the SemesterAvg application prompts the user to enter three test grades and then displays the average of the grades when Average is clicked:

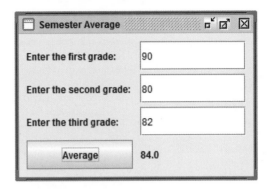

The swing package includes the JTextField class with the following constructors and methods:

### Class JTextField (javax.swing.JTextField)

### Constructor/Methods

`JTextField(int col)`

        creates a JTextField object with width `col`.

`JTextField(String text, int col)`

        creates a JTextField object displaying default text `text` in a field with width `col`.

`getText()`        returns a String containing the text in the JTextField.

`addActionListener(Object)`

        adds an object that listens for the user to press the Enter key in this component.

The information typed into a text field is a string, even when numeric data is entered. Conversly, the setText() method of a JLabel expects a string even when the data is numeric. Class methods in the Double and Integer classes can be used to convert data between numeric and String types:

### Class Double (java.lang.Double)

### Method

`parseDouble(String text)`

        returns the `double` value in the String `text`.

`toString(double num)`

        returns the String representation of `num`.

### Class Integer (java.lang.Integer)

### Method

`parseInteger(String text)`

        returns the `int` value in the String `text`.

`toString(int num)`

        returns the String representation of `num`.

The parseDouble() and parseInteger() methods are used to convert String data to numeric. The SemesterAvg application, shown on the previous page, uses parseDouble():

```java
import javax.swing.*;
import java.awt.*;
import java.awt.event.*;

public class SemesterAvg implements ActionListener {
  JFrame frame;
  JPanel contentPane;
  JLabel prompt1, prompt2, prompt3, average;
  JTextField grade1, grade2, grade3;
  JButton avgButton;

  public SemesterAvg(){
    /* Create and set up the frame */
    frame = new JFrame("Semester Average");
    frame.setDefaultCloseOperation(JFrame.EXIT_ON_CLOSE);

    /* Create a content pane with a GridLayout */
    contentPane = new JPanel();
    contentPane.setLayout(new GridLayout(0, 2, 10, 5));
    contentPane.setBorder(BorderFactory.createEmptyBorder
                                      (10, 10, 10, 10));

    /* Create and add a prompt and then a text field */
    prompt1 = new JLabel("Enter the first grade: ");
    contentPane.add(prompt1);

    grade1 = new JTextField(10);
    contentPane.add(grade1);

    /* Create and add a second prompt and
       then a text field */
    prompt2 = new JLabel("Enter the second grade: ");
    contentPane.add(prompt2);

    grade2 = new JTextField(10);
    contentPane.add(grade2);

    /* Create and add a third prompt and then a text field */
    prompt3 = new JLabel("Enter the third grade: ");
    contentPane.add(prompt3);

    grade3 = new JTextField(10);
    contentPane.add(grade3);

    /* Create and add button that will display the
       average of the grades */
    avgButton = new JButton("Average");
    avgButton.setActionCommand("Average");
    avgButton.addActionListener(this);
    contentPane.add(avgButton);

    /* Create and add a label that will display the
       average */
    average = new JLabel(" ");
    contentPane.add(average);

    /* Add content pane to frame */
    frame.setContentPane(contentPane);
```

*Chapter 10 GUIs and Event-Driven Programming*

```
                    /* Size and then display the frame. */
                    frame.pack();
                    frame.setVisible(true);
                }


                /**
                 * Handle button click action event
                 * pre: none
                 * post: The average of the grades entered has been
                 * calculated and displayed.
                 */
                public void actionPerformed(ActionEvent event) {
                    String eventName = event.getActionCommand();

                    if (eventName.equals("Average")) {
                        double avgGrade;
                        String g1 = grade1.getText();
                        String g2 = grade2.getText();
                        String g3 = grade3.getText();

                        avgGrade = (Double.parseDouble(g1) + Double.parseDouble(g2)
                                    + Double.parseDouble(g3))/3;
                        average.setText(Double.toString(avgGrade));
                    }
                }


                /**
                 * Create and show the GUI.
                 */
                private static void runGUI() {
                    JFrame.setDefaultLookAndFeelDecorated(true);

                    SemesterAvg myGrades = new SemesterAvg();
                }
```

...*main() method of SemesterAvg code*

In the actionPerformed() method, the strings are read from the text fields. To calculate the average grade, each string is parsed for a `double` value (with parseDouble()). The `avgGrade` value was then converted to a String with the Double class method toString().

## Review: DivisibleBy3

Create a DivisibleBy3 application that prompts the user for an integer and then displays a message when Check is clicked indicating whether the number is divisible by 3. The application interface should look similar to the following after the user has typed a number and clicked Check:

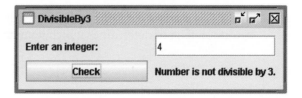

# Combo Boxes

A *combo box* offers a user a way to select from a limited set of choices. Combo boxes can offer choices without taking up much room on the interface. The user simply clicks the combo box arrow to display additional choices. The LatinPlantNames application allows the user to select a plant name from a combo box:

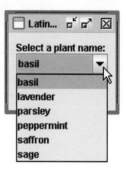

The swing package includes the JComboBox class for creating combo boxes:

**Class JComboBox** (javax.swing.JComboBox)

**Methods**

`JComboBox(Object[] items)`

> creates a JComboBox object that contains the items from the `items` array, which must be an array of objects.

`setSelectedIndex(int index)`

> makes the item at index `index` the selected item.

`getSelectedItem()`

> returns the String corresponding to the selected JComboBox item.

`setEditable(boolean)`

> allows text to be typed in the combo box when `true` is the `boolean` argument.

`addActionListener(Object)`

> adds an object that listens for the user to select an item from this component's list.

Handling an event from a JComboBox requires two lines of code that are similar to:

```
JComboBox comboBox = (JComboBox)event.getSource();
String itemName = (String)comboBox.getSelectedItem();
```

The first statement determines the source of the action event and then the second statement determines which item has been selected.

The LatinPlantNames application code includes a JComboBox object:

```java
import javax.swing.*;
import java.awt.*;
import java.awt.event.*;

public class LatinPlantNames implements ActionListener {
  JFrame frame;
  JPanel contentPane;
  JComboBox plantNames;
  JLabel plantListPrompt, latinName;

  public LatinPlantNames(){
  /* Create and set up the frame */
  frame = new JFrame("LatinPlantNames");
  frame.setDefaultCloseOperation(JFrame.EXIT_ON_CLOSE);

  /* Create a content pane with a BoxLayout and
     empty borders */
  contentPane = new JPanel();
  contentPane.setLayout(new BoxLayout(contentPane,
                                   BoxLayout.PAGE_AXIS));
  contentPane.setBorder(BorderFactory.createEmptyBorder
                                   (10, 10, 10, 10));

  /* Create a combo box and a descriptive label */
  plantListPrompt = new JLabel("Select a plant name: ");
  plantListPrompt.setAlignmentX(JLabel.LEFT_ALIGNMENT);
  contentPane.add(plantListPrompt);

  String[] names = {"basil", "lavender", "parsley",
                 "peppermint", "saffron", "sage"};
  plantNames = new JComboBox(names);
  plantNames.setAlignmentX(JComboBox.LEFT_ALIGNMENT);
  plantNames.setSelectedIndex(0);
  plantNames.addActionListener(this);
  contentPane.add(plantNames);

  /* Create and add a label that will display the
     Latin names */
  latinName = new JLabel("Ocimum");
  latinName.setBorder(BorderFactory.createEmptyBorder
                                       (20, 0, 0, 0));
  contentPane.add(latinName);

  /* Add content pane to frame */
  frame.setContentPane(contentPane);

  /* Size and then display the frame. */
  frame.pack();
  frame.setVisible(true);
}
```

```
/**
 * Handle a selection from the combo box
 * pre: none
 * post: The Latin name for the selected plant
 * has been displayed.
 */
public void actionPerformed(ActionEvent event) {
  JComboBox comboBox = (JComboBox)event.getSource();
  String plantName = (String)comboBox.getSelectedItem();

  if (plantName == "basil") {
    latinName.setText("Ocimum");
  } else if (plantName == "lavender") {
    latinName.setText("Lavandula spica");
  } else if (plantName == "parsley") {
    latinName.setText("Apium");
  } else if (plantName == "perppermint") {
    latinName.setText("Mentha piperita");
  } else if (plantName == "saffron") {
    latinName.setText("Crocus");
  } else if (plantName == "sage") {
    latinName.setText("Salvia");
  }
}
```

*…runGUI() and main() method of LatinPlantNames code*

The LatinPlantNames application displays the following output after sage has been selected:

# Review: MetricConversion

Create a MetricConversion application that allows the user to select a type of conversion from a combo box and then the corresponding formula is displayed in a label. To convert from the length measurement inches to centimeters, the formula is 1 inch = 2.54 centimeters. The formula 1 foot = 0.3048 meters converts the distance measurement feet to meters. The volume measurement gallon is converted to liters with the formula 1 gallon = 4.5461 liters. The formula 1 pound = 0.4536 kilograms converts the mass measurement pound to kilograms. The application interface should look similar to the following after the user has selected feet to meters:

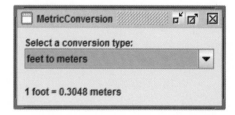

*Chapter 10 GUIs and Event-Driven Programming*

# Changing Colors

Swing components have methods for changing their colors. For example, the content pane can be green, buttons can be magenta, combo boxes can display text in pink. When making color choices, keep the end user in mind because colors can give an application a fun and exciting look or completely turn users away.

*Color class*  The java.awt package includes the Color class with numerous color constant members. The following methods, in the Swing component classes, can be used to change the background and foreground colors of the components:

```
setBackground(Color.constant)
```

> sets the background color of a component to `constant` from the Color class.

```
setForeground(Color.constant)
```

> sets the foreground color of a component to `constant` from the Color class.

How the color change affects the component varies. For a JLabel, the foreground color refers to the color of the text. For a JComboBox, the foreground color refers to the color of the text in the list.

The ColorDemo application demonstrates the color possibilities for components. The application GUI and the code, except for the runGUI() and main() methods, follow:

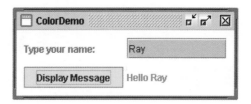

```java
import javax.swing.*;
import java.awt.*;
import java.awt.event.*;

public class ColorDemo implements ActionListener {
    JFrame frame;
    JPanel contentPane;
    JTextField name;
    JButton displayMessage;
    JLabel textFieldPrompt, hello;

    public ColorDemo(){
        /* Create and set up the frame */
        frame = new JFrame("ColorDemo");
        frame.setDefaultCloseOperation(JFrame.EXIT _ ON _ CLOSE);

        /* Create a content pane with a BoxLayout
           and empty borders */
        contentPane = new JPanel();
        contentPane.setBorder(BorderFactory.createEmptyBorder
                                        (10, 10, 10, 10));
        contentPane.setBackground(Color.white);
        contentPane.setLayout(new GridLayout(0, 2, 5, 10));
```

```
/* Create a text field and a descriptive label */
textFieldPrompt = new JLabel("Type your name:  ");
textFieldPrompt.setForeground(Color.red);
contentPane.add(textFieldPrompt);

name = new JTextField(10);
name.setBackground(Color.pink);
name.setForeground(Color.darkGray);
contentPane.add(name);

/* Create a Display Message button */
displayMessage = new JButton("Display Message");
displayMessage.setBackground(Color.yellow);
displayMessage.setForeground(Color.blue);
displayMessage.addActionListener(this);
contentPane.add(displayMessage);

/* Create a label that will display a message */
hello = new JLabel(" ");
hello.setForeground(Color.green);
contentPane.add(hello);

/* Add content pane to frame */
frame.setContentPane(contentPane);

/* Size and then display the frame. */
frame.pack();
frame.setVisible(true);
}


/**
 * Handle a the button click
 * pre: none
 * post: A message has been displayed.
 */
  public void actionPerformed(ActionEvent event) {
    String text = name.getText();

    hello.setText("Hello " + text);
  }
```

*...runGUI() and main() method of ColorDemo code*

## Adding Images

*GIF, JPG*

Images can make an application more informative, easier to to use, and fun. Labels and buttons are often used to display an image, but many Swing components support images. Images that are GIF and JPG format work best. Unless a different path is specified in the application code, the image files must be in the same location as the compiled code.

The JLabel class includes a constructor and a method for displaying images in a label:

### Class JLabel (javax.swing.JLabel)

### Constructor/Method
```
JLabel(ImageIcon pic)
```

                    creates a JLabel object containing `pic`.

```
setIcon(ImageIcon pic)
```

                    sets the JLabel to contain `pic`.

*Chapter 10 GUIs and Event-Driven Programming*

The JButton class includes a constructor and a method for displaying images in a button:

**Class JButton (javax.swing.JButton)**

**Constructor/Method**

`JButton(String str, ImageIcon pic)`

> creates a JButton object containing the text `str` and the image `pic`.

`JButton(ImageIcon pic)`

> creates a JButton object containing the image `pic`.

`setIcon(ImageIcon pic)`

> sets the JButton to contain `pic`.

The Roll application displays a die face. The user can click Roll Die to "roll the die" and display the outcome of the roll. The application GUI and the code, except for the runGUI() and main() methods, follow:

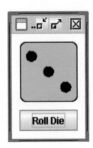

```
import javax.swing.*;
import java.awt.*;
import java.awt.event.*;
import java.lang.Math;

public class Roll implements ActionListener {
    JFrame frame;
    JPanel contentPane;
    JButton rollDie;
    JLabel dieFace;

    public Roll(){
        /* Create and set up the frame */
        frame = new JFrame("Roll");
        frame.setDefaultCloseOperation(JFrame.EXIT _ ON _ CLOSE);

        /* Create a content pane with a BoxLayout and
         empty borders */
        contentPane = new JPanel();
        contentPane.setBorder(BorderFactory.createEmptyBorder
                                    (10, 10, 10, 10));
        contentPane.setBackground(Color.white);
        contentPane.setLayout(new BoxLayout(contentPane,
                                    BoxLayout.PAGE _ AXIS));

        /* Create a label that shows a die face */
        dieFace = new JLabel(new ImageIcon("die3.gif"));
        dieFace.setAlignmentX(JLabel.CENTER _ ALIGNMENT);
        dieFace.setBorder(BorderFactory.createEmptyBorder
                                    (0, 0, 10, 0));
        contentPane.add(dieFace);
```

```
/* Create a Roll Die button */
rollDie = new JButton("Roll Die");
rollDie.setAlignmentX(JButton.CENTER _ ALIGNMENT);
rollDie.addActionListener(this);
contentPane.add(rollDie);

/* Add content pane to frame */
frame.setContentPane(contentPane);

/* Size and then display the frame. */
frame.pack();
frame.setVisible(true);
}


/**
 * Handle a button click
 * pre: none
 * post: A die has been rolled.  Matching image shown.
 */
public void actionPerformed(ActionEvent event) {
  int newRoll;

  newRoll = (int)(6 * Math.random() + 1);
  if (newRoll == 1) {
    dieFace.setIcon(new ImageIcon("die1.gif"));
  } else if (newRoll == 2) {
    dieFace.setIcon(new ImageIcon("die2.gif"));
  } else if (newRoll == 3) {
    dieFace.setIcon(new ImageIcon("die3.gif"));
  } else if (newRoll == 4) {
    dieFace.setIcon(new ImageIcon("die4.gif"));
  } else if (newRoll == 5) {
    dieFace.setIcon(new ImageIcon("die5.gif"));
  } else if (newRoll == 6) {
    dieFace.setIcon(new ImageIcon("die6.gif"));
  }
}
```

An image must be an object of the ImageIcon class for use in a Swing GUI. The ImageIcon class, from the java.swing package, has a constructor that accepts a file name as an argument and then converts that file to an ImageIcon object.

## Review: Roll

Modify the Roll application to roll two dice. Include an image for each die. Change the colors of the components to be more exciting, while still allowing the user to easily read the text on the button and to see the die images. The die images are name die1.tif, die2.tif, die3.tif, die4.tif, die5.tif, and die6.tif and are supplied as data files for this text.

# Using Nested Classes to Handle Events

A GUI can quickly become complex, as a combination of buttons, text fields, and other components that must handle events are added. When a variety of components are on a single interface, separate actionPerformed() methods should handle their events.

Up to this point, an instance of the controlling class (this) implemented an actionPerformed() method. This single method was used to handle events for every component on the GUI. This was sufficient for a simple GUI. However, a GUI with more than one type of component responding to an event should have multiple listeners. One way to implement multiple listeners in a single application is to create each listener from a nested class.

**TIP** A nested class is also called an inner class.

A *nested class* is a class within a class. A nested class is a member of the class it is within. As a class member, it has access to all the other members of the class, including private member variables and methods. A class that contains a class member is called an *outer class*. The Semester Stats application uses two nested classes to respond to events:

*outer class*

```
import javax.swing.*;
import java.awt.*;
import java.awt.event.*;

public class SemesterStats {
  JFrame frame;
  JPanel contentPane;
  JLabel prompt1, prompt2, prompt3, stat;
  JTextField grade1, grade2, grade3;
  JButton avgButton, minButton, maxButton;

  public SemesterStats(){
    /* Create and set up the frame */
    frame = new JFrame("Semester Stats");
    frame.setDefaultCloseOperation(JFrame.EXIT_ON_CLOSE);

    /* Create content pane with a GridLayout and empty borders */
    contentPane = new JPanel();
    contentPane.setLayout(new GridLayout(0, 2, 10, 5));
    contentPane.setBorder(BorderFactory.createEmptyBorder
                                          (10, 10, 10, 10));

    /* Create and add a prompt and then a text field */
    prompt1 = new JLabel("Enter the first grade: ");
    contentPane.add(prompt1);

    grade1 = new JTextField(10);
    contentPane.add(grade1);

    /* Create and add a second prompt and then a text field */
    prompt2 = new JLabel("Enter the second grade: ");
    contentPane.add(prompt2);

    grade2 = new JTextField(10);
    contentPane.add(grade2);

    /* Create and add a third prompt and then a text field */
    prompt3 = new JLabel("Enter the third grade: ");
    contentPane.add(prompt3);
```

```java
        grade3 = new JTextField(10);
        contentPane.add(grade3);

        /* Create and add button that will display the average grade */
        avgButton = new JButton("Average");
        avgButton.addActionListener(new AvgListener());
        contentPane.add(avgButton);

        /* Create and add button that will display the min grade */
        minButton = new JButton("Min");
        minButton.setActionCommand("Min");
        minButton.addActionListener(new MinMaxListener());
        contentPane.add(minButton);

        /* Create and add button that will display the max grade */
        maxButton = new JButton("Max");
        maxButton.setActionCommand("Max");
        maxButton.addActionListener(new MinMaxListener());
        contentPane.add(maxButton);

        /* Create and add a label that will display stats */
        stat = new JLabel(" ");
        stat.setBorder(BorderFactory.createEmptyBorder(10, 0, 10, 0));
        contentPane.add(stat);

        /* Add content pane to frame */
        frame.setContentPane(contentPane);

        /* Size and then display the frame. */
        frame.pack();
        frame.setVisible(true);
    }


    class AvgListener implements ActionListener {

        /**
         * Handle Average button click event
         * pre: none
         * post: The grade average has been calculated and displayed.
         */
        public void actionPerformed(ActionEvent event) {
            double avgGrade;
            String g1 = grade1.getText();
            String g2 = grade2.getText();
            String g3 = grade3.getText();

            avgGrade = (Double.parseDouble(g1) + Double.parseDouble(g2) +
                        Double.parseDouble(g3))/3;
            stat.setText(Double.toString(avgGrade));
        }
    }
```

```
class MinMaxListener implements ActionListener {

  /**
   * Handles the Min and Max button click events
   * pre: none
   * post: The minimum or maximum grade has been
   * determined and displayed.
   */
  public void actionPerformed(ActionEvent event) {
    String eventName = event.getActionCommand();
    double minGrade = 999;
    double maxGrade = 0;
    double[] grades = new double[3];

    grades[0] = Double.parseDouble(grade1.getText());
    grades[1] = Double.parseDouble(grade2.getText());
    grades[2] = Double.parseDouble(grade3.getText());

    if (eventName.equals("Min")) {
      for (int i = 0; i < 3; i++) {
        if (minGrade > grades[i]) {
          minGrade = grades[i];
        }
      }
      stat.setText(Double.toString(minGrade));
    } else if (eventName.equals("Max")) {
      for (int i = 0; i < 3; i++) {
        if (maxGrade < grades[i]) {
          maxGrade = grades[i];
        }
      }
      stat.setText(Double.toString(maxGrade));
    }
  }
}


  /**
   * Create and show the GUI.
   */
  private static void runGUI() {
    JFrame.setDefaultLookAndFeelDecorated(true);

    SemesterStats myGrades = new SemesterStats();
  }


  public static void main(String[] args) {
    /* Methods that create and show a GUI should be
       run from an event-dispatching thread */
    javax.swing.SwingUtilities.invokeLater(new Runnable() {
      public void run() {
        runGUI();
      }
    });
  }
}
```

One class (AvgListener) was used to implement a listener for the Average button and a second class (MinMaxListener) implements a listener for the Min and Max buttons. These buttons were combined into one listener because their algorithms closely match.

The SemesterStats application displays output similar to:

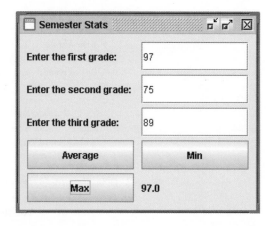

# Chapter 10 Case Study

In this case study, a Swing GUI will be created for an application that plays a carnival game called Break-A-Plate. The Break-A-Plate game allows a player to try to break all three plates. If all three plates are broken, a first prize is awarded, otherwise, a consolation prize is awarded.

### BreakAPlate Specification

The BreakAPlate application displays three unbroken plates at the start. Clicking Play plays the game, displays broken plates, and displays the prize won. If all three plates are broken, a tiger plush first prize is awarded. If less than three plates are broken, a sticker consolation prize is awarded. At the end of a game the Play button changes to Play Again. Clicking Play Again displays a set of unbroken plates and the button changes back to Play allowing the user to play repeatedly. The application ends when the user closes the window.

The BreakAPlate game uses random numbers to determine if a player has broken all three plates. When three 1s are generated by the random number generator then the application displays three broken plates. If zero, one, or two ones are generated, then the application displays two broken plates indicating a loss.

The BreakAPlate interface should be a GUI that includes a label for displaying the image of the plates, a button for allowing the user to play or play again, and a label for displaying the the prize won. The BreakAPlate GUI should look similar to the following before a game is played, after a losing game has been played, and after a winning game has been played:

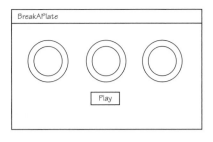

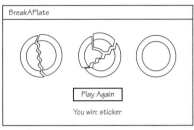

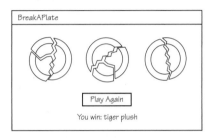

The BreakAPlate algorithm:

1. When a game is played, generate three random numbers between 0 and 1.

2. If three ones are generated, display three broken plates and the names of the first prize. Otherwise, display two broken plates and the name of the consolation prize.

### BreakAPlate Code Design

The BreakAPlate application simulates a game booth at a carnival. The game can therefore be modeled with a GameBooth object. The GameBooth class was created in Chapter 7 and contains the following methods:

**TIP** Refer to Chapter 7 for the GameBooth code.

### Class GameBooth

### Constructor/Methods

`GameBooth(int cost, String p1, String p2)`

creates a GameBooth object that charges `cost` amount to play, awards a first prize `p1`, and a consolation prize `p2`. If there is no charge for the game, or the charge is not a consideration, then 0 should be the argument for `cost`.

`start()`  simulates a a game that allows the player three plays. If the player succeeds all three times, then the name of the first prize is retuned. Otherwise, the name of the consolation prize is returned.

`getCost()`  returns the cost of the game.

The cost of the game is not a factor in this application, so 0 will be the argument for the `cost` parameter in the constructor, and the getCost() method will not be needed.

Based on the algorithm and the GameBooth class, the BreakAPlate actionPerformed() method pseudocode looks similar to:

```
String eventName = event.getActionCommand();
String prize;

if (Play) {
    prize = breakAPlate.start();
    if (prize is tiger plush) {
        display all broken plates;
    } else if (prize is sticker)) {
        display two broken plates
    }
    display prize won
    change button to Play Again
} else if (Play Again) {
    display unbroken plates
    clear prize won text
    change button to Play
```

### BreakAPlate Implementation

The BreakAPlate implementation involves creating the BreakAPlate java file and adding the GameBooth java file to the project.

The BreakAPlate application is implemented below:

```java
/**
 * BreakAPlate.
 */
import javax.swing.*;
import java.awt.*;
import java.awt.event.*;

public class BreakAPlate implements ActionListener {
    static final String FIRST_PRIZE = "tiger plush";
    static final String CONSOLATION_PRIZE = "sticker";
    JFrame frame;
    JPanel contentPane;
    JButton play;
    JLabel plates, prizeWon;
    GameBooth breakAPlate;

    public BreakAPlate(){
        /* initialize game booth and player */
        breakAPlate = new GameBooth(0, FIRST_PRIZE, CONSOLATION_PRIZE);

        /* Create and set up the frame */
        frame = new JFrame("BreakAPlate");
        frame.setDefaultCloseOperation(JFrame.EXIT_ON_CLOSE);

        /* Create a content pane with a BoxLayout and empty borders */
        contentPane = new JPanel();
        contentPane.setBorder(BorderFactory.createEmptyBorder(20, 20, 20, 20));
        contentPane.setBackground(Color.white);
        contentPane.setLayout(new BoxLayout(contentPane, BoxLayout.PAGE_AXIS));
```

```
    /* Create a label that shows the start of the game */
    plates = new JLabel(new ImageIcon("plates.gif"));
    plates.setAlignmentX(JLabel.CENTER_ALIGNMENT);
    plates.setBorder(BorderFactory.createEmptyBorder(10, 10, 20, 10));
    contentPane.add(plates);

    /* Create a Play button */
    play = new JButton("Play");
    play.setActionCommand("Play");
    play.setAlignmentX(JButton.CENTER_ALIGNMENT);
    play.addActionListener(this);
    contentPane.add(play);

    /* Create a label that will show prizes won */
    prizeWon = new JLabel(" ");
    prizeWon.setAlignmentX(JLabel.CENTER_ALIGNMENT);
    prizeWon.setBorder(BorderFactory.createEmptyBorder(20, 0, 0, 0));
    contentPane.add(prizeWon);

    /* Add content pane to frame */
    frame.setContentPane(contentPane);

    /* Size and then display the frame. */
    frame.pack();
    frame.setVisible(true);
}


/**
 * Handle the button click
 * pre: none
 * post: The appropriate image and message are displayed.
 */
public void actionPerformed(ActionEvent event) {
    String eventName = event.getActionCommand();
    String prize;

    if (eventName == "Play") {
        prize = breakAPlate.start();
        if (prize.equals(FIRST_PRIZE)) {
            plates.setIcon(new ImageIcon("plates_all_broken.gif"));
        } else if (prize.equals(CONSOLATION_PRIZE)) {
            plates.setIcon(new ImageIcon("plates_two_broken.gif"));
        }
        prizeWon.setText("You win: " + prize);
        play.setText("Play Again");
        play.setActionCommand("Play Again");
    } else if (eventName == "Play Again") {
        plates.setIcon(new ImageIcon("plates.gif"));
        prizeWon.setText(" ");
        play.setText("Play");
        play.setActionCommand("Play");
    }
}
```

```
/**
 * Create and show the GUI.
 */
private static void runGUI() {
    JFrame.setDefaultLookAndFeelDecorated(true);

    BreakAPlate carnivalGame = new BreakAPlate();
}


public static void main(String[] args) {
    /* Methods that create and show a GUI should be
       run from an event-dispatching thread */
    javax.swing.SwingUtilities.invokeLater(new Runnable() {
        public void run() {
            runGUI();
        }
    });
}
}
```

Running the BreakAPlate application displays a GUI similar to:

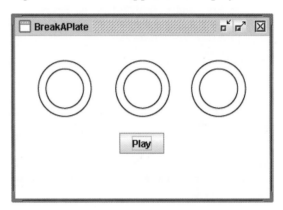

When Play is clicked, the user either wins or loses. The output below shows a losing game:

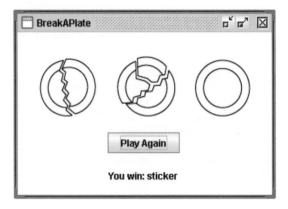

*Chapter 10 GUIs and Event-Driven Programming*

The application GUI below shows a winning game:

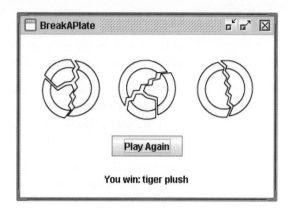

## BreakAPlate Testing and Debugging

The application should be tested by playing several games, making sure that the correct prize is named and that the buttons and images change appropriately.

# Review: BreakAPlate

Modify the BreakAPlate application to display a picture of the prize won rather than text naming the prize. The tiger_plush.gif, sticker.gif, and placeholder.gif are supplied as data files for this text. The placeholder.gif file is a white square that is the same size as the tiger_plush and sticker images. The placeholder.gif file should be displayed in the label at the start of each game. The modified BreakAPlate interface should look similar to the following after the user has played a winning game:

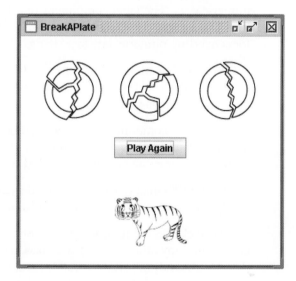

# Chapter Summary

This chapter introduced graphical user interfaces that use the Swing API. The Java swing package contains many component classes, including JFrames, JPanels, JLabels, JButtons, JComboBoxes, and JTextFields.

Applications with a GUI are event-driven. The GUI must be run from an event-dispatching thread. A GUI application responds to interactions from the user called events. An event executes a method called an event handler. A Swing event handler is also called an action event handler.

A frame is a container for content panels. A commonly used content panel is the JPanel component. A JPanel can contain other components such as labels and buttons. A label is a component that does not receive events. A button is a commonly used component for accepting input from the user.

Only components with a listener object can execute an event handler. A listener executes the actionPerformed() event handler, passing it the an ActionEvent object that contains the action command describing the event.

The layout of components in a JPanel can be controlled with layout manager and the use of borders and alignment. The FlowLayout, BoxLayout, and GridLayout are the three managers covered in this chapter. The placement of components within a layout can be controlled further with empty borders for padding and using alignment.

The text field component allows a user to type information into the interface. The information typed into a text field is a string. The Integer and Double classes include class methods for converting information to numeric data. The label component requires a string when setting the text. The Integer and Double classes also provide the toString() method for converting numeric data to a String.

Combo boxes allow the user to select from a limited set of choices. A combo box does not take up much space and displays a list of choices when its arrow button is clicked.

Most of the components include methods for setting the background and foreground colors. Color can make an application easier to use and more interesting, but should be selected with the user in mind.

GIF and JPG images can be included in an application GUI. A label or a button is commonly used to display an image.

Nested classes are used to implement multiple event handlers. Nested classes, like any other member of a class, have access to other members of the class, including private variables and method members. A class that contain a class member is called an outer class.

**Action command**  A string describing an event.

**Alignment**  The placement of components within a layout.

**BoxLayout manager**  A layout manager that places components one after the other in a column.

**Button**  A GUI component that the user can click.

**Combo box**  A GUI component that offers a user a way to select from a limited set of choices.

**Container**  A component that holds and displays all the other components of a GUI.

**Content frame**  A top-level container.

**Event**  A user interaction with an application's GUI.

**Event-driven application**  An application that responds to events.

**Event handler**  A method that executes in response to an event.

**FlowLayout manager**  A layout manager that places components one next to the other in a row.

**Frame**  A GUI window that contains a border, title, and maximize, minimize, and close buttons.

**GridLayout manager**  A layout manager that places components in a grid of rows and columns.

**Label**  A GUI component that displays text or an image and does not interact with the user.

**Layout**  The arrangement of components.

**Layout manager**  Used to specify the order of components on a content pane.

**Listener**  An object that listens for action events.

**Nested class**  A class that is a member of another class. A class within a class.

**Outer class**  A class that contains a class member.

**Text field**  A GUI component that allows a user to enter information at run time.

**Thread**  A process that runs sequentially from start to finish.

**ActionListener** The java.awt.event interface that contains the actionListener() method.

**actionPerformed()** A method that is implemented to respond to events. This method is the only method in the ActionListener interface.

**BorderFactory** The java.lang class with class methods for creating a border object.

**BoxLayout** A javax.swing class for setting the layout of a content pane.

**Color** The java.awt class that contains constants for changing component colors.

**Double** A java.lang class for converting numbers between numeric and text data.

**GridLayout** A java.awt class for setting the layout of a content pane.

**ImageIcon** A java.swing class for converting an image, such as a GIF or JPG, to an ImageIcon object.

**Integer** A java.lang class for converting numbers between numeric and text data.

**java.awt** The package containing the GridLayout class and Color class constants.

**java.awt.event** The package containing the ActionListener interface.

**java.swing** The package containing the Swing API classes.

**JButton** A java.swing class for creating a button in a GUI. The class includes methods for adding text or images to the label.

**JComboBox** A java.swing class for creating a combo box in a GUI.

**JFrame** A java.swing class for creating a window, also called a frame, in a GUI.

**JLabel** The java.swing class for creating a label in a GUI. The class includes methods for adding text or images to the label.

**JPanel** The java.swing class for creating a content panel for a frame. The class includes methods for adding and removing components.

**JTextField** The java.swing class for creating a text field.

**FlowLayout** A javax.swing class for setting the layout of a content pane.

**Swing API** A part of the Java Foundation Classes that contains numerous components for creating GUIs.

`this` The keyword for indicating an object itself.

1. What is a GUI?

2. Explain how code is executed in an event-driven application.

3. Can components be added directly to a frame? Explain.

4. Can a label respond to events? Explain.

5. Why do you think a GUI needs to be run from an event-dispatching thread?

6. What is the difference between a label and a button?

7. a) What does `this` indicate when used as the argument for the the addActionListener() method?
   b) What must the object listening for an event contain?

8. List three ways to control the layout of a content pane.

9. What type of borders are used to add padding around components?

10. List three layout managers and explain how each arranges the components on a content pane.

11. Which class is used to return an object for the setBorder() method?

12. Are borders for padding necessary when the GridLayout manager is used? Explain.

13. What must first be done with numeric data typed in a text field before it can be used in a calculation?

14. What is the value of `num1` in the last statement below?

```
double num1;
Double num2 = new Double(3);
String num3 = "5";
num1 = num2.doubleValue() +
       Double.valueOf(num3).doubleValue();
```

15. An application prompts a user to select a name from a list of six names. Which is a better component choice: a text field or a combo box? Explain.

16. Would white text on a pink background be a good color combination for a GUI? Why or why not?

17. What image types are supported in a Swing GUI?

18. Which components are often used to display an image?

19. What must an image be converted to in order to be displayed by a Swing component?

**True/False**

20. Determine if each of the following are true or false. If false, explain why.
    a) JFrame is a class in the javax.swing package.
    b) A button click is an event handler.
    c) Labels can be changed by the user.
    d) A JFrame object uses a content pane to hold GUI components.
    e) The index value for the first component on a content pane is 1.
    f) The JLabel class constant LEADING indicates right alignment.
    g) A thread is a sequential process that runs from start to finish.
    h) Swing components use listeners to determine if an event has occurred.
    i) A class that uses a listener must implement an ActionListener class.
    j) An empty border indicates that there is no space around a component.
    k) The FlowLayout manager places components one after the other in a column, with one column per line.
    l) All components on a GUI must have the same alignment.
    m) The class content PAGE_AXIS specifies that components should be arranged in a vertical line.
    n) The JLabel setAlignmentX() method is used to specify the horizontal alignment of the components within the layout.

o) Code using the BoxLayout manager requires an import java.awt.* statement.
p) Information is entered into a text field at run time.
q) A text field can only accept numeric data.
r) The JLabel foreground color refers to the text color.
s) A Swing GUI can have only one listener.
t) A nested class has access to the `private` variable members of the outer class.

*Chapter 10 GUIs and Event-Driven Programming*

# Exercises

## Exercise 1 ———————————————————————— LocalBankGUI

Create LocalBankGUI application that implements a GUI for the Local Bank case study in Chapter 9.

## Exercise 2 ———————————————————————— TicTacToeGUI

Create a TicTacToeGUI application that allows two players to play a computerized tic-tac-toe game. Refer to the TicTacToe application presented in Chapter 9. The TTT class code will need to be modified for the GUI version of the application. Use a button for each "box" in the tic-tac-toe board.

## Exercise 3 ———————————————————————— PhotoAlbum

Create a PhotoAlbum application that displays a new picture each time Next is clicked. Use the grayangel.jpg, scorpionfish.jpg, sponges.jpg, and starfish.jpg files supplied as data files for this text. The application should allow the user to continously cycle through the images.

## Exercise 4 ———————————————————————— Clacker

In the game Clacker, the numbers 1 through 12 are initially displayed. The player throws two dice and may cover the number representing the total or the two numbers on the dice. For example, for a throw of 3 and 5, the player may cover the 3 and the 5 or just the 8. Play continues until all the numbers are covered. The goal is to cover all the numbers in the fewest rolls.

Create a Clacker application that displays 12 buttons numbered 1 through 12. Each of these buttons can be clicked to "cover" it. A covered button displays nothing. Another button labeled Roll can be clicked to roll the dice. Include labels to display the appropriate die images for each roll. Another label displays the number of rolls taken. A New Game button can be clicked to clear the labels and uncover the buttons for a new game.

## Exercise 5 ☼ ———————————————————————— LifeGUI

Create a LifeGUI application that is based on the Life application created in Chapter 9, Exercise 14. The 20 x 20 grid should be buttons that initially display all 0s. To select the live cells for the first day, the user clicks the buttons in the positions of live cells. When clicked, a button changes from displaying a 0 to displaying a X. A Next button below the grid can be clicked repeatedly to display the next generations until the user quits or there are no more live cells.

*Chapter 10 GUIs and Event-Driven Programming*

# Chapter 11
# Files and Exception Handling

### Key Concepts

Using the File class
Writing exception handlers
Understanding file streams
Processing numeric data
Writing Keypress event procedures
Understanding object serialization and
deserialization processes

### Case Study

Local Bank 2 application

## What is a File?

Up to this point, the applications created in this text have stored data in the computer's memory. However, storage in memory is available only when the computer is on and an application is running. A *file* is a collection of related data stored on a persistent medium such as a hard disk or a CD. *Persistent* simply means lasting.

*persistent*

Files often store data used by an application. Files are also used to store the data generated by an application. In either case, a file is separate from the application accessing it and can be read from and written to by more than one application. Most applications require access to one or more files on disk.

## The File Class

*java.io*

The File class, part of the java.io package, is used for creating an object that represents a file. A File object can be used to create a new file, test for the existence of a file, and delete a file. Some of the File class methods include:

### Class File (java.io)

### Constructor/Methods

`File(String f)` creates a File object that refers to the file `f`.

`createNewFile()`

creates a new file using the file name specified in the constructor if the file does not already exist. Returns `true` if the file is created, `false` otherwise. This method throws an IOException exception if the file cannot be created.

`delete()` permanently deletes the file represented by the File object. Returns true if the file is deleted, false otherwise.

`exists()` Returns `true` if the file represented by the File object exists, `false` otherwise.

The application below checks for the existence of a file:

```java
import java.io.*;

public class TestFiles {

  public static void main(String[] args) {
    File textFile = new File("c:\\temp\\supplies.txt");
    if (textFile.exists()) {
      System.out.println("File already exists.");
    } else {
      System.out.println("File does not exist.");
    }
  }
}
```

The name of a file is specified as a String. If a path is included in the file name, escape sequences (\\) must be used to separate the drive, folder, and file names.

## Review: MyFile – part 1 of 2

Create a MyFile application that prompts the user for the name of a file and then displays a message that indicates whether the files exists or not.

## Handling Exceptions

*exception*

An *exception* is an error affecting program execution. If an exception is not taken care of, or *handled*, the application abruptly terminates. Although many types of exceptions may still require program termination, an exception handler can allow an application to terminate gracefully by providing the user with an informative error message.

*exception handler*
*try-catch-finally*

An *exception handler* is a block of code that performs an action when an exception occurs. The `try-catch-finally` statement can be used to write an exception handler. It takes the form:

```java
try {
  <statements>
} catch (exception err_code) {
  <statements>
} ...additional catch clauses
} finally (exception err_code) {
  <statements>
```

The `try` statements are the statements that could possibly generate an exception. The `catch` clause waits for the exception matching the `exception` parameter and then executes its code. If more than one type of exception is possible from the statements in the `try` clause, then a separate `catch` should be written for each type of exception. The `finally` clause is optional and executes its statements regardless of what happens in the `try-catch` portion of the error handler.

*Chapter 11 Files and Exception Handling*

An exception handler is required when calling certain methods. For example, the createNewFile() method in the File class generates an IOException exception when the specified file name cannot be used to create a file. The createNewFile() method includes code to *throw*, or generate, an exception object if it cannot complete its task.

*IOException*
*throw*

The modified TestFiles application checks for the existence of a file before creating a new one:

```
import java.io.*;

public class TestFiles {

  public static void main(String[] args) {
    File textFile = new File("c:\\supplies.txt");
    if (textFile.exists()) {
      System.out.println("File already exists.");
    } else {
      try {
        textFile.createNewFile();
        System.out.println("New file created.");
      } catch (IOException e) {
        System.out.println("File could not be created.");
        System.err.println("IOException: " + e.getMessage());
      }
    }
  }
}
```

### The Exception Stack

When an exception is thrown, the current block of code is first checked for an exception handler. Next, the calling method is checked for a handler, and so on until the Java interpreter is reached.

An exception, such as IOException, is an object of the Throwable class. Throwable objects have a getMessage() member that returns a String containing information about the exception. The *err stream* is used for displaying error messages on the screen.

*err stream*

## Review: MyFile – part 2 of 2

Create a MyFile application that creates a file named zzz.txt and then displays a message indicating that the file has been created. The application should prompt the user to either keep or delete the file. If the file is deleted, a message should notify the user when the file has been successfully deleted.

## The File Streams

**TIP** The Scanner class requires an input stream.

A file must be associated with a stream in order to perform operations such as reading the contents, writing over existing contents, and adding to the existing contents. A *stream* processes characters, and in Java, streams are implemented with classes.

*file position*

The file stream keeps track of the *file position*, which is the point where reading or writing last occurred. File streams are used to perform *sequential file access*, with all the reading and writing performed one character after another or one line after another.

*sequential file access*

## Data Streams

A stream applies to data input/output in general. For example, memory, information sent to a printer, and data sent and received from an Internet site can all be streamed.

A stream can be thought of as a sequence of characters. For example, a file containing a list of names and scores may look like the following when viewed in a word processor:

```
Drew 84
Tia 92
```

However, when thinking about file operations, the file should be visualized as a stream of data:

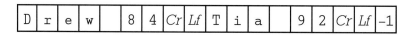

| D | r | e | w |  | 8 | 4 | $Cr$ | $Lf$ | T | i | a |  | 9 | 2 | $Cr$ | $Lf$ | –1 |

*line terminator, end of file*

The carriage return character (Cr) followed by a line feed character (Lf) is called a *line terminator*. A –1 is the *end of file*.

## The FileReader and BufferedReader Classes

*input file stream*

The FileReader and BufferedReader classes, both from the java.io package, are used together to read the contents of an existing file. The FileReader class is used to create an *input file stream*. Next, the BufferedReader class is used to read text from the stream. The following is a summary of the FileReader and BufferedReader classes:

### Class FileReader (java.io)

### Constructor/Method
`FileReader(File fileName)`

*FileNotFoundException*

creates an input file stream for the File object. This constructor throws a FileNotFoundException exception if the file does not exist.

`close()` closes the input file stream. This method throws an IOException exception if the file cannot be closed.

**TIP** A buffer stores a large number of characters from the stream so that more than one character at a time can be read, such as in a readLine().

### Class BufferedReader (java.io)

### Constructor/Methods
`BufferedReader(Reader stream)`

creates a buffered-input stream from `stream`. Reader is the FileReader superclass.

`read()` reads a single character from the input stream. This method throws an IOException exception if the stream cannot be read.

`readLine()` reads a line of text from the input stream. This method throws an IOException exception if the stream cannot be read.

`close()` closes the input file stream. This method throws an IOException exception if the stream cannot be closed.

## Reading Characters

The read() method returns an `int`, which corresponds to a Unicode value. In Unicode, a space corresponds to 32, a tab to 9, carriage return to 13, and line feed to 10.

The application on the next page reads an existing file line-by-line to show the contents of the file:

```
import java.util.Scanner;
import java.io.*;

public class ReadFile {

  public static void main(String[] args) {
    File textFile = new File("operating _ systems.txt");
    FileReader in;
    BufferedReader readFile;
    String lineOfText;

    try {
      in = new FileReader(textFile);
      readFile = new BufferedReader(in);
      while ((lineOfText = readFile.readLine()) != null ) {
        System.out.println(lineOfText);
      }
      readFile.close();
      in.close();
    } catch (FileNotFoundException e) {
      System.out.println("File does not exist or could
                          not be found.");
      System.err.println("FileNotFoundException:  "
                          + e.getMessage());
    } catch (IOException e) {
      System.out.println("Problem reading file.");
      System.err.println("IOException:  " + e.getMessage());
    }
  }
}
```

The ReadFile application reads and displays the file contents within a `try-catch` statement because both the FileReader and BufferedReader constructors and methods throw exceptions if there is a problem reading the file. A `try` can have multiple `catch` statements. The `catch` statements are in the order that they may occur. For example, the FileNotFoundException is handled first because the FileReader object is created first in the `try` statement.

The close() methods are used to close the FileReader and BufferedReader streams. It is important that the streams be closed in the reverse order that they were opened.

The ReadFile application displays the following output when run:

```
An operating system, or OS, is a software program.
An operating system enables the computer hardware to communicate and operate with the computer software.
Without a computer operating system, a computer would be useless.
Operating systems include Linux and Windows.
```

## Review: Assignment

Create a Assignment application that reads and then displays the contents of a file containing instructions for this assignment. Use Notepad or some other word processor to create the file. Be sure that the file is saved as a Text file (TXT). The Assignment application will need to include the correct path to the location of the file. If a path is not specified, the file must be placed in the same folder as the Assignment executable file.

# Processing Numeric Data

A file on disk is a set of characters, even when the file contains numeric data, such as test scores. An application written to process numeric data from a file must convert the data after it is read. The Double and Integer classes include class methods for converting a string to a primitive data type:

### Class Double (java.lang.Double)

### Method

`parseDouble(String text)`

> returns the `double` value in the String `text`.

### Class Integer (java.lang.Integer)

### Method

`parseInteger(String text)`

> returns the `int` value in the String `text`.

The AvgScore application reads tests scores that are stored one score per line in a text file and then reports the average:

```java
import java.io.*;

public class AvgScore {

  public static void main(String[] args) {
    File dataFile = new File("scores.dat");
    FileReader in;
    BufferedReader readFile;
    String score;
    double avgScore;
    double totalScores = 0;
    int numScores = 0;

    try {
      in = new FileReader(dataFile);
      readFile = new BufferedReader(in);
      while ((score = readFile.readLine()) != null ) {
        numScores += 1;
        System.out.println(score);
        totalScores += Double.parseDouble(score);
      }
      avgScore = totalScores / numScores;
      System.out.println("Average = " + avgScore);
      readFile.close();
      in.close();
    } catch (FileNotFoundException e) {
      System.out.println("File does not exist or could
                          not be found.");
      System.err.println("FileNotFoundException: "
                          + e.getMessage());
    } catch (IOException e) {
      System.out.println("Problem reading file.");
      System.err.println("IOException: " + e.getMessage());
    }
  }
}
```

## DAT Files

Text files that contain numeric data often have the file name extension `.dat`, also referred to as a DAT file.

The application produces the output:

```
88
92
76
95
67
82
91
Average = 84.42857142857143
```

## Review: Stats – part 1 of 2

Create a Stats application that reads names and scores from a data file named test1.dat, supplied with this text. The file contains a student name on one line followed by the student's test score on the next line. The Stats application should read and display each name and score. After all the scores have been displayed, the lowest score, highest score, and average score should be displayed.

## The FileWriter and BufferedWriter Classes

*output file stream*

The FileWriter and BufferedWriter classes, both from the java.io package, are used together to write data to a file. The FileWriter class is used to create an *output file stream*. A BufferedWriter class object is then used to send text to the stream. Some of the FileWriter and BufferedWriter classes methods include:

### Class FileWriter (java.io)

### Constructor/Method

`FileWriter(File fileName, boolean append)`

creates an input file stream for the File object. If `append` is true, then data written to the file will be added after existing data, otherwise the file will be overwritten. This constructor throws an IOException exception if the file cannot be created or opened.

`close()` closes the output file stream. This method throws an IOException exception if the file cannot be closed.

When a FileWriter object is created, the file referenced by the File object is automatically overwritten unless the FileWriter object is set to append. In either case, if the file does not yet exist, a new one will be created. Caution must be used so that a file is not inadvertently overwritten.

## Class BufferedWriter (java.io)

### Constructor/Methods

`BufferedWriter(Writer stream)`

 creates a buffered-writer stream from `stream`. Writer is the FileWriter superclass.

`newLine()` writes a newline character to the output stream. This method throws an IOException exception if the stream cannot be written to.

`write(String str)`

 writes the string `str` to the output stream. This method throws an IOException exception if the stream cannot be written to.

`write(char c)` writes the character `c` to the output stream. This method throws an IOException exception if the stream cannot be written to.

`close()` closes the output file stream. This method throws an IOException exception if the stream cannot be closed.

The CreateDataFile application prompts the user for names and scores and then writes them to a new file:

```java
import java.io.*;
import java.util.Scanner;

public class CreateDataFile {

  public static void main(String[] args) {
    File dataFile = new File("StuScores.dat");
    FileWriter out;
    BufferedWriter writeFile;
    Scanner input = new Scanner(System.in);
    double score;
    String name;

    try {
      out = new FileWriter(dataFile);
      writeFile = new BufferedWriter(out);
      for (int i = 0; i < 5; i++) {
        System.out.print(:Enter student name: ");
        name = input.next();
        System.out.print("Enter test score: ");
        score = input.nextDouble();
        writeFile.write(name);
        writeFile.newLine();
        writeFile.write(String.valueOf(score));
        writeFile.newLine();
      }
      writeFile.close();
      out.close();
      System.out.println("Data written to file.");
    } catch (IOException e) {
      System.out.println("Problem writing to file.");
      System.err.println("IOException: " + e.getMessage());
    }
  }
}
```

Note that the application will overwrite the StuScores.dat file each time that it is run. The CreateDataFile application displays output similar to that shown on the next page:

```
Enter student name: Tyra
Enter test score: 98
Enter student name: Carmen
Enter test score: 83
Enter student name: Mikayla
Enter test score: 77
Enter student name: Juan
Enter test score: 92
Enter student name: Andre
Enter test score: 67
Data written to file.
```

## Review: Stats – part 2 of 2

Modify the Stats application to allow the user to enter the names and grades of the students. The user should be prompted for the name of the file to create and for the number of student grades that will be entered. After the data has been entered and the written to a file, the file should be read and the lowest, highest, and average score displayed.

## Object Serialization

A file can also be used to store object data. Writing objects to a file is called *object serialization*. In this process, class information about an object is written out to a stream. If a class uses another class, this information is also written out, and so on. When information about an object is retrieved from a file, it is called *object deserialization*.

Object serialization and deserialization is performed with object output and input streams. The FileOutputStream and ObjectOutputStream classes, both from the java.io package, are used together to write objects to a file. The FileInputStream and ObjectInputStream classes, also from the java.io package, are used together to read objects from a file. Some of the methods from the classes for writing and reading objects include:

### Class FileOutputStream (java.io)

### Constructor/Method

`FileOutputStream(File fileName, boolean append)`

creates an output file stream for the File object. If append is true, then data written to the file will be added after existing data, otherwise the file will be overwritten or created if the file does not exist. This method throws a FileNotFoundException exception if the file cannot be opened or created.

`close()`  closes the output file stream. This method throws an IOException exception if the file cannot be closed.

In addition to methods for writing objects to the output stream, the ObjectOutputStream class also contains methods for writing primitive data types.

### Class ObjectOutputStream (java.io)

**Constructor/Method**

`ObjectOutputStream(FileOutputStream stream)`

creates an object stream from `stream`.

`writeObject(Object obj)`

writes object information to the output stream. This method throws an IOException exception if there are problems with the class or if the stream cannot be written to.

`writeInt(int num)`

writes an `int` to the output stream. This method throws an IOException exception if the stream cannot be written to.

`writeDouble(double num)`

writes a `double` to the output stream. This method throws an IOException exception if the stream cannot be written to.

`close()`

closes the output stream. This method throws an IOException exception if the stream cannot be closed.

Objects are read from a FileInputStream stream object:

### Class FileInputStream (java.io)

**Constructor/Method**

`FileInputStream(File fileName)`

creates an input file stream for the File object. This method throws a FileNotFoundException exception if the file cannot be read.

`close()`

closes the input file stream. This method throws an IOException exception if the file cannot be closed.

The ObjectInputStream class contains method for reading both objects and primitive data types.

### Class ObjectInputStream (java.io)

**Constructor/Method**

`ObjectInputStream(FileInputStream stream)`

creates an object stream from `stream`. This constructor throws an IOException exception if the stream cannot be read.

`readObject()`

reads an object from the input stream. This method throws exceptions IOException and ClassNotFoundException if the the stream cannot be read or a class cannot be deserialized.

`readInt()`

reads an `int` from the input stream. This method throws an IOException exception if the file cannot be read.

| | |
|---|---|
| `readDouble()` | reads a `double` from the input stream. This method throws an IOException exception if the file cannot be read. |
| `close()` | closes the input stream. This method throws an IOException exception if the file cannot be closed. |

The ObjectWriteRead application demonstrates writing and reading objects from a file:

```java
import java.io.*;

public class ObjectWriteRead {

  public static void main(String[] args) {
    File stuFile = new File("students.dat");

    try {
      /* write objects */
      FileOutputStream out = new FileOutputStream(stuFile);
      ObjectOutputStream writeStu = new ObjectOutputStream(out);
      writeStu.writeObject(new Student("Drew", 87));
      writeStu.writeObject(new Student("Tia", 92));
      writeStu.close();
      System.out.println("Data written to file.");

      /* read objects */
      FileInputStream in = new FileInputStream(stuFile);
      ObjectInputStream readStu = new ObjectInputStream(in);
      Student stu1 = (Student)readStu.readObject();
      Student stu2 = (Student)readStu.readObject();
      readStu.close();

      System.out.println(stu1);
      System.out.println (stu2);

    } catch (FileNotFoundException e) {
      System.out.println("File could not be found.");
      System.err.println("FileNotFoundException: "
                          + e.getMessage());
    } catch (IOException e) {
      System.out.println("Problem with input/output.");
      System.err.println("IOException: " + e.getMessage());
    } catch (ClassNotFoundException e) {
      System.out.println("Class could not be used to
                          cast object.");
      System.err.println("ClassNotFoundException: "
                          + e.getMessage());
    }
  }
}
```

The ObjectWriteRead application writes two Student objects to the students.dat file. The Student class is shown on the next page:

```
import java.io.*;

public class Student implements Serializable {
  private String stuName;
  private double stuGrade;

  /**
   * constructor
   * pre: none
   * post: A Student object has been created.
   * Student data has been initialized with parameters.
   */
  public Student(String name, double grade) {
    stuName = name;
    stuGrade = grade;
  }


  /**
   * Creates a string representing the student object
   * pre: none
   * post: A string representing the student object
   * has been returned.
   */
  public String toString() {
    String stuString;

    stuString = stuName + " grade: " + stuGrade;
    return(stuString);
  }
}
```

*Serializable interface*

If the objects of a class are to be written to a file, the class must implement the Serializable interface. This interface is part of the java.io package and contains no methods to implement. It simply allows information about an instance of the class to be written out.

Note that reading an object from a file requires casting. The readObject() method reads Object data from the file. It is up to the programmer to cast the object to the appropriate type.

The ObjectWriteRead application catches several exceptions. First, a FileNotFoundException occurs when there is a problem creating a File object. IOException is a more general exception and occurs for various input/output problems. If IOException were first in the `catch` clauses, the other more specific exceptions would not be caught and the user would not be able to read their descriptive error messages. Finally, the ClassNotFoundException occurs if the class for an object written to the file cannot be found.

# Review: Roster

Create a Roster application that prompts the user for the name of the file to store student names and then prompts the user for the number of students in a class. The application should then prompt the user for the first and last name of each student and write this data to a file. After all the data is written to a file, the application display the class roster with one name after the other in a list. Create a StuName class that has member variables `firstName` and `lastName` and a toString() member method.

*Chapter 11 Files and Exception Handling*

In this case study, a LocalBank2 application will be created. LocalBank2 is the Chapter 9 case study modified to read and write account information from a file.

## LocalBank2 Specification

The LocalBank2 application has the same specification as LocalBank. It allows accounts to be opened, modified, and closed. Each account has a unique account number, which is required for all transactions. Transactions include deposits and withdrawals. An account balance can also be checked.

The LocalBank2 interface will not change from LocalBank. It will provide a menu of options:

```
Deposit\Withdrawal\Check balance
Add an account\Remove an account
Quit

Enter choice: a
First name: Adriana
Last name: Lee
Beginning balance: 100
Account created. Account ID is: ALee

Deposit\Withdrawal\Check balance
Add an account\Remove an account
Quit

Enter choice: D
Enter account ID: ALee
Deposit amount: 22
ALee
Adriana Lee
Current balance is $122

Deposit\Withdrawal\Check balance
Add an account\Remove an account
Quit

Enter choice:
```

The LocalBank2 algorithm will not change from the LocalBank application algorithm.

## LocalBank2 Code Design

The LocalBank2 application will be modeled with a Bank object, Account objects, and Customer objects, just as LocalBank. However, the Bank object will store and retrieve accounts from a file. To do this, the Bank constructor should create a file stream for the File object specified when the Bank object is instantiated. The constructor should also load accounts from the file stream into an ArrayList. An updateAccounts() method will need to be added to the Bank class so that any account changes can be written back to the file.

Because account objects will be read from and written to a file, the Account class and any classes it uses must implement the Serializable interface. This includes the Customer class.

The LocalBank2 client code must be modified to create a File object that stores the account information. Before ending the LocalBank application, the updateAccounts() method is called to write account information back to the file. The pseudocode for the LocalBank2 client code follows:

```
File accountsFile =  new File("LBAccounts.dat");
Bank easySave = new Bank(accountsFile);

do {
    prompt user for transaction type

    if (add account) {
        easySave.addAccount();
    } else if (not Quit) {
        prompt user for account ID;
        if (deposit) {
          prompt user for deposit amount
          easySave.transaction(make deposit, acctID, amt);
        } else if (withdrawal) {
          prompt user for withdrawal amount
          easySave.transaction(make withdrawal, acctID, amt);
        } else if (check balance) {
          easySave.checkBalance(acctID);
        } else if (remove account) {
          easySave.deleteAccount(acctID);
        }
    }
} while (not quit);
easySave.updateAccounts(accountsFile);
```

## LocalBank Implementation

The LocaBank2 application is shown below:

```
/**
 * LocalBank2 client code.
 */

import java.io.*;
import java.util.Scanner;

public class LocalBank {

    public static void main(String[] args) {
        File accountsFile = new File("LBAccounts.dat");
        Bank easySave = new Bank(accountsFile);
```

```
        Scanner input = new Scanner(System.in);
        String action, acctID;
        Double amt;

        /* display menu of choices */
        do {
            System.out.println("\nDeposit\\Withdrawal\\Check balance");
            System.out.println("Add an account\\Remove an account");
            System.out.println("Quit\n");
            System.out.print("Enter choice: ");
            action = input.next();

            if (action.equalsIgnoreCase("A")) {
                easySave.addAccount();
            } else if (!action.equalsIgnoreCase("Q")) {
                System.out.print("Enter account ID: ");
                acctID = input.next();
                if (action.equalsIgnoreCase("D")) {
                    System.out.print("Enter deposit amount: ");
                    amt = input.nextDouble();
                    easySave.transaction(1, acctID, amt);
                } else if (action.equalsIgnoreCase("W")) {
                    System.out.print("Enter withdrawal amount: ");
                    amt = input.nextDouble();
                    easySave.transaction(2, acctID, amt);
                } else if (action.equalsIgnoreCase("C")) {
                    easySave.checkBalance(acctID);
                } else if (action.equalsIgnoreCase("R")) {
                    easySave.deleteAccount(acctID);
                }
            }
        } while (!action.equalsIgnoreCase("Q"));

        easySave.updateAccounts(accountsFile);      //write accounts to file
    }
}
```

The Bank class is shown below. The accounts are expected to be loaded from a file. Additionally, the number of accounts is also kept in the file. This number is the first data item in the file. It is read first and then used to determine how many accounts to read from the file. Throughout the class, the number of accounts is updated when a new account is added and when an account is deleted. When updateAccounts() is called, the number of accounts is written to the file first, followed by the accounts:

```
/**
 * Bank class.
 */

import java.util.ArrayList;
import java.io.*;
import java.util.Scanner;

public class Bank {
    private ArrayList accounts;
    private int numAccts;
```

```java
/**
 * constructor
 * pre: none
 * post: accounts have been loaded from acctFile.
 */
public Bank(File acctsFile) {
    accounts = new ArrayList();
    Account acct;

    /* Create a new file for accounts if one does not exist */
    if (!acctsFile.exists()) {
        try {
            acctsFile.createNewFile();
            System.out.println("There are no existing accounts.");
        } catch (IOException e) {
            System.out.println("File could not be created.");
            System.err.println("IOException: " + e.getMessage());
        }
        numAccts = 0;
    } else {     /* load existing accounts */
        try {
            FileInputStream in = new FileInputStream(acctsFile);
            ObjectInputStream readAccts = new ObjectInputStream(in);
            numAccts = (int)readAccts.readInt();
            if (numAccts == 0) {
                System.out.println("There are no existing accounts.");
            } else {
                for (int i = 0; i < numAccts; i++) {
                    acct = (Account)readAccts.readObject();
                    accounts.add(acct);
                }
            }
            readAccts.close();
        } catch (FileNotFoundException e) {
            System.out.println("File could not be found.");
            System.err.println("FileNotFoundException: " + e.getMessage());
        } catch (IOException e) {
            System.out.println("Problem with input/output.");
            System.err.println("IOException: " + e.getMessage());
        } catch (ClassNotFoundException e) {
            System.out.println("Class could not be used to cast object.");
            System.err.println("ClassNotFoundException: " + e.getMessage());
        }
    }
}


/**
 * Adds a new account to the bank accounts.
 * pre: none
 * post: An account has been added to the bank's accounts.
 */
public void addAccount() {
    Account newAcct;
    double bal;
    String fName, lName;
    Scanner input = new Scanner(System.in);

    System.out.print("First name: ");
    fName = input.nextLine();
    System.out.print("Last name: ");
    lName = input.nextLine();
    System.out.print("Beginning balance: ");
    bal = input.nextDouble();
```

*Chapter 11 Files and Exception Handling*

```
        newAcct = new Account(bal, fName, lName);    //create account object
        accounts.add(newAcct);                       //add account to bank accounts
        numAccts += 1;                               //increment number of accounts

        System.out.println("Account created. Account ID is: " + newAcct.getID());
    }


    /**
     * Deletes an existing account.
     * pre: none
     * post: An existing account has been deleted.
     */
    public void deleteAccount(String acctID) {
        int acctIndex;
        Account acctToMatch;

        acctToMatch = new Account(acctID);
        acctIndex = accounts.indexOf(acctToMatch);    //retrieve location of account
        if (acctIndex > -1) {
            accounts.remove(acctIndex);               //remove account
            System.out.println("Account removed.");
            numAccts -= 1;                            //decrement number of accounts
        } else {
            System.out.println("Account does not exist.");
        }
    }

/**
     * Performs a transaction on an existing account. A transCode of 1 is for deposits
     * and a transCode of 2 is for withdrawals.
     * pre: transCode is 1 or 2.
     * post: A transaction has occurred for an existing account.
     */
    public void transaction(int transCode, String acctID, double amt) {
        int acctIndex;
        Account acctToMatch, acct;

        acctToMatch = new Account(acctID);
        acctIndex = accounts.indexOf(acctToMatch);    //retrieve location of account
        if (acctIndex > -1) {
            acct = accounts.get(acctIndex);           //retrieve object to modify
            if (transCode == 1) {
                acct.deposit(amt);
                accounts.set(acctIndex, acct);        //replace object with updated object
                System.out.println(acct);
            } else if (transCode == 2) {
                acct.withdrawal(amt);
                accounts.set(acctIndex, acct);        //replace object with updated object
                System.out.println(acct);
            }
        } else {
            System.out.println("Account does not exist.");
        }
    }
```

```java
/**
 * Displays the account information, including the current balance,
 * for an existing account.
 * pre: none
 * post: Account information, including balance, has been displayed.
 */
public void checkBalance(String acctID) {
    int acctIndex;
    Account acctToMatch, acct;

    acctToMatch = new Account(acctID);
    acctIndex = accounts.indexOf(acctToMatch);       //retrieve location of account
    if (acctIndex > -1) {
        acct = accounts.get(acctIndex);              //retrieve object to display
        System.out.println(acct);
    } else {
        System.out.println("Account does not exist.");
    }
}


/**
 * Accounts are written to a file for storage.
 * pre: none
 * post: accounts have been written to acctFile.
 */
public void updateAccounts(File acctsFile) {

    try {
        FileOutputStream out = new FileOutputStream(acctsFile);
        ObjectOutputStream writeAccts = new ObjectOutputStream(out);
        writeAccts.writeInt(numAccts);
        for (Object acct : accounts){
            writeAccts.writeObject(acct);
        }
        writeAccts.close();
    } catch (FileNotFoundException e) {
        System.out.println("File could not be found.");
        System.err.println("FileNotFoundException: " + e.getMessage());
    } catch (IOException e) {
        System.out.println("Problem with input/output.");
        System.err.println("IOException: " + e.getMessage());
    }
}
```

The Account class need only be modified to implement the Serializable class:

```java
/**
 * Account class.
 */

import java.io.*;
import java.text.NumberFormat;

public class Account implements Serializable {
```

*...rest of Account class (refer to Chapter 9 case study)*

The Customer class need only be modified to implement the Serializable class:

```
/**
 * Customer class.
 */

import java.io.*;

public class Customer implements Serializable {
```

*...rest of Customer class (refer to Chapter 9 case study)*

Running the LocalBank2 application displays the same output as the LocalBank application:

```
Deposit\Withdrawal\Check balance
Add an account\Remove an account
Quit

Enter choice: a
First name: Wei
Last name: Lau
Beginning balance: 1500
Account created. Account ID is: WLau

Deposit\Withdrawal\Check balance
Add an account\Remove an account
Quit

Enter choice: d
Enter account ID: WLau
Enter deposit amount: 500
WLau
Wei Lau
Current balance is $2,000.00

Deposit\Withdrawal\Check balance
Add an account\Remove an account
Quit
```

### LocalBank2 Testing and Debugging

The LocalBank2 application should be tested to be sure that it works appropriately when no file exists, when a file with no accounts exists, and when a file with accounts exists.

## Review: LocalBank2

Modify the Bank class to keep track of accounts with low balances. A low balance is an account with less than $20.00. The number of low balance accounts should be stored after the number of accounts, but before the account objects in the account file. Have the number of low balance accounts displayed when a Bank object is created and again when the updateAccounts() method is called.

# Chapter Summary

This chapter discussed files and exception handling. A file is a data stored on a persistent medium such as a hard disk or CD. In Java, a File object is associated with a file name. A File object can be used to create or delete a file.

An exception is an error affecting program execution. An exception handler is a block of code that performs an action when an exception occurs. This chapter introduced the `try-catch-finally` statement for writing exception handlers.

A file must be associated with a stream in order to read and write to the file. A file stream processes characters and is used to perform sequential file access. The FileReader, BufferedReader, FileWriter, and BufferWriter classes are used to read and write to a file.

An application written to process numeric data from a file must convert the file data from a strings to numerics. The Double and Integer classes contain methods for converting numeric characters in a string to an `int` or a `double`.

Objects can be written to a file in a process called object serialization. Reading objects from a file is called object deserialization. Serialization and deserialization are performed with an object stream. The FileOutputStream, ObjectOutputStream, FileInputStream, and ObjectInputStream classes are used to write and read objects to a file. The ObjectOutputStream and ObjectInputStream classes can also be used to write and read primitive data to a file.

**ClassNotFoundException** An exception thrown if a stream cannot be read or a class cannot be deserialized.

**End of file** A –1 in the file stream.

**err stream** The stream used for displaying error messages to the user.

**Exception** An error affecting program execution.

**Exception handler** A block of code that performs an action when an exception occurs.

**File** A collection of related data stored on a persistent medium.

**FileNotFoundException** An exception thrown when a file does not exist.

**File position** The point at which reading or writing in the stream last occurred.

**Handle** Take care of.

**Input file stream** A file stream for reading a file.

**IOException** An exception thrown when a file cannot be created, or when there is a general input/output problem.

**Line terminator** A carriage return followed by a line feed in the file stream.

**Object deserialization** The process used to read objects from a file.

**Object serialization** The process used to write objects to a file.

**Output file stream** A file stream for writing to a file.

**Persistent** Lasting.

**Sequential file access** Reading and writing one character after another.

**Stream** The construct used for processing characters.

**Throw** Generate.

## Java

**BufferedReader** A java.io class used for creating a buffered file stream for reading a file.

**BufferedWriter** A java.io class used for creating a buffered file stream for writing to a file.

**Double** A java.lang class for converting numeric text in a string to a `double`.

**File** The java.io class used for creating an object that refers to a file.

**FileInputStream** A java.io class used for creating an object input stream.

**FileOutputStream** A java.io class used for creating an object output stream.

**FileReader** The java.io class used for creating a file stream for reading a file.

**FileWriter** The java.io class used for creating a file stream for writing to a file.

**Integer** A java.lang class for converting numeric text in a string to an `int`.

`try-catch-finally` Statement used to write an exception handler.

**ObjectInputStream** A java.io class used for creating an object for reading objects from a file.

**ObjectOutputStream** A java.io class used for creating an object for writing objects to a file.

1. Can data in memory be called a file? Explain.

2. Write the `import` statement required to access the File Class in an application.

3. Identify the error in the following statement:
   `File textFile = new File("c:\inventory.txt");`

4. a) Which statement is used to write an exception handler?
   b) Write an exception handler to handle an IOException if a specified file name cannot be used to create a file. The exception handler should display appropriate messages to the user.

5. a) What is the name of the stream for displaying error messages.
   b) Where are these messages displayed?

6. a) What does the file stream keep track of?
   b) What characters together make up a line terminator?

7. What two classes are used together to write data to a file?

8. Write a statement to convert account balances that have been read from a text file to a `double` value and add them to `totalBalance`.

9. Explain the difference between object serialization and object deserialization.

10. What interface must be implemented if objects of a class are to be written to a file?

11. Describe two situations where an IOException exception could be thrown, and write an example exception handler for each situation to output an appropriate message if the exception occurs.

**True/False**

12. Determine if each of the following are true or false. If false, explain why.
    a) An exception always results in program termination.
    b) Sequential file access reads and writes data one character after another or one line after another.
    c) Z–1 is the end of file.
    d) A file on disk is a set of numbers ranging from 0 to 9.
    e) Numeric data in a file must be converted to a primitive data type before it can be processed numerically.
    f) A FileNotFoundException exception is thrown if a file cannot be closed.
    g) The output file stream is a file stream for writing to the screen.
    h) Reading an object from a file requires casting.

## Exercise 1 ——————————————————————— WordCount

Create a WordCount application that displays the number of words and the average word length in a text file named source.txt. Consider a word to be any sequence of letters terminated by nonletters. For example, forty-nine is two words.

## Exercise 2 ——————————————————————— WordStats

a) Create a WordStats application that lists all the unique words in a file and how many times they occurred. WordStats should ignore capitalization. The application should provide a listing similar to:

```
WORD    OCCURENCES
the     57
and     12
zoo     3
```

b) Modify the WordStats application to list the words in alphabetical order. This can be done by either using the sorting algorithm presented in Chapter 9, Exercise 11 or by keeping the words in order as they are read.

## Exercise 3 ——————————————————————— TestProcessor

Test results for a multiple choice test can be stored in a text file as follows:

Line 1: The correct answers, one character per answer
Line 2: Name of the first student (length <= 30 chars)
Line 3: Answers for the student in line 2
The remaining lines: student names and answers on separate lines

For example:

```
BADED
Smithgall
BADDD
DeSalvo
CAEED
Darji
BADED
```

Create a TestProcessor application that processes the test results file for any number of students. The application should provide statistics similar to:

```
Smithgall   80%
DeSalvo     60%
Darji       100%
```

# Exercise 4 ———————————————————————— MadLib

A Mad-Lib story is a story where nouns and verbs in a paragraph are randomly replaced with other nouns and verbs, usually with humorous results. Create a MadLib application that displays a Mad-Lib story. The application will require three files:

- story.txt which contains a story with # signs as noun placeholders, and % signs as verb placeholders. For example:

```
Bugsy Kludge is a # with our company.
His job is to % all of the #s.
```

- verbs.txt which contains verbs, one per line. For example:

```
run
display
eat
```

- nouns.txt which contains nouns, one per line. For example:

```
banana
soprano
elephant
vegetable
```

Application output should display the story with apporpriate replacements made. A possible output would produce a MadLib similar to:

```
Bugsy Kludge is a vegetable with our company.
His job is to display all of the elephants.
```

# Exercise 5 ———————————————————————— MergeFiles

The idea of merging two or more files is an important one in programming. One approach is to merge the ordered data of two files into a third file, keeping the data in order.

Create a MergeFiles application that merges the integers ordered from low to high in two files into a third file, keeping the order from low to high. For example, two files of integers could contain:

```
File 1:   12 23 34 45 56 67 69 123 133
File 2:   4 5 10 20 35 44 100 130 150 160 180
```

The application should not use an array to temporarily store the numbers, but should merge the two files by taking one element at a time from each. After MergeFiles has been run, the third file should contain:

```
4 5 10 12 20 23 34 35 44 45 56 67 69 100 123 130 133 150 160 180
```

# Exercise 6  ———————————————————————— MergeLarge

The algorithm implemented in Exercise 5 is sometimes used as part of a sorting algorithm with data that is too large to be stored in memory at once. For example, to sort a large file large.dat that is twice as large as will fit in memory, half can be read into an array, the array sorted, and then written to a file numbers1.dat. Next, the second half of large.dat can be read into the array, sorted, and then written to numbers2.dat. Finally, the two files can be merged in order back into large.dat. Create a MergeLarge application that implements this algorithm. Test the application with a file that contains 30 integers sorted from low to high.

*Chapter 11 Files and Exception Handling*

# Exercise 7 ——————————————————————————————HTMLViewer

The early success of the Web is largely due to the simplicity of HTML (HyperText Markup Language), for designing a Web page. HTML documents are text documents containing content and tags that describe the format of the content. An HTML document could look similar to:

```
JUNE BUGS<p>June bugs RAM in megabytes of fleshy fruit,<br>downsize fine fat
figs<br>chip away at melon bits.<br>They monitor windows for open screens,<br>seeking
felicity in electricity.<br>Built-in memory warns of websites<br>hiding spiders
with sly designs.<br>Scrolling the scene of leaves and trees,<br>they network the
neighborhood in flashy green jackets,<br>each bug a browser, scanner, looter-
<br>not even knowing the word "computer."<p>by Avis Harley<p><hr>
```

Tags are enclosed in angle brackets, < >. The tag <br> means to start a new line. The tag <p> means to start a new paragraph (a blank line). The tag <hr> means to draw a horizontal rule. When these tags are interpreted, the HTML document above is displayed as:

```
JUNE BUGS

June bugs RAM in megabytes of fleshy fruit,
downsize fine fat figs
chip away at melon bits.
They monitor windows for open screens,
seeking felicity in electricity.
Built-in memory warns of websites
hiding spiders with sly designs.
Scrolling the scene of leaves and trees,
they network the neighborhood in flashy green jackets,
each bug a browser, scanner, looter-
not even knowing the word "computer."

by Avis Harley


------------------------------------------------
```

a) HTML documents are interpreted by browser software. Create an HTMLViewer application that interprets an HTML file to display the Web content as intended, similar to the way a browser decides how to display an HTML document.

b) Modify the HTMLViewer application to allow the user to specify the display line width. For example, a width of 35 should display the HTML document as:

```
JUNE BUGS

June bugs RAM in megabytes of
fleshy fruit,
downsize fine fat figs
chip away at melon bits.
They monitor windows for open
screens,
seeking felicity in electricity.
Built-in memory warns of websites
hiding spiders with sly designs.
Scrolling the scene of leaves and
trees,
they network the neighborhood in
flashy green jackets,
each bug a browser, scanner,
looter-
not even knowing the word
"computer."

by Avis Harley


-----------------------------------
```

## Exercise 8 ✦ ———————————————————————— CarRecall

Modify the CarRecall application created in Chapter 5, Exercise 4 to load the defective car model numbers from a file.

## Exercise 9 ✦ ———————————————————————— WordGuess

Modify the WordGuess case study from Chapter 5 to use a word from a file as the secret word. The file should contain a list of words, with one word per line. The WordGuess application should determine which word to use, by generating a random number that corresponds to one of the words in the file.

## Exercise 10 ———————————————————————— FindAndReplace

Create a FindAndReplace application that prompts the user for a file name, a search word or phrase, and a replacement word or phrase. After entering the replacement word or phrase, FindAndReplace finds all occurrences of the search word or phrase in a file and replaces them with the specified replacement word or phrase.

## Exercise 11 ———————————————————————— ApplicationDoc

Create an ApplicationDoc application that prompts the user for the file name of a Java source code file (the file name extension should be java) and then copies all the documentation comments (/** */) to a separate file.

## Exercise 12 ✦ ———————————————————————— MySavings

Modify the MySavings application from Chapter 7, Exercise 1 to store and load the PiggyBank object from a file.

## Exercise 13 ✦ ———————————————————————— Adder

Modify the Adder application from Chapter 7, Exercise 8 to keep track of player scores in a file. The application should prompt the player for his or her name and then create a file based on the player name. For example, if the player's name is Jo, then a file named JoScores.txt should be created. The application should write the player's score to their file at the end of the game and then display the player's previous scores.

## Exercise 14 ✦ ———————————————————————— CountVowels

Modify the CountVowels application created in Chapter 5, Exercise 20 to count the number of vowels in a text file. The application should prompt the user for the file name.

## Exercise 15 ✎ ───────────────────────────── Coder

Modify the Coder application created in Chapter 9, Exercise 10 to encode the text in one file and write it to a new file.


## Exercise 16 ✎ ──────────────────────── CourseGrades

Modify the CourseGrades application created in Chapter 9, Exercise 12 to write the GradeBook object to a file.


## Exercise 17 ✎ ───────────────────────────── Life

Modify the Life application created in Chapter 9, Exercise 14 to retrieve the initial life grid from a file.


## Exercise 18 ✎ ──────────────────────── Inventory

Modify the Inventory application created in Chapter 9, Exercise 16 to write the inventory items to a file.

Chapter 11 Files and Exception Handling

# Chapter 12
# Recursion and Advanced Algorithms

## Key Concepts

Implementing the selection sort algorithm
Implementing the insertion sort algorithm
Understanding recursion
Implementing the merge sort algorithm
Implementing the binary search algorithm
Analyzing algorithms for efficiency

## Selection Sort

Sorting is the process of putting items in a designated order, either from low to high or high to low. The *selection sort* algorithm starts by finding the lowest item in a list and swapping it with the first. Next, the lowest item among items 2 through the last is found and swapped with item 2, and then the lowest item among items 3 through the last is swapped with item 3. This process is continued until the last item is reached, at which point all the items are sorted.

The selection sort algorithm compares an element to the items in the array after the element. This algorithm can be implemented with nested `for` loops. The outer loop controls which element to compare and the inner `for` loop iterates through the array after the element (the subarray). The selection sort pseudocode for sorting an array of items from low to high appears like:

```
for (arrayIndex = 0 to numItems-1)
   for (subarrayIndex = arrayIndex to numItems-1)
     if (items[subarrayIndex] < items[arrayIndex]) {
       swap items[subarrayIndex] and items[arrayIndex]
     }
   }
}
```

The Sorts class on the next page implements a selectionSort() method:

```
public class Sorts {

  /**
   * Sorts an array of data from low to high
   * pre: none
   * post: items has been sorted from low to high
   */
  public static void selectionSort(int[] items) {

    for (int index=0; index<items.length; index++) {
      for (int subIndex=index; subIndex<items.length; subIndex++) {
        if (items[subIndex] < items[index]) {
          int temp = items[index];
          items[index] = items[subIndex];
          items[subIndex] = temp;
        }
      }
    }
  }
}
```

The TestSorts application generates an array of integers and then calls selectionSort() to sort the array elements:

```
import java.util.Scanner;
import java.util.Math;

public class TestSorts {

  public static void displayArray(int[] array) {
    for (int i = 0; i < array.length; i++) {
      System.out.print(array[i] + "  ");
    }
    System.out.println("\n");
  }

  public static void main(String[] args) {
    Scanner input = new Scanner(System.in);
    int numItems;
    int[] test;

    System.out.print("Enter number of elements: ");
    numItems = input.nextInt();

    /* populate array with random integers */
    test = new int[numItems];
    for (int i = 0; i < test.length; i++) {
      test[i] = (int)(101 * Math.random());
    }
    System.out.println("Unsorted:");
    displayArray(test);

    Sorts.selectionSort(test);

    System.out.println("Sorted:");
    displayArray(test);
  }
}
```

The TestSorts application produces output similar to:

```
Enter number of elements: 10
Unsorted:
79  50  10  18  77  31  64  18  14  96

Sorted:
10  14  18  18  31  50  64  77  79  96
```

## Sorting Objects

Relational operators, such as > and <, cannot be used to compare objects. Objects use methods of their class to determine if one object is greater than, less than, or equal to another. The equals() method in a class is used to determine equality. For determining order, the compareTo() method is used.

*Comparable interface*

Objects that are to be sorted must have a class that implements the Comparable interface. The String, Double, and Integer clases implement the Comparable interface. The Circle class in Chapter 8 also implements the Comparable interface.

*polymorphism*

An interface cannot be used to instantiate a class. However, an interface can be used as a data type. An interface data type can reference any class that implements it. This polymorphic behavior makes it possible to implement a generic sort that works with any list of objects that implement the Comparable interface.

The Sorts class has been modified to include an overloaded SelectionSort() method, which has a Comparable array parameter:

```
/**
 * Sorts an array of objects from low to high
 * pre: none
 * post: Objects have been sorted from low to high
 */
public static void selectionSort(Comparable[] items) {

  for (int index = 0; index < items.length; index++) {
    for (int subIndex=index; subIndex<items.length; subIndex++) {
      if (items[subIndex].compareTo(items[index]) < 0) {
        Comparable temp = items[index];
        items[index] = items[subIndex];
        items[subIndex] = temp;
      }
    }
  }
}
```

The TestSorts application, on the next page, has been modified to sort an array of Circle objects:

```
import java.util.Scanner;
import java.util.Math;

public class TestSorts {

  public static void displayArray(Circle[] array) {
    for (int i = 0; i < array.length; i++) {
      System.out.println(array[i] + "   ");
    }
    System.out.println("\n");
  }

    public static void main(String[] args) {
    Scanner input = new Scanner(System.in);
    int numObjects;
    Circle[] test;

    System.out.print("Enter number of objects:  ");
    numObjects = input.nextInt();
    input.close();

    /* populate array with Circle objects of varying radii */
    test = new Circle[numObjects];
    for (int i = 0; i < test.length; i++) {
      test[i] = new Circle((int)(10 * Math.random() + 1));
    }
    System.out.println("Unsorted:");
    displayArray(test);

    Sorts.selectionSort(test);

    System.out.println("Sorted:");
    displayArray(test);
  }
}
```

The TestSorts application produces output similar to:

```
Enter number of objects: 5
Unsorted:
Circle has radius 1.0
Circle has radius 3.0
Circle has radius 9.0
Circle has radius 5.0
Circle has radius 4.0


Sorted:
Circle has radius 1.0
Circle has radius 3.0
Circle has radius 4.0
Circle has radius 5.0
Circle has radius 9.0
```

Create an ArrayListSort application that implements a selection sort on an ArrayList object. Test the sort with an ArrayList containing Double objects.

## Insertion Sort

More efficient than the selection sort algorithm is the insertion sort algorithm. An *insertion sort* starts by sorting the first two items in a list. This sort is performed by shifting the first item into the second spot if the second item belongs in the first spot. Next, the third item is properly inserted within the first three items by again shifting items into their appropriate position to make room for the moved item. This process is repeated for the remaining elements.

The insertion sort is illustrated below with an array containing four elements. Step 1 shows the original list, which contains items 40, 10, 30, and 20. Step 2 shows that 40 is shifted to make room for the second item, 10. Next, 30 compared to the value in the previous position (40), 40 is shifted into position 3, 30 is then compared to the value in the previous position (10), and then 30 is placed at position 2. This process repeats for the remaining items.

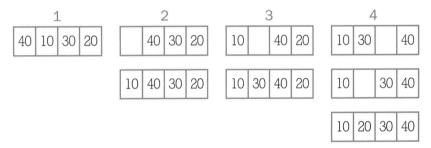

Based on the algorithm, the insertion sort pseudocode for an array of integers is:

```
for (index = 1 To array.length - 1) {
  temp = array[index]
  previousIndex = index - 1
  while (array[previousIndex] > temp && previousIndex > 0) {
    shift array[previousIndex] up one element
    previousIndex = previousIndex - 1
  }
  if (array[previousIndex] > temp) {
    swap the two elements
  } else {
    insert element at appropriate location
  }
}
```

The Sorts class has been modified to include an insertionSort() method:

```java
/**
 * Sorts an array of integer from low to high
 * pre: none
 * post: Integers have been sorted from low to high
 */
public static void insertionSort(int[] items) {
  int temp, previousIndex;

  for (int index = 1; index < items.length; index++) {
    temp = items[index];
    previousIndex = index - 1;
    while ((items[previousIndex] > temp) && (previousIndex > 0)) {
      items[previousIndex + 1] = items[previousIndex];
      previousIndex -= 1;         //decrease index to compare current
    }                             //item with next previous item
    if (items[previousIndex] > temp) {
      /* shift item in first element up into next element */
      items[previousIndex + 1] = items[previousIndex];
      /* place current item at index 0 (first element) */
      items[previousIndex] = temp;
    } else {
      /* place current item at index ahead of previous item */
      items[previousIndex + 1] = temp;
    }
  }
}
```

The TestSorts application has been modified to use the insertionSort() method to sort an array of integers:

```java
import java.util.Scanner;
import java.util.Math;

public class TestSorts {

  public static void displayArray(int[] array) {
    for (int i = 0; i < array.length; i++) {
      System.out.print(array[i] + "  ");
    }
    System.out.println("\n");
  }

  public static void main(String[] args) {
    Scanner input = new Scanner(System.in);
    int numItems;
    int[] test;

    System.out.print("Enter number of elements:  ");
    numItems = input.nextInt();

    /* populate array with random integers */
    test = new int[numItems];
    for (int i = 0; i < test.length; i++) {
      test[i] = (int)(100 * Math.random());
    }
    System.out.println("Unsorted:");
    displayArray(test);

    Sorts.insertionSort(test);
```

```
      System.out.println("Sorted:");
      displayArray(test);
    }
  }
```

The TestSorts application produces output similar to:

```
Enter number of elements: 10
Unsorted:
78 6 95 34 61 35 52 1 60 76

Sorted:
1 6 34 35 52 60 61 76 78 95
```

## Review: ObjectsInsertionSort

Create an ObjectsInsertionSort application that implements an insertion sort on an array of objects. Test the sort on an array of String objects.

## Recursion

*recursive call*

A method can call itself. This process is called *recursion* and the calls are referred to as *recursive calls*. The RecursiveDemo application contains a method that calls itself:

```
public class RecursiveDemo {

  public static void showRecursion(int num) {
    System.out.println("Entering method. num = " + num);
    if (num > 1) {
      showRecursion(num - 1);
    }
    System.out.println("Leaving method. num = "  + num);
  }


  public static void main(String[] args) {
    showRecursion(2);
  }
}
```

The call showRecursion(2) from the main() method is the initial call. In the showRecursion() method, a call is made to itself passing num – 1. When showRecursion is called with num equal to 1, the if is skipped and the remaining statement in the method is executed. At this point the stack of calls made before num was 1 are executed in the reverse order they were made, with each call executing the statement in the method after the recursive call (after the if).

The RecursiveDemo produces the output shown on the next page:

```
Entering method. num = 2
Entering method. num = 1
Leaving method. num = 1
Leaving method. num = 2
```

Recursion is a programming technique that can be used whenever a problem can be solved by solving one or more smaller versions of the same problem and combining the results. The recursive calls solve the smaller problems.

One problem that has a recursive solution is raising a number to a power. For example, $2^4$ can be thought of as:

$2^4 = 2 * 2^3$ which can be thought of as
$2^3 = 2 * 2^2$ which can be thought of as
$2^2 = 2 * 2^1$ which can be thought of as
$2^1 = 2 * 2^0$ which can be thought of as
1

In each case, the power problem is reduced to a smaller power problem. A more general solution is:

$$x^n = x * x^{n-1}$$

However, carefully analyzing this solution shows that there is no stopping point. For example, $2^3$ would be $2 * 2^2$, which would return $2 * 2^1$, which returns $2 * 2^0$, which returns $2 * 2^{-1}$, and so on. This solution would cause *infinite recursion*. To prevent this, a recursive solution must have a *base case* that requires no recursion. For this solution, when the power is 0, 1 should be returned.

*infinite recursion*
*base case*

The intPower() method in the Power application implements a recursive solution for calculating an `int` raised to an `int` power to return an `int` (as opposed to Math.pow(), which returns a `double`):

```java
public class Power {

    /**
     * Returns num to the power power.
     * pre: num and power are not 0.
     * post: num to the power power has been returned.
     */
    public static int intPower(int num, int power) {
        int result;
        if (power == 0) {
            result = 1;
        } else {
            result = num * intPower(num, power-1);
        }
        return(result);
    }


    public static void main(String[] args) {
        int x = intPower(2, 5);
        System.out.println(x);
    }
}
```

The Power application produces the output:

32

*Chapter 12 Recursion and Advanced Algorithms*

Create a RecursiveFactorial application that returns the factorial of an integer. The factorial of a number is the product of all positive integers from 1 to the number. For example, 5! = 5*4*3*2*1. Computing 5! could be thought of as 5*4! or more generally, n*(n–1)!. By definition, 0! is equal to 1. Compare your recursive solution to the nonrecursive solution created in the Factorial Review completed in Chapter 5.

## Mergesort

**TIP** Measuring an algorithm's efficiency is discussed later in this Chapter.

The selection sort is simple, but inefficient, especially for large arrays. Imagine using the selection sort process by hand for a pile of 1000 index cards. Searching through the cards for the lowest item would take a long time, but more importantly, after each search the remaining cards must be searched again! Each card ends up being examined about 500 times.

The *mergesort* algorithm takes a "divide-and-conquer" approach to sorting. Imagine the 1000 cards being divided into two piles of 500. Each pile could then be sorted (a simpler problem) and the two sorted piles could be combined (merged) into a single ordered pile. To further simplify the sorting, each subpile could be divided and sorted, and so on. This algorithm is best implemented recursively.

The mergesort pseudocode is:

```
if there are items remaining {
    mergesort the left half of the items
    mergesort the right half of the items
    merge the two halves into a completely sorted list
}
```

The mergesort subtasks are recursive calls to mergeSort() and a call to merge(). The mergesort() method will need arguments indicating which portion of the array is to be sorted. Similarly, merge() implements the merging of two halves and needs arguments indicating which portion of the array is to be merged.

The mergesort() method is defined as:

```
/**
 * Sorts items[start..end]
 * pre: start > 0, end > 0
 * post: items[start..end] is sorted low to high
 */
public static void mergesort(int[] items, int start, int end) {
  if (start < end) {
    int mid = (start + end) / 2;
    mergesort(items, start, mid);
    mergesort(items, mid + 1, end);
    merge(items, start, mid, end);
  }
}
```

The stopping condition for the recursive function is determined by comparing `start` and `end`. The middle of the array is calculated using integer division, which automatically truncates the decimal portion of the quotient.

The merge() method uses a temporary array to store items moved from two sorted portions of the items array. The elements are moved so that the temporary array is sorted. To illustrate the merge() algorithm, suppose at entry to merge() the array looks like:

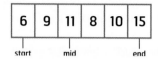

The array is sorted from start to mid and from mid+1 to end. The merge() method starts by examining the first element of each sorted portion, start and mid+1, as indicated by pos1 and pos2:

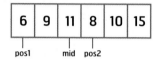

Since items[pos1] < items[pos2], the element items[pos1] is moved to the new array, and pos1 is incremented:

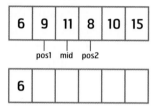

In this case, items[pos1] > items[pos2], so the the element items[pos2] is moved to the new array and pos2 incremented:

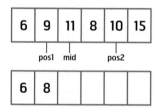

This process is repeated until all items have been moved. Since it is likely that one array portion will be exhausted before the other, merge() tests for this case and just moves items from the remaining list. Finally, merge() copies the merged items in the temporary array to the original array.

The Sorts class has been modified to include a mergesort() method. Note that the merge() method is private because it is a helper method:

```java
/**
 * Merges two sorted portion of items array
 * pre: items[start..mid] is sorted. items[mid+1..end] sorted.
 * start <= mid <= end
 * post: items[start..end] is sorted.
 */
private static void merge(int[] items, int start,
                              int mid, int end) {
  int[] temp = new int[items.length];
  int pos1 = start;
  int pos2 = mid + 1;
  int spot = start;

  while (!(pos1 > mid && pos2 > end)) {
    if ((pos1 > mid) ||
        ((pos2 <= end) && (items[pos2] < items[pos1]))) {
      temp[spot] = items[pos2];
      pos2 += 1;
    } else {
      temp[spot] = items[pos1];
      pos1  += 1;
    }
    spot += 1;
  }
  /* copy values from temp back to items */
  for (int i =  start; i <= end; i++) {
    items[i] = temp[i];
  }

}


/**
 * Sorts items[start..end]
 * pre: start > 0, end > 0
 * post: items[start..end] is sorted low to high
 */
public static void mergesort(int[] items, int start, int end) {
  if (start < end) {
    int mid = (start + end) / 2;
    mergesort(items, start, mid);
    mergesort(items, mid + 1, end);
    merge(items, start, mid, end);
  }
}
```

The if in the merge() method says that if the pos1 (left) subarray is exhausted, or if the pos2 (right) subarray is not exhausted and the pos2 element is less than the pos1 element, then move an item from the pos2 subarray to the temp array, otherwise move an item from the pos1 subarray. This process continues until both subarrays are exhausted.

The TestSorts application has been modified to use the mergesort() method to sort an array of integers:

```java
import java.util.Scanner;
import java.util.Math;

public class TestSorts {

  public static void displayArray(int[] array) {
    for (int i = 0; i < array.length; i++) {
      System.out.print(array[i] + "  ");
    }
    System.out.println("\n");
  }

  public static void main(String[] args) {
    Scanner input = new Scanner(System.in);
    int numItems;
    int[] test;

    System.out.print("Enter number of elements:  ");
    numItems = input.nextInt();

    /* populate array with random integers */
    test = new int[numItems];
    for (int i = 0; i < test.length; i++) {
      test[i] = (int)(100 * Math.random());
    }
    System.out.println("Unsorted:");
    displayArray(test);

    Sorts.mergesort(test, 0, test.length - 1);

    System.out.println("Sorted:");
    displayArray(test);
  }
}
```

The TestSorts application produces output similar to:

```
Enter number of elements: 10
Unsorted:
47 65 82 0 51 56 72 16 86 85

Sorted:
0 16 47 51 56 65 72 82 85 86
```

## Review: ObjectsMergesort

Create an ObjectsMergesort application that implements a mergesort on an array of objects. Test the sort on an array of String objects.

## Binary Search

**TIP** The linear search algorithm was introduced in Chapter 9. A linear search, also called a sequential search, is much less efficient than a binary search. However, a linear search does not require a sorted list.

Arrays are sorted in order to perform a more efficient search. A binary search is used with a sorted list of items to quickly find the location of a value. Like the mergesort algorithm, the binary search algorithm also takes a divide-and-conquer approach. It works by examining the middle item of an array sorted from low to high, and determining if this is the item sought, or if the item sought is above or below this middle item. If the item sought is below the middle item, then a binary search is applied to the lower half of the array; if above the middle item, a binary search is applied to the upper half of the array, and so on.

For example, a binary search for the value 5 in a list of items 1, 2, 3, 4, 5, 6, and 7 could be visualized as:

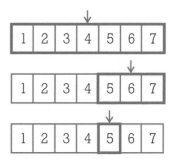

The binary search algorithm is very efficient. For example, an array of 100 elements checks no more than 8 elements in a search, and in an array of one million items no more than 20 items are checked. If a list of the entire world's population were to be searched using this algorithm, less than 40 checks are made to find any one person.

The binary search algorithm can be implemented recursively. The pseudocode for a recursive solution appears like:

```
if (goal == items[mid]) {
    return(mid)
} else if (goal < items[mid]) {
    return(binarySearch(lowerhalf)
} else {
    return(binarySearch(upperhalf)
}
```

The Searches class on the next page implements a binary search:

```
public class Searches{

    /**
     * Searches items array for goal
     * pre: items is sorted from low to high
     * post: Position of goal has been returned,
     * or -1 has been returned if goal not found.
     */
    public static int binarySearch(int[] items, int start,
                                        int end, int goal) {

      if (start > end) {
        return(-1);
      } else {
        int mid = (start + end) / 2;
        if (goal == items[mid]) {
          return(mid);
        } else if (goal < items[mid]) {
          return(binarySearch(items, start, mid-1, goal));
        } else {
          return(binarySearch(items, mid+1, end, goal));
        }
      }
    }
}
```

The TestSorts application has been modified to sort an array of integers and then prompt the user for a number to search for:

```
import java.util.Scanner;
import java.util.Math;

public class TestSorts {

public static void displayArray(int[] array) {
  for (int i = 0; i < array.length; i++) {
    System.out.print(array[i] + "   ");
  }
  System.out.println("\n");
}

public static void sortIntArray() {
  Scanner input = new Scanner(System.in);
  int numItems, searchNum, location;
  int[] test;

  System.out.print("Enter number of elements:  ");
  numItems = input.nextInt();

  /* populate and sort array */
  test = new int[numItems];
  for (int i = 0; i < test.length; i++) {
    test[i] = (int)(101 * Math.random());
  }
  Sorts.mergesort(test, 0, test.length - 1);
  System.out.println("Sorted:");
  displayArray(test);
```

```
/* search for number in sorted array */
System.out.print("Enter a number to search for:  ");
searchNum = input.nextInt();
while (searchNum != -1){
  location = Searches.binarySearch(test, 0,
                                    test.length-1, searchNum);
  System.out.println("Number at position: " + location);
  System.out.print("Enter a number to search for: ");
  searchNum = input.nextInt();
  }
}


public static void main(String[] args) {
  sortIntArray();
  }
}
```

The modified TestSorts application displays output similar to:

```
Enter number of elements: 15
Sorted:
1 4 4 10 14 15 16 27 37 46 47 56 58 59 95

Enter a number to search for: 47
Number at position: 10
Enter a number to search for: 4
Number at position: 1
Enter a number to search for: 14
Number at position: 4
Enter a number to search for: 27
Number at position: 7
Enter a number to search for: -1
```

## Review: SearchLocations

Create a SearchLocations application that displays the positions examined during a binary search. The application output should look similar to:

```
Sorted:
1  2  3  6  6  7  10 10 10 10 11 12 13 14 14 14 14 14 15 15 15 16 17 17 18 19 22
22 23 23 23 24 25 25 25 25 26 26 26 27 27 27 28 28 29 29 30 31 32 33 35 36
36 36 37 38 38 38 40 41 41 42 43 44 44 44 44 45 45 47 47 49 49 49 51 52 52
52 53 53 55 56 56 56 57 58 59 60 60 61 62 64 65 65 65 66 66 66 67 67 67 68
68 68 69 69 71 72 73 76 76 78 79 80 81 81 81 81 82 83 84 84 85 85 86 86 86
86 87 88 89 89 89 92 93 93 94 94 94 95 96 96 97 97 97 98 99 99 99 100

Enter a number to search for: 80
Examining 74
Examining 112
Examining 131
Examining 121
Examining 116
Examining 114
Examining 113
Number at position: 113
Enter a number to search for:
```

## Review: ObjectsBinarySearch

Create an ObjectsBinarySearch application that implements a binary search on an array of objects. Test the search on an array of String objects.

## Review: BinarySearch2

Create a BinarySearch2 application that implements a nonrecursive binary search. The binary search algorithm can be implemented without recursion by doing the following:

- Enclose the method body with a `do-while` loop
- Replace the recursive calls with appropriate assignments to the values of `start` or `end`.

## Depth-First Searching

Many programs generate and search through a series of possibilities, such as:

- different paths through a maze
- different possible ways of making change
- different possible plays in a game
- different schedules for a student in a school
- different pixels reachable from an initial pixel

All these tasks can be solved through the recursive technique called *depth-first searching*. The depth-first searching algorithm works by searching from a given starting position, processing that position, and then (recursively) searching from all adjacent positions.

Depth-first searching can be illustrated in a DetectColonies application that allows a researcher to determine the number and size of distinct colonies of bacteria on a microscope slide. The slide has been converted to digital format, where a * represents a cell that is part of a colony, and a – represents the background color of the slide. A slide file has the format:

First line: length of slide
Second line: width of slide
Remaining lines: slide data.

For example, a slide file could look similar to:

```
7
9
---------
___*__*__
__***_**_
***___*__
**_**____
___****__
___*__*__
```

Cells are considered to be part of the same colony if they touch horizontally or vertically. The example slide contains three colonies. Counting rows and columns starting from zero, one colony has a cell at (1, 3) and contains 9 elements. Another colony has four elements with a cell at (1, 6), and the third has eight elements with a cell at (4, 3). Note that the first and third colonies are considered separate because they touch across a diagonal but not horizontally or vertically.

The DetectColonies application analyzes the slide and displays the following output:

```
Colony at (1,3) with size 9
Colony at (4,3) with size 8
Colony at (1,6) with size 4
```

A depth-first search is appropriate here because once a colony cell is detected, all the possible directions for connected cells must be searched. If a connected cell is a colony cell, then all the possible directions for that cell must be searched, and so on. The basic idea is that, given a starting cell at (row, col) in a colony, the total number of connected cells in that colony can be found as:

1 for the starting cell

+ count of connected cells starting with (row+1, col)

+ count of connected cells starting with (row–1, col)

+ count of connected cells starting with (row, col+1)

+ count of connected cells starting with (row, col–1)

The latter four lines are recursive calls. To find the starting cells, each cell in the slide is tested with a nested `for` loop.

When implementing a depth-first search algorithm, code must be included to avoid infinite recursion. For example, a starting cell of (1, 3) generates a recursive call with cell (2, 3), which generates a call with (1, 3) again, which generates a call with (2, 3), and so on. For this application, a cell will be changed to the background color once it has been examined. This makes counting colonies a destructive algorithm.

The DetectColonies application can be modeled with a Slide class. The constructor will load the slide data into variable member slideData, which is a two-dimensional array appropriate for modeling the slide. Method members displaySlide() and displayColonies() will display the slide and determine the colonies. Member constants COLONY and NON_COLONY will represent * and –.

The displayColonies() method checks each cell of the entire slide, and whenever a colony cell is encountered, displayColonies() determines the colony size and displays data about the colony. To determine the size, displayColonies() calls a private member method collectCells(), which changes a cell to the background once it is counted.

The Slide class is implemented on the next page:

```java
import java.io.*;

public class Slide {
  private char COLONY = '*', NON_COLONY = '-';
  private char[][] slideData;

  /**
   * constructor
   * pre: Slide file contains valid slide data in the format:
   * first line: lenght of slide
   * second line: width of slide
   * remaining lines: slide data
   * post: Slide data has been loaded from slide file.
   */
  public Slide(String s) {

    try {
      File slideFile = new File(s);
      FileReader in = new FileReader(slideFile);
      BufferedReader readSlide = new BufferedReader(in);
      int length = Integer.parseInt(readSlide.readLine());
      int width = Integer.parseInt(readSlide.readLine());
      slideData = new char[length][width];
      for (int row = 0; row < length; row++) {
        for (int col = 0; col < width; col++) {
          slideData[row][col] = (char)readSlide.read();
        }
        readSlide.readLine(); //read past end-of-line
      }
      readSlide.close();
      in.close();
    } catch (FileNotFoundException e) {
      System.out.println("File does not exist or could not
                          be found.");
      System.err.println("FileNotFoundException: "
                          + e.getMessage());
    } catch (IOException e) {
      System.out.println("Problem reading file.");
      System.err.println("IOException: " + e.getMessage());
    }
  }


  /**
   * Determines a colony size
   * pre: none
   * post: All colony cells adjoining and including
   * cell (Row, Col) have been changed to NON_COLONY,
   * and count of these cells is returned.
   */
  private int collectCells(int row,  int col) {

    if ((row < 0) || (row >= slideData.length) ||
        (col < 0) || (col >= slideData[0].length)
        || (slideData[row][col] != COLONY)) {
      return(0);
    } else {
        slideData[row][col] = NON_COLONY;
        return(1+
          collectCells(row+1, col)+
          collectCells(row-1, col)+
          collectCells(row, col+1)+
          collectCells(row, col-1));
    }
  }
}
```

*Chapter 12 Recursion and Advanced Algorithms*

```
/**
 * Analyzes a slide for colonies and displays colony data
 * pre: none
 * post: Colony data has been displayed.
 */
public void displayColonies() {
  int count;

  for (int row = 0; row < slideData.length - 1; row++) {
      for (int col = 0; col < slideData[0].length; col++) {
        if (slideData[row][col] == COLONY) {
          count = collectCells(row, col);
          System.out.println("Colony at (" + row + "," + col
                                    + ") with size " + count);
        }
      }
    }
  }


/**
 * Displays a slide.
 * pre: none
 * post: Slide data has been displayed.
 */
public void displaySlide() {

  for (int row = 0; row < slideData.length; row++) {
    for (int col = 0; col < slideData[0].length; col++) {
      System.out.print(slideData[row][col]);
    }
    System.out.println();
  }
}
}
```

The depth-first search algorithm is implemented in the helper method
collectCells(). The first `if` statement checks to see that the current position
is on the slide and contains a colony cell. This eliminates the need to check
before each recursive call. As good programming style, it is better to check
data at the start of the recursive function rather than before each call.

The DetectColonies application is relatively simple:

```
public class DetectColonies {

  public static void main(String[] args) {

    Slide culture = new Slide("slide.dat");
    culture.displaySlide();
    culture.displayColonies();
  }
}
```

The DetectColonies application displays output similar to:

```
---------
---*--*--
--***-**-
***---*--
**-**----
---****--
---*--*--
Colony at (1,3) with size 9
Colony at (1,6) with size 4
Colony at (4,3) with size 8
```

## Review: DetectColonies – part 1 of 3

How must the DetectColonies application be modified if the definition of a colony allowed the colony to be connected across diagonals? What colonies would be reported by DetectColonies for the sample slide?

## Review: DetectColonies – part 2 of 3

Modify the DetectColonies application to display the slide colonies from largest to smallest.

## Review: DetectColonies – part 3 of 3

What slide will be output by the second `culture.displaySlide()` statement if DetectColonies contained the statements below? Explain.

```
public static void main(String[] args) {

    Slide culture = new Slide("slide.dat");
    culture.displaySlide();
    culture.displayColonies();
    culture.displaySlide();
}
```

## Algorithm Analysis

*Algorithm analysis* includes measuring how efficiently an algorithm performs its task. A more efficient algorithm has a shorter running time. *Running time* is related to the number of statements executed to implement an algorithm. It can be estimated by calculating statement executions. Running time estimations are usually based on a worst-case set of data. For example, an array that is already sorted or nearly sorted may require fewer statement executions than an array of data that is in reverse sorted order. Since the original state of the data is usually unknown, the worst case should be assumed.

As a first analysis, consider the selection sort algorithm, which uses nested `for` loops to sort items. If the sort is thought of in simplified terms, with each `for` statement containing a single statement, for an array of $n$ items, $n * n$ statements are executed. The selection sort is therefore said to have a running time of $n^2$.

**TIP** Theoretical running times can be written in Big Oh notation, which is a theoretical measure of an algorithm's efficiency.

*Chapter 12 Recursion and Advanced Algorithms*

The insertion sort algorithm seems more efficient because a `while` loop is used within a `for` loop. This could allow for a faster sort in some cases, but in the worst case, the insertion sort algorithm executes $n$ statements * $n-1$ statements for a running time of about $n^2$.

The mergesort is a more complicated algorithm, but a divide and conquer approach can be much more efficient than a linear approach. Because this algorithm divides the array and each subarray in half until the base case of one element is reached, there are $\text{Log}_2 n$ calls to mergesort() and then $n$ calls to merge. The mergesort algorithm is said to have running time of $n \text{Log}_2 n$.

The binary search also implements a divide and conquer approach. However, the elements are already ordered. The algorithm is simply performing a search. Because this algorithm divides the array and each subarray in half until the base case of one element is reached, there are $\text{Log}_2 n$ calls to binarySearch(). Therefore, the algorithm is said to have a running time of $\text{Log}_2 n$.

## Chapter Summary

Sorting is the process of putting items in a designated order, either from low to high or high to low. The selection sort, insertion sort, and mergesort algorithms were presented in this chapter. The merge sort algorithm takes a divide-and-conquer approach to sorting. It is implemented recursively and is much faster than the selection and insertion sorts.

Objects cannot be compared with relational operators. Therefore, lists of objects are sorted by implementing an algorithm that uses the Comparable interface. Interfaces can be used as data types, which allows a generic implementation of an algorithm that sorts objects. Objects that are to be sorted must have a class that implements the Comparable interface.

A method can call itself in a process called recursion. Recursion is a programming technique that can be used whenever a problem can be solved by solving one or more smaller versions of the same problem and combining the results. To prevent infinite recursion, a base case that requires no recursion must be part of the recursive solution.

A binary search algorithm can be used to find an element in a sorted array. Binary search is implemented recursively and is very efficient. The depth-first searching algorithm can be used to search through a series of possibilities. When implementing depth-first searching, code must be included to avoid infinite recursion.

Algorithm analysis includes how efficiently an algorithm performs its task. A more efficient algorithm has a shorter running time.

## Vocabulary

**Binary search** A searching algorithm that recursively checks the middle of a sorted list for the item being searched for.

**Base case** The part of a recursive solution that requires no recursion.

**Depth-first search** A searching algorithm that recursively checks a starting position, processes that position, and then searches adjacent positions.

**Infinite recursion** A recursive solution which has no base case.

**Mergesort** A sorting algorithm that recursively divides a list into halves, sorting those halves, and then merging the lists so that the items are in order.

**Insertion sort** A sorting algorithm that repeatedly inserts an item into the appropriate position of a subarray until the subarray has no items left to insert.

**Recursion** The process in which a method calls itself. A programming technique that can be used whenever a problem can be solved by solving one or more smaller versions of the same problem and combining the results.

**Recursive call** A call to a method from within the same method.

**Selection sort** A sorting algorithm that repeatedly selects the lowest item in a subarray of an array and moves it to the position just before the subarray until the subarray has no items left to search.

## Java

**Comparable** A java.lang interface that is required to be implemented by a class if their objects are to be sorted. Comparable can also be used as a data type.

1. For the list 4, 6, 2, 10, 9, show how the numbers are ordered after each loop iteration of the algorithms:
   a) selection sort
   b) insertion sort

2. What must be done to a list of items in order to use a binary search to find a specific item?

3. Use the recursive method below to answer the questions:

```
public void ct(int n) {
  System.out.println("Starting " + n);
  if (n > 0) {
    ct(n/3);
    System.out.println("Middle " + n);
  }
}
```

   a) What output is generated when ct(13) is called?
   b) What output is generated when ct(3) is called?
   c) What output is generated when ct(0) is called?

4. Use the recursive method below to answer the questions:

```
public void ct(int n) {
  System.out.println(n);
  if (n > 0) {
    if (n % 2 == 1) {
      ct(n/3);
    } else {
      ct(n/2);
    }
  }
}
```

   a) What output is generated when ct(13) is called?
   b) What output is generated when ct(14) is called?
   c) What output is generated when ct(15) is called?

5. Use the recursive method below to answer the questions:

```
public void ct(int n) {
  if (n > 0) {
    ct(n/10);
    System.out.println(n % 10);
  }
}
```

   a) What output is generated when ct(13) is called?
   b) What output is generated when ct(124) is called?
   c) What output is generated when ct(21785) is called?
   d) What in general does this method do?

6. Use the recursive method below to answer the questions:

```
public void whatzItDo() {
  Scanner input = new Scanner(System.in);
  String letter = input.next();
  if (!letter.equals(".")) {
    whatzItDo();
    System.out.print(letter);
  }
}
```

   a) What output is generated when the user enters T, E, S, T, . ?
   b) What in general does this method do?

7. A sorting algorithm is said to be "stable" if two items in the original array that have the same "key value" (the value to be sorted on) maintain their relative position in the sorted version. For example, assume an array with the following data:

| Ann | Jon | Mel | Tom | Kim |
|-----|-----|-----|-----|-----|
| 20  | 19  | 18  | 19  | 22  |

When the array is sorted by age, a stable sort would guarantee that Jon would stay ahead of Tom in the sorted array, as in:

| Kim | Ann | Jon | Tom | Mel |
|-----|-----|-----|-----|-----|
| 22  | 20  | 19  | 19  | 18  |

and not:

| Kim | Ann | Tom | Jon | Mel |
|-----|-----|-----|-----|-----|
| 22  | 20  | 19  | 19  | 18  |

Which of the sorts presented in this chapter (selection, mergesort) is stable? For each which is not stable, give an example of data to illustrate this.

**True/False**

8.  Determine if each of the following are true or false. If false, explain why.

    a) Sorting always puts items in order from low to high.

    b) One measure of the efficiency of a sorting algorithm is the speed at which it can complete a sort.

    c) The selection sort algorithm is more efficient than the insertion sort.

    d) A method can call itself.

    e) The merge sort algorithm is more efficient than the selection sort algorithm for large arrays.

    f) A binary search is used to sort a list of items.

    g) A binary search starts by examining the last item in an array.

    h) The more statements required to complete a task, the more efficient the algorithm.

    i) An interface can be used as a data type.

    j) A recursive solution that has no base case results in infinite recursion.

    k) An insertion sort recursively divides a list into halves, sorting those halves, and then merging the lists in order.

*Chapter 12 Recursion and Advanced Algorithms*

## Exercises

## Exercise 1 ———————————————————————— Friends

Create a Friends database application that maintains a file of Friend objects that contain names, telephone numbers, and email addresses. The Friends application should load Friend records from a file and then allow the user to add new friends, remove friends, display a list of all friends by either first name or last name, and search for a friend. The application should display a menu similar to:

```
1. List Friends.
2. Add a friend.
3. Remove a friend.
4. Find a friend.
Enter 0 to quit
Enter you choice:
```

## Exercise 2 ———————————————————————— TernarySearch

Modify the Searches class to include a ternarySearch() method. A ternary search, similar to a binary search, divides an array into three pieces rather than two. A ternary search finds the points that divide the array into three roughly equal pieces, and then uses these points to determine where the goal should be searched for.

## Exercise 3 ———————————————————————— InterpolationSearch

Modify the Searches class to include an interpolationSearch() method. An interpolation search is a variation of the binary search. The idea is to look in a likely spot, not necessarily the middle of the array. For example, if the value sought is 967 in an array that holds items ranging from 3 to 1022, it would be intelligent to look nearly at the end of the array. Mathematically, because 967 is about 95% of the way from 3 to 1022, the position to start searching at is a position 95% of the way down the array. For example, if the array holds 500 elements, the first position to examined is 475 (95% of the way from 1 to 500). The search then proceeds to a portion of the array (either 1..474 or 476..500) depending upon whether 967 is greater or less than the 475th element.

## Exercise 4 ———————————————————————— NumDigits

Create a NumDigits application that includes a recursive method numDigits() that returns the number of digits in its integer parameter. Numbers –9 through 9 have one digit; numbers –99 to –10 and 10 to 99 have two digits, and so on. (Hint: the number of digits of a number n is one more than the number of digits in n/10.)

# Exercise 5 —————————————————————— DetectColonies2

Create a DetectColonies2 application that is based on DetectColonies presented in this chapter. This application gives improved colony results because slides are now digitized to report color. For example, a slide file could look similar to:

```
00550000
00050000
00005500
01200000
01111000
00000030
```

The digits 1 through 9 represent various colors. The digit 0 represents black (background color).

The DetectColonies2 application should display a listing of the size, location, and color value of each colony on the slide. A colony is defined as a connected (horizontally or vertically) sequence of cells holding the same color value. For the above slide, the application should report:

| Color | Size | Location |
|-------|------|----------|
| 5     | 3    | 1, 3     |
| 5     | 2    | 3, 5     |
| 1     | 5    | 4, 2     |
| 2     | 1    | 4, 3     |
| 3     | 1    | 6, 7     |

# Exercise 6 —————————————————————— Knapsack

A well-known problem in computer science is called the *knapsack problem*. A variation is as follows:

> Given a collection of weights of (possibly) different integral values, is it possible to place some of the weights in a knapsack so as to fill it to some exact total weight?

> For example, if the weights are 3, 5, 6, and 9, then it is possible for such totals as 3, 8, 11, 14, 17, etc. to be made exactly, but 2, 4, 22, etc. are not possible.

Create a Knapsack application that solves this problem. The fillKnapsack() method handles the first weight, and then recursively handles the remaining weights with an isPossible() helper method. fillKnapsack() and isPossible() have the following declarations:

```
/* Returns true if there exists a subset of the items in
 * weights[start..weights.length] that sum to goal.
 * pre: items in weights[start..weights.length] > 0
 * post: true has been returned if there exists a subset
 * of items in weights[start..weights.length] that sum to goal.
 */
fillKnapsack(int[] weights, int goal, int start)


/* Returns true if there exists a subset of the items in
 * weights that sum to goal.
 * pre: items in weights > 0
 * post: true has been returned if there exists a subset
 * of items in weight that sum to goal.
 */
isPossible(int[] weights, int goal)
```

The fillKnapsack algorithm determines if the goal can be found in all of the items not including the first, or if it can be found by including the first in the subset. The pseudocode is:

```
if (simple case) {
    handle simple cases
} else {
    if (fillKnapsack(weights, goal, start+1)) {
        return(true);
    } else if (fillKnapsack(weights, goal-weights[start], start+1)) {
        return(true);
    } else {
        return(false);
    }
}
```

Note that the simple cases will need to be determined and handled properly.

# Exercise 7 &mdash;&mdash;&mdash;&mdash;&mdash;&mdash;&mdash;&mdash;&mdash;&mdash; Maze

A maze can be defined in a file using X characters to represent walls, space characters to represent paths, and a $ character to represent the goal. For example, a file containing a maze could look similar to:

```
8
10
XXXXXXXXXX
X        X
XX XXX XXX
XX   X   X
XXXX X X X
X    X XXX
X XXXX  $X
XXXXXXXXXX
```

The starting point is assumed to be location (1, 1) and the maze is assumed to have a border. Create a Maze application that displays the sequence of positions in a path from the start to the goal, or indicate if no path is available. For example, for the maze above, the application should report:

```
Path:  (1,1)  (1,2)  (1,3)  (1,4)  (1,5)  (1,6)
       (2,6)  (3,6)  (4,6)  (5,6)  (6,6)  (6,7)  (6,8)
```

# Exercise 8 ———————————————————————— MyBoggle

The game of Boggle is played on a square board with random letters. The object is to find words formed on the board by contiguous sequences of letters. Letters are considered to be touching if they are horizontally, vertically, or diagonally adjacent. For example, the board:

```
Q W E R T
A S D F G
Z X C V B
Y U A O P
G H J K L
```

contains the words WAS, WAXY, JOB, and others, but not the word BOX. Words can contain duplicate letters, but a single letter on the board may not appear twice in a single word, for example POP is not contained on this board.

Create a MyBoggle application that displays a board of random letters, and allows the user to enter words found on the board. The application should report if the word entered by the user is indeed on the board.

*Hint*: Search the board for the first letter of the word entered, and then recursively search around the found letter for the remaining letters of the word.

# Chapter 13
# Data Structures

## Key Concepts

Using data structures to organize data
Implementing data structures
Choosing appropriate data structures
LIFO and FIFO structures

## The Stack Data Structure

A data structure organizes data. The *stack* data structure can contain many data items just as an array can. Additionally, it has a set of operations that can be performed on the data.

*top*  A stack structure has a *top*. For example, the stack shown below holds three integers. The value 11 is the top item in the stack:

```
 11  | top
 34  |
 12  |
```

*pop*  There are two standard operations that can be performed on the items in a stack, and only the top item of a stack can be processed. The *pop* operation removes the top item. For example, when a pop is executed on the stack above, the top value, 11, is removed:

```
 34  | top
 12  |
```

The next item, 34, is now at the top of the stack, and is the only item that can be accessed.

*push*  Another operation is the *push* operation, which adds an item to the top of the stack. For example, if the value 27 is pushed onto the stack, the stack becomes:

```
 27  | top
 34  |
 12  |
```

Other stack operations include the *isEmpty* query, which returns true when there are no items in the stack, and false otherwise. The *size* operation determines the number of items in a stack. A stack can be emptied with the *makeEmpty* operation.

Since the stack is designed so that the last item pushed on is the first item to be popped, it is sometimes referred to as a *last-in-first-out* (LIFO) data structure. There are a number of applications of stacks, particularly in writing compiler software. For example, each of the following is generally performed using a stack:

- Matching of braces, { and }. In Java, a close brace, }, always goes with the last open brace, {.

- Matching `else` with `if`: An `else` always goes with the last `if`.

- Matching of parentheses in an expression: A closing parenthesis always goes with the last open parenthesis.

- Recursion: After completion of a recursive call, control returns to the last call that was executed. In fact, recursion is sometimes replaced with a stack.

## The Stack Class

A data structure has a specific set of operations that can be performed on the data it stores. Therefore, a class is often used to implement the data structure.

The StackDemo application uses a stack:

```java
public class StackDemo {

    public static void main(String[] args) {
        Stack s = new Stack(10);

        System.out.println("Adding 10 and 13 to stack.");
        s.push(10);
        s.push(13);
        System.out.println("Top of stack: " + s.top());
        System.out.println("Items in stack: " + s.size());
        System.out.println("Removing top item.");
        s.pop();
        System.out.println("Top of stack: " + s.top());
        System.out.println("Items in stack: " + s.size());
        System.out.println("Adding a new item.");
        s.push(40);
        System.out.println("Top of stack: " + s.top());
        System.out.println("Items in stack: " + s.size());
    }
}
```

The StackDemo produces the output:

```
Adding 10 and 13 to stack.
Top of stack: 13
Items in stack: 2
Removing top item.
Top of stack: 10
Items in stack: 1
Adding a new item.
Top of stack: 40
Items in stack: 2
```

The Stack class below is a very simple stack implementation that stores data in an array:

```java
public class Stack {
   private int[] data;
   private int top;


   /**
    * constructor
    * pre: none
    * post: An empty stack that can hold up to maxItems
    * has been created.
    */
   public Stack(int maxItems) {
     data = new int[maxItems];
     top = -1;       //no items in the array
   }


   /**
    * Returns the top item without removing it from the stack.
    * pre: Stack contains at least one item.
    * post: The top item has been returned while leaving it
    * on the stack.
    */
   public int top() {
     return(data[top]);
   }


   /**
    * Removes the top item from the stack and returns it.
    * pre: Stack contains at least one item.
    * post: The top item of the stack has been removed
    * and returned.
    */
   public int pop() {
     top -= 1;
     return(data[top + 1]);
   }
```

```
/**
 * Adds an item to the top of the stack if there is room.
 * pre: none
 * post: A new item has been added to the top of the stack.
 */
public void push(int num) {
  if (top < data.length - 1) {
    top += 1;
    data[top] = num;
  }
}



/**
 * Determines if there are items on the stack.
 * pre: none
 * post: true returned if there are items on the stack,
 * false returned otherwise.
 */
public boolean isEmpty() {
  if (top == -1) {
    return(true);
  } else {
    return(false);
  }
}



/**
 * Returns the number of items in the stack.
 * pre: none
 * post: The number of items in the stack is returned.
 */
public int size() {
  if (isEmpty()) {
    return(0);
  } else {
    return(top + 1);
  }
}



/**
 * Empties the stack.
 * pre: none
 * post: There are no items in the stack.
 */
public void makeEmpty() {
  top = -1;
}
}
```

The Stack class implements a stack for `int` values. A generic implementation would use objects. This implementation is completed in the Stack2 review.

## Review: Stack2

Create a Stack2 class that implements a stack data structure for data type Object. Since Object is the superclass of other objects, a Stack2 object can store objects from any class. Write appropriate client code to test the Stack2 class.

## The Queue Data Structure

*rear, front*   A *queue* is a data structure similar to a stack in that it holds a number of data items. However, one end of the queue is referred to as the *rear* and the other end the *front*. For example, the queue shown below holds three items:

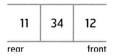

All insertions are made at the rear and all removals are made at the front.

*dequeue*   There are two standard operations that can be performed on a queue. The *dequeue* operation removes an item from the front. For example, when a dequeue is executed on the queue above, the value at the front, 12, is removed from the queue:

*enqueue*   The *enqueue* operation adds an item to the rear of the queue. For example, if the value 27 is enqueued, the queue becomes:

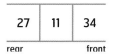

Other queue operations include the *front* operation, which returns the front item without removing it from the queue. The *isEmpty* query returns true when there are no items in the queue, and false otherwise. The *size* operation determines the number of items in a queue. A queue can be emptied with the *makeEmpty* operation.

*FIFO*   A queue is analogous to a line at a ticket counter where "first come, first served," and is sometimes referred to as a *first in first out* (FIFO) data structure. There are a number of real-world situations that can be represented as a queue structure. For example:

- Lines at a toll booth or bank teller

- Waiting lists for tickets on planes

- Pages of data queued up for a printer

- Performing breadth-first-searching where all items near the starting position are examined before looking at those farther away.

## The Queue Class

The QueueDemo application uses a queue:

```java
public static void main(String[] args) {
    final int MAX_ITEMS = 3;
    Queue q = new Queue(MAX_ITEMS);
    Scanner input = new Scanner(System.in);
    String choice;
    int num;

do {
        System.out.print("Add/Remove/Count/Front/Quit: ");
        choice = input.next();
        if (choice.equalsIgnoreCase("a")) {
          if (q.size() < MAX_ITEMS) {
            System.out.print("Number to add: ");
            num = input.nextInt();
            q.enqueue(num);
          } else {
            System.out.println("Queue is full.");
          }
        } else if (choice.equalsIgnoreCase("r")) {
          System.out.println("Dequeueing: " + q.dequeue());
        } else if (choice.equalsIgnoreCase("c")) {
          System.out.println("Items in queue: " + q.size());
        } else if (choice.equalsIgnoreCase("f")) {
          System.out.println("Front of queue: " + q.front());
        } else {
          System.out.println("quitting");
        }
    } while (!choice.equalsIgnoreCase("q"));
  }
```

The QueueDemo produces the output:

```
Add/Remove/Count/Front/Quit: a
Number to add: 10
Add/Remove/Count/Front/Quit: a
Number to add: 25
Add/Remove/Count/Front/Quit: c
Items in queue: 2
Add/Remove/Count/Front/Quit: f
Front of queue: 10
Add/Remove/Count/Front/Quit: r
Dequeueing: 10
Add/Remove/Count/Front/Quit: q
quitting
```

The Queue class on the next two pages is a very simple queue implementation that stores data in an array:

*Chapter 13 Data Structures*

```
public class Queue {
  private int[] data;
  private int front, rear, maxSize;


  /**
   * constructor
   * pre: none
   * post: An empty queue that can hold up to maxItems
   * has been created.
   */
  public Queue(int maxItems) {
    data = new int[maxItems];
    front = -1;          //no items in the array
    rear = -1;
    maxSize = maxItems;
  }


  /**
   * Returns the front item without removing it from
   * the queue.
   * pre: Queue contains at least one item.
   * post: The front item has been returned while leaving
   * it in the queue.
   */
  public int front() {
    return(data[front]);
  }


  /**
   * Removes the front item from the queue and returns it.
   * pre: Queue contains at least one item.
   * post: The front item of the queue has been removed
   * and returned.
   */
  public int dequeue() {
      front = (front + 1) % maxSize;
    return(data[front - 1]);
  }


  /**
   * Adds an item to the queue if there is room.
   * pre: none
   * post: A new item has been added to the queue.
   */
  public void enqueue(int num) {
    if (isEmpty()) {        //first item queued
      rear = 0;
      front = 0;
      data[rear] = num;
    } else {
      rear = (rear + 1) % maxSize;
      data[rear] = num;
    }
  }
```

```
/**
 * Determines if there are items on the queue.
 * pre: none
 * post: true returned if there are items on the queue,
 * false returned otherwise.
 */
public boolean isEmpty() {
  if (front == -1 && rear == -1) {
    return(true);
  } else {
    return(false);
  }
}


/**
 * Returns the number of items in the queue.
 * pre: none
 * post: The number of items in the queue is returned.
 */
public int size() {
  if (isEmpty()) {
    return(0);
  } else {
    return(rear - front + 1);
  }
}


/**
 * Empties the queue.
 * pre: none
 * post: There are no items in the queue.
 */
public void makeEmpty() {
  front = -1;
  rear = -1;
}
}
```

Because the queue is limited to the number of items it can store, the front and rear pointers must cycle through the spots available in the array. Therefore, the front and rear values are calculated using modular arithmetic (%).

The Queue class implements a queue for `int` values. A generic implementation would use objects. This implementation is left as a review.

## Review: Queue2

Create a Queue2 class that implements a queue data structure for data type Object. Since Object is the superclass of other objects, a Queue2 object can store objects from any class. Write appropriate client code to test the Object2 class.

## Review: Queue3

The Queue class is limited because the queue size cannot change from its initial size. Create a Queue3 class that implements a queue data structure using an ArrayList. Write appropriate client code to test the class.

## The Linked List Data Structure

Another way of storing lists of data in memory requires each item to store information that indicates where the next item is stored. The additional information is a reference, or pointer, to a data location. This kind of list data structure is called a *linked list*, and can be illustrated like:

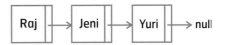

*head, tail*
*node*

The first item in a linked list is called the *head*. The last item points to null and is called the *tail*. Each element of a linked list is called a *node*. There are three nodes in the list above.

**TIP** Objects stored in memory are stored in dynamic memory. Dynamic memory is allocated from an area called the *heap*, which is used during program execution.

Because each item in a linked list must contain data and a pointer, an item is best modeled with a class. Therefore, a linked list is a list of objects. The objects in a linked list are organized because they point to each other. There is no need to place them in a structure, such as an array, for organization. This mean that linked links are not restricted by the size of an array.

*addAtFront*

There are two standard operations that can be performed on a linked list. The *addAtFront* operation adds a new node to the front of the list. When a new node is added to the front of a linked list, it is simply designated the head and its pointer is set to the current head. For example, if Raj was the head, adding a new item means that the new object is now the head and its pointer points to the Raj object:

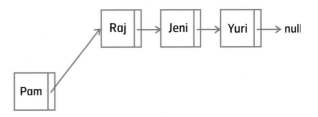

*remove*

The *remove* operation removes an item from the linked list. Removing an item from a linked list means that the pointer of the previous item is changed to point to the item after the one to be removed. For example, removing Raj from the list below means that the object is no longer referenced by another object in the list:

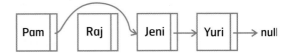

Linked lists are useful for maintaining dynamic lists because the number of items in a linked list can shrink and grow as needed.

The LinkedListDemo application uses a linked link:

```
public class LinkedListDemo {

    public static void main(String[] args) {
        LinkedList list = new LinkedList();

        list.addAtFront("Sachar");
        list.addAtFront("Osborne");
        list.addAtFront("Suess");
        System.out.println(list);

        list.remove("Suess");
        list.remove("Sachar");
        list.remove("Osborne");
        System.out.println(list);
    }
}
```

The LinkedListDemo produces the output:

```
Suess
Osborne
Sachar

There are no items in list.
```

*nested class*

*outer class*

The LinkedList class below contains a nested class. A *nested class* is a class within a class. A nested class is a member of the class it is within. As a class member, it has access to all the other members of the class, including private member variables and methods. A class that contains a class member is called an *outer class*. The Node class is a nested class because its members should only be accessed by a LinkedList object:

```
public class LinkedList {
    private Node head;


    /**
     * constructor
     * pre: none
     * post: A linked list with a null item has been created.
     */
    public LinkedList() {
        head = null;
    }


    /**
     * Adds a node to the linked list.
     * pre: none
     * post: The linked list has a new node at the head.
     */
    public void addAtFront(String str) {
        Node newNode = new Node(str);
        newNode.setNext(head);
        head = newNode;
    }
```

```
/**
 * Deletes a node in the linked list.
 * pre: none
 * post: The first node containing str has been deleted.
 */
public void remove(String str) {
  Node current = head;
  Node previous = head;

  if (current.getData().equals(str)) {
    head = current.getNext();
  } else {
    while (current.getNext() != null) {
      previous = current;
      current = current.getNext();
      if (current.getData().equals(str)) {
        previous.setNext(current.getNext());
      }
    }
  }
}


/**
 * Creates a string that lists the nodes of the
 * linked list.
 * pre: none
 * post: The linked list has been written to a string.
 */
public String toString() {
  Node current = head;
  String listString;

  if (current != null) {
    listString = current.getData() + "\n";
    while (current.getNext() != null) {
      current = current.getNext();
      listString += current.getData() + "\n";
    }
    return(listString);
  } else {
    return("There are no items in list.");
  }
}


private class Node {
  private String data;
  private Node next;


  /**
   * constructor
   * pre: none
   * post: A node has been created.
   */
  public Node(String newData) {
    data = newData;
    next = null;
  }
```

**TIP** Nested classes were also introduced in Chapter 10.

```
/**
 * The node pointed to by next is returned
 * pre: none
 * post: A node has been returned.
 */
public Node getNext() {
  return(next);
}


/**
 * The node pointed to by next is changed to newNode
 * pre: none
 * post: next points to newNode.
 */
public void setNext(Node newNode) {
  next = newNode;
}


/**
 * The node pointed to by next is returned
 * pre: none
 * post: A node has been returned.
 */
public String getData() {
  return(data);
}
  }
}
```

## Review: LinkedList – part 1 of 3

Modify the LinkedList class to include a member function size() that returns the number of items in the list.

## Review: LinkedList – part 2 of 3

Modify the LinkedList class to include a member function addAtEnd() that adds a new item to the end of the linked list.

## Review: LinkedList – part 3 of 3

Modify the LinkedList class to include a member function makeEmpty() that removes all the items in the list

*Chapter 13 Data Structures*

## Chapter Summary

The stack, queue, and linked list data structures were introduced in this chapter. Each data structure organizes data and can be used to perform a set of operations on that data.

The stack data structure is also called a LIFO structure because the last item in the first item out. A stack has a top. Operations that can be performed on a stack include pop, push, isEmpty, size, and makeEmpty.

The queue data structure is also called a FIFO structure because the first item in is the first item out. A queue has a front and rear. Operations that can be performed on a queue include enqueue, dequeue, isEmpty, size, and makeEmpty.

The linked list data structure is a list of objects that point to each other. The linked list does not have the size limitations of a data structure implemented using an array. A linked list has a head and a tail. Each item in a linked list is called a node. Operations that can be performed on a linked list include addAtFront and remove.

## Vocabulary

**addAtFront** A linked list operation where an item is added to the front of the list.

**Dequeue** A queue operation that removes the item at the front of the queue.

**Enqueue** A queue operation that adds an item to the rear of the queue.

**FIFO** First In First Out. A queue data structure.

**Front** The start of a queue.

**Head** The first node in a linked list.

**isEmpty** A stack or queue operation that returns true when there are no items in the data structure and false otherwise.

**LIFO** Last In First Out. A stack data structure.

**Linked list** A data structure that has a head and tail and contains nodes that point to each other.

**Nested class** A class that is a member of another class. A class within a class.

**Node** A linked list element. A node contains the item and a pointer to the next node.

**Outer class** A class that contains a class member.

**Pop** A stack operation where the top item is removed.

**Push** A stack operation where a new item is added.

**Queue** A data structure that has a front and rear and organizes data so that the first item in is the first item out.

**Rear** The end of a queue.

**Remove** A linked list operation where an item is removed from the list.

**Size** A stack or queue operation that returns the number of items in the data structure.

**Stack** A data structure that has a top and organizes data so that the last item in is the first item out.

**Tail** The last node in a linked list. The tail points to `null`.

**Top** The last item pushed onto a stack.

1. Explain the similarities between an array and a stack.

2. Describe how a programmer might use a stack when writing compiler software.

3. What output is generated by the following statements if s is a Stack object?

```
Stack s = new Stack(10);
s.push(5);
s.push(8);
int x = s.pop();
s.push(x);
s.push(12);
s.push(13);
int y = s.pop();
System.out.println(x + " " + y);
y = s.pop();
x = s.top();
System.out.println(x + " " + y);
```

4. Consider the "hot plate" problem: In a busy restaurant, fresh salad plates are brought out and added to the existing pile of plates. This means that, even though there may be plates that were washed long ago, the customer is frequently stuck with a warm plate for salad. Explain how this is analogous to a stack.

5. What output is generated by the following statements if q is a Queue object?

```
Queue q = new Queue(10);
q.enqueue(5);
q.enqueue(8);
int x = q.dequeue();
q.enqueue(x);
q.enqueue(12);
q.enqueue(13);
int y = q.dequeue();
System.out.println(x + " " + y);
y = q.dequeue();
x = q.front();
System.out.println(x + " " + y);
```

6. Explain the difference between a FIFO and a LIFO data structure.

7. List two real-world situations that could be represented as a queue structure other than those listed in the chapter.

**True/False**

8. Determine if each of the following are true or false. If false, explain why.
   a) A stack data structure has a front and a rear.
   b) A stack can be emptied.
   c) In a stack, top refers to the first item pushed onto a stack.
   d) The isEmpty operation returns an int value.
   e) A queue can hold more than one data item.
   f) In a queue, all removals are made at the rear.
   g) The enqueue operation adds an item to the front of the queue.
   h) The first item in a linked list is called the head.
   i) A node refers to an item in a stack.
   j) The number of items in a stack or queue can be determined with the length operation.
   k) In a linked list, the tail points to null.

## Exercise 1 ——————————————————————————————StackList

The Stack class implemented a stack using an array. A stack can also be implemented using a linked list. Create a StackList class that implements a stack using a linked list that can store Object data. The StackList class should implement the standard stack operations. Note that the standard linked list operations will not be implemented when the linked list is implementing a stack. What are the advantages or disadvantages of using a linked list rather than an array?

## Exercise 2 ——————————————————————————————— ReverseList

Create a ReverseList application that uses a stack to reverse a set of integers entered by the user. The user should be prompted to enter up to 10 numbers or to terminate the list of numbers by entering 999. Application output should look similar to:

```
Enter a number (999 to quit): 10
Enter a number (999 to quit): 25
Enter a number (999 to quit): 44
Enter a number (999 to quit): 16
Enter a number (999 to quit): 999
The list reversed is: 16 44 25 10
```

## Exercise 3 ——————————————————————————————— ParenChecker

To analyze an expression with parentheses, the computer must be able to determine which left parenthesis any given right parenthesis matches.

a) Create a ParenChecker application that prompts the user to enter an expression with parentheses, and then displays a list of the positions of pairs of parentheses. The application should store the positions of the left parentheses on a stack when they are found. Application output should look similar to:

```
Enter an expression: (a-b*(c-d))
Pair: 10 6
Pair: 11 1
```

b) Modify the ParenChecker application to detect the two errors below and display appropriate error messages:

1. Attempt to pop an empty stack.

2. Stack not empty at the end of the program.

# Exercise 4 ——————————————————— QueueList

The Queue class implemented a queue using an array. A queue can also be implemented using a linked list. Create a QueueList class that implements a queue using a linked list that can store Object data. The QueueList class should implement the standard queue operations. Note that the standard linked list operations will not be implemented when the linked list is implementing a queue. What are the advantages or disadvantages of using a linked list rather than an array?

# Exercise 5 ——————————————————— Stats

a) Create a Stats interface that declares methods sum(), min(), and max(). The member methods should return an `int` value that represents the sum of the items in a list, the minimum value in a list, and the maximum value in a list.

b) Create a LinkedList class that implements the Stats interface and stores `int` values. Write client code that tests the modified class.

# Exercise 6 ——————————————————— DoublyLinkedList

The nodes in a doubly-linked list point to the next and previous nodes, and can be thought of as:

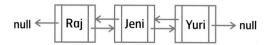

The node of the doubly-linked list may be represented as:

```
private class Node {
    private String data;
    private Node next;
    private Node prev;
...rest of class
```

The previous field of the head is set to `null`.

a) What advantages does this structure offer? What disadvantages?

b) Compare the doubly-linked list with the singly linked list implemented in this chapter. When would you choose to use one rather than the other?

c) Create a DoublyLinkedList class. Include member methods addAtFront(), addAtEnd(), remove(), and displayList() and displayReverseList().

# Appendix A
# Unicode

Every letter of an alphabet (Latin, Japanese, Cherokee, and so on) and symbols of every culture (=, @, ½, and so on) have been given a representation in a digital code called Unicode. Unicode uses a set of sixteen 1s and 0s to form a 16-bit binary code for each symbol. For example, the uppercase letter V is Unicode 00000000 01010110, which can be thought of as the base 10 number 86 (8610). Lowercase v has a separate code of 00000000 01110110, or 11810. Below is a table of some Unicode symbols and their corresponding decimal and binary equivalents.

| Decimal | Binary | Unicode Symbol | Decimal | Binary | Unicode Symbol | Decimal | Binary | Unicode Symbol |
|---|---|---|---|---|---|---|---|---|
| 32 | 00000000 00100000 | space | 64 | 00000000 01000000 | @ | 96 | 00000000 01100000 | ` |
| 33 | 00000000 00100001 | ! | 65 | 00000000 01000001 | A | 97 | 00000000 01100001 | a |
| 34 | 00000000 00100010 | " | 66 | 00000000 01000010 | B | 98 | 00000000 01100010 | b |
| 35 | 00000000 00100011 | # | 67 | 00000000 01000011 | C | 99 | 00000000 01100011 | c |
| 36 | 00000000 00100100 | $ | 68 | 00000000 01000100 | D | 100 | 00000000 01100100 | d |
| 37 | 00000000 00100101 | % | 69 | 00000000 01000101 | E | 101 | 00000000 01100101 | e |
| 38 | 00000000 00100110 | & | 70 | 00000000 01000110 | F | 102 | 00000000 01100110 | f |
| 39 | 00000000 00100111 | ' | 71 | 00000000 01000111 | G | 103 | 00000000 01100111 | g |
| 40 | 00000000 00101000 | ( | 72 | 00000000 01001000 | H | 104 | 00000000 01101000 | h |
| 41 | 00000000 00101001 | ) | 73 | 00000000 01001001 | I | 105 | 00000000 01101001 | i |
| 42 | 00000000 00101010 | * | 74 | 00000000 01001010 | J | 106 | 00000000 01101010 | j |
| 43 | 00000000 00101011 | + | 75 | 00000000 01001011 | K | 107 | 00000000 01101011 | k |
| 44 | 00000000 00101100 | , | 76 | 00000000 01001100 | L | 108 | 00000000 01101100 | l |
| 45 | 00000000 00101101 | - | 77 | 00000000 01001101 | M | 109 | 00000000 01101101 | m |
| 46 | 00000000 00101110 | . | 78 | 00000000 01001110 | N | 110 | 00000000 01101110 | n |
| 47 | 00000000 00101111 | / | 79 | 00000000 01001111 | O | 111 | 00000000 01101111 | o |
| 48 | 00000000 00110000 | 0 | 80 | 00000000 01010000 | P | 112 | 00000000 01110000 | p |
| 49 | 00000000 00110001 | 1 | 81 | 00000000 01010001 | Q | 113 | 00000000 01110001 | q |
| 50 | 00000000 00110010 | 2 | 82 | 00000000 01010010 | R | 114 | 00000000 01110010 | r |
| 51 | 00000000 00110011 | 3 | 83 | 00000000 01010011 | S | 115 | 00000000 01110011 | s |
| 52 | 00000000 00110100 | 4 | 84 | 00000000 01010100 | T | 116 | 00000000 01110100 | t |
| 53 | 00000000 00110101 | 5 | 85 | 00000000 01010101 | U | 117 | 00000000 01110101 | u |
| 54 | 00000000 00110110 | 6 | 86 | 00000000 01010110 | V | 118 | 00000000 01110110 | v |
| 55 | 00000000 00110111 | 7 | 87 | 00000000 01010111 | W | 119 | 00000000 01110111 | w |
| 56 | 00000000 00111000 | 8 | 88 | 00000000 01011000 | X | 120 | 00000000 01111000 | x |
| 57 | 00000000 00111001 | 9 | 89 | 00000000 01011001 | Y | 121 | 00000000 01111001 | y |
| 58 | 00000000 00111010 | : | 90 | 00000000 01011010 | Z | 122 | 00000000 01111010 | z |
| 59 | 00000000 00111011 | ; | 91 | 00000000 01011011 | [ | 123 | 00000000 01111011 | { |
| 60 | 00000000 00111100 | < | 92 | 00000000 01011100 | \ | 124 | 00000000 01111100 | | |
| 61 | 00000000 00111101 | = | 93 | 00000000 01011101 | ] | 125 | 00000000 01111101 | } |
| 62 | 00000000 00111110 | > | 94 | 00000000 01011110 | ^ | 126 | 00000000 01111110 | ~ |
| 63 | 00000000 00111111 | ? | 95 | 00000000 01011111 | _ | | | |

*Appendix A Unicode*

# Appendix B
# Using JCreator

There are a number of IDEs that can be used to edit, compile, and run Java source code. This appendix explains how to use the JCreator LE IDE. It also discusses other IDEs.

## The JCreator IDE

JCreator is an *integrated development environment* (IDE). An IDE provides a workspace that allows for editing, compiling, and running of source code. The JCreator IDE has a graphical user interface, which makes it easy to learn and use. The JCreator IDE can be used to create Java applications and applets. JCreator maintains each application and applet as a *project*. Projects are created in a workspace environment, which consists of several windows:

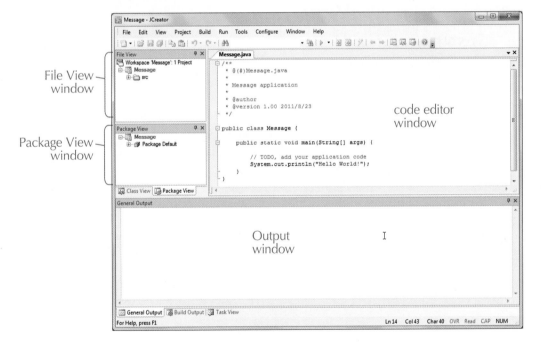

- The File View window displays the folders and files associated with the project workspace.

- The Package View window displays the classes associated with the project workspace.

- The code editor window is used to type and edit Java and HTML code.

- The Output window displays Java program output, build errors, a task list, and debug output.

JCreator LE can be downloaded for free from www.jcreator.com. When installing JCreator LE, you will be prompted to install the JDK if a recent version of the JDK is not installed on the computer. You will also be prompted to install a recent version of the JDK JavaDocs.

To start JCreator LE, double-click [JC] on the Desktop or select Start → All Programs → JCreator LE → JCreator LE. When JCreator is started, if an existing workspace is open, it is important to select File → Close Workspace before creating a new project because a workspace can contain more than one project.

## Compiling and Running a Program

In JCreator, a Java application or applet must be compiled before it is run. *Compiling* automatically saves the program file and converts the Java source code to bytecode. Select Build → Build Project (F7) to compile the program. If the program compiles successfully, the message "Process completed." will appear in the Build Output window. Next, select Run → Run Project (F5) to run the program and display the program output in a window.

## Review: Message

You will create a project named Message.

① **START JCREATOR**

The Start page is displayed:

② **CREATE A NEW PROJECT**

a. Select File → New → Project. The Project Wizard dialog box is displayed:

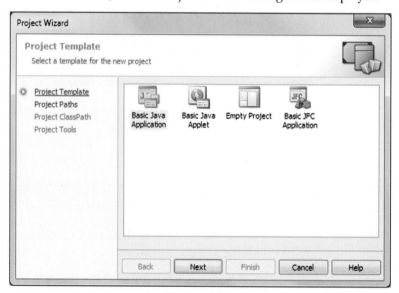

b. In the Project Wizard dialog box, select **Empty Project**.

c. Select **Next**. The second Project Wizard dialog box is displayed.

d. In the **Name** box, type `Message`:

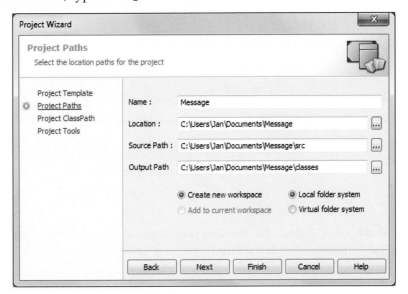

e. Verify that the project paths are correct in the **Location, Source Path,** and **Output Path** boxes. If the project paths are not correct, click ⬚ beside the corresponding box and select the appropriate path from the Select Directory dialog box.

f. Select **Create new workspace,** if it is not already selected.

g. Select **Next**. The third Project Wizard dialog box is displayed:

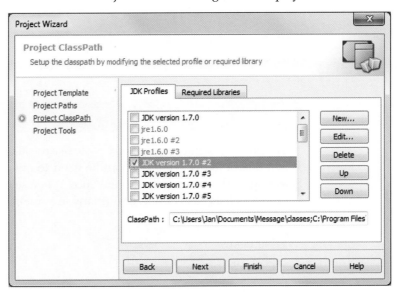

h. Select the JDK profile and then click **Next**.

i. Select Finish. The `Message` workspace file and project folder are displayed in the File View window.

③ *ADD A FILE TO THE PROJECT*

a. On the toolbar, click the New File ⬚ button. The File Wizard dialog box is displayed.

b. Select **File Type** if it is not already selected.

c. Select Empty Java File and then select Next.

d. In the Name box, type `Message`.

e. Select Finish. A `Message.java` file is created.

④ *ENTER A JAVA PROGRAM*

In the code editor window, type the following program:

```
1    /*This program displays Hello World.*/
2
3    public class Message {
4        public static void main (String args[])
5        {
6            System.out.println ("Hello World!");
7
8        }
9    }
```

⑤ *COMPILE AND RUN MESSAGE*

a. Select Build → Build Project. The `Message.java` file is saved and the message "Process completed." is displayed in the Build Output window:

```
Build Output                                                                          ⊡ ✕
--------------------Configuration: Message - JDK version 1.7.0 #2 <Default> - <Default>--------------------

Process completed.
```

b. Select Run → Run Project. The program output window is displayed:

```
General Output                                                                        ⊡ ✕
--------------------Configuration: Message - JDK version 1.7.0 #2 <Default> - <Default>--------------------
Hello World!

Process completed.
```

# Other IDEs

The previous section explained how to use the JCreator LE IDE. JCreator is just one of many IDEs that can be used to create Java applications. Selecting an IDE is a personal preference. When selecting an IDE, look at features such as ease of use, cost (many are free), and debugging tools. Other IDEs include:

- NetBeans
- CodeWarrior
- Eclipse
- JBuilder
- JPad Pro
- jGrasp

# Appendix C
# Applets and Web Programming

## The World Wide Web

The most widely used Internet service is the World Wide Web (WWW), also called the Web. The *Web* is used to search and access information available on the Internet. A *web browser application*, such as Internet Explorer provides a graphic interface to present information from a website:

*A web page displayed in a web browser*

Most web pages are created using HTML (HyperText Markup Language) and other code. *HTML* is a markup language that is well suited for the Web because it supports hypertext and multimedia. *Hypertext* is a database system where objects, such as text and images, can be linked. *Multimedia* includes images, video, audio, and Java applets, which can be embedded in an HTML document.

Millions of people all over the world are able to view and author web content because the World Wide Web Consortium (W3C) continuously develops standards for the Web. These standards include HTML standards to ensure that HTML documents display similarly in different browsers and across different platforms. They have also developed Web accessibility standards for those with disabilities.

---

### Browsers

Commonly used web browser applications include Internet Explorer, Opera, Firefox, and Safari.

# HTML

HTML uses a set of codes, called *tags*, to "mark up" plain text so that a browser application, such as Internet Explorer, knows how to interpret the text. A tag is comprised of an *element* inside angle brackets (<>). For example, `<title>` is called the title tag, where `title` is the element. Tags affect the text they surround, and are usually paired to indicate the start and end of an instruction. A slash (/) before the element indicates the end of an instruction, such as `</title>`.

A web page with one line of text will be displayed when the HTML document below is opened in a browser:

```
<html>

<head>
<title>An example HTML document</title>
</head>

<body>
<p>Hello world!</p>
</body>

</html>
```

Text marked up with `<title>` and `</title>` is displayed in the title bar or tab of the browser window. The text `Hello world!` is marked to be displayed as a paragraph (`<p>` and `</p>`) in the body of the browser window (`<body>` and `</body>`). When viewed in Internet Explorer, the HTML tags are interpreted sequentially and the document appears similar to:

# Creating an HTML Document

HTML documents are plain text files and can be created using any text editor, such as Notepad, or by using a word processor. In general, the structure of an HTML document should be similar to:

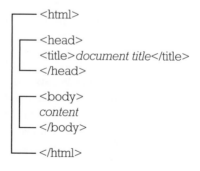

*An HTML document contains pairs of tags*

*Appendix C Applets and Web Programming*

The html, head, title, and body tags are called *document tags*:

- The `<html>` tag tells the browser that the file contains HyperText Markup Language.

- The `<head>` tag defines the section that contains information about the document, including its title. This section will not be displayed as part of the document content.

- The `<title>` tag marks the document title. The title section must be within the head section. The document title should be descriptive and meaningful because it is displayed in the title bar of the browser's window and is also used when the user adds the document to the browser's Favorites list.

- The `<body>` tag defines the body section, which contains the document's content. All content must be enclosed in the appropriate tags. For example, on the previous page, the content is marked as a paragraph.

HTML documents are *free-form*, which means that spaces and blank lines generally have no effect on how the document is interpreted. Therefore, the document:

```
<html><head><title>An example HTML document</title>
</head>
<body>  <p>Hello world!</p></body></html>
```

*Poorly structured HTML document*

displays exactly the same as the HTML document on the previous page. However, editing a poorly structured document can be time-consuming and error-prone.

## Review: Computer Viruses Website – part 1 of 3

Create a properly structured HTML document that displays the text "Computer Viruses." Include the title "Computer Viruses". Save the document as `computer_virus.htm` in a folder named Computer Viruses. View the HTML document in a browser.

## JavaScript

*Scripts* are used to add dynamic content to an HTML document and consist of a list of commands that execute without user interaction. Scripts are written in a scripting language, such as JavaScript. *JavaScript* is a scripting language that is interpreted by a browser's built-in JavaScript engine.

In an HTML document, JavaScript code is written as a script block between `<script>` and `</script>` tags. Scripts are typically found in the head section, but can be placed anywhere in an HTML document. Displaying a message in an alert dialog box is one form of dynamic content that can be added to an HTML document using a script:

```
<head>
<title>JavaScript Greeting</title>
<script type="text/javascript">
// Display a greeting
alert("Hello World!");
</script>
</head>
```

- The `type` attribute in the `script` tag specifies which scripting language is used to define the script.

- `//` is used to add a single line comment that explains the script.

- `alert()` displays an alert dialog box with the specified text message.

- A semicolon is used to end each JavaScript statement.

The script above is interpreted when the HTML document is loaded:

JavaScript can also be used to prompt the user for information:

```
<head>
<title>JavaScript User Name</title>
<script type="text/javascript">
//initialize a variable with a null value
var name = null;
// Ask user for their name
name = prompt("Please enter your first name", " ");
//Greet the user
alert("Welcome " + name);
</script>
</head>
```

- A variable called `name` is initialized to represent the user's name.

- `prompt()` displays the specified message in a prompt dialog box. The empty string, `" "`, after the message indicates the prompt box is to be blank when the dialog box is first displayed. When the user enters their name, it is assigned it to the variable `name`.

- The text message and variable are joined by a +.

The script above generates output similar to:

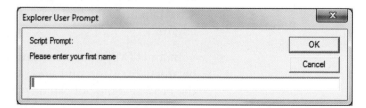

## Review: Computer Viruses Website – part 2 of 3

Modify `computer_virus.htm` to include a script block that prompts the user for their first name when the page loads and then displays "Ready to Learn About Computer Viruses *Name*?", replacing *Name* with the user's name, in an alert dialog box.

## Using Scripts to Enhance a Website

JavaScript can also be used to display the current date and time on a web page:

```
<head>
<title>JavaScript Current Date</title>
<script type="text/javascript">
// Display the current date
var now = new Date();
document.write(now);
</script>
</head>
```

- A new date object called `now` is created.

- `document.write` is used to display output on the web page:

Web applications are often programmed to display differently depending on the user's browser, platform, and whether Java is enabled. These settings can be detected using JavaScript:

```
<head>
<title>JavaScript Setting Detector</title>
<script type="text/javascript">
// Detect the browser
var browser = navigator.appName;
// Detect the platform
var platform = navigator.platform;
//Detect Java enabled
var JavaCheck = navigator.javaEnabled();
alert(browser +" \n" + platform + " \n" + "Java is enabled: "
+ JavaCheck);
</script>
</head>
```

- `navigator.appName` detects the browser name.
- `navigator.platform` detects the operating system.
- `navigator.javaEnabled()` detects whether Java is enabled and returns a value of true or false.
- `\n` creates a new line.

The script will generate output similar to:

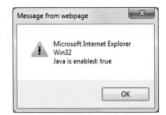

## Review: Computer Viruses Website – part 3 of 3

Modify `computer _ virus.htm` to display the current time and date on the first line of the web page.

## Review: System Check – part 1 of 2

Create an HTML document that detects the browser, platform, and whether the browser is Java enabled. Display the output in an alert dialog box.

## Java Applets

A *Java applet* is a small Java application that is embedded in an HTML document and run in a browser window. When a browser interprets a document that contains a Java applet, the program files are downloaded onto the user's machine and then the browser's Java interpreter runs the applet. Java applets are well suited for the Web because they are able to run on different hardware and across different platforms. Applets are secure because they do not have the ability to read or write to files on a user's computer.

Numerous applets can be downloaded from the Web and embedded in an HTML document to add dynamic content. Applets take various forms, such as animated banners, stock ticker tapes, photo cubes, and animated video clips. Original applets can also be created.

## Creating Java Applets

An applet is created in a Java compiler, such as JCreator. The Java code for the applet is saved with a `.java` extension and then compiled to convert the Java code to bytecode. The bytecode is saved with a `.class` extension.

The code below is for a basic applet that paints the message "My first Java applet" at a specific screen location:

```
/*
 * Example _ Applet.java
 */

import java.awt.*;
import java.applet.*;

public class Example _ Applet extends Applet {

    String message;

    public void init() {
        message="My first Java applet";
    }

    public void paint(Graphics g) {
        g.setColor(Color.blue);
        g.drawString(message, 50, 60 );
    }
}
```

**TIP** The example applet uses the Applet class, which is part of the `java.applet` package, and the Graphics class, which is part of the `java.awt` package.

- The two `import` statements indicate which Java packages are used.

- A class is used to define an applet and extend the Applet class. Applets are always an extension of the Applet class.

- The `init()` method is used to initialize variables to starting values. The variable `message` is assigned the text string, "My first Java applet".

- The `paint()` method is used to paint text, shapes, and graphics onto the screen. In this example, the `paint()` method defines a Graphics object named `g`.

- The `setColor()` method sets the text color.

- The `drawString()` method draws the message on the screen at the specified coordinates.

The JDK includes a tool called an appletviewer, which can be used to interpret, execute, and test an applet. When executed, the example applet above will appear similar to:

### Coordinates

A picture painted on the screen is made up of series of pixels (picture elements.) Each pixel maps to a screen location. Screen locations are represented using (x,y) values. The top-left corner has the coordinates (0,0) with the x-axis running horizontal and the y-axis running vertical.

Original applets can be created to draw colorful images. The applet below illustrates how shapes can be drawn and filled and how the background and foreground colors are set:

```
/*
 * Drawing Shapes and Changing Color Example
 */
import java.awt.*;
import java.applet.*;

public class Shapes_Color extends Applet {

    public void paint(Graphics g) {
        setBackground (Color.darkGray);
        g.setColor(Color.pink);
        g.drawRect(50, 50, 40, 40);
        g.setColor(Color.blue);
        g.fillRect(100, 100, 150, 150);
        g.setColor(Color.green);
        g.drawLine(20, 20, 300, 20);
        g.setColor(Color.red);
        g.fillOval(250, 250, 50, 50);
    }
}
```

When executed, the applet looks similar to:

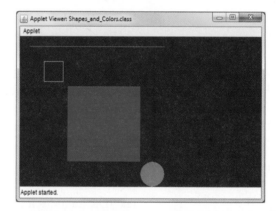

The different shapes require specified coordinates. For example:

- drawLine (x1, y1, x2, y2)   Paints a line from coordinates (x1, y1) to (x2, y2).

- drawOval (x, y, width, height)   Paints an oval with the upper left corner at position (x, y) with the specified width and height.

- drawRect (x, y, width, height)   Paints a rectangle with the upper left corner at position (x, y) with the specified width and height.

- drawArc (x, y, width, height, startAngle, arcAngle)   Paints an arc with the upper left corner at position (x, y) with the specified width, height, starting angle, and arc angle.

# Review: Hot Air Balloon

This review requires a Java compiler. Experiment with drawing shapes and adding color by creating an applet that paints a picture of a hot air balloon on the screen. Compile the applet and view it in the appletviewer.

## Placing an Applet in an HTML Document

An applet is embedded in an HTML document within the `<applet>` and `</applet>` tags. The tags can surround an alternative text message that will be displayed if the applet cannot run in the browser:

```
<html>

<head>
<title>Embedding an Applet</title>
</head>

<body>
<applet code = "FirstApplet.class" width = "300" height = "60">
You are unable to view the applet.
</applet>
</body>
```

**TIP** In JCreator, a Basic Java Applet template generates both a .java file and an .html file.

The `<applet>` tag has three required attributes:

- code=*"name"* specifies the name of the applets to run

- width=*"value"* specifies the width for the applet display in pixels

- height=*"value"* specifies the height for the applet display in pixels

## Applet Parameters

*Parameters* allow users to specify custom values to use in a Java applet. In an HTML document, parameter information is specified in a `<param>` tag, which requires two attributes, name and value. For example, the HTML document below specifies a specific image file, `scenery.gif`, to use in the applet.

```
<body>
<applet code = "AppletParam.class" width = "300" height = "60">
<param name ="image" value = "scenery.gif">
You are unable to view the applet.
</applet>
</body>
```

An applet available at the Oracle website, `http://java.sun.com/applets`, is an analog clock. Modify the body section of the System Check HTML document as follows, which embeds the `JavaClock.class` applet data file:

```
<applet  code="JavaClock.class" width="150" height="150">
<param  name="bgcolor"  value="ffffff">
<param  name="border"  value="5">
<param  name="ccolor"  value="dddddd">
<param  name="cfont"  value="TimesRoman¦BOLD¦18">
<param  name="delay"  value="100">
<param  name="hhcolor"  value="0000ff">
<param  name="link"  value="http://java.sun.com/">
<param  name="mhcolor"  value="00ff00">
<param  name="ncolor"  value="000000">
<param  name="nradius"  value="80">
<param  name="shcolor"  value="ff0000">
</applet>
```

Save the modified System Check HTML document in the `classes` folder in the CLOCK folder, which is included as a data file for this text.

# Index

bug 36, 106
built-in data types 53
bus topology 7
byte 9
bytecode 38, 354
Byte class 221

## C

C 5
C++ 6
cable modem 13
cache 3
calling a method 19
carpal tunnel syndrome 31
case clause 80
case sensitivity, identifiers 62
casting, see type casting
cellular radio 7
Central Processing Unit 3
chaos theory 123
char 53
   array 212
char array, initializing 212
charAt(), String class 212
Children's Online Privacy
   Protection Act of 1998 17
circuit boards 3
class 150
   abstract 190
   base 182
   body 158
   constructor 151
   declaration 158
   derived 182
   designing 154
   extending 181
   inner 150, 263
   naming 151
   nested 263, 344
   outer 263
   variables 150
   wrapper 221
   writing 150
ClassCastException 156
classes using classes 157
class method 129
ClassNotFoundException 290
client code 150
client/server network 7
close() 55
close(), BufferedReader class 282
close(), BufferedWriter class 286
close(), FileInputStream class 288
close(), FileOutputStream class 287
close(), FileReader class 283
close(), FileWriter class 285
close(), ObjectInputStream class 289
close(), ObjectOutputStream class 288
coaxial cable 7

COBOL 5
code conventions 41, 67, 90, 116, 141, 
collection 256
collections framework 220
colors, Swing API 259
combo box, Swing API 256
comments 37
   block 38
   documentation 38
   for debugging 107
   inline 79
   method 136
   multiline 38
   postcondition documentation 134
   precondition documentation 134
Comparable interface 193
compiler 5, 38
compression 11
computers 2
concatenation 52, 108
conditional control structure 77
constant 61
constructor 150, 153
cookie 17
copyright 19
counters 103
CPU 3
crackers 20
createNewFile() 279

## D

data
   boundary values 138
   passing to a method 130
   processing 55
   processing from a file 284
   reading from a file 282
   reading objects from a file 287
   testing a method 138
   writing objects to a file 287
   writing to a file 285
data structure
   array 207
   ArrayList 220
data structures
   linked list 343
   queue 339
   stack 335
data type
   abstract 54
   primitive 51
debugging
   commenting out statements 107
   debugger 106
   variable trace 106
   with println() 107
Debug Window 106
decimal number system 10
decision structure 77

declaration
   array 207
   class 150
   method 129
   two-dimensional array 216
   variable 52
decrement operator 105
delete(), File class 279
depth-first searching 322
dequeue, queue 339
derived class 134
desktop computer 2
documentation
   comments 37
downloading 15
dynamic lists 343

## E

ECPA 17
E-FOIA 17
Electronic Communications Privacy
   Act of 1986 17
Electronic Freedom of Information
   Act of 1996 17
electronic mail 15
element
   array 220
   ArrayList 220
   ArrayList, adding 220
   ArrayList, finding 220
   ArrayList, removing 220
e-mail 14
   etiquette 15
   software 15
employee monitoring 15
e, natural logarithm 98
encapsulation 149
encryption 18
end of file 282
endsWith(), String class 110
enqueue, queue 339
environment 4
environmental concerns 18
equal sign 52
equals(), String class 110
equals(), use by ArrayList 220
ergonomics 18
ethical implications of computer
   use 18
ethical responsibilities, IT
   professional 21
exabyte 12
exp(), Math class 98
exponentiation 85
exception
   handling 280
extranet 13

## L

label, Swing API 243
LAN 6
laser printer 2
lastIndexOf(), String class 110
layout manager, Swing API 249
leased/dedicated lines 14
length, array 208, 216
length(), String class 108
library 36
Life 240
    with GUI 277
Linear Congruential Method 81
linear search 214, 319
line feed character 282
line terminator 282
linked list 343
Linux 4
listener, Swing API 247
list, linked 343
Listserv 15
logic error 63
logical operators 16, 83
logical topology 8
loop structure 101

## M

machine code 38
machine language 5
Mac OS X 4, 243
magnetic technology 12
mailing list server 15
mainframe 2
main memory 3
main() method 37
Majordomo 15
makeEmpty, queue 336
malicious code 19
mantissa 11
Mastermind 237
Math class 85, 100
Mbps 14
median, determining 237
megabytes 10
megahertz 3
member, accessing 54
members, class 54
memory, dynamic 343
memory keys 2
memory-resident 4
mergesort 315
mergesort algorithm analysis 327
method 129
    accessing 183
    accessor 152
    calling 85
    helper 152
    main() 37
    modifer 152
    program development 129
    naming 130

    overloading 132
    parameters 130
    returning a value 129
    writing 129
MLA 16
mouse 2
multiplication 57

## N

natural logarithm 98
necklace problem 122
nested class 158, 263, 344
nested statements 79
NET Act 17
NetBeans 356
netiquette 9
network 6
    architecture 7
    client/server 7
    interface card 7
    peer-to-peer 7
newLine(), BufferedWriter class 286
nextBoolean(), Scanner class 55
nextDouble(), Scanner class 55
nextInt(), Scanner class 55
node, linked list 343
No Electronic Theft Act of 1997 17
NOT 16, 84
NullPointerException 109
number systems 9

## O

OASIS industry consortium 11
object 35, 54, 149
    argument 131
Object class 155, 181
object deserialization 287
ObjectInputStream class 288
object-oriented development 161
object-oriented programming 6
ObjectOutputStream 287
ObjectOutputStream class 288
ObjectOutputStream(),
    ObjectOutputStream class 288
Object parameter 156
object serialization 287
objects, sorting 309
object, to be written to a file 290
ODT file 11
offset array index 211
online profiling 17
OOP 6
Open Document file format 11
OpenOffice.org 11
operand 58
operating system software 4
operations, order of 58
operator 57
    relational 77
operator precedence 58
operators, built-in 57

optical technology 12
Or 83
    evaluation 84
    order of operations 84
OS 4
outer class 263
Outlook 15
overriding
    methods 156, 285

## P

package 36
    documentation 54
    naming 37, 55
package statement 37
pack(), JFrame 244
parameter
    array 209
    array, two-dimensional 216
    Object 131
    method 130
    pass by value 131
parentheses 58, 84
parseDouble(), Double class 284
parseInteger(), Integer class 253, 284
Pascal 5
pass by value 131
passing data to a method 210
PC card 7
peripheral devices 2
persistent data 279
persistent media 12
petabyte 12
phishing 20
PI, Math class 85
piracy 19
pixel 249
platform 4
platform-dependent languages 38
platform independence 6
PLC 13
podcasting 14
polymorphism 35, 181, 184
polymorphism, interfaces 309
POP3 15
pop, stack 335
ports 2
    Bluetooth 2
    FireWire 2
    parallel 2
    serial 2
power line communications 15
precondition, method
    documentation 134
prefix 105
primitive data type 53
println() 39, 52
    debugging 107
programming language
    low-level 5